How to TEPS 실전 900 독해편

지은이 김철용
펴낸이 임상진
펴낸곳 (주)넥서스

출판신고 1992년 4월 3일 제311-2002-2호 ㉴
10880 경기도 파주시 지목로 5
Tel (02)330-5500 Fax (02)330-5555

ISBN   978-89-5797-573-2 13740
          978-89-5797-575-6 （SET）

www.nexusEDU.kr
NEXUS Edu는 (주)넥서스의 초·중·고 학습물 전문 브랜드입니다.

가장 쉽고 빠르게 점수를 올려 주는

How to
TEPS
하우투 텝스

실전
900

김철용 지음

독해편

NEXUS Edu

필자는 매달 TEPS 시험을 본다. 고사장에서 매번 볼 수 있는 장면은 '시험 종료 5분 남았습니다'라는 방송과 함께 바빠지는 응시자들의 모습이다. 풀지 못한 독해 문제를 푸느라, 정답 마킹을 하느라 분주해지는 것이다. TEPS 독해 문제를 시간을 맞추어 제대로 푸는 응시자는 교실당 한두 명에 불과할 것이다.

TEPS 독해는 단순히 영어 해석 능력을 묻는 것이 아니라 영어로 논리적 사고를 얼마나 잘하며 빨리 할 수 있는지를 묻는 시험이다. 따라서 응시자의 영어 실력이 어느 정도의 수준에 올랐다고 보고, 얼마나 내재화되어 영어로 논리적 사고를 할 수 있는지 확인하는 문제가 많다. 따라서 한두 달 전문 학원을 다니거나 TEPS 책으로만 공부를 해서는 점수가 크게 오르기 쉽지 않다. TEPS 고득점을 목표로 하는 학습자들은 다음을 기억하기 바란다.

☞ TEPS는 보통 영어 실력 이상의 어려운 시험이다.
☞ 독해 고득점 없이 900점은 없다.
☞ 독해 40문제 중 37문제 이상은 맞혀야 한다.

TEPS 학습자는 영어 공부와 함께 논리적 사고 훈련도 병행해야 한다. 따라서 매일 영자 신문도 읽고, 영어 원서도 보고, TEPS 시험이 다가오면 독해 모의고사를 실전처럼 여러 번 풀어야 한다. 이 모든 것은 TEPS 학습자인 여러분의 몫이다. 결국 공부는 혼자서 하는 것이기에. TEPS 학습자는 단순히 영어를 공부한다는 마음이 아니라 마치 사법고시를 준비하듯 비장한 각오로 임해야 한다.

그럼 이 책의 의미는 무엇일까? 30여 회 이상 TEPS 시험에 응시한 필자가 지금까지 나온 어떤 TEPS 독해 책에서도 언급되지 않았고 응시자가 간과하고 있던 TEPS 독해의 비밀과 전략을 이 책에 담았다. 따라서 학습자들은 모의고사나 정기 시험에 이 전략을 잘 적용하여 시간에 쫓기는 일 없이 정확도를 더욱 높여서 고득점을 올릴 수 있길 바란다.

끝으로 더 큰 TEPS 강사가 되도록 물심양면 지원을 아끼지 않으시는 신동표 원장님께 깊은 존경과 감사의 마음을 전한다.

Contents

Actual Test

정답 및 해설 (별책부록)

Structure

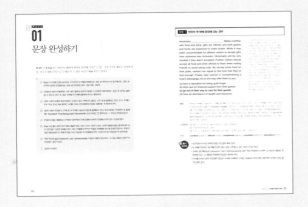

유형별 독해 전략

TEPS 독해의 가장 기본인 유형별 접근을 통해 각 유형별 전략을 완벽하게 익힐 수 있다.

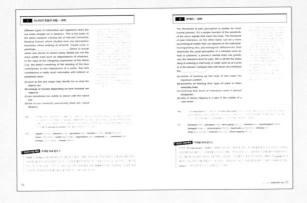

고난도 주제별 독해

독해 만점을 위한 필수적인 고난도 토픽 10개를 선정, 집중 공략법을 소개한다.

풀이 접근법

• 첫 문장이 단락의 주제 문장일 가능성이 매우 높다.

• 두 번째 문장이나 세 번째 문장만 봐도 답을 추론할 수 있는 경우가 더러 있다.

• 그러나 중간에 But/ However/ Yet/ Unfortunately와 같은 역접 연결어는 읽어야 하고, 그 내용을 반영해서 정답을 찾아야 한다.

• 단락에 숫자가 많이 언급되면 정답은 수치와 구체적인 단어를 포함하고 있지 가능성이 높다.

풀이 접근법

꼼꼼하게 유형을 이해하고 제한된 시간 내 어떤 문제도 효율적으로 풀 수 있도록 한다.

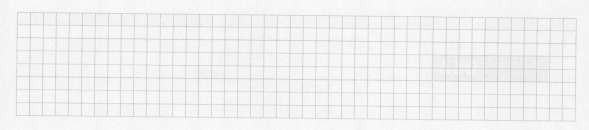

Actual Test 5회분

최신 기출 경향에 가장 유사한 문제를 풀면서 실전처럼 TEPS를 연습할 수 있다.

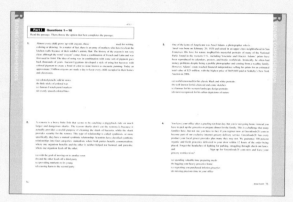

용쌤의 비법 특강

800점대 수험생들이 결정적으로 놓치기 쉬운 문제 풀이 노하우를 일목요연하게 제시한다.

http://www.nexusbook.com

본 교재 학습이 끝난 수험생들은 넥서스북에 접속하여 무료 어휘 리스트 및 점검 테스트를 제공받을 수 있다.

도서 → How to TEPS 실전 900 독해편 검색 → 다섯 번째 카테고리 클릭

1 / TEPS란?

TEPS 는 Test of English Proficiency developed by Seoul National University의 약자이며, 서울대학교 언어 교육원에서 개발하고 TEPS관리위원회에서 주관, 시행하는 국가 공인 영어 시험입니다. 본 시험은 수험생들의 영어 실력을 Reading, Listening, Grammar, Vocabulary 총 4개의 영역으로 나누어 평가하는 시험이며, 총 200문항, 990점 만점의 시험입니다. 이 중 Reading Part는 3개의 Part로 구성되어 있으며, Part 1은 빈칸 채우기 문제로 한 단락의 글이 자연스럽게 이어지도록 빈칸에 적절한 내용을 고르는 문제입니다. 그리고 Part 2는 내용 이해도를 평가하는 문제로 한 단락의 글을 읽고 질문에 알맞은 내용을 고르는 문제이며, 주로 주제, 지문과 일치하는 내용, 유추할 수 있는 내용을 찾는 문제로 나뉩니다. 마지막으로 Part 3는 한 단락의 글에서 흐름상 어색한 문장 하나를 고르는 문제입니다. 시험은 지역에 따라 다르나 매달 한 번씩 토요일 또는 일요일에 있으며, 접수는 인터넷 접수(www.teps.or.kr) 또는 방문 접수가 가능합니다. 성적 확인은 시험 후 2주 이내에 가능합니다.

2 / TEPS 시험 구성

영역	Part별 내용	문항수	시간/배점
청해 Listening Comprehension	Part I : 문장 하나를 듣고 이어질 대화 고르기 Part II : 3문장의 대화를 듣고 이어질 대화 고르기 Part III : 6~8 문장의 대화를 듣고 질문에 해당하는 답 고르기 Part IV : 담화문의 내용을 듣고 질문에 해당하는 답 고르기	15 15 15 15	55분 400점
문법 Grammar	Part I : 대화문의 빈칸에 적절한 표현 고르기 Part II : 문장의 빈칸에 적절한 표현 고르기 Part III : 대화에서 어법상 틀리거나 어색한 부분 고르기 Part IV : 단문에서 문법상 틀리거나 어색한 부분 고르기	20 20 5 5	25분 100점
어휘 Vocabulary	Part I : 대화문의 빈칸에 적절한 단어 고르기 Part II : 단문의 빈칸에 적절한 단어 고르기	25 25	15분 100점
독해 Reading Comprehension	Part I : 지문을 읽고 빈칸에 들어갈 내용 고르기 Part II : 지문을 읽고 질문에 가장 적절한 내용 고르기 Part III : 지문을 읽고 문맥상 어색한 내용 고르기	16 21 3	45분 400점
총계	13개 Parts	200	140분 990점

☆ **IRT** (Item Response Theory)에 의하여 최고점이 990점, 최저점이 10점으로 조정됨

Listening Comprehension 60문항

● Part I

Choose the most appropriate response to the statement. (15문항)

문제유형 질의 응답 문제를 다루며 한 번만 들려주고, 내용은 일상의 구어체 표현으로 구성되어 있다.

> W   I wish my French were as good as yours.
> M   _____

(a) Yes, I'm going to visit France.　　　　✔ (b) Thanks, but I still have a lot to learn.
(c) I hope it works out that way.　　　　　(d) You can say that again.

번역　W 당신처럼 프랑스어를 잘하면 좋을 텐데요.
　　　　M _____

(a) 네, 프랑스를 방문할 예정이에요.　　　(b) 고마워요. 하지만 아직도 배울 게 많아요.
(c) 그렇게 잘되기를 바라요.　　　　　　(d) 당신 말이 맞아요.

● Part II

Choose the most appropriate response to complete the conversation. (15문항)

문제유형 두 사람이 A–B–A–B 순으로 대화하는 형식이며, 한 번만 들려준다.

> W   I wish I earned more money.
> M   You could change jobs.
> W   But I love the field I work in.
> M   _____

(a) I think it would be better.　　　　　✔ (b) Ask for a raise then.
(c) You should have a choice in it.　　　　(d) I'm not that interested in money.

번역　W 돈을 더 많이 벌면 좋을 텐데요.
　　　　M 직장을 바꾸지 그래요?
　　　　W 하지만 난 지금 일하고 있는 분야가 좋아요.
　　　　M _____

(a) 더 좋아질 거라고 생각해요.　　　　　(b) 그러면 급여를 올려 달라고 말해요.
(c) 그 안에서 선택권이 있어야 해요.　　　(d) 돈에 그렇게 관심이 있지는 않아요.

● Part III
Choose the option that best answers the question. (15문항)

문제유형 비교적 긴 대화문. 대화문과 질문은 두 번. 선택지는 한 번 들려준다.

> M   Hello. You're new here, aren't you?
>
> W   Yes, it's my second week. I'm Karen.
>
> M   What department are you in?
>
> W   Customer service, on the first floor.
>
> M   I see. I'm in sales.
>
> W   So, you'll be working on commission, then.
>
> M   Yes. I like that, but it's very stressful sometimes.

Q: Which is correct according to the conversation?

(a) The man and woman work in the same department.

✔ (b) The woman works in the customer service department.

(c) The man thinks the woman's job is stressful.

(d) The woman likes working for commissions.

번역

M 안녕하세요. 새로 오신 분이시죠?

W 예. 여기 온 지 2주째예요. 전 캐런이에요.

M 어느 부서에서 근무하시나요?

W 1층 고객 지원부에서 일해요.

M 그렇군요. 전 영업부에서 일해요.

W 그러면 커미션제로 일하시는군요.

M 네. 좋기는 하지만 가끔은 스트레스를 많이 받아요.

Q: 대화에 따르면 옳은 것은?

(a) 남자와 여자는 같은 부서에서 일한다.

(b) 여자는 고객 지원부에서 일한다.

(c) 남자는 여자의 일이 스트레스가 많다고 생각한다.

(d) 여자는 커미션제로 일하는 것을 좋아한다.

● Part IV

Choose the option that best answers the question. (15문항)

문제유형   담화문의 주제, 세부 사항, 사실 여부 및 이를 근거로 한 추론 등을 다룬다.

> Confucian tradition placed an emphasis on the values of the group over the individual. It also taught that workers should not question authority. This helped industrialization by creating a pliant populace willing to accept long hours and low wages and not question government policies. The lack of dissent helped to produce stable government and this was crucial for investment and industrialization in East Asian countries.

Q: What can be inferred from the lecture?
(a) Confucianism promoted higher education in East Asia.
(b) East Asian people accept poverty as a Confucian virtue.
✔ (c) Confucianism fostered industrialization in East Asia.
(d) East Asian countries are used to authoritarian rule.

번역   유교 전통은 개인보다 조직의 가치를 강조했습니다. 또한 노동자들에게 권위에 대해 의문을 제기하지 말라고 가르쳤습니다. 이것은 장시간 노동과 저임금을 기꺼이 감수하고 정부의 정책에 의문을 제기하지 않는 고분고분한 민중을 만들어 냄으로써 산업화에 도움이 되었습니다. 반대의 부재는 안정적인 정부를 만드는 데 도움이 되었고, 이는 동아시아 국가들에서 투자와 산업화에 결정적이었습니다.

Q: 강의로부터 유추할 수 있는 것은?
(a) 유교는 동아시아에서 고등교육을 장려했다.
(b) 동아시아 사람들은 유교의 미덕으로 가난을 받아들인다.
(c) 유교는 동아시아에서 산업화를 촉진했다.
(d) 동아시아 국가들은 권위주의에 익숙하다.

● Part I

Choose the best answer for the blank. (20문항)

문제유형   A, B 두 사람의 짧은 대화 중에 빈칸이 있다. 동사의 시제 및 수 일치, 문장의 어순 등이 주로 출제되며, 구어체 문법의 독특한 표현들을 숙지하고 있어야 한다.

> A   Should I just keep waiting _____ me back?
>
> B   Well, just waiting doesn't get anything done, does it?

(a) for the editor write

✔ (b) until the editor writes

(c) till the editor writing

(d) that the editor writes

번역   A 편집자가 나한테 답장을 쓸 때까지 기다리고만 있어야 합니까?

         B 글쎄요, 단지 기다리고 있다고 해서 무슨 일이 이루어지는 건 아니겠죠?

● Part II

Choose the best answer for the blank. (20문항)

문제유형   문어체 문장을 읽고 어법상 빈칸에 적절한 표현을 고르는 유형으로 세부적인 문법 자체에 대한 이해는 물론 구문에 대한 이해력도 테스트한다.

> All passengers should remain seated at _____ times.

(a) any

(b) some

✔ (c) all

(d) each

번역   모든 승객들은 항상 앉아 있어야 합니다.

● Part III

Identify the option that contains an awkward expression or an error in grammar. (5문항)

문제유형   대화문에서 어법상 틀리거나 어색한 부분이 있는 문장을 고르는 문제로 구성되어 있다.

> (a)   A Where did you go on your honeymoon?
> (b)   B We flew to Bali, Indonesia.
> ✔ (c)   A Did you have good time?
> (d)   B Sure. It was a lot of fun.

번역   (a)   A 신혼여행은 어디로 가셨나요?

   (b)   B 인도네시아 발리로 갔어요.

   (c)   A 좋은 시간 보내셨어요?

   (d)   B 물론이죠. 정말 재미있었어요.

● Part IV

Identify the option that contains an awkward expression or an error in grammar. (5문항)

문제유형   한 문단 속에 문법적으로 틀리거나 어색한 문장을 고르는 유형이다.

> (a) Morality is not the only reason for putting human rights on the West's foreign policy agenda. (b) Self-interest also plays a part in the process. (c) Political freedom tends to go hand in hand with economic freedom, which in turn tends to bring international trade and prosperity. (d) A world in which more countries respect basic human rights would be more peaceful place.

번역   (a) 서양의 외교정책 의제에 인권을 상정하는 유일한 이유가 도덕성은 아니다. (b) 자국의 이익 또한 그 과정에 일정 부분 관여한다. (c) 정치적 자유는 경제적 자유와 나란히 나아가는 경향이 있는데, 경제적 자유는 국제 무역과 번영을 가져오는 경향이 있다. (d) 더 많은 국가들이 기본적인 인권을 존중하는 세상은 더 평화로운 곳이 될 것이다.

Vocabulary 50문항

● Part I
Choose the best answer for the blank. (25문항)

문제유형 A, B 대화 빈칸에 가장 적절한 단어를 넣는 유형이다. 단어의 단편적인 의미보다는 문맥에서 어떻게 쓰였는지 아는 것이 중요하다.

> A   Let's take a coffee break.
> B   I wish I could, but I'm ＿＿＿＿＿＿ in work.

✔ (a) up to my eyeballs   (b) green around the gills
(c) against the grain   (d) keeping my chin up

번역 A 잠깐 휴식 시간을 가집시다.
B 그러면 좋겠는데 일 때문에 꼼짝도 할 수가 없네요.

(a) ~에 몰두하여   (b) 안색이 나빠 보이는
(c) 뜻이 맞지 않는   (d) 기운 내는

● Part II
Choose the best answer for the blank. (25문항)

문제유형 문어체 문장의 빈칸에 가장 적절한 단어를 고르는 유형이다. 고난도 어휘의 독특한 용례를 따로 학습해 두어야 고득점이 가능하다.

> It takes a year for the earth to make one ＿＿＿＿＿＿ around the sun.

(a) conversion   (b) circulation
(c) restoration   ✔ (d) revolution

번역 지구가 태양 주위를 한 번 공전하는 데 일 년이 걸린다.
(a) 전환   (b) 순환
(c) 복구   (d) 공전

● Part I

Choose the option that best completes the passage. (16문항)

문제유형　지문의 논리적인 흐름을 파악하여 문맥상 빈칸에 가장 적절한 선택지를 고르는 문제이다.

> This product is a VCR-sized box that sits on or near a television and automatically records and stores television shows, sporting events and other TV programs, making them available for viewing later. This product lets users watch their favorite program _____ . It's TV-on-demand that actually works, and no monthly fees.

　　✔ (a) whenever they want to
　　(b) wherever they watch TV
　　(c) whenever they are on TV
　　(d) when the TV set is out of order

번역　이 제품은 텔레비전 옆에 놓인 VCR 크기의 상자로 TV 공연, 스포츠 이벤트 및 다른 TV 프로그램을 자동으로 녹화 저장하여 나중에 볼 수 있게 해준다. 이 제품은 사용자 자신이 가장 좋아하는 프로그램을 원하는 시간 언제나 볼 수 있게 해준다. 이것은 실제로 작동하는 주문형 TV로 매달 내는 시청료도 없다.

　　(a) 원하는 시간 언제나
　　(b) TV를 보는 곳 어디든지
　　(c) TV에 나오는 언제나
　　(d) TV가 작동되지 않을 때

Part II

Choose the option that best answers the question. (21문항)

문제유형   지문에 대한 이해를 측정하는 유형으로 주제 파악, 세부 내용 파악, 논리적 추론을 묻는 문제로 구성되어
있다.

> The pace of bank mergers is likely to accelerate. Recently Westbank has gained far
> more profit than it has lost through mergers, earning a record of $2.11 billion in 2003.
> Its shareholders have enjoyed an average gain of 28% a year over the past decade,
> beating the 18% annual return for the benchmark S & P stock index. However, when big
> banks get bigger, they have little interest in competing for those basic services many
> households prize. Consumers have to pay an average of 15% more a year, or $27.95, to
> maintain a regular checking account at a large bank instead of a smaller one.

Q: What is the main topic of the passage?

(a) Reasons for bank mergers

✔ (b) Effects of bank mergers

(c) The merits of big banks

(d) Increased profits of merged banks

번역   은행 합병 속도가 가속화될 전망이다. 최근 웨스트 뱅크가 2003년 21억 1천만 달러의 수익을 기록함으로써 합
병으로 잃은 것보다 훨씬 더 많은 수익을 얻었다. 웨스트 뱅크 주주들은 지난 10년간 S & P 지수의 연간 수익률
18%를 웃도는 연평균 수익률 28%를 누려 왔다. 하지만 규모가 더욱 커진 대형 은행들은 많은 가구가 중요하게
생각하는 기본 서비스에 대한 경쟁에는 별 관심을 두고 있지 않다. 소비자들은 작은 은행 대신 대형 은행의 보통
당좌예금 계정을 유지하기 위해 연평균 15% 이상, 즉 27달러 95센트를 지불해야 한다.

Q: 지문의 소재는?

(a) 은행 합병의 이유

(b) 은행 합병의 영향

(c) 대형 은행의 장점

(d) 합병된 은행들의 수익 증가

● Part III
Identify the option that does NOT belong. (3문항)

문제유형   한 문단에서 전체의 흐름상 어색한 내용을 고르는 유형이다.

> Communication with language is carried out through two basic human activities: speaking and listening. (a) These are of particular importance to psychologists, for they are mental activities that hold clues to the very nature of the human mind. (b) In speaking, people put ideas into words, talking about perceptions, feelings, and intentions they want other people to grasp. (c) In listening, people decode the sounds of words they hear to gain the intended meaning. (d) Language has stood at the center of human affairs throughout human history.

번역   언어로 이루어지는 의사소통은 두 가지 기본적인 인간 활동인 말하기와 듣기에 의해 수행된다. (a) 이 두 가지는 심리학자들에게 각별한 중요성을 지니는데, 이는 두 가지가 인간의 심성 본질 자체에 대한 단서를 쥐고 있는 정신적 활동이기 때문이다. (b) 말할 때 사람들은 다른 사람들이 이해하기를 원하는 지각과 감정, 의도 등을 말하면서 아이디어들을 단어로 표현한다. (c) 들을 때 사람들은 의도된 뜻을 간파하기 위해 들리는 단어의 소리를 해독한다. (d) 언어는 인류의 역사를 통틀어 인간 활동의 중심에 있어 왔다.

TEPS 등급표

등급	점수	영역	능력검정기준(Description)
1+급 Level 1+	901-990	전반	외국인으로서 최상급 수준의 의사소통 능력 : 교양 있는 원어민에 버금가는 정도로 의사소통이 가능하고 전문분야 업무에 대처할 수 있음. (Native Level of Communicative Competence)
1급 Level 1	801-900	전반	외국인으로서 거의 최상급 수준의 의사소통 능력 : 단기간 집중 교육을 받으면 대부분의 의사소통이 가능하고 전문분야 업무에 별 무리 없이 대처할 수 있음. (Near-Native Level of Communicative Competence)
2+급 Level 2+	701-800	전반	외국인으로서 상급 수준의 의사소통 능력 : 단기간 집중 교육을 받으면 일반분야 업무를 큰 어려움 없이 수행할 수 있음. (Advanced Level of Communicative Competence)
2급 Level 2	601-700	전반	외국인으로서 중상급 수준의 의사소통 능력 : 중장기간 집중 교육을 받으면 일반분야 업무를 큰 어려움 없이 수행할 수 있음. (High Intermediate Level of Communicative Competence)
3+급 Level 3+	501-600	전반	외국인으로서 중급 수준의 의사소통 능력 : 중장기간 집중 교육을 받으면 한정된 분야의 업무를 큰 어려움 없이 수행할 수 있음. (Mid Intermediate Level of Communicative Competence)
3급 Level 3	401-500	전반	외국인으로서 중하급 수준의 의사소통 능력 : 중장기간 집중 교육을 받으면 한정된 분야의 업무를 다소 미흡하지만 큰 지장은 없이 수행할 수 있음. (Low Intermediate Level of Communicative Competence)
4급 Level 4	201-400	전반	외국인으로서 하급수준의 의사소통 능력 : 장기간의 집중 교육을 받으면 한정된 분야의 업무를 대체로 어렵게 수행할 수 있음. (Novice Level of Communicative Competence)
5급 Level 5	101-200	전반	외국인으로서 최하급 수준의 의사소통 능력 : 단편적인 지식만을 갖추고 있어 의사소통이 거의 불가능함. (Near-Zero Level of Communicative Competence)

TEPS
Test of English Proficiency
developed by
Seoul National University

SCORE REPORT

NAME	**REGISTRATION NO.**
HONG GIL DONG	0123456
DATE OF BIRTH	**TEST DATE**
JAN. 01. 1980	MAR. 02. 2008
GENDER	**VALID UNTIL**
MALE	MAR. 01. 2010

NO : RAAAA0000BBBB

TOTAL SCORE AND LEVEL

SCORE	LEVEL
768	**2+**

SECTION	SCORE	LEVEL	%	0% 100%
Listening	307	2+	77 / 59	
Grammar	76	2+	76 / 52	
Vocabulary	65	2	65 / 56	
Reading	320	2+	80 / 61	

■ your percentage   ■ average

OVERALL COMMUNICATIVE COMPETENCE

768

89.89%

A score at this level typically indicates an advanced level of communicative competence for a non-native speaker. A test taker at this level is able to execute general tasks after a short-term training.

SECTION			PERFORMANCE EVALUATION
Listening	PART I	86%	A score at this level typically indicates that the test taker has a good grasp of the given situation and its context and can make relevant responses. Can understand main ideas in conversations and lectures when they are explicitly stated, understand a good deal of specific information and make inferences given explicit information.
	PART II	66%	
	PART III	86%	
	PART IV	66%	
Grammar	PART I	84%	A score at this level typically indicates that the test taker has a fair understanding of the rules of grammar and syntax and has internalized them to a degree enabling them to carry out meaningful communication.
	PART II	75%	
	PART III	99%	
	PART IV	21%	
Vocabulary	PART I	72%	A score at this level typically indicates that the test taker has a good command of vocabulary for use in everyday speech. Able to understand vocabulary used in written contexts of a more formal nature, yet may have difficulty using it appropriately.
	PART II	56%	
Reading	PART I	68%	A score at this level typically indicates that the test taker is at an advanced level of understanding written texts. Can abstract main ideas from a text, understand a good deal of specific information and draw basic inferences when given texts with clear structure and explicit information.
	PART II	90%	
	PART III	66%	

THE TEPS COUNCIL

Section 1
유형별
TEPS 독해

문장 완성하기

TEPS 독해 Part 1은 1번부터 16번까지이며, 빈칸에 들어갈 수 있는 가장 적절한 내용을 찾아야 한다. 결국 논리와 글의 흐름 문제라 할 수 있다. 다음은 Part 1의 특징이다.

⊙ Part 1의 문제 유형은 4가지다. 1) 빈칸이 첫 번째 문장에 있는 경우, 2) 빈칸이 단락 중간에 있는 경우, 3) 빈칸이 마지막 문장에 있는 경우, 4) 연결어를 묻는 경우 (15~16번)

⊙ 1번부터 10번 문제까지는 1분 내로 풀어서 비교적 어려운 11번부터 16번까지는 조금 더 시간을 할애할 수 있도록 한다. 즉, 평균 1분에 한 문제씩 풀어야 한다고 생각하자.

⊙ 13번, 14번 문제가 특히 어렵다. 문장이 길고 선택지의 함정도 수준 높게 출제되고 있다. 이 두 문제는 주로 역사, 문학, 과학 분야를 소재로 하며, 총점 900점 이상을 위해서는 꼭 맞아야 한다.

⊙ 15번, 16번 연결어 두 문제 중 한 문제가 비교적 어렵게 출제되고 있다. 특히 어려운 연결어로 잘 출제되는 Granted/ That being said/ Henceforth 등의 의미를 잘 챙겨두자. (⇒ 유형 4 연결어 참고)

⊙ 연결어 문제를 제외하고 1번부터 14번까지 문제 중에서 마지막 문장에 빈칸이 있는 유형이 많다.

⊙ Part 1을 풀다 보면 빈칸 앞뒤 내용만 봐도 답이 나오는 경우가 있다. 하지만 900 이상을 생각한다면 이런 접근법은 가급적 피해야 한다. 지문 전체에서 빈칸의 역할을 파악해 주제 문장인지, 주제 문장을 뒷받침하는지, 주제 문장을 다시 진술하는지 이해해야 한다. 요령이 아니라 정공법으로 돌파하자.

⊙ 역접 연결어 but/ however/ yet/ unfortunately 다음의 내용이 중요하다. 그 다음 내용이 정답으로 직결되는 경우가 많다.

⊙ 결국은 논리다!

Ukrainians _____. Tables overflow with food and drink, gifts are offered, and both guests and hosts are expected to make toasts. While it may seem uncomfortable for affluent visitors to accept gifts from someone less fortunate, Ukrainians will be very insulted if they aren't accepted. Further, visitors should accept all food and drink offered to them when visiting friends to avoid being rude. By saving some food on their plate, visitors can signal to the host that they've had enough. Finally, take caution in complimenting a host's belongings; he or she may offer them to you.

(a) have a reputation for being quite frugal
(b) often ask for financial support from their guests
(c) go out of their way to care for their guests
(d) have an abundance of wealth and resources

우크라이나 사람들은 지극 정성으로 손님을 모신다. 식탁에는 음식과 음료로 넘쳐나고 손님에게 선물도 주며 손님과 집주인은 축배를 들 것이다. 잘사는 사람이 못사는 사람에게 선물을 받는 것이 불편할 수 있지만 우크라이나 사람들은 선물을 주었는데 상대방이 이를 거부하면 모욕을 당했다고 생각할 것이다. 게다가 친구의 집에 방문했을 때 무례하다는 인상을 주지 않기 위해 대접받는 모든 음식과 음료를 받아야 한다. 손님은 접시에 어느 정도의 음식을 남겨서 자신이 배가 부르다는 것을 집주인에게 알려 줄 수 있다. 마지막으로 집주인이 가지고 있는 것을 칭찬하는 데에 각별히 신경을 써야 한다. 당신에게 그 물건을 줄 수도 있기 때문이다.

(a) 근검절약하는 것으로 명성이 자자하다.
(b) 손님에게 종종 금전적 지원을 요구한다.
(c) 지극 정성으로 손님을 모신다.
(d) 막대한 부와 재력을 갖추고 있다.

해설 빈칸이 첫 번째 문장에 있다. 두 번째, 세 번째 문장을 읽고도 답을 찾을 수 있는 유형으로 첫 번째 문장이 주제 문장인 두괄식 단락이다. 뒤에 연결어 further와 finally를 보면 같은 성격의 내용이 이어질 것이라고 예측할 수 있다. 즉, 이 문제는 단락 전체를 다 읽지 않고도 답을 쉽게 찾을 수 있다. 이런 유형은 1분 내로 풀고 시간을 절약해서 Part 1의 후반부 문제에 좀 더 시간을 투자하는 것이 현명하다. 선택지를 보면 '비상한 노력을 하다'라는 뜻인 go out of one's way 라는 표현이 사용되었지만 혹시 이 표현을 몰랐다 해도 나머지 선택지가 확실히 답이 아님은 알 수 있다. 따라서 정답은 (c)이다.

오답분석 (a) 지문은 근검절약하는 내용이 아니라 오히려 그 반대이다.
(b) 돈과 관련된 이야기는 없다.
(d) 손님을 후하게 대한다는 내용이지 엄청난 재력을 가지고 있다는 내용은 아니다.

어구 overflow 넘치다 | affluent 부유한 | compliment 칭찬하다 | reputation 평판, 명성 | abundance 부유함

풀이 접근법
• 첫 문장이 단락의 주제 문장일 가능성이 매우 높다.
• 두 번째 문장이나 세 번째 문장만 봐도 답을 추론할 수 있는 경우가 더러 있다.
• 그러나 중간에 But/ However/ Yet/ Unfortunately와 같은 역접 연결어가 나오면 그 이후의 내용을 꼭 읽어야 하고, 그 내용을 반영해서 정답을 찾아야 한다.
• 단락에 숫자가 많이 언급되면 정답은 수치와 구체적인 단어를 포함하고 있지 않은 일반적인 문장이 답일 가능성이 높다.

> The President calls Holbrooke a true giant of American foreign policy, while acknowledging he was a tough man to work with.
> 대통령은 홀브룩을 미국 외교 정책의 진정한 위인이라 칭하는 한편, 같이 일하기에는 힘든 사람이었다는 것은 인정한다.
>
> Although the occupancy rate changed, the rate of the owner-occupied housing and renter-occupied was similar.
> 입주율에 변화가 있었음에도, 주택 소유자 입주율과 세입자 입주율은 비슷했다.

글쓴이는 콤마 이전 내용을 강조하려는 것일까, 콤마 이후 내용을 강조하려는 것일까? 이 문장 다음부터는 콤마 이후 내용에 좀 더 초점을 두고 계속 언급할 것이다. 따라서 정답도 콤마 이후 내용과 관련될 가능성이 크다.

In the Philippines, western culture dominates the urban areas; however, tribal people still maintain some of their heritage in rural regions. They encourage others to meet with their tribes to enjoy old rituals and customs. One of the most popular _____ is called Tinikling, which is done by two or more people holding two or more bamboo sticks known as Kawayan. Participants start moving the bamboo sticks as the people place their feet in between them quickly in and out. Kamayan, as the participants are called, has the literal meaning of "eating with hands."

(a) arenas for public debate
(b) tenets of the native folklore
(c) features of a holy custom
(d) ritualistic dances

필리핀에서는 서양 문화가 도시 지역을 장악한다. 하지만 시골 지역에서는 아직도 부족민들이 일부 유산을 보존하고 있다. 그들은 타인에게 자기 부족과 만나 오랜 의식과 관습을 즐기기를 권한다. 가장 인기 있는 의식무 중 하나는 티니클링인데 두 명 이상이 카와안이라 불리는 대나무 막대 두 개 이상을 손에 들고 춤을 춘다. 춤을 추는 사람들은 대나무 막대 사이 안팎으로 발을 재빨리 놓으면서 막대기를 움직이기 시작한다. 이 춤을 추는 이들을 카마얀이라 부르는데 글자대로의 의미는 '손으로 먹기'이다.

(a) 공론의 장
(b) 토착 민속의 규율
(c) 신성한 관습의 특징
(d) 의식무

해설 빈칸이 단락 중간에 있다. 빈칸 다음에 오는 내용을 보고 무엇에 관해 설명하고 있는지 파악해야 한다. 사람들이 대나무 막대 안쪽으로 재빨리 들어갔다 나왔다 하는 동작을 떠올릴 수 있고 첫 문장에서 필리핀 부족민의 유산을 언급하고 있으므로 (d)가 정답이다.

오답분석 (a) 토론을 하는 내용은 아니다.
(b) 규율이나 규칙을 설명한 글은 아니다.
(c) 신성하다는 근거를 찾을 수 없다.

어구 dominate 지배하다 | tribal 부족의 | heritage 유산 | literal 글자대로의 | arena 원형 경기장 | tenet 규율, 교리 | feature 특징 | ritualistic 의식적인

• 주제 문장을 찾는 문제도 있지만, 주로 주제 문장을 뒷받침하는 문장들 사이의 논리적 연결 관계를 묻는 문제가 많이 출제되고 있다.
• 뒷받침 문장은 예시, 부연, 상술, 인과, 대조 형태로 등장한다.
• 빈칸이 단락 중간에 있으면 글의 흐름과 논리가 더욱 중요해지므로 앞뒤의 논리적 관계를 잘 따져야 한다.

✏ **용쌤의 비법 특강** **만점 비법 2**

첫 문장이 Many people believe that/ Many people say/ It is believed that/ It is widely held that 등으로 시작하면 이 문장은 별로 중요하지 않다. 그 다음 문장에서 But/ However/ In fact/ Nevertheless와 같은 역접 연결어가 나오기 때문이다. 첫 문장은 그 다음 문장을 위한 밑밥이며 역접 연결어가 있는 문장에 정답의 결정적 단서가 있다. 문장을 이렇게 배치함으로써 필자의 의도를 좀 더 효과적으로 전달할 수 있기 때문이다.

The philosophy of existentialism regards the individual as being the sole agent of his or her own life's meaning. Further, it posits that people should live their lives passionately and honestly while fighting the "distractions" life places in a person's path such as negative emotions and actions as well as responsibility for other people and their possessions. Many of these thinkers attempted to seek out the consequential outcomes relating to the existence or non-existence of God. This philosophy became popular after World War 2 as the focus on an individual's _____.

(a) self-esteem and freedom was in vogue
(b) right to bear arms in public was at stake
(c) need for acceptance was at its highest
(d) family planning and cooperation was required

실존주의 철학은 개인을 각기 인생의 의미에서 유일한 요소로 간주한다. 더군다나 실존주의 사람들이 삶이 개인의 길에 놓아둔 타인과 그들의 소유물에 대한 책임감은 물론 부정적인 감정과 행동 같은 '방해 요소들'과 싸움과 동시에 열심히, 정직하게 살아야 한다고 단정한다. 다수의 실존주의 사상가들은 신이 존재하는가, 존재하지 않는가와 관련된 중대한 결론을 도출하려고 시도했다. 실존주의 철학은 제2차 세계 대전 이후 개인의 자존감과 자주성이 유행할 때 그 중심으로서 인기를 얻었다.

(a) 자존감과 자유가 인기를 얻으면서
(b) 공공연히 무기를 지닐 수 있는 권리가 위태로워지면서
(c) 수용해야 한다는 필요성이 절정에 달하면서
(d) 가족 계획과 협력이 요구되면서

해설   빈칸이 마지막에 있는 고난도 문제이다. 실존주의 철학의 정의를 내리고 있는 첫 번째 문장이 사실상 주제 문장이라 할 수 있다. 그 다음부터는 실존주의 철학에 대한 뒷받침 문장이 나열되고 있다. 첫 주제 문장과 나머지 뒷받침 문장과의 흐름을 잘 파악한 후에 마지막 문장 밑줄에 들어갈 내용을 판단한다.

첫 번째 문장: 실존주의 정의에 따르면 개인이 중심임을 알 수 있다.
→ 두 번째 문장: 실존주의에 대한 부연 설명 1
→ 세 번째 문장: 실존주의에 대한 부연 설명 2
→ 네 번째 문장: 실존주의 철학이 유명해졌다.

실존주의 철학이 유명해진 이유는 무엇일까? 실존주의가 추구하는 개인에 대한 중요성이 강조되었기 때문일 것이다. 즉, 개인과 관련된 요소가 부각되었던 것이다. 따라서 개인적 요소인 자부심과 자유가 언급되어 있는 (a)가 정답이다.

오답분석   (b) 제2차 세계 대전이 나왔다고 해서 무기에 관한 이야기는 아니다.
(c) 수용하는 자세와 개인적 가치를 중시하는 실존주의는 맞지 않다.
(d) 가족 계획과 협력은 본문에서 전혀 언급되지 않았다.

어구   existentialism 실존주의 | sole 유일한 | agent 요소 | posit 단정하다 | distraction 방해 요소
consequential 중대한 | self-esteem 자존감 | in vogue 유행하여 | bear (무기를) 몸에 지니다 | at stake
위태로운 | acceptance 수용하는 자세 | at its highest 절정에

· 빈칸 앞 문장만 보고 답을 찾으려는 우를 범하지 말자. 처음부터 끝까지 다 읽는 것이 가장 확실한 방법이다.

· 지문이 완결성이 없는 글일 때 마지막 문장에 밑줄이 있으면 좀 더 어려운 문제 유형으로 13, 14번에 잘 배치된다.

· 첫 번째 문장이 주제 문장이고 마지막 문장에 이를 다시 한번 풀어서 쓰는 양괄식일 경우 첫 번째 문장에 가장 확실한 힌트가 있고 이런 유형은 비교적 쉬운 문제에 속한다.

· 마지막 문장에 빈칸이 있는 문제는 비교적 어려우므로 900점 돌파를 위해 이 유형을 많이 연습하자.

용쌤의 비법 특강   만점 비법 3

For years, experts have embraced the idea that oil prices will continue to skyrocket due largely to geopolitical uncertainties. But starting this year, the prices remain stable, as new technologies have helped the OPEC countries pump more oil than before.

수년간 전문가들은 유가가 지정학적 불안정성으로 인해 계속 치솟을 것이라는 생각을 받아들였다. 그러나 올해부터 새로운 기술 개발로 OPEC 국가들이 원유를 전보다 더 많이 퍼냄에 따라 유가가 여전히 안정적이다.

어떤 문장에서 '현재완료시제 ~ (so far)'가 사용되었다고 하자. 다음 문장에서는 그와 반대되는 내용이 나올 가능성이 크다. 즉, '지금까지는 이렇게 해왔다. 그러나 이제는 아니다'라는 식으로 전개하는 경우가 많다. 앞으로 TEPS 독해를 하면서 이런 글의 흐름에 익숙해지기 바란다.

Many researchers over the years have claimed that they are making progress in terms of understanding how to treat cancer. _____, seldom do these claims result in an actual strategy to implement. Finally, according to four new studies published in the September issue of *Cell Cycle*, researchers are claiming that they now have learned of new potential therapies. The study shows that a body's support cells called fibroblasts produce the stroma which are connective tissues that surround tumor cells. The stroma provide nutrients to the tumor. A key finding in these studies was the fact that tumor cells can die when they aren't provided the nutrients from the stroma so drugs have been developed to break this tumor feeding cycle.

(a) By the same token

(b) However

(c) Incidentally

(d) Henceforth

수년간 많은 연구자들은 암 치료 방법을 이해하는 데에 진전이 있다고 주장해왔다. 그러나 이와 같은 주장은 암 치료를 위한 실행에 옮길 수 있는 실질적인 방법으로까지 좀처럼 이어지지 못하고 있다. 〈셀 사이클〉 9월호에 실린 새로운 연구 4건에 따르면 연구자들은 마침내 이제 새로운 잠재적 치료법을 알아냈다고 주장하고 있다. 이 연구에 따르면 섬유아 세포라 불리는 신체 지지 세포가 종양 세포를 둘러싸는 연결 세포인 기질을 만들어 낸다고 한다. 기질은 종양에 영양분을 공급해 준다. 이 연구의 중요한 발견은 종양이 기질로부터 영양을 공급받지 못하면 죽을 수 있다는 사실로, 종양을 키우는 사이클을 끊도록 약이 개발된 것이다.

(a) 같은 이유로

(b) 그러나

(c) 덧붙여 말하자면

(d) 지금부터

해설 Part 1은 모두 논리 문제이지만 15, 16번에 등장하는 연결어 문제야말로 논리의 결정판이라 할 수 있다. 이 문제는 쉽게 생각하면 어렵지 않게 풀 수 있는데 오히려 지문을 끝까지 다 읽으면 매우 어려워질 수 있다. 연결어 문제는 일반적으로 앞뒤 문장만 봐도 어느 정도 답을 찾을 수 있다. 일단 첫 번째 문장과 두 번째 문장만 살펴보자. 첫 문장은 암 치료에 대한 진전이 있었다는 내용이다. 그러나 두 번째 문장에서는 실질적인 치료법을 만들어 내지 못한다는 내용이 이어진다. 이 두 문장만 봐도 역접 관계임을 알 수 있으므로 바로 정답 (b)를 찾을 수 있다. 세 번째 문장은 Finally로 시작한다. 결국 암 치료법을 발견했으며, 치료법에 대해 설명하는 내용이 이어진다.

오답분석 나머지 선택지는 다음 풀이 접근법의 연결어 목록을 참고하길 바란다.

어구 implement 실행하다 | publish 발행하다 | fibroblast 섬유아 세포 | stroma 기질 (단백질을 주성분으로 하는 엽록체와 미토콘드리아 기초 물질) | connective 연결하는 | tumor 종양 | nutrient 영양분

- 시간이 부족할 경우 빈칸 앞뒤 문장만 유의해서 읽어도 실제로 답을 찾을 수 있는 경우가 있다.
- 그러나 고득점을 얻기 위해서는 전체를 다 읽는 마음가짐이 바람직하다.
- 다음은 시험에 나온 바 있는 어려운 연결어 목록이다. 지문 독해는 제대로 했는데 연결어의 의미를 정확히 몰라서 틀리는 경우도 더러 있기 때문에 이번 기회에 까다로운 연결어를 자기 것으로 만들자.

❶ Granted (상대방의 말에) 인정해, 맞아 (다음 문장에 보통 역접 연결어 But이 온다.)

Granted, North Korea had its own justifiable reason to open fire on the territory. But it harmed civilians.

북한이 그 영토에 공격을 가한 합당한 이유가 있었다는 점은 인정한다. 그러나 민간인이 다쳤다.

❷ Subsequently 이어서, 나중에 (드물지만 '결과적으로'라는 뜻도 있다.)

The President showed up with his secretaries. Subsequently, he issued a statement to all White House correspondents.

대통령은 장관들과 함께 등장했다. 이어서 백악관 출입 기자 모두에게 성명서를 발표했다.

❸ Consequently 결과적으로

The new employees have never received any formal training. Consequently, their productivity at work is very low.

신입 사원들은 어떠한 정식 교육도 받지 못했다. 결과적으로 회사에서 그들의 생산성은 매우 낮다.

❹ Likewise 마찬가지로

Public transportation is almost unavailable in the remote region. Likewise, its hospitals are also inaccessible.

외딴 지역에서 대중교통은 거의 이용할 수 없다. 마찬가지로 그 지역의 병원도 이용하기 힘들다.

❺ Alternatively 그렇지 않으면, 대신에

The company can make business trip arrangements for you. Alternatively, you can prepare for what is needed for the trip by yourself.

회사는 당신을 위해 해외 출장 준비를 해줄 수 있다. 그렇지 않으면 출장에 필요한 것을 당신 혼자서 준비해도 된다.

❻ Conversely 거꾸로, 반대로

If you increase taxes to pay for government programs, you're virtually making them expensive. Conversely, if you decrease taxes, you're making the programs cheaper.

세금을 인상하여 정부 프로그램을 마련한다면 프로그램은 사실상 비싸지는 것이다. 반대로 세금을 인하하면 정부 프로그램이 더 싸지는 것이다.

❼ By the same token 같은 이유로, 마찬가지로

The death penalty should be abolished on the ground that it infringes on human rights. By the same token, corporal punishment should be eliminated in the school.

사형 제도는 인권을 침해하기 때문에 폐지되어야 한다. 같은 이유로 학교에서의 체벌도 폐지되어야 한다.

❽ Henceforth 지금부터, 지금 이후로

Henceforth, students are not allowed to use their cell phones during classes.

지금부터 학생들은 수업 시간에 휴대 전화를 사용할 수 없다.

❾ Incidentally 말이 난 김에 말하자면, 덧붙여 말하자면 (새로운 내용을 언급할 때)

Many confidential documents are still being released by Wikileaks, which have caused a stir around the world. Incidentally, you can read some secret information about the two Koreas on the website.

많은 기밀 정보가 위키리크스를 통해 여전히 유출되고 있는데, 이는 전 세계적으로 반향을 일으켰다. 말이 나와서 하는 말인데 한국과 북한에 대한 기밀 정보도 홈페이지에서 읽을 수 있다.

⑩ Accordingly 따라서

Some of the laws recently passed have room for misinterpretation. Accordingly, they should be more clarified.

최근에 통과된 법규 중 일부는 잘못 해석될 여지가 있다. 따라서 이 법규들은 좀 더 명백히 설명되어야 한다.

⑪ In sum 요약해서 말하자면

In sum, everything boils down to cause and effect.

요약해서 말하자면, 모든 것은 원인과 결과로 귀결된다.

⑫ That being said/ Having said that/ This having been said/ That said

그렇다 하더라도, 그래도

Just like most of the smart phones, the company's new smart phones have a plethora of features. Having said that, they come with big sizes and unattractive colors.

대부분의 스마트폰과 마찬가지로 그 회사가 새로 출시한 스마트폰은 매우 많은 기능을 가지고 있다. 그렇다 하더라도 그 제품은 크기도 크고 색깔도 매력적이지 않다.

⑬ In fact vs. Indeed

이 두 연결어를 사전에서 찾아보면 '사실은,' '실제로'로 비슷한 뜻인 것처럼 보이는데, 사실은 다르다. In fact는 역접 연결어로 앞의 내용과 상반되는 내용을 유도한다. 반대로 Indeed는 앞의 내용을 더욱 강조하는 역할을 한다.

Korea and Japan prepared in earnest for the 2022 World Cup, having high hopes for it. In fact, Qatar was chosen to host the event.

한국과 일본은 2022년 월드컵 경기 개최 준비를 열심히 하였고, 기대감도 컸다. 그러나 카타르가 개최지로 선정되었다.

The US has nothing against diversity. Indeed, it wants more of it.

미국은 다양성에 대해 어떠한 부정적인 감정도 없다. 사실, 더 많은 다양성을 원한다.

✏️ **용쌤의 비법 특강** 만점 비법 4

TEPS 독해는 3~7문장 정도이며, 단어 수는 약 90개에서 130개이다. 이 범위 내에서 한 단락에는 내용상의 완결성과 함께 전달하고자 하는 하나의 메시지가 담겨 있다. 〈한 단락+하나의 메시지+3~7문장+90~130단어〉 포맷에서 문제가 만들어진다.

02-1
대의 파악하기

TEPS 독해 Part 2의 첫 번째 유형인 대의 파악 문제는 17번부터 22번까지이다. 요지, 주제, 제목, 목적 등을 찾는 문제가 출제되고 있고 각 개념을 정확하게 이해할 필요가 있다. TEPS 독해 타 유형보다 비교적 쉬운 편이므로 1분 내로 풀고 6문제를 모두 다 맞아야지 900점대 달성을 꿈꿀 수 있다.

→ 한 시험에 요지, 주제, 제목, 목적 문제가 모두 출제되는 경우는 드물다. 매 시험 지문의 주제와 목적을 묻는 문제는 빠지지 않고 출제되며. 요지 문제는 3번 시험 보면 2번 출제되는 빈도이다. 제목 문제는 3~5개월에 한번씩 나오는 추세이다.

→ 대의 파악 능력을 평가하기 때문에 답도 당연히 전반적인 것이 답이 되어야 한다. 선택지 중에서 한두 개는 글의 세부 내용을 언급하는 경우가 많으므로 혼동하지 말아야 한다.

→ 한 문제당 지문은 길지 않지만 하나의 완결성을 가지고 있다. 따라서 단락 후반부에 역접 연결어가 나오지 않는다면 앞의 두세 문장만 읽어도 답이 나오는 경우가 있다.

→ TEPS 독해 문제는 1분에 1문제를 푸는 것으로 원칙으로 한다. 그러나 17번부터 22번까지의 대의 파악 6문제는 난이도가 높지 않아 한 번 쭉 읽은 다음 선택지를 보면 되기 때문에 4분에 6문제를 풀 수도 있다. 대의 파악 문제를 빨리 풀어 시간을 절약한 다음 세부 내용 문제와 추론 문제에 시간을 더 확보해야 고득점이 가능하다.

Sustainable development is the current philosophy in the resource industries in this time of environmental concern. Its main premise is to make certain that there are enough resources for the human race today and the future while concurrently ensuring the needs of the natural environment are being met. To do this, companies are always on the lookout to cut down the energy they consume, reduce their carbon footprint, and find new ways to minimize other types of waste. Companies taking a longer term view of profit with the idea of being socially responsible through sustainable development are being rewarded both with government support and by consumers as they make their purchases.

Q: What is the main point of the passage?
(a) Government subsidies are the only reason for sustainable development.
(b) Resource companies seem to be embracing sustainable development.
(c) Consumers are using up too many valuable resources unsustainably.
(d) Companies with a short term view may not be sustainable.

지속 가능한 개발은 환경 문제가 대두되고 있는 시점에서 자원 산업 분야의 철학 경향이라 할 수 있다. 지속 가능한 개발은 현재와 미래에 인류가 사용할 충분한 자원을 확보하는 한편 자연 환경이 필요로 하는 것을 동시에 충족시켜 주는 것을 주요 전제로 한다. 그러기 위해서 회사는 사용하는 에너지를 줄이고 탄소 발자국을 낮추며 다른 종류의 폐기물 발생을 최소화할 새로운 방법을 모색하는 데 항상 노력을 기울이고 있다. 지속 가능한 개발을 통해 사회적 책임감을 가지고 장기적 관점에서 수익을 추구하는 회사는 정부의 지원과 소비자가 자사 제품을 구입함으로써 보상을 받을 수 있다.

Q: 글의 요지는 무엇인가?
(a) 정부의 보조금이 지속 가능한 개발을 하는 유일한 이유이다.
(b) 자원 회사는 지속 가능한 개발을 받아들이고 있는 것으로 보인다.
(c) 소비자들은 너무 많은 소중한 자원을 유지할 수 없게 고갈시키고 있다.
(d) 단기적 관점을 지닌 회사는 지속 가능하지 않을 것이다.

해설 요지 문제는 필자가 진정으로 하고자 하는 말이 무엇인지 파악하는 것이 관건이다. 이러한 문제는 특정 문장만을 읽고 답을 찾는 것이 아니라 한 단락을 정확하게 꿰뚫어야 찾을 수 있다. 그 작업이 쉽지 않을 경우 선택지에서 하나씩 오답을 걸러 내야 한다. 첫 번째 문장은 지속 가능한 개발의 입지, 두 번째 문장은 지속 가능한 개발의 정의, 세 번째 문장은 지속 가능한 개발을 위해 기업들이 어떻게 움직이고 있는지, 마지막 문장은 지속 가능한 개발을 실천함으로써 받는 보상으로 내용이 전개되고 있다. 필자가 결국 오늘날의 회사가 지속 가능한 개발을 받아들이고 있음을 말하고 싶었던 것으로 정답은 (b)이다.

오답분석 (a) 마지막 문장에서 정부 보조금과 함께 소비자가 자사의 물건을 더 구입한다고 한다.
(c) 소비자들이 너무 많은 자원을 낭비하고 있다고 언급된 바 없다.
(d) 본문은 장기적 관점을 언급하고 있다.

어구 sustainable development 지속 가능한 개발 | concern 걱정거리 | premise 전제 | concurrently 동시에 be on the lookout 경계하는 | carbon footprint 탄소 발자국 (온실 효과를 유발하는 이산화탄소의 배출량) subsidy 보조금 | embrace 받아들이다 | unsustainably 지속 가능하지 않게

- 요지는 main point 또는 main idea이다. main topic과 혼동하지 말자.
- 요지란 한 단락에서 필자가 진정으로 하고자 하는 메시지이다.
- 일반적으로 선택지에서 요지는 문장으로 등장한다.
- 요지는 필자가 말하고자 하는 바이므로 단순한 사실(fact) 전달과는 거리가 멀다.
- must/ have to/ should/ need to가 있는 문장은 주의 깊게 볼 필요가 있다. 진정으로 하고자 하는 말이라면 '〜해야 한다'는 의미의 조동사가 있는 문장에 무게가 실리기 때문이다. 정답 고르기가 애매할 때 이와 같은 조동사가 있는지 잘 살펴보고, 그 내용이 반영된 문장이라면 답이 될 가능성이 높다.
- It is crucial[important/ imperative/ necessary/ mandatory/ compulsory/ obligatory] that이 있는 문장을 예의 주시하자. that 이하의 내용이 중요하다는 말이므로 이 문장은 요지일 가능성이 크다.
- 최상급 문장을 유의하자. 영어에서 최상급은 자주 쓰이는 편이 아니다. 그래서 최상급이 쓰였다면 특히 그 문장을 강조하고 싶다는 의도이다. 즉, 요지일 가능성이 크다. 예를 들어 한 단락의 마지막 문장에 The best thing in life is to help people out of poverty라고 나오면 이 문장이 한 단락을 정리하면서 마무리하는 문장으로 필자의 핵심 의도가 되는 것이다.

용쌤의 비법 특강 **만점 비법 5**

선택지에 only/ always/ any/ all/ every가 들어 있으면 조심해야 한다. 이 단어들은 내용을 단정하는 성격이 강하고 다른 의미상의 여지를 남겨두지 않는다. 본문에 언급된 내용이 선택지에서 알맞게 paraphrasing이 되었어도 이런 단어가 들어가면 그 의미가 달라져 오답일 가능성이 크다.

Measuring about 1/3 the size of the United States, the Kerguelen Plateau is a massive underwater plateau that was forged by enormous volcanic eruptions. Based on analysis of the soil layers in the basalt rock, it appears that much of the plateau was above the sea for 3 periods between 100 million and 20 million years ago. Today, while most of it is underwater, the Kerguelen Islands, Heard Island, and the McDonald Islands remain above sea level and are located about 3,000 km southwest of Australia. Scientists studying the formation believe that undersea volcanoes such as these may have caused changes in ocean currents, world climate, and sea levels in the past.

Q: What is the main topic of the passage?
(a) All underwater mountain ranges were above sea level in the past.
(b) Australia could have been forged by a massive subsea volcanic eruption.
(c) A chain of underwater volcanoes connect the Kerguelen Plateau and Australia.
(d) Underwater volcanic activity can change the geology of earth over time.

미국 면적의 약 1/3 크기인 케르겔렌 판은 거대한 수중 평지로 대규모의 화산 활동으로 형성되었다. 현무암 토양층을 분석해본 결과 케르겔렌 판은 1억만 년에서 2천만 년 전 사이에 해수면보다 높이 위치한 적이 3번 있었던 것으로 보인다. 현재 대부분이 수중에 잠겨 있지만 케르겔렌 섬과 허드 섬, 맥도날드 섬은 수면 위에 남아있고 호주 남서쪽에서 3천 킬로미터 떨어진 곳에 위치해 있다. 케르겔렌 판의 형성을 연구하는 과학자들은 이와 같은 해저 화산이 과거의 해류와 세계 기후, 해수면에 변화를 주었을지도 모른다고 생각한다.

Q: 다음 글의 주제는 무엇인가?
(a) 모든 해저 산맥은 과거 해수면 위에 있었다.
(b) 호주는 거대한 규모의 해저 화산 폭발로 형성될 수 있었다.
(c) 일련의 해저 화산이 케르겔렌 판과 호주를 연결시키고 있다.
(d) 해저 화산 활동은 시간이 지나면서 지구의 지질을 변화시킬 수 있다.

해설 주제 찾기 문제로 한두 문장만 보고는 답을 찾을 수 없도록 만든 문제이다. 단락을 다시 한번 읽어보기 바란다. 두괄식, 양괄식, 미괄식 중 어떤 형태의 단락인가? 바로 미괄식이다. 첫 세 문장은 마지막 주제 문장을 뒷받침하는 문장이다. 케르겔렌 판이 아니라 해저 화산 활동이 중요한 말이고 해저 화산 활동으로 인해 여러 변화가 있을 수 있다는 내용이 글의 주제이다. 따라서 정답은 (d)이다.

오답분석 (a) 선택지에서 all은 항상 조심해야 한다.
(b) 호주 대륙에 관한 내용이 아니다.
(c) 해저 화산의 화산 활동이 케르겔렌 판과 호주 대륙을 연결시킨다는 내용은 없다.

어구 forge 형성시키다 | soil layer 토양층 | basalt 현무암 | sea level 해수면 | current 해류 | mountain range 산맥

• 질문은 What is the main topic of the passage?로 주어진다.
• TEPS 독해 시험에서 주제라 함은 '이 글은 무엇에 관한 것인가?'라고 생각하면 된다.
• 실제로 단락의 첫 두세 문장만 봐도 답이 나오는 문제가 자주 출제되고 있다. 필자가 첫 문장에서 주제를 명시하고 나머지 문장에서 이를 뒷받침하기 때문에 두 문장만 읽어봐도 정답을 유추할 수 있다.

〈to+동사원형〉이 문장 맨 앞에 위치할 경우 그 다음은 거의 '~해야 한다'는 의무의 내용이 온다.

> To stay afloat in times of global economic crisis, companies must have their own edge that differentiates their rivals.
> 세계 경제 위기에 버텨내기 위해서는 회사가 경쟁사와 차별화할 수 있는 자체 우위를 반드시 갖추어야 한다.

유형 3 제목 찾기

Cardiomyopathy or 'Broken Heart Syndrome' is the sudden and potentially fatal condition that occurs in the body when someone is undergoing a surge of stress hormones. It was first discovered in Japan in 1991 and was originally named Takotsubo cardiomyopathy after a type of trap that Japanese fishermen used to capture octopuses. Japanese doctors X-raying a patient with Broken Heart Syndrome have reported that the heart's shape is similar to this trap. Upon the discovery of its cause, the condition became known as Broken Heart Syndrome. Recovery from this syndrome usually takes about a week if treated quickly.

Q: What is the best title for the passage?
(a) Broken Hearts and Octopuses Traps: The Connection
(b) Japanese Heart Conditions Related to the Octopus
(c) The Stress Induced by Octopus Traps
(d) Japanese Research on Broken Heart Syndrome

심근증 혹은 '상심증후군'은 스트레스 호르몬이 급격히 증가할 때 신체에서 발생하는 갑작스럽고 잠재적으로 치명적인 질환이다. 이 병은 1991년 일본에서 최초로 발견되었으며 원래는 일본 어부들이 문어를 잡을 때 사용하는 덫의 이름을 따서 타코츠보 심근증이라고 이름 붙여졌다. 상심증후군을 앓는 환자를 X선 촬영한 일본 의사들이 환자의 심장 모양이 이 덫과 비슷하다고 보고했다. 그리고 병의 원인을 파악하자마자, 이런 상태는 상심증후군인 것으로 알려졌다. 조속한 치료를 받으면 회복하는 데 약 일주일이 걸린다.

Q: 가장 적절한 제목은 무엇인가?
(a) 상심증후군과 문어 덫, 그 관련성
(b) 문어와 관련된 일본의 심장 질환
(c) 문어 덫에 의해 발생하는 스트레스
(d) 상심증후군에 관한 일본의 연구

해설   제목 찾기 문제는 글의 대의를 파악해야 하는 문제이다. 첫 번째 문장에서는 심근증에 대한 소개. 두 번째 문장과 세 번째 문장에서는 병명의 기원. 마지막에는 병의 치료에 관해 소개되고 있다. 심근증에 관한 글임을 알 수 있고, 각 문장의 내용을 다 포괄할 수 있는 단어를 선택지에서 찾으면 research가 적절하므로 정답은 (d)이다.

오답분석   (a) 상심증후군과 문어 덫은 한 단락의 일부 내용만을 담고 있다.
  (b) 문어는 병명의 기원을 설명하기 위한 것이고, 문어가 직접적으로 상심증후군을 일으킨다는 내용은 없다.
  (c) 문어 덫은 병명의 기원을 설명하기 위한 것이지 스트레스와는 관련이 없다.

어구   cardiomyopathy 심근증 | Broken Heart Syndrome 상심증후군 | surge 갑작스러운 증가 | induce 야기하다

- 질문은 What is the best title for the passage?로 주어진다.
- TEPS 독해에서 제목은 글 전반의 내용을 포함하며 주제보다는 조금 더 추상적이고 함축적으로 표현되는 경우가 많다.
- 대의 파악 문제이기 때문에 세부적이거나 지엽적인 내용을 언급하는 선택지는 바로 오답으로 처리한다.
- 선택지의 명사나 동사에 유의한다. 본문 문장과의 관련성을 따져 보자. 앞 문제의 경우 (d)의 research는 내용 전반을 포함하고 있다.
- 제목 문제는 주제, 목적 문제와 달리 보통 3개월에 한두 문제 출제된다.
- TEPS 독해 제목 유형을 소위 '착한 제목'과 '나쁜 제목'으로 분류할 수 있다. Japanese Research on Broken Heart Syndrome이 착한 제목으로 혼동되지 않고 딱딱 떨어지는 느낌이 있다. 이런 제목은 일반적으로 예측 가능한 제목이다. 문제는 '나쁜 제목' 유형이다. 이 경우 아래와 같이 신문의 헤드라인처럼 드라마틱하게 쓴다거나 극단적인 최상급을 쓸 수 있고 말장난(pun)을 사용할 수도 있다.
A Grandma Goes To Court Because Of Mickey Mouse
할머니 미키 마우스 때문에 법정에 가다
The Worst-Ever Economic Crisis That May Take Toll On The Global Economies
최악의 경제 위기, 전 세계 경제에 큰 영향 미칠 수 있어

용쌤의 비법 특강 만점 비법 7

독해 중 모르는 부사가 나왔을 때는 그냥 very라고 생각하고 넘어가자. 50% 이상 뜻이 통한다. 아니면 그 부사를 아예 없다고 생각하고 독해하길 바란다. 단, rarely/ hardly/ scarcely와 같은 부정 의미를 담고 있는 부사는 제외한다.

Dear Mrs. Derranger,

I was extremely shocked to learn about Terri's passing and I would like to express my sincere sympathy to you and your family on behalf of the senior management team here at Jamieson's Meats. As I'm sure you are aware from attending many of our company events over the years, Terri was highly respected by managers and employees alike throughout the entire company. Further, he was regarded as a visionary leader by anyone who ever worked with him and his contributions to this company will never be forgotten. Please accept our heartfelt condolences at this difficult time and if we can be of any assistance, please don't hesitate to contact us.

With sympathy,
Henry Lamington
CEO

Q: What is the main purpose of the letter?
(a) To apologize for Terry feeling that he had to leave the company
(b) To ask a manager's wife to attend more company functions
(c) To support a manager's family in his retirement plans
(d) **To offer support to a manager's family after his untimely death**

더렌저 부인께

테리 씨가 돌아가셨다는 소식을 접하고 매우 충격을 받았습니다. 제이미슨 미트의 선임 경영팀을 대표하여 부인과 가족분들에게 진심으로 애도의 말을 전합니다. 지난 몇 년간 회사 행사에 참여해서 아실 거라고 생각하지만 테리 씨는 회사의 매니저는 물론 직원들 모두로부터 매우 존경을 받았습니다. 그리고 테리 씨와 함께 일한 분들은 한결같이 테리 씨는 미래를 내다보는 리더라고 평가했습니다. 테리 씨가 회사에 바친 공헌은 절대로 잊혀지지 않을 것입니다. 힘든 시기에 회사의 애도를 받아 주시고 저희가 도움이 될 일이 있다면 주저 말고 언제든지 연락 주십시오.

CEO
헨리 래밍턴

Q: 서신의 목적은 무엇인가?
(a) 테리가 회사를 떠날 수 밖에 없다고 느꼈던 것에 대해 사과하기 위해
(b) 매니저 아내에게 회사 행사에 더 많이 참석해달라고 요청하기 위해
(c) 은퇴 계획이 있는 매니저 가족을 지원하기 위해
(d) 매니저의 갑작스러운 죽음 뒤 가족에게 힘을 주기 위해

해설 express my sincere sympathy/ will never be forgotten/ condolence에서 힌트를 얻어 편지 수신인의 남편이 사망한 것에 대해 애도를 표함을 알 수 있다. 따라서 정답은 (d)이다. Part 2 대의 파악 문제 중 목적을 묻는 문제가 가장 쉬운데, 아주 쉬운 문제는 첫 문장만 봐도 바로 답을 찾을 수 있고 조금 난이도가 높은 문제는 마지막에 결정적인 힌트가 나온다.

오답분석 (a) 테리는 회사를 떠난 것이 아니다.
(b) 과거에 행사에 참석한 것을 기억한다고 했지 행사 참석을 요청하지 않았다.
(c) 은퇴에 관한 내용은 언급되지 않았다.

어구 passing 사망 | express one's sincere sympathy 진심으로 애도를 표하다 | on behalf of ~을 대표하여 visionary 미래를 내다보는 | heartfelt 진심이 담긴 | condolence 애도 | function 〈회사의〉 행사

풀이
접근법

- 질문은 What is the main purpose of the letter?로 주어진다.
- 첫 문장에 I am writing to 혹은 I am writing this letter to가 나오면 그 문장에 정답의 힌트가 나올 가능성이 크다.
- 목적 문제는 시간 절약형 문제다. 뒤의 추론 문제를 위해 빨리 풀어서 시간을 아껴두자.

용쌤의 비법 특강 만점 비법 8

글을 빨리 읽기 위해서는 뒤에서부터 해석하는 습관을 버리고, 읽어가면서 바로 이해하고 넘어가야 한다. 특히 문장을 읽다가 after나 before가 나오면 의미를 염두에 두며 해석을 뒤에서부터 하지 않고 보이는 대로 읽고 넘어가면서 시간을 절약하는 것도 간단한 독해 전략이다.

> The residents in the remote island evacuated before Hurricane Alex touched down on it.
> 외딴 섬에 거주하는 주민들은 대피했고 그 후 허리케인 알렉스가 그 섬에 상륙했다.
>
> The young child was hospitalized after he choked on plastic toys.
> 어린 아이는 플라스틱 장난감이 목에 걸리자 병원에 입원했다.

Brazil has commenced auctioning parts of its rainforest to private logging companies. One million hectares are being made available as logging concessions this year and this amount is expected to rise to 11 million hectares within five years. While this may sound like an environmentalist's worst nightmare, the Brazilian government claims it will reduce demand for illegal logging and make sure the forests are managed in a sustainable way. The biggest drivers of deforestation are clearance for cattle grazing, growing soy beans, illegal roads and small-scale slash and burn farming. The concessions will allow companies to take only about four to six trees per hectare. Is this a legitimate plan or a recipe for disaster?

Q: What is the news article mainly about?
(a) **Outlining the government's rationale for approving private logging in the Amazon**
(b) Environmentalists' misguided views on conservation over economic stability
(c) The selling off of the world's largest rainforest to the highest bidder
(d) Allowing logging in the Amazon reduces the need for illegal slash and burn

브라질은 열대 우림의 일부를 민간 벌목 업체에게 경매 형식으로 팔기 시작했다. 올해 벌목 영업권으로 백만 헥타르를 사용할 수 있게 되고 이는 향후 5년 내로 천백만 헥타르로 증가할 것으로 보인다. 환경론자의 관점에서는 최악의 상황인 것처럼 보이지만 브라질 정부는 불법 벌목 수요를 줄이고 열대 우림 지역을 지속 가능한 방식으로 관리할 수 있을 것이라 주장한다. 산림 황폐의 가장 큰 주범은 가축 방목 허가, 콩 재배, 불법 도로, 소규모 화전 농법이다. 이번 영업권 승인으로 인해 벌목 회사는 1헥타르당 4그루에서 6그루만 벌목할 수 있게 된다. 과연 합당한 계획일까, 아니면 재앙으로 가는 길일까?

Q: 뉴스 기사는 무엇에 관한 내용인가?
(a) 아마존 열대 우림에서의 민간 벌목을 승인한 정부의 결정 근거에 대한 설명
(b) 경제적 안정성보다 보존에 관한 환경론자의 잘못된 견해
(c) 세계 최대의 열대 우림을 가장 높은 가격을 제시한 입찰자에게 매각함
(d) 아마존 벌목 승인이 불법 화전의 필요성을 줄여 줌

해설 대의 파악 문제는 매달 등장하는 유형으로 그리 어렵지는 않다. 아마존 열대 우림의 벌목 승인이라는 사실(fact)이 먼저 언급되었고 정부가 왜 그런 결정을 내렸는지 이유를 설명하고 있다. 따라서 정답은 (a)이다.

오답분석 (b) 환경론자들의 의견을 대변하는 글이 아니다.
(c) 단락에서 언급되지 않은 내용이다.
(d) 화전 내용이 언급은 되었지만 세부 내용이 아니기 때문에 정답이 될 수 없다.

어구 commence 시작하다 | auction 경매하다 | logging 벌목 | concession 영업권 | sustainable 지속 가능한 | deforestation 산림 황폐 | clearance 허가 | slash and burn farming 화전 농법 | a recipe for disaster 재난으로 가는 방법 | rationale 근거 | misguided 잘못된 | stability 안정성 | selling off 매각 bidder 입찰자

• 질문은 What is the article[passage] mainly about? 혹은 What is the article[passage] mainly talking about[discussing]?으로 주어진다.

• 주제 찾기 문제와 비슷하며, 실제 시험에서 그리 어렵지 않게 출제되고 있어 빨리 풀어서 시간을 절약할 수 있는 문제다.

용쌤의 비법 특강 **만점 비법 9**

TEPS 독해는 문학, 예술, 정치, 경제, 사회, 문화 등 거의 모든 영역이 소재가 되고 있다. 그중에서도 최신 시사 내용이 자주 출제되고 있는 점에 주목해야 한다. 일례로 2010년 12월 5일 정기 TEPS 독해 5번 문제는 NASA가 극단적인 환경에서 살 수 있는 미생물(extremophile)을 발표하는 내용이 출제되었다. 당시 실제로 NASA는 독성 물질 비소를 먹고 사는 새로운 생명체에 대한 중대 발표를 한 바 있다. 이런 예는 과거 TEPS 독해 시험에서도 얼마든지 있었다. 한 기업이 집단 소송(class action suit)을 당해 징계적 처벌(punitive damages)과 보상적 처벌(compensatory damages)을 받아야 한다는 내용, 한 금융인(financier)의 천문학적인 (astronomical) 사기 사건(scam)에 관한 글, 오바마 대통령의 한국 교육의 우수성 인정에 관한 글 등 매 시험에 적어도 하나 이상은 시사성이 있는 지문이 출제되고 있다. TEPS 독해와 청해 Part 4는 시사적 내용을 많이 알 수록 큰 효과를 낼 수 있다. 영어 실력뿐만 아니라 지적 능력까지 향상시킬 수 있는 영자 신문 보기를 권한다.

Part

02-2
세부 내용 찾기

TEPS 독해 Part 2의 두 번째 유형인 세부 내용 문제는 23번부터 32번까지로 총 10문제가 출제되고 있다. 앞에서 학습한 대의 파악과 정반대 성격의 문제이다. 말 그대로 세부적인 내용을 물어보기 때문에 하나하나 내용을 대조하느라 선택지 문장도 제대로 못 읽는 상황이 발생할 수 있다. 2010년 1월 시험부터는 새로운 세부 내용 유형의 문제가 등장한 것이 주목할 만하다.

⊙ 문제를 어떻게 풀지 미리 결정한다.

(1) 단락 → 질문 → 선택지: 세부적인 내용을 물어보기 때문에 단락을 다 읽고 선택지를 보면 독해력과 기억력이 매우 탁월한 이상 자칫하면 다시 단락을 읽어야 하는 상황이 발생한다.

(2) 질문 → 선택지 → 단락: 단점은 잘못된 정보 3개를 가지고 읽기 때문에 독해 속도가 느려질 수 있고 선택지를 4개 외워서 독해하는 것이 쉽지 않다.

(3) 읽으면서 선택지 보기: 본문을 읽으면서 선택지도 같이 보자. 즉, 본문 한두 문장을 읽고 선택지 한두 개를 본다. 그 타이밍은 학습자의 몫이다. 1분에 1문제를 푸는 데 가장 효율적인 방법이 아닐까 한다.

⊙ 세부 내용 문제 10문제 중 후반부 3, 4문제가 까다로운 편이므로 앞 문제는 빨리 빨리 풀어야 한다.

⊙ 필자가 실제로 TEPS 시험을 30회 이상 보고 시중에 나와 있는 기출 문제를 분석한 결과 세부 내용 문제에서 (a)와 (b) 그리고 (c)와 (d)의 정답 비율은 4:6이다. 또한 정답이 되는 근거는 단락 후반부에 주로 위치한다. 하지만 (c), (d)가 답으로 잘 나온다는 점이 중요한 것이 아니다. (a), (b) 정답이 열 문제 중 4문제 가량 나온다는 사실이 중요하다. 단락의 한두 문장, 많으면 세 문장까지만 읽고도 선택지를 보면 빠른 시간에 답을 고를 수 있다는 말이기 때문이다. 답이 확실하게 나왔다고 판단이 되면 그 다음 문장과 선택지는 읽지 않고 바로 넘어간다. 그래야 시간을 절약할 수 있고 까다로운 추론 문제를 여유 있게 풀 수 있기 때문이다.

⊙ 단락에 숫자가 나오면 정답이든 오답이든 반드시 문제화되니 숫자에 유의하자.

⊙ 최근 Which of the following claims is made in the passage? 또는 Which of the following claims is made about … in the passage? 유형의 문제가 새롭게 등장했다.

Section 1 유형별 TEPS 독해 43

Dear Mr. Brown,

It gives me great pleasure to recommend Mark McKenzie, a former tenant of mine for over two years, as a tenant for your apartment complex. Without fail, his rent was taken care of every month in a timely manner and others in the complex always had nothing but positive things to say about him. Initially, there was an issue regarding a door knocker mounted on his door which was in violation of the apartment code; however, upon discussing it with him, he was quick to comply and removed it. Finally, I would like to note that upon making the decision to move to a larger apartment, he gave me ample notice to find a replacement tenant.

Sincerely,

Jane Austen

Complex Manager

Q: Which of the following is correct according to the letter?

(a) Mr. McKenzie failed to pay his rent in a timely manner often.

(b) Mr. McKenzie knocked down his door just after he first moved in.

(c) The complex manager took great pleasure in getting rid of Mr. McKenzie.

(d) The complex manager had sufficient time to find a new tenant.

브라운 씨께

저의 건물에 지난 2년간 지냈던 세입자 마크 맥켄지 씨를 귀하의 아파트 단지 세입자로 추천할 수 있게 되어 기쁘게 생각합니다. 월세를 단 한번도 어긴 적 없이 제때 납부했고 아파트 단지의 다른 사람들도 맥켄지 씨에 대해 긍정적인 말만 합니다. 초기에 문에다 도어 노커를 설치해서 아파트 규칙에 어긋나는 일이 있었지만 문제를 상의한 후 그는 아파트 규칙에 즉각 동의하고 제거했습니다. 마지막으로 맥켄지 씨는 좀 더 큰 집으로 옮기기로 결정하자마자 제게 다음 세입자를 구할 수 있도록 충분한 시간을 주었습니다.

아파트 매니저

제인 오스틴

Q: 서신에 따르면 다음 중 옳은 것은?

(a) 맥켄지 씨는 종종 제때 월세를 내지 못했다.

(b) 맥켄지 씨는 처음 이사 오고 나서 그의 문을 부수었다.

(c) 아파트 매니저는 맥켄지 씨를 아파트에서 내보낼 수 있게 되어 매우 기뻐했다.

(d) 아파트 매니저는 새로운 세입자를 찾을 충분한 시간을 확보했다.

해설 아파트에서 한 입주자를 다른 아파트에 추천해주는 내용의 편지글이다. 마지막 문장에서 맥켄지 씨가 이사 가기로 결정한 뒤 다음 세입자를 찾을 충분한 시간을 주었다는 언급이 있으므로 정답은 (d)이다. 두 번째 문장까지 읽고 선택지 (a)를, 세 번째 문장을 읽고 선택지 (b)를, 선택지 (c)를 읽고 get rid of가 잘못되었음을 파악하고 걸러낸다. (a), (b), (c)가 확실히 답이 아니므로 (d)는 읽지 않고 바로 답으로 선택하고 다음 문제로 넘어간다.

오답분석 (a) 맥켄지 씨는 항상 제때 월세를 냈다.

(b) 문을 부순 것이 아니라 문에 도어 노커를 설치한 내용이었다.

(c) 전체적으로 맥켄지 씨가 훌륭한 입주자였다는 내용이므로 맞지 않다.

어구 tenant 세입자, 입주자 | timely 시의 적절한 | initially 처음에 | regarding ~에 관해서 | door knocker 도어 노커 (문 두드리는 쇠고리) | comply 준수하다 | ample 충분한

- 질문은 Which of the following is correct according to the passage?로 주어진다.
- 정답은 본문에 언급된 내용이 paraphrasing되어 나온다.
- 본문에 숫자가 나오면 정답이든 오답이든 반드시 선택지에 나오지만 주로 오답으로 등장한다.
- 특히 시간 부족할 경우, 첫 두 문장을 읽고 답이 나오면 바로 다음 문제로 넘어간다.
- 최상급에 유의한다. 단락에 one of the 최상급이 언급되고 선택지에 최상급으로 나오면 오답 처리해야 한다. the 최상급과 one of the 최상급은 의미가 다르다.
- 비교급에도 유의하자. 본문에 비교급이 언급되고 선택지에는 최상급으로 나오는 경우가 있다.
- 지문에 긍정적인 내용이 선택지에 부정적인 내용으로 언급될 수 있고, 그 반대일 수도 있음에 유의하자.

🖋 용쌤의 비법 특강 만점 비법 10

TEPS는 청해, 문법, 어휘 다음으로 독해 시간을 준다. 전체 시간 약 2시간 20분에서 앞의 세 영역을 1시간 35분 동안 전투를 치르듯 풀고 지친 상태에서 독해 영역을 푸는 것이다. 이런 체력적 부담을 없애기 위해서 매달 TEPS에 응시할 필요가 있다. 집에서 모의고사로 푸는 것은 한계가 있다. 낯선 장소에서 낯선 사람과 부대끼면서 시험 상황에 익숙해져야 한다. 옆에서 다리 떠는 학생, 기침하는 학생, 잡음이 들리는 스피커, 감독관 확인으로 인해 끊기는 집중력 등, 이 모든 변수를 극복하는 훈련이 필요하다. 가능한 시험을 많이 봐서 TEPS 독해를 거뜬히 풀 수 있는 체력과 집중력을 키우자. 매달 TEPS에 응시하면서 일 년에 두세 번 정도 찾아오는 '대박 달'도 노릴 수 있다.

According to three researchers, Strayer, Drews, and Crouch in their study titled, "A Comparison of the Cell Phone Driver and the Drunk Driver," using a cell phone while driving can be just as dangerous as driving while intoxicated. Distracted while using a cell phone, drivers miss traffic signals and generally react more slowly to driving conditions. Frighteningly, the National Highway and Traffic Safety Association estimates that more than 100 million U.S. drivers use their cell phone while driving and about 8% of drivers on the freeway at any given moment in the day are either conversing or texting on their cell phone.

Q: Which of the following claims is made in the passage?

(a) Driving intoxicated is just as acceptable as driving while using a cell phone.

(b) Slowly reacting to general driving conditions is only a problem with drunk drivers.

(c) A passenger using a cell phone in a car can easily distract the driver.

(d) While driving, cell phone use can be just as hazardous as inebriation.

〈운전 중 휴대 전화 사용과 음주 운전에 관한 비교〉라는 제목의 연구를 한 3명의 과학자 스트레이어, 드류, 크라우치에 따르면 운전 중 휴대 전화 사용은 음주 운전만큼이나 위험할 수 있다고 한다. 운전 중 휴대 전화를 사용하면 주의가 분산되기 때문에 운전자가 교통 신호를 놓칠 수 있고 일반적으로 운전 상황에 더 느리게 대응한다. 놀랍게도 전국 고속 도로 교통 안전청에서 추산하는 바에 따르면 미국의 1억 명이 넘는 운전자들이 운전 중에 휴대 전화를 사용하고 있고 하루 중 어느 때이고 고속 도로 운전자의 8%가 휴대 전화로 대화를 하거나 문자를 주고받는다.

Q: 다음 중 지문에서 언급된 주장은?
(a) 음주 운전은 운전 중 휴대 전화 사용만큼이나 용인할 수 있다.
(b) 일반적인 도로 상황에서 느리게 대응하는 것이 음주 운전의 유일한 문제이다.
(c) 차에서 휴대 전화를 사용하는 탑승자는 운전자의 주의를 쉽게 분산시킬 수 있다.
(d) 운전 중 휴대 전화 사용은 음주 운전만큼이나 위험하다.

해설 첫 번째 문장에서 운전 중 휴대 전화 사용은 음주 운전만큼이나 위험하다고 언급하고 있다. (d)를 보면 dangerous 가 hazardous로 바뀌었고 driving while intoxicated가 inebriation으로 바뀌었다. 세부 내용 문제는 이렇게 같은 내용을 다른 단어로 바꾸어 정답 선택지를 만든다는 점을 기억하자. 정답은 (d)이다.

오답분석 (a) 위험하다고 했지 용인 가능하다고 하지 않았다.
(b) 선택지에 only가 나오면 오답일 가능성이 크다. 유일한 문제인지는 알 수 없고 언급되지도 않았다.
(c) 차량 탑승자가 운전자의 주의를 분산시킨다는 언급은 없다.

어구 intoxicated 술에 취한 | distracted 주의가 분산된 | estimate 추산하다 | converse 대화하다
text 문자를 보내다 | acceptable 받아들일 수 있는 | driving conditions 도로 상황 | inebriation 술에 취함

풀이 접근법

- 최근에 등장하기 시작한 세부 내용 유형 문제로 질문이 Which of the following claims is made in the passage?로 주어진다.
- 단락에 언급된 주장과 일치하는 것을 찾으면 되는데, 앞서 설명한 세부 내용 유형 문제와 같은 접근법으로 풀면 된다.

용쌤의 비법 특강 **만점 비법 11**

타 영어 시험에 비해 TEPS는 영어 공부를 많이 해도 점수 올리기가 쉽지 않다. TEPS는 영어적 지식을 바탕으로 한 수험자의 논리력과 사고력을 묻는 시험이기 때문이다. 주어, 동사, 목적어를 끊어 가며 해석하는 지엽적인 학습법으로는 결코 TEPS 독해에서 고득점을 보장하기 힘들다. 점수가 일정 수준에 도달하면 더 이상 오르기 힘든 것이다. 평소 영문 독서를 통해 논리적으로 생각하는 연습을 하자. 당장은 고통스럽고 결과가 눈에 보이지 않더라도 꾸준히 연습하면 그 대가는 반드시 온다. TEPS 시험을 보면서 급격히 늘어난 자신의 독해 실력에 놀랄 것이고, 점수를 통해 그 노력을 눈으로 확인할 수 있을 것이다. 다시 한번 강조한다. TEPS는 영어 지식을 묻는 시험이 아닌 논리력과 사고력의 시험이다.

02-3
추론하기

TEPS 독해를 풀 때는 Part 3 → Part 1 → Part 2 순서로 푸는 것이 바람직하다. Part 3은 배점이 높으면서도 쉽기 때문에 먼저 푸는 것이다. 이런 순서로 문제를 풀면 마지막에는 Part 2의 추론 5문제만 남는다. 바로 이 5문제에서 TEPS 독해 점수가 결정된다고 해도 과언이 아니다. 독해 고득점을 위해서는 바로 앞 세부 내용 10문제를 10분 내에 풀고 7~8분 정도 확보한 상태에서 추론 5문제에 접근하는 것이 관건이다.

- ➔ 33번부터 37번까지 5문제가 출제되고 있다. 사실상 독해 중 가장 어려운 문제 유형으로 배점도 상대적으로 높다.

- ➔ 세부 내용 문제와 달리 추론 문제이기 때문에 지문 전체를 조망할 수 있어야 한다. 지문을 다 읽은 다음에 문제를 푸는 것이 바람직하다.

- ➔ 추론 문제이긴 하지만 세부 내용 문제처럼 특정 문장만 보고 답을 찾아낼 수 있는 경우가 있다. 이런 문제는 쉬운 문제이다.

- ➔ 특히 37번 문제가 매우 어렵게 출제되고 있다. 내용도 어렵거니와 이해하기 벅찬 문장도 나온다.

- ➔ 추론 5문제 중에서 두 문제 이상 틀리면 안 된다.

- ➔ 행간의 의미를 파악하면서 글쓴이의 태도와 뉘앙스를 잘 읽어내야 한다.

According to Dr. Ian Joint, carbon dioxide increase in the atmosphere is turning the world's oceans into weak acids that are affecting marine life and oxygen levels. Further, the effect on marine life may be significant enough to cause loss of a major food source for humankind. Millions of types of bacteria called microbes are responsible for keeping the planet's oceans fertile and assist in reducing the amount of toxins in the oceans. Currently, they are at risk of dying due to the imbalance being created by the acidification of oceans. The gravity of this situation is quite severe, given that this plant matter in the oceans creates almost half of the oxygen globally. Putting microbes at risk puts humanity and the planet at risk.

Q: What can be inferred from the passage?
(a) **Microbes are essential to maintaining oxygen levels in the world.**
(b) Carbon dioxide increases the amount of toxic bacteria in the world's oceans.
(c) Humans may soon be consuming seafood too rich in carbon dioxide.
(d) Acidification of the world's oceans is caused by too many marine microbes.

이안 조인트 박사에 따르면 대기 중 이산화탄소 증가로 인해 전 세계의 해양이 약산성으로 변하고, 그로 인해 해양 생물과 산소량에 영향을 미치고 있다고 한다. 게다가 해양 생물에 대한 영향은 인류가 주요 음식 공급원을 잃을 수 있을 정도로 크다. 미생물이라 불리는 수백만 종류의 박테리아로 인해 지구의 바다 영양분을 풍부하게 유지하고 바다의 독성 물질을 줄이는 데 도움이 된다. 현재 해양의 산성화로 인한 불균형 때문에 미생물이 사라질 위험에 처해 있다. 현 상황은 바다의 미생물이 전 세계적으로 산소의 약 절반을 만들어 낸다는 점을 고려할 때 매우 심각한 수준이다. 미생물을 위험에 빠뜨리면 인류와 지구도 위험에 빠진다.

Q: 다음 글을 통해 유추할 수 있는 것은?
(a) 미생물은 지구의 산소량을 유지하는 데 매우 중요하다.
(b) 이산화탄소는 전 세계 해양의 독성 박테리아 양을 증가시킨다.
(c) 인간은 머지않아 이산화탄소가 지나치게 함유된 해산물을 먹게 될 것이다.
(d) 해양의 산성화는 너무 많은 해양 미생물에 의해 발생한다.

해설 미생물이 해양에 미치는 여러 긍정적인 효과가 언급되면서 지문 전반을 통해 미생물의 중요성이 강조되고 있다. 전 세계 절반 가량의 해양 산소를 생성하는 미생물이 산성화로 인해 폐사할 위기에 처해 있으므로 평균 산소량을 유지하기가 쉽지 않을 것이다. 따라서 정답은 (a)이다. 특정 문장만 보고 답을 찾을 수도 있지만 글 전체를 꿰뚫은 상태에서 답을 찾는 것이 고득점의 지름길이다.

오답분석 (b) 증가시키는 것이 아니라 감소시킨다.
(c) 이산화탄소 증가로 인한 영향은 해산물에 관한 것이 아니라 해양의 산성화이다.
(d) 해양의 산성화는 이산화탄소의 증가로 인한 것이다.

어구 carbon dioxide 이산화탄소 | weak acid 약산성 | microbe 미생물 | fertile 비옥한, 영양이 풍부한
toxin 독소 | acidification 산성화 | gravity 중대성 | put … at risk ~을 위험에 빠뜨리다

풀이
접근법
• 질문은 What can be inferred from the passage?로 주어진다.
• 단락 전반의 흐름을 이해해야 쉽게 풀 수 있다. 행간의 의미를 파악하고 필자가 글을 쓰는 이유를 파악해야 한다.
• 단락 내 쟁점이 되는 중요한 내용이 문제로 만들어진다. 지엽적이거나 세부적인 내용은 정답이 될 가능성이 낮다.

평소 TEPS 독해 문제를 풀 때 40문제 한 세트를 통째로 풀기 보다는 유형별로 문제를 집중 공략한다. Part 1의 빈칸 16문제, Part 2의 대의 파악 5문제 · 세부 내용 10문제 · 추론 5문제, Part 3의 3문제씩 유형별로 집중해 풀면 출제자의 의도를 꿰뚫을 수 있어 해석이 잘 되지 않더라도 정답을 맞힐 수 있는 감(感)까지 얻을 수 있다. 그런 후 시험 3~4일 전에 실전처럼 독해 모의고사 40문제를 한번에 푸는 연습을 한다.

유형 2 세부적인 내용 추론

The Vatican is the world's smallest independent city-state and has a population of 800 people living on 44 hectares of land. The city is an enclave surrounded completely by the city of Rome and is divided into 2 areas, the Holy See and Vatican City. For the residents in the Holy See, diplomatic and service passports are issued. Outside of the Holy See in Vatican City, regular Vatican passports are issued. Additionally, the Vatican has its own military guards, its own national anthem, and its own form of currency that is accepted throughout the EU. While a group of cardinals appointed by the Pope have authority for legislative and judicial purposes, the Pope has absolute power in this jurisdiction.

Q: What can be inferred from passage?
(a) **Though surrounded by Rome, the Vatican remains an independent state.**
(b) The government structure of the Vatican is an exact duplicate of Rome.
(c) The Vatican has its own money not usable in the rest of Europe.
(d) The holy land of the Vatican does not allow any secular residents.

바티칸은 세계에서 가장 작은 독립 도시 국가로 44 헥타르 면적에 800명의 인구가 살고 있다. 도시는 로마에 완전히 둘러싸인 소수 집단의 거주지로 교황청과 바티칸 시로 나뉜다. 교황청에 거주하는 사람들에게는 외교관 여권 및 일반 여권이 발급된다. 교황청 밖의 바티칸 사람들에게는 일반 바티칸 여권이 발급된다. 또한 바티칸은 자체 군사 병력, 자체 국가, EU 내에서 통용되는 자체 통화를 보유하고 있다. 교황이 임명하는 추기경에게 입법 및 사법 목적으로 권한이 있지만 바티칸에 대한 절대적인 권한은 교황에게 있다.

Q: 글에서 유추할 수 있는 것은 무엇인가?
(a) 바티칸은 로마에 둘러싸여 있지만 독립 국가로 남아 있다.
(b) 바티칸의 정부 구조는 로마와 꼭 닮았다.
(c) 바티칸은 나머지 유럽 지역에서 통용되지 않는 자체 통화가 있다.
(d) 바티칸 성지는 어떠한 세속 거주자도 허용하지 않는다.

해설   바티칸을 소개하는 글이다. 첫 번째 문장과 두 번째 문장에서 바티칸이 독립 국가이며 로마에 둘러싸여 있다고 언급하므로 정답은 (a)이다. 이 문제는 글 전체를 읽고 추론하는 문제가 아니라 특정 부분만 읽고도 답을 알 수 있다. 세부 내용 문제와 비슷한 쉬운 문제이므로 반드시 맞춰야 한다.

오답분석   (b) 바티칸의 정부 구조가 로마와 닮았다는 언급은 없다.

                  (c) 자체 통화가 유럽에서 통용된다고 했다.

                  (d) 세속 거주자를 배제한다는 내용은 없다.

어구   enclave 소수 민족[집단] 거주지 | currency 통화 | cardinal 추기경 | legislative 입법의 | judicial 사법의
duplicate 복제(품) | secular 속세의

・질문은 What can be inferred from the passage?로 주어진다.

・전체 내용보다는 특정 문장만 봐도 답을 추론할 수 있는 세부 추론형 문제라 할 수 있다.

・숫자를 유의해서 보되 그 숫자가 글에서 의미하는 바를 잘 잡아내야 한다.

용쌤의 비법 특강   **만점 비법 13**

TEPS 독해는 한 단락을 바탕으로 문제가 출제된다. 평소 TEPS 공부를 할 때 TEPS 문제집만 가지고 공부를 할 것이 아니라 〈뉴스위크〉, 〈타임〉, 〈이코노미스트〉 같은 영어 잡지로 공부하는 것도 만점을 위한 방법이다. 문제집에 있는 한 단락에만 연연하지 말고 여러 단락으로 구성된 한 편의 글을 읽으면서 단락과 단락이 어떤 논리로 전개되는지 살펴봐야 한다. 이런 훈련을 거친 후 TEPS 독해 문제를 보면 매우 쉽게 느껴질 것이다. 몸에 납 주머니를 매고 운동을 하다가 실전에서 납 주머니를 떼고 경기에 임하면 몸이 매우 가벼워져 더 좋은 결과를 만들 수 있다고 한다. TEPS 공부를 할 때에도 목표를 100% 달성하기 위해 100%의 노력만 할 것이 아니라 120% 이상의 노력을 쏟아야 한다.

03

통일성을 해치는 문장 찾기

TEPS 독해의 마지막 유형 Part 3은 38번에서 40번까지 총 3문제이며 TEPS 독해 중 가장 배점이 높은 유형으로 최대 15점까지 주어진다. 다섯 문장으로 구성된 한 단락에서 완결성을 해치는 문장 하나를 골라내면 된다.

→ 어휘 영역이 끝나고 독해 1번 문제부터 풀기보다는 Part 3부터 먼저 풀도록 한다. Part 3는 배점이 높은 반면 문제가 그리 어렵지 않기 때문에 3문제 다 맞힐 수 있다. 그래서 혹시나 시간이 부족해서 찍어야 하는 상황이 발생할 경우 배점이 낮은 문제를 찍는 것이 바람직하다.

→ 일반적으로 3문제가 모두 쉽게 출제되는 편이지만, 2~3달에 한번은 3문제 중에서 한 문제가 어렵게 나오는 경우가 있다. Part 3은 배점이 크기 때문에 시간을 조금 더 들여서라도 꼭 맞아야 한다. 17번부터 32번까지 대의파악과 세부 내용 문제에서 시간을 충분히 줄일 수 있기 때문에 Part 3은 다 맞아야 한다. 그러나 아무리 까다롭더라도 절대로 2분 이상 넘겨서는 안 된다. 독해 전체 시간 관리에 차질을 빚을 수 있다.

→ 첫 번째 문장이 제일 중요하다. Part 3에서 첫 번째 문장이 단락의 주제 문장으로 등장하는 경우가 3문제 중 2문제 정도 등장하는 경우가 많다. 이런 유형은 비교적 쉽게 문제를 풀 수 있다.

→ 그러나 첫 번째 문장이 주제 문장이 아닐 경우, 즉 나열식 문장이거나, 단락의 완결성은 떨어지지만 문장과 문장 사이의 논리는 살아있는 문제가 특히 어렵다.

→ 나무보다는 숲을 보는 마음으로 Part 3에 임하자. 위에서 내려다보는 마음으로, 세부적이거나 지엽적인 내용에 연연하지 말고 전체를 조망하는 마인드를 견지해야 한다.

Contrary to traditional belief, smelling the cork before drinking a wine reveals little about the wine. (a) Servers offer you the cork to allow you to read the date or any other information, should there actually be any written on it. (b) Further, you should inspect it for mold, drying, cracking, or breaks which indicates poor storage of the wine. **(c) Cork material from Portugal tends to be the most popular in the world.** (d) Wines with a musty smell, similar to wet cardboard or mold, often are referred to as "corked," meaning that they have gone off and are undrinkable.

통념과 달리 와인을 마시기 전에 코르크 냄새를 맡는 것으로 와인에 대해 알 수 있는 것은 거의 없다. (a) 서빙하는 이는 코르크에 어떤 내용이 적혀 있다면 당신이 날짜와 다른 정보를 읽을 수 있도록 코르크를 내어 줄 것이다. (b) 더욱이 당신은 곰팡이, 건조 상태, 금이 간 상태 등 와인이 잘못 보관되었음을 알려 주는 파손 상태를 검사해야 한다. (c) 포르투갈산 코르크 재료가 세계에서 가장 인기가 많다. (d) 젖은 마분지 냄새나 곰팡이와 비슷한 퀴퀴한 냄새가 나는 와인은 '코르크트 와인'이라고 하는데 와인이 상하거나 마실 수 없는 상태임을 의미한다.

해설 와인의 코르크에 관한 내용이다. 코르크가 갖고 있는 정보와 코르크 상태에 따라 와인의 상태를 알 수 있다는 글이다. 포르투갈산 코르크 재질이 인기 있음을 언급한 (c)는 전체 내용의 통일성을 해치므로 정답은 (c)이다. 문제가 조금 쉽다고 느낄지 모르는데, 실제 Part 3에서는 이 정도 수준의 문제가 출제되고 있다. 따라서 비교적 쉬우면서도 배점이 높은 Part 3을 먼저 공략하는 것이 고득점 전략 중 하나이다.

오답분석 첫 번째 문장: 코르크가 핵심어임을 알 수 있다.
(a) 코르크가 제공하는 정보를 언급하므로 뒤의 내용과 연결될 수 있다.
(b) 코르크의 상태에 따라 와인 보관이 어떠한지 알 수 있다.
(d) 코르크트 와인에 대해 언급하고 있다.

어구 reveal 드러내다 | inspect 검사하다 | drying 건조 | cracking 금이 감 | storage 보관 | musty 곰팡내 나는 | cardboard 마분지 | refer 언급하다 | corked 코르크 마개 냄새가 나는 | go off 음식이 상하다

- 3문제 중에서 2문제는 첫 문장이 주제 문장이다. 첫 문장에서 핵심어가 무엇인지 파악해야 한다. 그러고 나서 나머지 선택지 문장을 읽고 첫 문장과 관련 없는 것을 고른다.
- 남은 한 문제는 다섯 문장간의 유기적인 논리 관계를 따져야 하는 어려운 문제이다. 단락 전체 내용을 보면서 세부적인 내용도 같이 봐야 하기 때문에 1분 안에 풀기에는 까다로운 편이다.
- 아무리 확실한 답이 나왔다 해도 무조건 선택지 (d)까지 읽어야 한다. TEPS의 함정은 교묘한데 특히 Part 3의 경우가 그렇다. 신중한 자세가 필요하다.

용쌤의 비법 특강 만점 비법 14

TEPS 독해에서 고득점을 받기 위해서는 당연히 독해 실력이 좋아야 하겠지만 그것이 다는 아니다. 2시간 30분에 이르는 시험을 거뜬히 치러낼 수 있는 '**TEPS 체력**'이 필요한데, 이에 못지 않게 중요한 것이 시간 관리이다. Part 1과 Part 3은 총 19문제로 19분 안에 푼다. Part 2는 대의 파악과 세부 내용 16문제를 13~14분 내로, 추론 5문제를 7~8분 내로 풀고, 마킹에 2분, 애매한 문제 고민에 3분을 쓰면 독해 시간 관리는 성공이다.

Section 2
주제별
TEPS 독해

□ TEPS 독해 지문을 주제별로 나누어 보면 과학, 경제, 금융, 정치, 사회, 문화, 예술, 스포츠, 역사, 종교, 문학, 광고, 비즈니스 서신 등 거의 모든 주제를 다루고 있으므로 독해 실력이 출중할지라도 특정 분야의 내용을 잘 모르면 어려울 수 있다. TEPS 독해 문제는 배경 지식을 기반으로 푸는 문제는 출제되지 않지만, 배경 지식을 알면 그만큼 지문에 친숙하게 빨리 다가갈 수 있다. 따라서 본인이 취약한 분야의 내용을 영문과 국문으로 자주 읽어서 대비해야 한다. 이 장에서는 필자가 30회 넘게 TEPS 시험에 응시하면서 수험자들이 특히 어려움을 호소했던 내용을 선별하여 재구성한 문제를 풀어 보는 시간을 갖는다.

Different types of information are registered when the eye looks straight on or askance. This is the basis of the latest research coming out of Harvard University Medical School which studies how our perception functions when looking at artwork. Visual cues in paintings _____. Direct or foveal vision was shown to detect sharp details but not the more subtle ones such as degradations of shadows. In the case of the intriguing expression of the *Mona Lisa*, the artist's rendering of the shading of the face contributes to the impression of a smile. But this contribution is really most noticeable with indirect or peripheral vision.

(a) such as line and shape help identify for us what the objects are
(b) emerge or recede depending on how focused our vision is
(c) are sometimes too subtle to detect with the naked eye
(d) aid in our correctly perceiving what are visual illusions

눈의 시선이 정면을 향하거나 혹은 옆을 향할 때 다른 종류의 정보가 입력된다. 이는 우리가 예술 작품을 볼 때 인지 능력이 어떻게 기능을 하는지에 대한 하버드 의과 대학의 최근 연구의 근간이다. 그림의 시각적 신호는 사람의 시각이 어떻게 집중되느냐에 따라 나타나거나 사라진다. 직접적 혹은 망막 중심의 시각은 뚜렷한 부분을 감지할 수 있지만 명암 퇴색과 같은 좀 더 미세한 부분은 잡아내기 어려운 것으로 나타났다. 〈모나리자〉의 흥미로운 표현을 예로 들어보면, 화가가 모나리자 얼굴에 표현한 음영 때문에 미소 짓는 인상을 받는다. 그러나 간접적 혹은 측면 시선으로 보면 이런 미소가 가장 두드러진다.

(a) 선, 모양 같은 신호가 대상이 무엇인지 알아보는 데 도움을 준다
(b) 사람의 시각이 어떻게 집중되느냐에 따라 나타나거나 사라진다
(c) 가끔 육안으로 감지하기에 너무 미세하다
(d) 무엇이 시각적 착각인지 정확하게 인지하는 데 도움을 준다

해설 첫 번째 문장이 주제 문장이고 두 번째 문장은 주제 문장을 뒷받침하기 위한 연구를 제시하고 있다. 연구의 골자가 밑줄로 처리되었으니 첫 번째 문장을 염두에 둔 상태에서 빈칸 다음 내용을 읽는다. 이해를 돕기 위해 〈모나리자〉의 미소를 예로 들고 있다. 정면보다 측면으로 보면 미소가 더 잘 보인다고 했으므로 미소가 사라지거나 나타나는 것으로 볼 수 있기 때문에 emerge or recede가 있는 (b)가 정답이라고 할 수 있다.

어구 register 기록하다 | askance 옆으로 | perception 인지 | function 기능하다 | foveal 망막 중심의 sharp 뚜렷한, 선명한 | subtle 미묘한, 미세한 | degradation 퇴색 | rendering 표현 | peripheral 측면의 emerge 나오다, 나타나다 | recede 멀어지다

용쌤의 비법 특강 주제별 독해 분석 1

TEPS 독해 Part 1 14번에 위와 같은 내용의 문제가 출제된 적이 있다. 모나리자의 웃음에 관한 내용까지는 파악했는데 정작 지문의 핵심은 모르는 수험자가 대부분이었다. 모든 어휘를 다 알 수도 없고 모든 주제를 다 아는 것도 불가능하다. 그럴수록 글의 논리를 따라 읽어 내려 가자. TEPS가 어려운 시험이기는 하지만 어려운 단어를 제시해서 단어 때문에 독해 문제를 못 풀게 하지는 않는다.

The threshold of pain perception is similar for most normal persons. It's a simple function of the sensitivity of the nerve signals that reach the brain. The threshold of pain tolerance, on the other hand, can be a more psychological matter that can depend on the individual. Disregarding any physiological differences that deactivate the usual perception of a stimulus such as heat or pressure, a person's mental state can greatly vary the tolerance level for pain. We've all felt the sharp sting of entering a cold body of water such as at a pool or in the shower. Compare that with those who embrace the _____.

(a) notion of turning up the heat of the water for maximum comfort
(b) benefits of feeling this type of pain in their everyday lives
(c) lowering this level of tolerance until it almost disappears
(d) idea of skinny dipping in a lake in the middle of a cold winter

고통을 인지하는 한계치는 대부분의 일반인에게 있어 비슷하다. 두뇌로 전달되는 신경 신호의 자극 반응성의 단순한 기능이다. 한편 고통을 참아낼 수 있는 한계치는 개인에 따라 다를 수 있는 심리적인 문제라 할 수 있다. 열 또는 압력과 같은 자극의 일반적인 인식을 비활성화시키는 생리적인 차이점을 무시한다면 한 사람의 심리적 상태가 고통을 참아낼 수 있는 한계치는 매우 다를 수 있다. 우리는 모두 수영장이나 샤워장에서 차가운 물 속에 들어가 살이 에이는 듯한 느낌을 받은 적이 있다. 일상에서 이런 고통을 느끼는 혜택을 받아들인 사람들과 비교해보자.

(a) 최대한의 편안함을 위해 뜨거운 물을 틀어야 한다는 생각
(b) 일상에서 이런 고통을 느끼는 혜택
(c) 고통이 사라질 때까지 한계치 수준을 낮추는 것
(d) 추운 한겨울 호수에서 알몸으로 수영하는 생각

해설   한계치(threshold)에 관한 내용이다. On the other hand가 있는 문장부터는 새로운 사실을 도입하고 있다. 사람의 심리 상태에 따라 한계치를 받아들이는 정도가 다름을 설명하고 있고, 생리적인 면과 대조적인 내용이 나올 것임을 예측할 수 있다. 선택지 (b)가 한계치에 대해서 긍정적인 상태를 의미하므로 정답이다.

어구   threshold 한계점 | perception 인지 | nerve signals 신경 신호 | tolerance 참음 | psychological 심리적인
disregard 무시하다 | physiological 생리적인 | deactivate 비활성화시키다 | stimulus 자극
sting 찌르는 듯한 아픔 | embrace 받아들이다 | skinny dipping 알몸 수영

✎ 용쌤의 비법 특강   **주제별 독해 분석 2**

한계점 개념(threshold)은 TEPS 독해에서 여러 번 출제된 바 있다. 자극에 대해 반응하기 시작하는 한계치, 한계점에 관한 내용으로 한계치에 도달하기 전에는 의식하지 못하고, 사람마다 오감에 대한 한계치가 다르다는 내용과 심리적인 상황이 크게 영향을 미친다는 부분에서 문제가 만들어진다. 이때 동사 register가 함께 나올 가능성이 큰데 원래 뜻은 '기록하다, 〈계기판이 숫자를〉 가리키다'이지만 '느끼다'로 이해하면 쉽다. subject도 '피실험자'의 뜻으로 함께 나올 수 있다.

_____ a new paper published in the journal *Science*. It centers on the discovery of a supposed new strain of rod bacteria designated GFAJ-1 which may be capable of unusually substituting at least some of its phosphorus atoms in its DNA structures with arsenic atoms. This finding by Felisa Wolfe-Simon of NASA represents the first ever such instance among any living organism, increasing the possibility for finding life in the universe where toxic arsenic is abundant even if phosphorus is not. Nonetheless, Wolfe-Simon faces some skeptics who wonder if the laboratory procedures followed were adequate enough to remove all doubt. These scientists argue that proper controls were not in place to absolutely guarantee the validity of the conclusions drawn.

(a) The effect of arsenic on DNA mutation is the subject of study in

(b) New practical applications of bacteria are being proposed in

(c) A debate about our traditional definitions of life has been sparked by

(d) Peer review by fellow researchers in the field are all in support of

생명에 관한 전통적인 개념에 대한 논쟁이 〈사이언스〉 저널에 실린 논문에 의해 야기되었다. 이 논문은 특이하게 DNA 구조에서 적어도 일부 인 원자를 비소 원자로 대체할 수 있을지도 모르는 GFAJ-1로 지정된 소위 새로운 변종 막대 박테리아의 발견에 중심을 둔다. NASA의 펠리사 울프-사이먼의 이번 발견은 살아 있는 유기체 중 최초의 사례이며, 비록 인은 아닐지라도 독성 비소가 풍부한 우주에서 생명체를 발견할 가능성을 높였다. 그럼에도 불구하고 모든 의심을 불식시킬 만큼 실험 절차가 적절했는지에 대해 몇몇 회의적인 시각도 있다. 이런 과학자들은 그 결론의 타당성을 완벽히 보장하는 제대로 된 대조군을 사용하지 않았다고 주장한다.

(a) DNA 변종에 있어서 비소의 영향이 연구 주제이다.

(b) 박테리아에 대한 새롭고 실용적인 응용 방법이 제안되었다.

(c) 생명에 관한 전통적인 개념에 대한 논쟁이 야기되었다.

(d) 해당 분야 동료 연구원들의 평가가 전적으로 지지한다.

해설   글의 전반적인 내용을 보면 새로운 연구 결과가 〈사이언스〉 저널에 실렸으며 연구 내용에 대한 설명이 있고 이 연구 결과의 타당성을 의심하는 과학자들의 의견이 이어지고 있다. 그러므로 한 사안에 대한 찬반 양론이 있는 (c)가 가장 적절하다.

어구   center on ~을 초점으로 하다 | strain 변종 | rod bacteria 막대 박테리아, 간균 | designate 지정하다
phosphorus 인 | arsenic 비소 | abundant 충분한 | skeptic 회의론자 | controls 대조군 | validity
타당성

용쌤의 비법 특강 주제별 독해 분석 3

TEPS는 시사성이 있는 주제를 독해 지문으로 출제하기도 한다. 2010년 말 NASA가 새로운 생명체를 발견했다는 뉴스가 있었고 그 다음 달 TEPS 시험에 새로운 생명체 발견과 유사한 지문이 출제된 바 있다. 사전에 이런 최신 뉴스를 업데이트 해 둔 수험자는 그 글을 비교적 쉽게 그리고 빨리 이해할 수 있었을 것이다.

An old English law practice that remains today in the American judicial system is the class action lawsuit. Its function is to hold one representative trial on behalf of a large group or class of potential plaintiffs. This is seen as both time and labor-saving. It would also allow suits not worth prosecuting by a single plaintiff to be brought to court as a class action. For example, if the damage to a plaintiff is only a small financial amount, a lawyer can bring up a class action suit to punish the wrongdoer who might otherwise not be prosecuted. But the cynical view in this case might be that it is the lawyer who really profits and the group of plaintiffs may not see much compensation in the end.

Q: What can be inferred from the passage?
(a) Class action lawsuits are usually better for the lawyers than the plaintiffs.
(b) The English antecedents of class action lawsuits started in Europe.
(c) Class action suits increase the number of trivial cases brought to court.
(d) Lawyers bringing a class action lawsuit represent several plaintiffs.

미국 사법 체계에 오늘날까지 남아있는 오래된 영국의 변호사업은 집단 소송 제도이다. 집단 소송 제도의 기능은 대규모의 단체나 계층의 잠재적 원고를 대표해 한 명의 변호사를 두고 재판을 진행하는 것이다. 이는 시간과 노동을 절약할 수 있는 것으로 보인다. 또한 한 명의 원고에 의해 처벌할 가치가 없는 소송을 집단 소송 제도로 법정으로 끌고 갈 수 있다. 예를 들어, 원고에게 끼친 피해가 소액에 불과할 때, 변호사가 집단 소송을 제기하여 자칫 처벌받지 않을 수도 있는 범법자를 처벌할 수 있다. 그러나 이런 경우 실제로 이득을 챙기는 쪽은 변호사측이고 원고 집단은 결국 충분한 보상을 받지 못할 것이라고 부정적으로 보는 시각도 있다.

Q: 글을 통해 유추할 수 있는 것은?
(a) 집단 소송 제도는 보통 원고보다 변호사에 더 좋다.
(b) 영국의 집단 소송 제도는 유럽에서 시작되었다.
(c) 집단 소송 제도는 법정으로 가는 작은 재판 건수를 증가시킨다.
(d) 집단 소송을 수임하는 변호사는 여러 명의 원고를 대변한다.

해설 두 번째 문장에 집단 소송의 기능은 한 단체나 여러 명의 원고를 대표하여 변호사가 소송을 거는 것이라고 언급하고 있다. (a)는 usually로 인해 오답이다. (b)는 미국 집단 소송 제도가 영국에서 왔다고 했지 영국의 집단 소송 제도가 어디에서 유래했는지는 추론할 수 없다. (c)는 집단 소송 제도로 인해 작은 재판 건수가 증가한다는 근거는 지문에서 찾을 수 없다.

어구 law practice 변호사업 | judicial 사법의 | class action lawsuit 집단 소송 제도 | representative 변호사 | on behalf of ~을 대신하여 | plaintiff 원고 | prosecute 고발하다 | wrongdoer 범법자 | cynical 냉소적인 | profit 이득을 챙기다 | compensation 보상 | antecedent 선행하는 것 | trivial 사소한 | represent 대변하다

독해 37번 문제는 추론 문제이며 난이도가 높아 배점이 크다. 이 문제를 틀리면 타격이 클 수밖에 없다. 안 그래도 시간이 촉박해서 글이 눈에 잘 들어오지 않는 데다가 어려운 소재와 주제가 등장해서 더욱 헤맬 수 있었다. 다음은 필자가 **TEPS**를 30회 이상 보면서 자주 등장했고 수험자들이 지문을 접했을 때 이해하기 힘들어 했던 독해 주제이다. 개념을 정확히 잡고 관련 영문 텍스트를 찾아서 추가 학습하길 바란다.

❶ Affirmative Action 소수 인종 우대 정책

미국은 다문화 사회이고 WASP(White Anglo-Saxon Protestant), 즉 기존의 앵글로색슨계의 신교도 백인이 미국 사회의 주류이다. 아프리카 미국인, 라틴 아메리카인, 아시아인은 상대적으로 주류 사회의 진입을 모색하지만 여전히 장애가 많은 것이 현실이다. 그래서 정책적으로 회사나 학교에서 전체 인원의 일부를 소수 인종에게 쿼터를 주어 의무적으로 선발하도록 하고 있다. 소수 인종 또는 유색 인종을 배려하는 정책인 것이다. 그러나 소수 인종 우대 정책이 오히려 역차별이라는 주장도 있다. 실력으로 대학이나 회사에 들어가야지 소수 인종이라는 이유로 다른 실력이 있는 학생이나 지원자가 낙방하는 경우가 발생하기 때문이라는 것이다.

❷ Sedentary Life Style 사무적 생활 양상

비만(obesity)과 당뇨병(diabetes)는 **TEPS** 독해 지문에 자주 등장하는 토픽으로 비만과 당뇨의 원인 중 하나는 바로 좌식 위주의 생활 또는 부족한 신체 활동량 때문이라는 것이다. 정답이든 오답이든 sedentary가 문제화되기 때문에 이 단어를 반드시 알아야 한다.

❸ Federal Reserve Board 연방 준비 제도 이사회

한국의 중앙 은행은 한국 은행이며 미국의 중앙 은행은 연방 준비 제도 이사회 Federal Reserve Board(FRB)이다. 중앙 은행의 주요 기능 중 하나는 재할인율(rediscount rate, 중앙은행과 시중은행 간 여신금리) 등 금리 결정, 재무부 채권(bond) 매입(purchasing)과 발행(issuing), 지급준비율(reserve ratio) 결정 등의 권한을 가진다. **FRB**는 각 지역 은행장들이 주요 기업가, 경제학자, 시장전문가 등의 경제 상황 의견을 종합해 작성하는 베이지 북(Beige Book)을 1년에 여덟 번 발행한다.

❹ PTSD(Post Traumatic Stress Disorder) 외상 후 스트레스 장애

전쟁, 화재나 어린 시절의 끔찍한 경험을 한 후 나타나는 정신적 질병을 의미한다. 전쟁을 경험한 병사들이 귀환하고 난 후 악몽을 계속 꾼다거나 과민 반응을 보이는 경우가 한 예이다. 신체적 장애뿐만 아니라 정신적 장애(mental illness)를 호소한다는 내용이 출제된다.

❺ Expectation Confirmation Theory 기대 일치 이론

기존에 사형 제도를 찬성했던 이가 사형 제도를 찬성하는 설문 결과를 확인하고는 더욱 찬성하는 경향을 보인다는 내용이 출제된 적 있다. 다른 이름으로 기대 불일치 이론(Expectation Disconfirmation Theory)이 있으며 마케팅에서 제품이 소비자의 기대치를 초과하면 구매 후 만족이 발생하고 이를 긍정적 불일치(Positive Disconfirmation)라고 하며, 그 반대는 부정적 불일치(Negative Disconfirmation)라고 한다.

❻ English is a Lingua Franca 영어는 국제 공통어

영어가 국제 공용어임을 부인하는 사람은 없다. 이런 독해 문제는 내용은 평이하지만 lingua franca라는 다소 생소한 단어가 등장해서 어리둥절할 수 있다. lingua franca는 국제어, 공통어라는 뜻이다.

❼ Global Warming 지구 온난화

역사적으로 봤을 때 지구는 오늘날과 같이 더운 적이 여러 번 있었다. 지구 온난화와 관련해 찬반양론이 한 창이지만 확실한 것은 지금 지구가 과거보다 더운 것은 맞지만 아직까지는 지구 온난화가 이론에 불과하다는 점이다. 지구 온난화가 아직은 팩트(fact)가 아니라 이론(theory)이라는 사실을 기억하자. 다음은 지구 온난화와 관련하여 자주 등장하는 단어다.

UN Framework Convention on Climate Change 유엔 기후 변화 협약

CO2 emission rights 이산화탄소 배출권

Carbon sinks 이산화탄소 흡수계

Chlorofluorocarbon(CFC) 프레온 가스

coolant 냉각제

❽ Pros and Cons of Globalization 세계화의 장단점

세계화 문제와 관련하여 농업 보조금(agricultural subsidy)에 관한 내용이 출제된 적이 있다. 강대국이 자국 농업 보조금을 지원함으로써 아프리카의 농업 국가는 오히려 큰 타격을 받는다는 내용이었다. 세계화가 진행되면서 오히려 득(blessing)보다 실(scourge)이 크다는 내용이 주로 등장한다.

❾ Henry David Thoreau's *Walden* 헨리 데이비드 소로의 작품 〈월든〉

영문학도에게 익숙한 작품 *Walden*은 TEPS 독해뿐만 아니라 청해 Part 4에도 출제된 바 있다. 소로는 1845년부터 1847년까지 물욕, 인습의 사회와 인연을 끊고 월든의 숲 속에서 금욕적이고 간소한 생활을 하면서 자연과 인생을 직시하는 내용을 다루고 있다. 그러나 월든은 소로의 자택에서 불과 2마일 떨어져 있었다는 내용이 나온 적이 있다. 포인트는 소로가 2년 동안 완전히 문명과 도시 생활로부터 격리된 것은 아니고 주말마다 그의 집으로 가서 세상 돌아가는 소식을 모두 접했다는 부분이다.

Dear Mr. Floyd,

This is to inform you that we shall be terminating our regular orders with your company effective the 20th of this month. We regret this unfortunate turn of events but we feel that we can no longer tolerate the constant delays in shipments that we have experienced as of late. As our business model _____, we need to ensure our supplies are replenished in a timely and reliable manner. Therefore, please consider our July order to be the last one we will require of you. Again, we regret that it has come to this after our partnership of many months, but we would ask for your understanding on the matter.

Sincerely,

Joseph Marlon

(a) relies on prompt service to our customers
(b) demands on-time delivery to your facilities
(c) is constantly being postponed by delays
(d) is facing stiff competition from other companies

플로이드 씨께

이 서신은 이번 달 20일부로 귀사와의 정기 주문 해지를 알려 드리기 위함입니다. 이런 애석한 상황 변화에 대해서 유감입니다만 최근에 있었던 계속된 주문 지연을 더 이상 묵인할 수 없습니다. 본사의 비즈니스 모델은 고객에게 신속한 서비스를 제공하는 것에 있기 때문에 물품이 제시간에 신뢰할 만한 방식으로 공급되어야 합니다. 따라서 7월 주문을 마지막 주문이라고 생각하시면 됩니다. 수개월간의 제휴 관계 뒤 이런 일이 발생하여 다시 한번 유감을 표하며, 이 사안에 대해 귀사의 양해를 부탁합니다.

조셉 말론

(a) 고객에게 신속한 서비스를 제공하는 것에 있다.
(b) 귀하의 시설에 정기적인 배달을 요구한다.
(c) 지연 사태로 인해 계속 연기되고 있다.
(d) 타사로부터 치열한 경쟁에 직면해 있다.

해설　서신은 업체의 주문 지연이 계속되어 제휴를 끊는다는 내용이다. 그 근거로 회사의 정책은 고객에게 '신속한' 서비스를 공급하는 데 있다는 (a)가 가장 적절하다.

어구　terminate 해지하다, 해약하다 | turn of events 상황 반전 | as of late 최근에 | replenish 공급하다
on-time 정기적인 | stiff competition 치열한 경쟁

🖊 **용쌤의 비법 특강** 주제별 독해 분석 5

서신 문제는 비교적 쉬운 편에 속한다. 그러나 비즈니스 서신일 경우 아직 회사 생활을 못해본 학습자에게는 어려울 수 있다. 이것은 익숙함의 문제이기 때문에 이런 유형은 10문제 정도 풀면 쉽게 해결될 것이다.

There is a nifty little strategy to save money on mortgage payments that not many people know about. It's called recasting and it is paying off the money on the principal amount early _____. Let's say you still owe $360,000 in principal for the remaining 15 years on your 30-year fixed-rate mortgage. Then your monthly payments will be $2,000 per month, excluding interest. If you now pay a lump sum of $60,000, the total remaining amount you owe will be $300,000. Then you can recast your future monthly payments down to $1,666.66 per month. This strategy is especially useful if the interest rate on your mortgage is high. But if the mortgage interest rate is low, it may not be needed at all.

(a) so that you can pay off your mortgage sooner
(b) and readjusting the monthly payments accordingly
(c) to reduce the interest rate on your mortgage
(d) thereby paying only the interest on your mortgage

주택 대출 상환 시에 돈을 절약할 수 있는 사람들이 잘 모르는 요긴한 전략이 있다. 이는 리캐스팅이라 불리는데 원금을 조기 상환하고 이에 따라 월별 납부금은 재조정하는 것이다. 30년 고정 금리로 앞으로 15년간 36만 달러의 원금을 빚지고 있다고 생각해 보자. 그러면 월별 납입금은 이자를 제외하고 2천 달러가 될 것이다. 만약 6만 달러라는 큰 액수를 납부하면 남은 액수는 30만 달러이다. 이렇게 하고 나면 앞으로 월별 납부금을 매달 1,666.66달러로 다시 계산할 수 있다. 이 전략은 주택 대출 금리가 높을 때 유용한 방법이다. 그러나 주택 대출 금리가 낮으면 이 방법은 전혀 필요하지 않을 수도 있다.

(a) 당신의 주택 대출을 더 빨리 갚을 수 있도록
(b) 그리고 이에 따라 월간 납부금을 재조정하는
(c) 당신 주택 대출의 금리를 낮추기 위해서
(d) 그럼으로써 당신의 주택 대출의 금리만 납부하는

해설 빈칸 뒤인 세 번째 문장부터 확인해 보자. 원금 납입을 2천 달러씩 계속 낼 때와 처음 납입액을 6만 달러 낼 때를 비교하고 있다. 6만 달러를 내면 앞으로 내야 할 이자가 낮아진다고 단락 후반부에 언급하고 있으므로 정답은 (b)이다.

어구 nifty 멋진, 재치 있는 | pay off 전액을 갚다 | principal 원금 | fixed-rate 고정 금리 | excluding 배제하고 | lump sum 많은 액수[양] | accordingly 그에 따라서 | thereby 그것에 의하여

용쌤의 비법 특강 주제별 독해 분석 6

TEPS 독해 Part 2 세부 내용 문제를 제외하고 Part 1에서 숫자가 많이 나오는 지문은 숫자가 의미하는 바를 정확히 파악하여 빈칸에 들어갈 수 있는 내용을 논리적으로 찾아야 한다. 이런 지문은 그 흐름을 잡지 못하면 읽었던 내용을 또 읽게 돼서 시간만 잡아 먹는다. 숫자가 많이 나오는 지문을 따로 모아서 집중 연습하도록 한다.

The FCC is considering approval of a merger between two giants in the telecom industry. The internet service provider Prime Net is proposing to join forces with media broadcaster DSE. Prime Net currently holds 34 percent share in the nation's broadband market according to industry stats. A company representative says that it is hoped that with this merger, that percentage will increase to 40 percent. A survey shows that 30 percent of Prime Net's 52,000,000 users utilize the internet service for games, 24 percent use it for news, and 18 percent use it for movies. The $29 billion deal is said to be decided on later this month, but sources say that the FCC chairman believes that it will serve the public interest. The current rate for high-speed internet access on Prime Net is $19.95 per month.

Q: Which is correct according to the passage?
(a) Prime Net is worth $29 billion as a company.
(b) DSE holds only 18 percent of the media market.
(c) Prime Net serves about a third of its market.
(d) The merger will increase the market share of DSE.

연방 통신 위원회는 전기 통신 업계 두 거대 업체의 합병 승인을 고려하고 있다. 인터넷 서비스 공급 업체 프라임 넷은 미디어 방송사 DSE와 합병을 제안했다. 업계 통계에 따르면 프라임 넷은 현재 미국 브로드밴드 시장에서 점유율 34%이다. 한 회사 대표에 의하면 이번 합병으로 시장 점유율이 40%까지 올라갈 것으로 보인다. 설문 조사 결과, 프라임 넷 5천 2백만 사용자 중에서 30%가 게임 목적으로 인터넷 서비스를 이용하고 24%는 뉴스, 18%는 영화를 보기 위해 이용한다. 290억 달러 규모에 달하는 이번 합병 건은 이달 말에 결정 날 것이라고 하며, 정보통에 따르면 연방 통신 위원장은 공익을 위한 합병이 될 것으로 본다고 한다. 프라임 넷에서 초고속 인터넷을 사용 요금은 현재 매달 19.95달러이다.

Q: 글에 따르면 옳은 것은?
(a) 프라임 넷은 회사로서 가치가 290억 달러이다.
(b) DSE의 언론 시장 점유율은 단지 18%에 불과하다.
(c) 프라임 넷은 시장의 약 3분의 1을 차지하고 있다.
(d) 합병으로 DSE의 시장 점유율이 상승할 것이다.

해설 이번 합병의 규모가 290억 달러라고 했지 현재 프라임 넷 회사의 가치를 의미하는 것은 아니므로 (a)는 오답이다. 본문에서 18%는 프라임 넷 유저가 영화를 보기 위해 인터넷을 사용한다고 말한 수치이므로 (b)의 내용과 일치하지 않는다. 이번 합병에서 DSE의 시장 점유율은 언급되지 않았기 때문에 (d)는 오답이다. 세 번째 문장에서 프라임 넷은 브로드밴드 시장에서 34%의 주식을 보유하고 있다고 했으므로 정답은 (c)라 할 수 있다. 본문에서는 34%가 선택지에서 3분의 1로 바꾸어 말했다는 점을 염두에 두자. 세부 내용 문제는 paraphrasing이 핵심이다.

어구 FCC(Federal Communications Commission) 연방 통신 위원회 | merger 합병 | join forces 힘을 합치다 share 주식 | stats 통계 | representative 대표자 | utilize 이용하다, 활용하다 | market share 시장 점유율

용쌤의 비법 특강 **주제별 독해 분석 7**

Part 2의 세부 내용에는 숫자가 유난히 많이 등장하는 지문이 최소 한 문제씩은 반드시 출제되고 있다. 선택지가 보통 내용 흐름에 맞게 순서대로 나열되기 때문에 숫자가 있는 문장을 읽고 선택지와 비교해서 정답과 오답을 가려내는 것이 효과적이다.

Besides the ostensible conflict between religions in the Crusades, internal pressures within the medieval Roman Catholic Church itself could be cited as helping to propel the call to holy war. The years following the turn of the first millennium were tumultuous times for Christendom. The Great Schism separated the church into Eastern Orthodox and Roman Catholic. The Byzantine Empire was suffering from attack by the Seljuk Turks. The Investiture Controversy continued to rage in Europe as a power struggle between secular rulers and bishops to appoint church leaders. When it came to calls for help in the ongoing armed conflict with Muslim forces on the Iberian Peninsula or the Levant, some in the church at least partially felt that it might be an opportunity to reassert the church's authority and unity.

Q: Which is correct according to the passage?
(a) The Crusades were primarily caused by the Great Schism.
(b) The Church wanted to strengthen itself through the Crusades.
(c) Christianity at the time of the Crusades was surrounded by enemies.
(d) The rulers of Europe did not really support the Church's Crusades.

십자군 전쟁은 표면상의 종교간 갈등 외에도 중세 로마 가톨릭 교회의 내부 압력이 성전을 부추겼다고 할 수 있다. 첫 천 년이 시작되고 몇 년 동안 기독교계는 혼란의 시기를 겪었다. 대분열로 교회는 동방 정교회와 로마 가톨릭 교회로 분리되었다. 비잔틴 제국은 셀주크 투르크족으로부터 공격을 받고 있었다. 교회 지도자를 선출하는 데 있어 세속 통치자와 주교 사이의 권력 투쟁으로서 서임권 투쟁은 유럽에서 계속 휘몰아쳤다. 이베리아 반도와 레반트 지역에서 이슬람 세력과 전쟁이 진행되고 있는 가운데 도움을 받아야 할 상황이 되자 교회의 일부 지도자들은 적어도 부분적으로는 교회의 권위와 통일을 다시 주장할 수 있는 기회일지도 모른다고 생각했다.

Q: 글과 일치하는 것은?
(a) 십자군 전쟁의 주된 원인은 대분열 때문이었다.
(b) 교회는 십자군 전쟁을 통해 세력을 강화하려 했다.
(c) 십자군 전쟁 당시 기독교는 적에 포위된 상황이었다.
(d) 유럽의 통치자들은 사실 기독교의 십자군 전쟁을 지지하지 않았다.

해설 글에서는 십자군 전쟁의 주된 원인으로 교회 내부의 압력을 언급하므로 (a)는 오답이다. 십자군 전쟁 당시 셀주크 투르크족으로부터 공격을 받았지만 적들에 포위된 내용은 없으므로 (c)는 오답이다. 유럽 통치자들이 십자군 운동 지지 여부는 언급되지 않았으므로 (d)도 오답이다. 내부적으로 갈등을 겪고 있는 교회는 십자군 운동을 통해 교회의 입지를 다지려 했다고 마지막 문장에 언급되어 있으므로 정답은 (b)이다.

어구 ostensible 표면상의 | crusade 십자군 | medieval 중세의 | cite 인용하다 | propel 몰고 가다
tumultuous 격변의 | Christendom 기독교계 | rage 계속 맹위를 떨치다 | secular 세속적인

용쌤의 비법 특강 주제별 독해 분석 8

십자군 전쟁과 같은 역사적 사건에 대한 지문은 관련 지식이 없으면 까다롭게 느껴질 수 있다. 게다가 쉽지 않은 고유 명사도 더러 등장하기 때문에 이해가 되지 않는 상태에서 계속 읽으면 풀지도 못하고 시간만 소비하기 일쑤다. TEPS 독해는 배경 지식이 없더라도 글의 흐름을 따라 가면 풀 수 있도록 출제되지만, 배경 지식을 알면 지문에 쉽게 다가갈 수 있다.

The reverberations of the Romantic era can be said to yet continue to echo in our time. Rousseau's admiration of the noble savage as more natural and pure than civilized man is reflected in the exalting of native peoples. Hugo's hunchback or Shelley's Frankenstein are primal monsters who nonetheless have admirable characters. Focusing on individualism as opposed to societal values is another lasting legacy of romanticism. Unlike the classical attitude of universal standards, the individual is free to determine value and meaning in the world. Holding intuition and imagination in the highest regard, above even that of the faculty of reason, is a romanticist notion. Then again, this only seems natural to a movement that is thought to be a reaction to the rationalism of the preceding Enlightenment period.

Q: What is the main point of the passage?

(a) **The present era still feels the influence of romanticism.**

(b) Romanticism emphasized that all men are good inside.

(c) The thinkers of the romantic era rejected reason and logic.

(d) Romanticist sensibility embraced the brotherhood of man.

낭만주의 시대의 영향은 아직까지도 오늘날 계속해서 이어지고 있다고 할 수 있다. 루소의 문명화된 인간보다도 고결한 야만인이 더 자연스럽고 순수하다는 예찬은 원시적 사람들의 칭송으로 나타난다. 위고의 꼽추나 셸리의 프랑켄슈타인은 원시적인 괴물이지만 그럼에도 좋아할 만한 특징이 있다. 사회적 가치에 반대되는 개인주의에 초점을 둔 것도 낭만주의의 또 하나의 남아 있는 유산이라 할 수 있다. 보편적 기준이라는 전통적인 태도와는 달리 각 개인은 세상의 가치와 의미를 자유롭게 정한다. 직관과 상상력을 심지어 이성보다도 더 높이 여기는 것이 낭만주의의 개념이다. 그러나 이것은 오직 앞선 계몽주의 시기의 합리주의에 대한 반응이라고 여겨지는 자연스러운 움직임으로 보인다.

Q: 글의 요지는?

(a) 현 시대에서도 여전히 낭만주의의 영향을 느낄 수 있다.

(b) 낭만주의는 모든 사람의 내면은 선하다고 강조했다.

(c) 낭만주의 사상가들은 이성과 논리를 거부했다.

(d) 낭만주의자들의 감수성은 인류애를 받아들였다.

해설   첫 번째 문장이 주제 문장이고 나머지 문장들은 첫 번째 문장을 뒷받침하고 있다. 첫 문장만 보고도 바로 답을 찾을 수 있는 문제로 결국 과거의 낭만주의가 오늘날까지 영향을 미친다는 내용이므로 정답은 (a)이다.

어구   reverberation 영향 | echo 반향하다 | noble savage 고결한 야만인 | exalt 〈신분·지위 등을〉 높이다
primal 원시적인 | admirable 좋아할 만한 | hold ... in high regard ~를 높게 평가하다 | intuition 직관
faculty of reason 이성 | rationalism 합리주의 | preceding 앞선 | emphasize 강조하다
embrace 포옹하다 | brotherhood 인류애

TEPS는 문학 지문을 선호하는 경향이 있다. 그렇다고 해서 시나 소설이 나오는 것은 아니지만 낭만주의, 인상주의, 입체주의 등 문학 사조의 정의나 해당 시대의 유명한 예술가와 작품을 소개하는 글이 다수 출제되고 있다. 다음은 TEPS 독해에 등장했거나 등장할 수 있는 문학 사조이다. 주제에 대해 더 검색하고 영어 원서로 읽어 보길 바란다.

- **Classicism** 고전주의

  낭만주의와 대비되는 사조로 정형화된 형식을 특징으로 하며 그리스와 로마 예술을 기반으로 한다.

- **Romanticism** 낭만주의

  자유와 개성을 강조하는 문예 사조 및 예술 운동으로 18세기 말부터 19세기 초에 걸쳐 독일, 영국, 프랑스 등에서 유행했다. 고전주의에 반발하여 생겨났는데 현실보다는 이상을 추구한다.

- **Realism** 사실주의

  19세기 후반 낭만주의에 반기를 들고 프랑스에서 전개된 문예 사조이다. 작품의 소재를 있는 그대로 표현한다. 인간의 본질을 역사적이며 사회적인 맥락에서 바라보며 실증적인 객관주의와 비개인성을 중시한다.

- **Hyperrealism**(Radical realism, Super realism) 극사실주의

  1960년대 후반 미국에서 일어난 회화와 조각의 새로운 경향으로 말 그대로 현실을 완벽하게 재현하려는 경향이다.

- **Enlightenment** 계몽주의

  15세기 말 영국, 네덜란드 등지에서 일어나 18세기 후반 프랑스에서 전성기였던 사상 운동으로 민중을 대상으로 하며 이성과 합리성을 기반으로 한 교훈주의 문학이라 할 수 있다.

- **Impressionism** 인상주의

  19세기 후반에서 20세기 초 프랑스를 중심으로 일어난 근대 예술 운동 중 하나로 작품 소재에 대해 순간적인 시각적 인상을 중시하고 주로 회화나 조각에 이런 성향이 두드러진다.

다음은 TEPS 문학 독해 지문에 잘 등장하는 문학 관련 어휘이다.

- **figures of speech** 비유적 표현
- **empathy** 감정 이입
- **parody** 패러디
- **motif** 주제
- **denotation** 지시적 의미, 명시적 의미
- **rhyme** 운
- **stanza** (시의) 연

- **simile** 직유법
- **metaphor** 은유법
- **personification** 의인법
- **satire** 풍자
- **connotation** 함축적 의미
- **catharsis** 카타르시스
- **alliteration** 두운

A fabled literary coterie of Americans living in Paris, the self-styled "Lost Generation" famously included the journalist and novelist Hemingway. (a) Along with working as a war correspondent in Europe, Hemingway wrote several novels in his time abroad such as *The Sun Also Rises*. (b) His writing is known for its matter-of-fact style, unadorned to the point of being satirized today as simplistic and artless. **(c) The idea of nature as a place in which men could recuperate or even rediscover things is a recurring motif.** (d) He once explained that he found that the less is explicitly stated, the stronger the story became and this characteristic minimalism can almost be said to be as recognizable as the works themselves.

파리에 사는 미국인으로 구성된 전설적인 문학 소규모 단체인 자칭 '로스트 제너레이션'에는 언론가이자 소설가였던 헤밍웨이가 몸담고 있었다. (a) 헤밍웨이는 유럽에서 종군 기자로 활동하면서 해외에 있을 때 〈해는 또다시 떠오른다〉 등을 포함해 소설 여러 작품을 남겼다. (b) 그의 작품은 무미건조한 스타일로 유명한데 오늘날 단순하고 예술적 느낌이 없다고 풍자될 정도로 꾸밈이 없는 편이다. (c) 사람이 회복할 수 있고 심지어 사물을 재발견할 수도 있는 곳으로서의 자연은 반복해서 등장하는 주제이다. (d) 그는 한 때 노골적인 표현을 더 적게 할수록 스토리는 더 탄탄해진다고 말했는데 이런 특징적인 미니멀리즘은 작품 그 자체만큼 식별이 가능하다고 말할 수 있다.

해설   이런 유형의 문제에서는 첫 번째 문장이 특히 중요하다. 첫 번째 문장을 보고 헤밍웨이에 관해서 이야기를 하겠구나 예측을 할 수 있어야 한다. (a)는 헤밍웨이의 직업과 작품 소개를 하고 (b)는 그의 문체에 관한 내용으로 첫 번째 문장의 연장선상에 있다. (d)는 헤밍웨이 문체의 특징 혹은 장점을 언급하고 있으므로 (b)와 연결이 되지만, 그 사이의 (c)는 헤밍웨이의 문체에 대한 것이 아닌 주제에 관해 언급하고 있으므로 (c)가 정답이다.

어구   fabled 전설적인 | coterie 〈목적을 같이 하는〉 소규모 집단 | self-styled 자칭의 | matter-of-fact 무미건조한 | unadorned 꾸밈이 없는 | satirize 풍자하다 | artless 꾸밈없는 | recuperate 회복하다 | recurring 되풀이하여 발생하는 | motif 주제 | explicitly 명쾌하게, 노골적으로 | minimalism 미니멀리즘 (최소한의 표현주의)

✍용쌤의 비법특강 주제별 독해 분석 10

TEPS에는 문학 작품이나 문학 인물을 소개하는 글이 한 문제는 등장한다. 다음은 TEPS 학습자들이 챙겨야 할 문학가 및 예술가 혹은 학자이다. 관련 영문 텍스트를 찾아보고 다른 문학 작품이나 인물을 알고 있는 것이 TEPS 독해에 도움이 될 것이다.

• *The Road Not Taken* by Robert Frost 로버트 프로스트의 '가지 않은 길'
• *Interpretation of Dream* by Sigmund Freud 지그문트 프로이트의 〈꿈의 해석〉
• *Adventures of Huckleberry Finn* by Mark Twain 마크 트웨인의 〈허클베리 핀〉
• *Walden* by Henry David Thoreau 헨리 데이비드 소로의 〈월든〉
• El Greco, the architect of the Spanish Renaissance 스페인 르네상스의 핵심 인물, 엘 그레코
• Leonardo da Vinci's Versatility 레오나르도 다빈치의 천재성
• Benjamin Franklin's Versatility 벤자민 프랭클린의 천재성

Actual Test

ACTUAL TEST 1

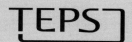

Reading
comprehension

Part I   Questions 1—16

Read the passage. Then choose the option that best completes the passage.

1.   Almost every child grows up with crayons, those _____ used for writing, coloring or drawing. As a matter of fact, there is an army of mothers who have to clean the kitchen walls because of their toddler's artistic flair. The history of the crayon is not very clear, although the word "crayon" comes from a combination of French and Latin and was first used in 1644. The idea of using wax in combination with some sort of pigment goes back thousands of years. Ancient Egyptians developed a style of using hot beeswax with colored pigment to create a bond of color to stone known as encaustic painting. Today an approximate 5 billion crayons are made a day to keep every child occupied in their homes and classrooms.

(a) colored pencils sold in stores
(b) little sticks of colored wax
(c) famous French pastel markers
(d) evenly spaced colored lines

2.   A remora is a brave little fish that seems to be catching a piggyback ride on much larger and dangerous sharks. The reason sharks don't eat the remora is because it actually provides a useful purpose of cleaning the shark of bacteria, while the shark provides security for the remora. This type of relationship is called symbiosis, or more specifically, they have a mutual symbiotic relationship. Scientists have classified symbiotic relationships into four categories: mutualism, where both parties benefit, commensalism, where one organism benefits and the other is neither helped nor harmed, and parasitic, where one organism feeds off the other, _____.

(a) with the goal of moving on to another soon
(b) and the other feeds off a third party
(c) providing nutrients to its young
(d) causing harm to the second party

3.   One of the icons of Americana was Ansel Adams, a photographer who is _____.
Ansel was born on February 20, 1920 and raised in an upper class neighborhood in San
Francisco. His love for nature inspired his masterful portraits of many of the National
Parks found in the western U.S., including Yosemite and Glacier. Adams' prints have
been reproduced in calendars, posters, and books worldwide. Ironically, he often had
money problems despite being a prolific photographer and coming from a wealthy family.
However, Adams' estate reached financial independence selling his prints for an estimated
total value of $25 million, with the highest price of $609,600 paid at Sotheby's New York
Auction in 2006.

(a) world renowned for his classic black and white portraits
(b) well known for his charcoal and conté sketches
(c) famous for his western landscape design portraits
(d) most recognized for his urban depictions of nature

4.   You leave your office after a grueling ten hour day, but you're not going home, instead you
have to pick up the groceries to prepare dinner for the family. This is a challenge that many
families have, but not one you have to face if you register now at Greenfoods2U.com to
become part of our exclusive internet grocery delivery service. Greenfoods2U has every
product your local grocer provides plus many they may not. We guarantee 100 percent
organic and fresh groceries delivered to your door within 12 hours of the order being
placed. Forget the headaches of fighting for parking, struggling through check-out lanes,
and _____. Sign up for Greenfoods2U.com now and leave your
grocery worries to us!

(a) spending valuable time preparing meals
(b) lugging your heavy groceries home
(c) regretting you purchased inferior groceries
(d) missing precious time in your office

5.   Roughly 250 million years ago during the Paleozoic and Mesozoic periods, _____. Instead of the seven continents we know today, there was one super continent called Pangea. Yet, over the Earth's 4.6 billion year history, scientists speculate there may have been many other supercontinents. Scientists believe that Pangea split in three stages starting roughly 175 million years ago. How does the science community support the Pangea hypothesis? They have been able to identify molten glass on every continent that was caused by a tremendously violent asteroid strike in the Sahara desert. This shows that the continents were connected and is just one of the many historical clues that confirm the presence of Pangea and its subsequent split.

(a) the Earth was a totally different place
(b) our planet experienced sudden changes
(c) the sun had a sudden shift on its axis
(d) an asteroid slammed into the Earth

6.   In 2010, Christian Kandlbauer became the first European to successfully utilize a "mind-controlled" robotic arm. Kandlbauer, an Austrian, lost both his arms in a horrendous electrical accident. But today, thanks to BCI (brain-computer interface) all he has to do is think about what he wants the joints on his prosthetic arm to do, and they obey his commands. Christian is able to dress himself and is the first person to be able to drive with this type of prosthetic. BCI is promising technology not only for patients that lose their limbs, but for other handicaps such as blindness. Yet, _____ of this technology because of the non-humanitarian applications it could be used for, such as evil "terminator" type cyborgs.

(a) not every patient is a suitable candidate
(b) there is very little need to be apprehensive
(c) test have discovered many additional benefits
(d) there will always be critics and watchdogs

7.

To Kaito Yoshida, President,

I am sorry to inform you that the Better Business Bureau(BBB) has revoked Kaito Construction's membership application because of two unresolved disputes regarding contracting work at Lund's Megamall and The Hampton Hotel. However, both companies are willing to rescind their complaints to the BBB if a proper agreement is found. As you know, it is the BBB's mission to provide third party assessment of a company's business ethics and practices. Unless you are able to come to an acceptable resolution to these two rows, we will not be able to stand behind you as a BBB member. We hope you will endeavor to _____ and resubmit your application.

Sincerely,
Jennifer Keller, BBB chief auditor

(a) improve your company's image and reputation
(b) remedy these differences with the above parties
(c) increase client satisfaction by providing incentives
(d) seek the assistance of a good public relations company

8. Among all the branches in the U.S. military, no other unit is as _____ as the Marine Scout Sniper. This is because these specialized warriors are silent and stealthy, moving in teams of two and evading the watching eyes of their foes. Following the motto of "One shot, one kill", a qualified sniper will spend days stalking down his high valued target and then eliminate him from a mile away. The Marine Scout Sniper training course runs two months and qualified candidates come from all branches of the military. Yet, despite this fact, the training program has an attrition rate of over 50 percent. Once a candidate passes the course, he joins a brotherhood of the most elite soldiers ever.

(a) highly in demand for rear support
(b) flamboyant and visually intimidating
(c) frequently glorified in film
(d) feared and reviled by the enemy

9.   Five times a day, devoted Muslims _____ over the loudspeakers attached to the tall minarets of a mosque. A mosque is a Muslim house of worship characterized by its grand entryways, domes, tall minarets and prayer halls. They are often wide open spaces and can date back to the 7th century. Once only found on the Arabian Peninsula, mosques are now found in every inhabited country in the world. Just like many holy houses of worship, the mosque also serves as a community center where followers can be educated and even settle disputes.

(a) practice their formal salat, or prayers
(b) around the world are called to prayer
(c) passionately debate concepts of their faith
(d) gather in their homes to hear music

10.   Have you ever asked for a "Coke" instead of a soda? Many people refer to tissues as "Kleenex," medical adhesive bandages are better known as "Band Aids" and peanut butter is simply referred to as "Jiffy." The reason behind these "mislabels" is mass marketing's powerful effect on the public's exposure to certain products. If you are bombarded by advertisements on the radio, TV, internet, newspaper, billboard and pretty much anywhere you look, then the brand name that is being advertised can actually replace the product's name. So, _____ a "Q-tip," be sure to remember the actual product is a cotton swab.

(a) if you need a refreshing break and reach for
(b) when people tell you to protect yourself with
(c) the next time you clean your ears with
(d) if there's a sale at the hardware store for

11. The first music video to be shown on August 1, 1981, was the appropriately entitled song "Video Killed the Radio Star" by The Buggles. This started a musical revolution all thanks to the debut of a little known channel called Music Television, or better known as MTV. This cutting-edge channel brought not only the most popular songs to our living rooms but also the singers themselves. MTV experienced a meteoric rise and expanded way beyond just music videos with live concerts, MTV unplugged, cartoons, music awards shows and many other programs. We can also thank MTV for _____ would have previously not been given the spotlight as they did with MTV.

(a) exposing us to non-mainstream music and artists who
(b) providing a variety of social and charitable programs that
(c) improving radio programs, DJs and advertisers who
(d) the attention given to television's obvious dominance it

12. _____ in human evolution. Once our ancient ancestors acquired a taste for meat, they were able to consume more protein. Not only did that protein provide more physical energy, it also supplied more nutrients for the brain. In addition, in order to catch their prey, which was generally much larger than them, hunters had to invent weapons, set traps and work together strategically. All of these factors combined to improve our reasoning and cognitive abilities as well as create social order. The better hunter you were, the more attractive you were to the clan as both a provider and leader.

(a) Many changes in dietary habits and social orders are seen
(b) Scientists to this day still argue the relevance hunting had
(c) Various geological and extra-terrestrial factors changed the direction
(d) Few people realize the importance meat-eating played

13. _____ in luxury vehicles, from the ancient palanquin, driven by man power, to today's modern day stretch limousine. The first limousine was made in 1902 and the first stretch limo in 1928. Today, limo manufacturers can modify just about any car, whether it's a Hummer, Cadillac Escalade or Rolls Royce. The process is relatively simple in theory; just cut the vehicle in half and extend it as long as desired. Limos possess all the luxurious amenities one would find in five-star hotels such as televisions, bars, dance lights, video games and more. The world's longest stretch limo reaches over 100 feet in length, requires 26 tires and boasts several beds, a heated Jacuzzi and even a helipad!

(a) Not everyone will get an opportunity to ride
(b) There are many ways to get from point A to point B
(c) For ages the wealthy and elite traveled
(d) The history of transport and travel evolved

14. In spite of many people's belief that a rainforest and jungle are one and the same, there are distinct differences between the two. A rainforest is usually surrounded by a jungle and what sets them apart is not the amount of rainfall or climate variations. Rather, a rainforest has a very tall and thick canopy that prevents sunlight from penetrating to the ground. This in turn means there is very little plant life and vegetation due to the lack of sunlight. In contrast, a jungle has a thick undergrowth of plants. When you see images of people _____, they are most likely in a jungle and not a rainforest.

(a) trekking under a solid covering of trees
(b) hacking their way through thick vegetation
(c) hunting in tall grasses near a body of water
(d) picking nuts and fruits from relatively tall trees

15.   Still to this day, there is no definitive proof of football's origins. Some historians note a game played in China around 3,000 years ago called Tsu Chu that involved kicking a stuffed ball of animal skin through an elevated hole. Around the same time, the Japanese played a game called Kemari where participants kicked a ball through two bamboo shoots. The Romans also played a game similar to today's football and brought it to Britain. The first recorded instance of a game that resembles football is from England in 1,100, albeit that game may have better been described as an all out brawl with little to no rules. _____ of the origins, football remains the number one game worldwide.

(a) In light
(b) As an exception
(c) In spite
(d) As a consequence

16.   It is recommended that once you receive an assignment that you begin it right away. Unfortunately, in the real world, procrastination tends to trump logic. How many times have you had to scramble to finish a task before the deadline? We have all regretted getting a late start because of our own laziness. This type of behavior is human nature, but can get us into a lot of hot water. If you start a project well before it is due, that gives you that much more time to react to any unexpected challenges. _____, no matter how often we hear this same advice, we tend to tell ourselves we'll follow it on the next project, not this one.

(a) For instance
(b) Correspondingly
(c) Notwithstanding
(d) As an alternative

Read the passage and the question. Then choose the option that best answers the question.

17.   Hydroblasting is a technique of removing unwanted materials off of surfaces such as dirt and rust. This method relies entirely on the energy of water striking a surface with tremendous 10,000 pounds per square inch (psi), and ultra-high, utilizing over 25,000 psi. Ultra-high hydroblasting water pressure is extremely dangerous and can sever a human limb in seconds. Unlike traditional sand and grit blasting, with hydroblasting there is no dispersal of spent abrasives or harmful chemicals into the ecosystem. Therefore, with more water–efficient hydroblasting machinery, we can be green even without toxic industrial strength cleaners.

Q: What is the main purpose of the passage?
(a) To classify the two types of hydroblasting techniques
(b) To highlight the advantages of using hydroblasting
(c) To spotlight the many uses of hydroblasting
(d) To illustrate the dangers of hydroblasting

18.   Today's most popular type of footwear gets its name from the 1800s when a London police officer created a rubber-soled shoe so he could "sneak" up on criminals without them hearing him. This innovation sparked the birth of today's global multi-billion dollar sneaker market. Sneakers are made of flexible materials, usually with a rubber sole and leather or canvas top. Besides serving its original purpose as active footwear, the sneaker has created a whole new subculture in itself. They have been an integral part of American hip-hop culture since the 70s and really took off internationally with the growing popularity of sports like basketball.

Q: What is the best title of the passage?
(a) From Beat-Cop to Backbeat, the Story of the Sneaker
(b) The History of America's Most Expensive Footwear
(c) The Reason Behind a Multi-Million Dollar Industry
(d) How the Sneaker Changed the Music Industry

19.

> Attention all P-Mart shoppers,
>
> In an effort to provide the best products at the lowest prices, we are extending our popular green-light specials. For the next week, whenever a green-light flashes above any product aisle, P-Mart shoppers will be entitled to an additional 30 percent off our already low, low prices! Be sure to take advantage of this promotional offer and look for additional coupons in this Sunday's *Daily Times Newspapers*. We recognize how attractive our low prices are, but unfortunately we have to limit the number of products per customer on a product to product basis. Thank you for your continued loyalty to P-Mart, we look forward to providing you with the lowest prices for your everyday needs.

Q: What is the main purpose of the announcement?
(a) To remind customers of a purchasing limit on sale items
(b) To inform customers of a limited time sales initiative
(c) To encourage customers to read the Sunday newspapers
(d) To win over customers from a competing company

20.

Studies performed over a long period of time have shown clear and strong links between the clearing of vegetation and the decline of annual rainfall. This has also led to more extreme periods of drought and increased vulnerability to extreme climatic changes. Vegetation systems offer crucial feedback to mechanisms that buttress water vapor recycling in micro and meso scales. Having a variety of heterogeneous forms of vegetation can ensure an atmospheric condition suitable to precipitation and therefore, increase the resilience of agro-ecosystems to drought and extreme climates. On the other hand, if we continue to develop landscapes with our current state of mind, climate change will only be exasperated and long term hazards will be harder to suppress.

Q: Which of the following claims is made in the passage?
(a) Extreme climates occur predominantly in areas of heavy vegetation.
(b) Changing methods of land development won't slow climate change.
(c) Having diverse vegetation makes the land susceptible to drought.
(d) Vegetation density has a positive correlation to precipitation levels.

21. After World War II, America began to prosper again and young people took to gathering at their favorite soda shops or diners to hang out with their friends. Even today, teens adopt the image of the music or musicians they listen to and in essence, it defines them. Thus, an integral part of this experience was the jukebox, a freestanding, coin-operated machine that played songs a customer chose by punching in a combination of letters and numbers. Later, an individual wall-mounted jukebox could also be found at every customer's table. The term "jukebox" comes from a Gullah (African Americans living in Southeast North Carolina) word that means "rowdy, disorderly, or wicked," which amply described the hangouts of rambunctious American teens.

Q: What is the best title of the passage?
(a) Hot American Trends Post WWII
(b) The Jukebox, an American Original
(c) The Jukebox Soda Shop Revolution
(d) How the Jukebox Propelled America

22. Magnetic resonance imaging, or MRI, is a medical technique used in the field of radiology to visualize internal structures in detail. It offers better contrast between the various soft tissues of the body and thus, makes it ideal for imaging the brain, muscles, heart and cancers. In comparison to alternative medical imaging technology like computer tomography or X-rays, MRI does not use potentially harmful ionizing radiation. The first MRI studies performed on humans were published in 1977, long after the first X-rays on humans that were performed in 1895. Today, MRIs can give medical professionals a 3D image, which has revolutionized how certain diseases and injuries are diagnosed and treated.

Q: What is the main idea of the passage?
(a) MRI has a short but successful history in radiology
(b) The revolutionary influence of MRIs to internal medicine
(c) MRI is an evolutionary step ahead for the medical industry
(d) MRI offers superior and safer imaging than other methods

23. Humans have always created or found sources of recreation. One unique example is sandboarding, which bears many similarities to snowboarding. A major hurdle to sandboarding is the fact that it is very difficult to build lifts in the desert. So, boarders must either take an excruciating trek back to the top of the dunes, or catch a lift on a buggy or all-terrain vehicle. Sandboarding has adherents on every continent, obviously with most of them near deserts. The Sahara desert is a favorite destination amongst boarders because it is the oldest desert on the planet, which results in sand grains that are nearly perfect polished spheres. This type of sand allows for the smoothest and fastest rides.

Q: Which of the following is correct about sandboarding?
(a) It is gaining popularity in non-desert regions
(b) Most participants are from equatorial countries
(c) It takes more stamina because of the heat
(d) Lack of lifts present unique challenges

24. Stretching over 2 kilometers with stacks of merchandise reaching over four stories, the fully automated warehouse of IKEA is a constant buzz of people and machines filling orders and restocking shelves. IKEA was founded in 1943 by a seventeen year old Swede by the name of Ingvar Kamprad. To fill in the rest of the acronym, "E" stands for Elmtaryd, the name of the farm Ingvar grew up in and "A" is for his home parish of Agunnard, Sweden. IKEA can be found in nearly every industrialized nation, many operating 24 hours a day. It's no wonder that in 2006, *Forbes* ranked the founder the sixth wealthiest man in the world with assets amounting over $26 billion.

Q: Which of the following is correct about IKEA?
(a) Its namesake is an acronym for the founder's name and hometown
(b) State-of-the art mechanization is used in its enormous warehouse
(c) Stores can be found in both developed and underdeveloped nations
(d) Store hours differ from country to country with most closing late at night

25.   According to a study done by Professors William A. Luke and Patricia Hughes of St. Cloud State University, charitable giving has for a long time provided substantial amounts of funding for nonprofit organizations. However, this source of income is highly variable. The study theorizes a possible explanation for the variability lies in the measurement of income. Furthermore, it investigates how the variability of income rises with the level of household income and varies depending on the source of income. By distinguishing types of income, permanent or transitory, the study also identifies factors in decision making by married couples. The study concludes that great variability in the flow of yearly household income has a direct negative effect on the total giving.

Q: Which of the following is correct about charitable giving?
(a) Charitable giving, although a major source of support, is inconsistent.
(b) Charitable giving is greater with married couples with transitory income.
(c) The more variable the income the greater the charitable giving.
(d) Charitable giving has been a small part of nonprofits' yearly budgets.

26.   Japanese teppanyaki-style restaurants have become a huge hit in America. Not to be confused with hibachi which is an open grill fueled by charcoal or gas, teppanyaki cooking is done on a solid griddle-type surface. Teppanyaki restaurants are known to be "where dinner is the show," with chefs being the center of attention, cooking at the table and vociferously sharing jokes. They have to be highly trained in order to juggle razor sharp cooking knives, flip grilled shrimp deftly onto customer's plates and adroitly spin uncooked eggs on a spatula. Besides having a wonderfully cooked meal, customers always leave with full stomachs and smiles on their faces because of an unforgettable experience.

Q: Which of the following is correct about teppanyaki cooking?
(a) Customers enjoy the smoky, flame-grilled steak and seafood.
(b) Chefs are typically Japanese in their soft spoken coyish ways.
(c) Customers are able to interact directly with the chefs.
(d) It is often cooked in conjunction with hibachi-style cooking.

27. During medieval times, being brought to the rack was one of the worst sentences a prisoner could face. The rack was often a raised wooden frame with two ropes attached to the top and bottom connected to a roller. Victims' arms were tied to the top ropes and legs to the bottom and a handle connected to the roller, when turned, stretched the limbs. Bones would often dislocate from their joints with a loud crack, the victims' limbs being completely ripped off their bodies in extreme cases. The purpose of the rack was to extract confessions from the victim. Failure to confess meant the torturer had permission to turn the handle more.

Q: Which of the following is correct about the rack?
(a) It was one of the most humane tools of torture.
(b) Its goal was to force admissions of guilt from prisoners.
(c) It was an unpopular interrogation technique of the time.
(d) It left prisoners with nominal physical and mental harm.

28.

Notice: Beginning next Monday, the Humanities Building will close the top two floors for three weeks in order to remove asbestos. This means students attending art classes on the fourth and fifth floors will be relocated to the basement level. Assigned classrooms will be posted at both the main and rear entrances of the Humanities building. As you should know, asbestos is an older insulating material that has been found to be carcinogenic. Of course all safety precautions will be in place, including, but not limited to, increased ventilation, industrial strength plastic curtains and dust free disposal. Please take note of the changes and we apologize for the inconvenience.

Sincerely,
Jeanette Torres, University Building and Maintenance

Q: Which of the following is correct about the Humanities Building?
(a) It will be closed for the next three weeks.
(b) Asbestos removal will take under a month.
(c) Art classes will be relocated to the first floor.
(d) Additional fire safety measures will be installed.

29.   Who would have thought that America's longest running sitcom would be a satirical cartoon? *The Simpsons* debuted on December 17, 1989 after having a few shorts run on the *Tracy Ullman Show* on Fox and hasn't stopped poking fun at modern day society. The creator, Matt Groening, based the characters of Homer, Marge, Bart, Lisa and Maggie on his real-life parents and family. *The Simpsons* is aired in over 60 countries worldwide and has had a notable impact on real life as evidenced in the many universities that teach classes based on the cartoon. As a matter of fact, at the University of California, Berkeley, *The Simpsons* has made it onto the syllabus of one of their philosophy classes.

Q: Which of the following is correct about *The Simpsons*?
(a) It started as a cameo filler to another Fox show.
(b) It is a sardonic lampoon of the working elite.
(c) It has garnered a limited cult following in the U.S.
(d) It has attracted the attention of academics worldwide.

30.   Racing down the fresh powder covered hills, curving like a pro, you're ready to hit that jump but all of a sudden, your goggles fog up! CRASH! This is a skier or snowboarder's worst nightmare, but it doesn't have to be for you. Introducing Cat's Eyes X-treme lens cleaner with their patented anti-fog veneer. With a clean, non-abrasive cloth, gently rub a pea-size amount on your goggles for a cleaner and fog-free skiing and snowboarding experience. No more do you have to worry about losing your sight as you fly down your favorite hill!

Q: Which of the following is correct about Cat's Eyes X-treme?
(a) It improves a winter sports enthusiast's proficiency.
(b) It can make you stand out amongst all others.
(c) It requires a bit of work to apply but is worth it.
(d) It leaves a revolutionary anti-fog covering on goggles.

31. With the increase in working hours, more consideration has been put into making sure that employees have both the right equipment and environment. This concern has led to the development of ergonomics, the study of designs that best fit the human body. Spending hours in front of a computer monitor and typing repetitively can lead to repetitive stress disorders. Ergonomics in the workplace involves making sure the computer monitor is at eye level, to prevent neck strain, placing an ergonomic keyboard at the right level, and making sure the office chair is straight and at the right height. With these safeguards in place, the worker will be more productive and will be less susceptible to mental and physical strain.

Q: Which of the following is correct about ergonomics?
(a) It can reduce employee retention if used properly.
(b) It is a standard that all employees strive to achieve.
(c) It concentrates on human interactions with equipment.
(d) It hasn't attracted many followers and practitioners.

32. The Very Large Array, or VLA, is a set of 27 radio antennae that are 10 stories high with a 25 meter diameter parabola dish. The individual antennae are arranged in a Y pattern and are moved four times in a 16 month period. The reason behind the routine relocation of the antennae is to change the resolution of the images captured, kind of like the zoom on your camera. VLA is highly valued because unlike conventional telescopes, radio waves can penetrate gases and clouds that can block the view of a telescope. Contrary to popular belief originating from showing VLA in movies such as *Contact* and *Independence Day*, VLA is not used to search for extra-terrestrials.

Q: Which of the following is correct about the passage?
(a) VLA is superior to telescope observatories.
(b) VLA has inspired many movies about aliens.
(c) VLA is the largest set of stationary radio antennae.
(d) VLA is like a camera and can quickly zoom in and out.

33. Lent is the Catholic penitential time leading up to Easter and is a period marked with sacrifice and self-discipline to show your devotion to God. Mardi Gras, on the other hand, is a last hurrah before the solemn Lenten season, which begins on Ash Wednesday. French for "Fat Tuesday," Mardi Gras is celebrated in New Orleans, Louisiana, and transpires during the same time as other Carnival festivals like in Rio de Janeiro, Brazil. This period is marked by an over indulgence of fatty and rich foods, alcohol and dancing. Revelers tend to dress up in exotic costumes and are known to party for many nights on end.

Q: What can be inferred from the passage?
(a) Mardi Gras pales in size and length compared to Carnival in Brazil.
(b) New Orleans is a peaceful city until Mardi Gras fans descend upon it.
(c) Mardi Gras allows devotees a last chance for debauchery before Lent.
(d) Costumes worn during Mardi Gras are symbolic of Christ's sacrifice.

34. Since the advent of the automobile, over 20 million fatalities have been recorded. Even as late as the 1950's, car manufacturers stood by the claim that it was impossible to make vehicles any safer than they were because the physical forces of a crash were too great to overcome. At the same time, after testing with cadavers, the first crash test dummy was unveiled. A crash test dummy is a full-scale anthropomorphic test device (ATD) that resembles the human body in weight, proportions, and movement. Today's dummies are equipped with sensitive high-tech sensors that provide vital crash test data. Thanks to these silent heroes, humans have the greatest chances of surviving fatal accidents than they have ever had.

Q: What can be inferred from the passage?
(a) Cadavers provided important feedback on automobile crashes.
(b) Auto manufacturers in the 50's just worried about making money.
(c) Crash test dummies aren't acknowledged enough for their contributions.
(d) Understanding of physics in the 50's was much less than today.

35. The best horror films always involve a demonic spirit possessing a poor, innocent victim. The possessed is transformed into the evil spirit and acts violently, speaking in tongues and scaring those around them. Every culture around the world has a similar tale of spirit possession as well as a cure for the possessed. Often referred to as an exorcism, a priest or spiritual healer uses prayers, religious symbols, gestures, etc. to remove the haunting spirit from the possessed body. The possessed is not considered evil themselves, rather just a hapless victim. Therefore, the exorcism in itself is considered a cure rather than a punishment. Exorcism rites can be found in Judaism, Christianity and Islam as well as in Buddhism.

Q: What can be inferred from the passage?
(a) The major religions practice the same rituals to cure the possessed.
(b) Evil spirits prey on the weak of mind and feeble of heart.
(c) Exorcisms have been practiced for hundreds of years.
(d) Spiritual healers have supernatural powers to expunge evil spirits.

36. Paul Bunyan and his companion Babe the Blue Ox are mythical figures whose origins are still in dispute. Some claim the myths originated with French Canadians who spun the yarns during their rebellion against the Queen of England. Others claim the legends were a marketing ploy by the lumber industry. In the folklores, Paul Bunyan is a giant of a lumberjack and Babe the Blue Ox is equally as large. The stories give credit to Paul Bunyan for creating the Grand Canyon by dragging his axe behind him, digging the Great Lakes as a watering hole for Babe, and forming Mount Hood by piling rocks on top of his campfire to extinguish it. Now that's a tall tale!

Q: What can be inferred from the passage?
(a) Paul Bunyan is a favorite tale told in the southern regions of America.
(b) Paul Bunyan was a myth conceived by lumberjacks in North America.
(c) Both Americans and Canadians stack claims to the invention of Paul Bunyan.
(d) Babe the Blue Ox is responsible for the creation of many geological sites.

37.

To Caroline Schoenberg, HR Director,

I want to thank you again for the opportunity to interview with your firm. Working for Brandon&Partners has been a goal of mine since I entered the field of intellectual property rights. Over my eight year career representing inventors across our state I have established a fantastic network of inventors. I have won over 16 cases for my clients, the most notable being Jesper Hassan, the inventor of America's most popular anti-snoring treatment, Snore-no-more facemask. I know that I can be a highly valuable asset to Brandon&Partners. Thank you again for your time and I look forward to hearing from you soon.

Sincerely yours,
Jeff Johnson

Q: What can be inferred from the passage?
(a) Jeff can bring many clients to Brandon&Partners.
(b) Caroline is an intellectual property rights lawyer.
(c) Brandon&Partners is the largest patent law firm.
(d) Jeff has more wins than losses for his clients.

Part III Questions 38—40

Read the passage. Then identify the option that does NOT belong.

38. Tattoos have become a popular fashion trend these days with over 25% of Americans sporting at least one. (a) For a long time Westerners thought only sailors and criminals got tattoos. (b) However, evidence of tattooing dates back about 5000 B.C. as evidenced in the discovery of Ötzi the iceman who was found in the Ötz valley in the Alps and had an estimated 57 carbon tattoos. (c) Tattooing has also been found on Egyptian mummies dating around the end of the second millennium B.C. and Japanese tattooing is believed to date nearly 10,000 years ago. (d) Western tattooing comes from Polynesia and when 18th century explorers were first exposed to tattoos, it became instantly popular with the sailors.

39. One of history's first incredibly dramatic film footage came on May 6, 1937, when the German passenger airship LZ 129 Hindenburg was engulfed in flames over Lakehurst, New Jersey. (a) The Hindenburg was a hydrogen-filled airship with 97 crew and passengers. (b) Its initial landing was delayed because of thunderstorms but was cleared later that day. (c) During the time the Hindenburg was waiting to land, it made its way towards Manhattan, which caused quite the stir as people scrambled to get a glimpse of the floating silver ship. (d) At approximately 7:25 p.m., the Hindenburg suddenly went up in flames, which prompted Herbert Morrison to exclaim the historical words, "Oh the humanity!" during his WLS radio broadcast.

40. Life for the blind was forever changed for the better after a blind Frenchman by the name of Louis Braille invented the Braille system for reading and writing. (a) Braille characters, or cells, are constructed of a six dot position system, arranged in a rectangle with two columns containing three raised dots each. (b) Not everyone was excited for the innovation Braille had created, but it still became the standard for the blind. (c) Braille came from a method of communication created for Napoleon who demanded a silent way for soldiers to communicate on the field without light. (d) Although this system was originally rejected because of its complexity, the blind around the world hail it as a godsend.

ACTUAL TEST 2

Reading
COMPREHENSION

Part I Questions 1—16

Read the passage. Then choose the option that best completes the passage.

1. When you think of a 12-16 meter long mammal weighing approximately 36,000 kilograms, _____. Yet, this describes the humpback whale, which is known to breach the water in a graceful display that would make any figure skater green with envy. One of the most amazing behaviors of the humpback whale is its yearly migration to Hawaii. Humpbacks migrate from three areas; some from Baja, Mexico, others from near Japan, and about 60 percent make the 3,500 mile trek from Alaska. Humpbacks migrate to Hawaii because it provides a safe haven for the young pups. The majority return to Alaska to feed on the small fish schools and krill rich waters, whereas Hawaii's waters are free of these smaller organisms.

(a) you envision a giant monster straight out of Hollywood
(b) an acrobatic leviathan usually doesn't come to mind
(c) you probably are thinking about an enormous sea animal
(d) there is no present day organism that can fit this bill

2.

Dear Mr. McGraw,

As per our discussion regarding the new marketing initiative, _____ the mailings by next month. Our target market was determined by zip codes of the upper 10 percent income earning households. These are "at risk" clients because they have no field agents or planners and are thus considered home office accounts. The cost of this campaign is a little over the budget for this fiscal year, but we have reserve funds which will compensate for next year. Please take the time to review the numbers and the marketing materials to make sure they are in compliance. Please email me with any questions, thank you again for your time!

Sincerely,
Aaron Flanagan, Marketing and Research

(a) our accounting department should expect
(b) this firm's biggest competitor will distribute
(c) television and radio stations will send
(d) we need your final approval to launch

3. Around 79 A.D. the city of Pompeii and its sister city of Herculaneum were completely obliterated by the eruption of Mount Vesuvius. It wasn't until over 1,500 years later that the two ancient cities were accidentally rediscovered under 4 to 6 meters of pumice and ash. Because of the volcanic debris, Pompeii gives us a remarkably clear glimpse into the lives of the Roman people at the height of the empire. The excavated town gives us a snapshot of Roman life such as the forums, the baths, numerous houses, and some out of town villas. Today Pompeii is one of _____ over 2.5 million visitors a year.

(a) Italy's most frequently visited tourist spots with
(b) the Renaissance's best preserved cities for
(c) Romania's most valued and remarkable cities with
(d) the world's most active volcanic spectacles

4. It's a hot muggy one out there today and by the look of things from the News 5 Eye in the Sky helicopter, many people are _____. We got two cars pulled over on the westbound interstate highway 15 at mile post 164, but after that things are clear sailing. Over on the beltline heading to Santa Cruz there's a car pulled over with its hood up, looks like overheating problems there. Traffic's a little packed behind the overheated car, it looks like too many people are more interested in the broken down car than on the freeway. Other than that, doesn't look to bad out there in the greater metropolis.

(a) seeking shelter under the highway over passes
(b) bundling up and putting on more layers
(c) trying to flee the city to head to the beach
(d) queuing up at the gas station and car washes

5.   For millenniums, the sword determined who ruled the land. Interestingly enough, the sword developed from the dagger and the oldest sword-like weapon dates back to 3300 B.C. in Turkey. However, this weapon is considered more of an extended dagger than an actual sword. It wasn't until stronger alloys such as steel and better heat treatment processes were developed that swords longer than 60 centimeters were produced. This is because the tensile strength of bronze decreases tremendously the longer the weapon is and thus bends easily. Perhaps it is more accurate that _____ for thousands of years.

    (a) swords were more popular than pens
    (b) the bronze age was defined by the dagger
    (c) swords and daggers were treasured by men
    (d) the sword was mightier than the pen

6.   Tired of pulling out that garden hose and all the other pool cleaning equipment to _____ your pool every week? With the Solar Breeze robotic pool cleaner, you no longer have that worrisome headache. Unlike other pool cleaners that make you wait until debris sinks to the bottom of the pool and clogs the pipes, the Solar Breeze lightly skims the surface automatically picking up floating particles there may be. Leaves, bugs and other debris usually float on the top of the water for over three hours, the whole time leeching contaminants into your pool. At only $500, the Solar Breeze is a worthy investment that is not only convenient and safe, but also environmentally friendly, order now!

    (a) make your tool shed clean and neat
    (b) keep the litter and debris out of
    (c) moisten and maintain water temperature in
    (d) thoroughly preserve the water quality of

7. Imagine a competition involving running a track of 253.3 meters over two wet and dry obstacles while carrying another competitor who has to weigh at least 49 kilograms with a goal of winning your own weight in beer. Every year in Finland and the states of Wisconsin and Michigan, the Wife Carrying competition is held. Legend has it that this unusual game originated in Finland at the end of the 18th century, inspired by a man named Herkko Rosvo-Ronkanien who was a leader of a gang of thieves notorious for stealing not only goods from towns, but women as well. Today _____ and certainly can make or break a marriage depending on if you drop your spouse or not.

(a) the race is highly regarded in all circles
(b) competitors rigorously train year round
(c) this spectacle has become world-renowned
(d) racers can be found in all shapes and sizes

8. Dr. Martin Cooper is considered the inventor of the first portable telephone and the one to _____. A former general manager for the systems division in Motorola, Dr. Cooper revealed the cell phone in April of 1983, calling his rival at Dell laboratories in a gesture akin to sticking one's tongue. Motorola's DynaTAC was a 9X5X1.75 inches, weighed a whopping 2.5 pounds and had a talk time of only 35 minutes. That pales in comparison to today's smart phones that are only 4.5X2.31X0.37 inches, weighing as little as 4.8 ounces with features such as text messaging, internet browsing, video phone, talk times of up to 14 hours and much more.

(a) bring it out of the military and into the public
(b) place the first cellular call in history
(c) market it effectively in Europe and Asia
(d) breathe life into a flagging industry

9.   With fewer and fewer couples marrying in developed nations, many sociologists, psychologists, and other experts have been fretting over declining birthrates. What is it in our society today that is either keeping people from marrying or leading them so easily to divorce? Some argue our everyday workload has increased significantly, especially in the last 20 years. Couple that with an accompanying rise in communications and electronic devices, which ironically should assist us in having closer relationships but unfortunately often has the opposite effect. We need to prioritize our lives and determine what is really important to us. So instead of browsing your social networks soon as you get home, try doing some face to face interaction, _____.

(a) you'll find it just as or even more rewarding
(b) via video phone or video chatting online
(c) rather than logging on and surfing the internet
(d) it may help you with your job and career

10.   Nearly everyone knows of Walt Disney and his enormous Disney enterprise, but what people tend to forget is that if it weren't for two brothers from Germany, _____.
The Brothers Grimm are Jakob and Wilhelm Grimm born at the end of the 1700's and died around the mid 1800's. The two collected German folktales and are credited for re-introducing now classic fairytales such as Cinderella, The Frog Prince, Hansel and Gretel, Sleeping Beauty, Snow White and many more. The Brothers Grimm published a manuscript containing several dozen fairytales in 1810. It has been rumored that they only collected stories by word of mouth from peasants, but in reality, many of the storytellers were middle-class or aristocrats that heard the stories from their servants.

(a) Disney would have settled into the newspaper industry
(b) Mickey and Minnie Mouse may not have been born
(c) Disney may never have been such a success
(d) Disneyworld and Pixar would never have existed

11.

Dear Gabby,

Recently my 16-year-old daughter has been nagging me _____ her driver's license and I am a little worried. I know today's cars are much safer than when we grew up, but I also know that today's kids have mobile phones which makes it that much more dangerous for them to drive. My daughter keeps saying that her friends have cars so why can't she? She won't see the logical reasoning I give her to wait until college to have a car and we haven't talked to each other in almost a week. I just don't know what to do!

Desperate in Arizona,
Susan Kraemer

(a) to take her to a private tutor for
(b) for a new car but she just got
(c) to pay for the annual renewal of
(d) for a greater weekly allowance and

12.

Tired of spending hours searching for an errant tee shot? Have your golf buddies stopped calling you because of your terrible slice? Then improve your swing quickly and effortlessly with the new Golf-Pal magnetic pointer. This simple, yet highly effective golf aid attaches to your club head and points to where you want your ball to fly. After only one week of practicing with the Golf-Pal magnetic pointer, your golf score will go down five strokes! Order now for the low introductory rate of $49.99 and not only will you make your money back _____, but you'll also be the envy of the golf course!

(a) by improving your golf handicap
(b) in various local golf tournaments
(c) to pay for a single golf season
(d) by not losing so many golf balls

13. One of the world's most revolutionary building materials is concrete. During the Roman Empire, concrete was widely utilized and spawned the Roman Architectural Revolution. Originally made from quicklime, pozzolana and an aggregate of pumice, concrete freed the Romans from the restrictive chains of bricks and stones. Concrete allowed for innovation and a marked increase in architectural complexity for Roman architects, with examples such as the Roman Pantheon, still the world's largest unreinforced concrete dome. Today's concrete structures use a different mixture of materials as well as iron or steel reinforcement. Furthermore, modern concrete has allowed us to keep pushing the envelope _____.

(a) for the tallest structures in the world
(b) to better ways of constructing domes
(c) of human ingenuity and competence
(d) for building green and eco-friendly

14. Baseball as we know it today requires some specialized equipment, none more so than _____. Interestingly enough, the early players of this game didn't wear gloves. It wasn't until 1875 that a St. Louis outfielder Charles Waitt sported a pair of fleshed-colored gloves. The concept slowly caught on with other players as they experimented with different types of gloves. The early gloves were most suitable for picking up ground balls and did not include the webbing between the first finger and thumb as we see in today's modern baseball glove.

(a) the unique ball and bat combination itself
(b) other sports such as soccer or football
(c) the baseball glove with its unique design
(d) the baseball diamond the game is played on

15. Long before we had sprawling mega malls to find every item we may need or want, there was the bazaar. The word, bazaar, originated in ancient Persia and represented a permanent area to sell merchandise. Characterized by their lively atmosphere and plethora of products, today's modern bazaars do not differ that greatly from ancient ones and have flourished globally. _____, bazaars are found in countries near the Middle East such as Azerbaijan as well as in distant countries like Ireland and China.

(a) In the end
(b) At the same time
(c) Consequently
(d) Notwithstanding

16. Life-giving water is a figure of speech on several levels. We need water itself to sustain our lives but seas and rivers also provide food. This is one of the reasons civilizations have sprung up around bodies of water or rivers. Ancient Egyptians and Chinese were using fishing rods, hooks and lines as early as 2000 B.C. even though a majority of fishermen used simple handlines. Early fishing lures were made of bone or bronze, the latter being strong but very thin and not easily visible to the fish. It wasn't until the 1900's that an American company started manufacturing lures for commercial use, _____ lures were made by individual craftsmen for private use.

(a) prior to that
(b) instead of when
(c) where
(d) even though

Part II   **Questions 17—37**

Read the passage and the question. Then choose the option that best answers the question.

17.   Residents of Grand Rapids awoke to a thunderous explosion as Becker's Grain and Feed grain silo 14 exploded around six in the morning Tuesday. The explosion was a result of a perfect storm of dry conditions followed by an unseasonal electrical storm. Any finely ground organic material is highly flammable; especially flour which is what was being stored at Becker's farm. Silo 14 and two nearby grain elevators were completely destroyed. Fire fighters worked past noon to keep the blaze under control and prevent it from spreading to other nearby farm structures. Fortunately no human injuries were reported, although some livestock had to be treated for minor burns.

Q: What is mainly discussed in the news passage?
(a) The devastating effects of an electric shock
(b) The dangers of using elevators to store grain
(c) A grain elevator explosion at a local farm
(d) The effects of a detrimental situation on a grain farm

18.   It's the little things in life that have made the biggest impact on our civilization. A great example of this is the peppercorn, or black pepper. Not to be confused with the long pepper fruit, black pepper is derived from the spherical peppercorn and has been used in India since at least 2000 B.C. In early times, all pepper found in Europe came from India and the surrounding areas. Pepper became so popular that it was even used as collateral or even currency. Pepper and other spices from India led the Portuguese and other European countries to find a quicker route to India. This in turn led to the discovery and colonization of the Americas and has forever changed world history.

Q: What is the best title of the passage?
(a) How the Pepper Found Its Way to India
(b) How the Pepper Changed Civilization
(c) Pepper, the Spice of the Silk Road
(d) How the Pepper Divided the East from the West

19. The other day I was walking to the campus library when I bumped into Jenny, a friend of a high school classmate. We never really talked much and I really didn't have a good first impression of her at the homecoming football game. When asked where I was going, I told her that I had a paper due and was heading to the library. She asked what class it was for, and I told her the paper was for my poli sci 211 class with Professor Adkins and it was already a day late. Jenny offered to help since she had remarkably had that same professor the previous semester. I was shocked at her willingness to help me, a virtual stranger. Guess it proves you can't judge a book by its cover!

Q: What is the main topic of the passage?
(a) It's impossible to make a first impression again.
(b) People's perception is their reality.
(c) Friends can appear suddenly out of thin air.
(d) First impressions aren't necessarily correct.

20.

Dear valued customer,

You have received this email as a nationwide customer outreach program and this is not an advertisement. MBH Incorporated has recognized your continued patronage of our open source operating system and want to invite you to continue adding your valuable contents and comments. We have vastly improved the response time and eradicated many glitches due to your feedback. In honor of your service to MBH Inc., we would like to do a profile spotlight on you with your permission. Please respond at your earliest convenience to this email or on the website at www.mbh.com.

With gratitude,
Christine Sayers, Customer Response Team

Q: What is mainly discussed in the letter?
(a) The value of open source content and comments
(b) An invitation to subscribe to the profile spotlight page
(c) Acknowledging a customer's contribution to the company
(d) Recognizing the flaws in open source content

21. The human body has about 7,000 different types of protein molecules in the average cell. Some of these protein molecules control the movement of materials in and out of the cell. Others send signals from the outside of the cell to the inside. Protein molecules are often the target of drug manufacturers with over half the drugs on the market working and interacting with these proteins. However, in the past it has been difficult to study the efficacy of these drugs with the proteins without depriving the proteins of other crucial elements and chopping them up. A new method for studying these protein molecules has been discovered using a laser without disturbing or altering the proteins themselves. This technique has promising potential for both research and treatment as not all patients react the same to certain drugs.

Q: What is mainly discussed in the passage?
(a) A breakthrough in studying drugs effects with protein molecules
(b) The two main uses of protein molecules in the human body
(c) Drug manufacturers' manipulation of protein molecules
(d) The difficulty with current methods of combining drugs with proteins

22. An announcement of a less than friendly M&A between two of the largest telecommunications giants has many business leaders in the U.S. apprehensive. Moreover, if the merger is approved by Congress, then there will only be three companies to choose from. This could have major implications for businesses who make operating systems for smartphones and provide apps. Unnamed company sources say they are concerned that the merger will make the purchasing company powerful enough that they could control the environment around smartphones and their accessories. Furthermore, the merger could mean that the biggest player will also unfairly determine price.

Q: What is the best title of the passage?
(a) Imminent M&A Will Test America's Resolve
(b) Major Telecom Merger to be Mulled on Wall Street
(c) Deal for Telecom Takeover Raises Concerns
(d) Business Leaders Agree About M&A

23.   The word scuba is an acronym for "self-contained underwater breathing apparatus" and is commonly thought of having been invented by an Australian by the name of Ted Eldred who improved on Jacques-Yves Cousteau's aqualung invention. Prior to the self-contained tank, divers relied on oxygen to be pumped to them from the surface through a long hose. This was incredibly dangerous as divers were helpless if any mechanical problems arose during their dive. Early problems of oxygen toxicity were experienced with Cousteau's aqualung rebreather system but are now remedied with modern scuba equipment.

Q: Which of the following is correct about scuba diving?
(a) It was originally developed by Jacques-Yves Cousteau.
(b) It was a great improvement from previous diving methods.
(c) It requires hours of training and certification courses.
(d) It is the safest way to experience underwater sightseeing.

24.   Forming a musical band really is not as difficult as it may seem. All you need is some like-minded friends with the same tastes in music as you. Ideally, these friends should have some formal musical training, but as history has proved, it is not absolutely necessary. Many self-taught musicians have made it big. One guitar legend comes to mind, and that is Eric Clapton. Clapton taught himself how to play the guitar at a young age and was known to lock himself in his room for hours listening to music over and over and copying it. He has been a headliner for over four decades as an internationally acclaimed blues and R&B guitarist and singer. Pretty good for a do-it-yourselfer!

Q: Which of the following is correct about Eric Clapton?
(a) He started playing the guitar in high school.
(b) He has been highly sought for over forty years.
(c) He had little formal training in grade school.
(d) His style of music originated in Europe.

25. Many cultures originated from nomadic tribes that never settled in any particular area permanently. Referred to as "itinerants" in society today, surprisingly there are still approximately 30-40 million nomads around the world. Nomads fall into one of three categories based on their economic specialization. The first group is by far the oldest of the three and is known as the hunting and gathering nomads. This group drives and follows wild game and plant life according to the seasons. The second category is pastoral nomads who raise livestock and drive and move with them in patterns to maintain pasture sustainability. The last group is the peripatetic nomads who contribute specialized skills and crafts to their society and are most commonly found in industrialized nations.

Q: Which of the following is correct about nomads?
(a) Some follow the seasonal migration of their prey.
(b) Many eventually settle in industrialized nations.
(c) Pastoral nomads are the most common today.
(d) Nomadic life has triggered environmental hazards.

26. Nearly everyone dreams of striking it rich by winning the lottery. Ironically, how many of these people actually buy lottery tickets? The largest prize ever won with a single lottery ticket in the United States was a whopping $177,270,519.67, split amongst eight co-workers at a Nebraska meat processing plant in 2006. The actual amount before taxes was $365 million and the workers wisely chose the lump sum cash payout rather than a lifetime payout that in the end pays you much less. Surprisingly enough, all eight workers said they would continue on with the jobs as usual. However, this golden pot at the end of the rainbow doesn't always guarantee a fairy story ending. As a matter of fact, nearly three out of every five lottery winner files for bankruptcy within five years of their winning.

Q: Which of the following is correct about the lottery?
(a) Only one person can claim a winning ticket.
(b) Choosing the right payout is crucial for value.
(c) Winnings are received free of state and federal tax.
(d) Lottery winners usually stay at their jobs.

27.   Rare earth metals, contrary to their namesake, are actually quite common on the planet, but not usually in highly concentrated amounts like other minerals and ore. Uses for rare earth metals range from rare microwave filters to lasers and X-ray machines. They are also crucial for many other electronic components such as batteries for laptops and mobile phones and camera lenses. Mining rare earth metals can pose some serious environmental risks including radioactive slurry and other toxic elements seeping into the groundwater or escaping into the air. The Burik Merah mine in Malaysia is currently under a $100 million clean-up effort after many residents blamed the refinery for birth defects and cases of leukemia.

Q: Which of the following is correct about rare earth metals?
(a) Only a few industries depend on them for essential components.
(b) They may soon be traded at equal or greater value than gold.
(c) There are many hazards in mining, refining and storing the waste.
(d) They are expensive because they are not commonly found on the planet.

28.   Various sausages are produced the world over, but none may beat the uniqueness of haggis. This dish is often attributed to Scotland in spite of the first written recipe coming from Lancashire in North West England in 1430. The traditional way to prepare haggis is to stuff a sheep's stomach with its 'pluck,' that is heart, liver and lungs, minced onions, oatmeal and other spices. The filling is also mixed with a stock, and left to simmer for about three hours. Many people consider haggis as a sausage or even a pudding. Although one might at first think haggis sounds unappetizing, it has legions of fans around the world.

Q: Which of the following is correct about haggis?
(a) It has its origins in North West Wales.
(b) It is not considered a type of sausage.
(c) It utilizes the major organs of the sheep.
(d) It is a quick and easy dish to prepare.

29. Besides being the principal author of the Declaration of Independence and the third president of the United States, Thomas Jefferson was also an extraordinary architect. In addition to the nearby University of Virginia, Jefferson also designed his magnificent estate "Monticello." Jefferson based the house design on the neoclassical principles written in the book by the Italian Renaissance architect Andrea Palladio. Its image has adorned the back side of the U.S. nickel since 1938 as well as appearing on the two dollar bill and a 1956 postage stamp. Jefferson remodeled Monticello after he returned from spending seven years as the Minister of the U.S. to France and had the opportunity to see in person the building he had only read about.

Q: Which of the following is correct about Monticello?
(a) It was designed by a famous Italian architect.
(b) It revolutionized currency and postage stamps design.
(c) It was remodeled after Jefferson returned from England.
(d) It is an example of neoclassical Italian Renaissance design.

30. Have you ever daydreamed about inventing that next hit product? In 2009, there were 4,548,072 patents granted worldwide. Not all inventions of course are a big hit, for example the "toilet snorkel," a patent granted in 1983 for a tube that allows a person to utilize the fresh air found at the back of a toilet when faced with a house fire. Also part of the "not so practical" invention category is the "cheese filtered" cigarette patented in 1966, as if smoking wasn't disgusting enough without adding the mellow flavor of a Gouda or sharp tang of cheddar. Last on the list is the "bulletproof desk" patent that was granted in 2001. This school desk has a clear bulletproof glass top with a handle that allows the terrorized student to hide behind the protective glass. Needless to say, public schools and universities around the country have not yet taken a shine to this desk.

Q: Which of the following is correct about patents?
(a) Criteria for patent grants have become stricter.
(b) Millions of patent applications are filed every year.
(c) Patents are only granted for inventions deemed useful.
(d) Inventors have a limit for the number of patents a year.

31. For every holiday, there are always accompanying games. The dreidel is a spinning top with four-sides played during the Jewish holiday of Hanukkah. Each side has a symbol that forms an acronym that stands for "a great miracle happened here," the miracle referring to what once happened in Israel. For adults, the four symbols stand for the rules of a gambling game. The symbolism of the dreidel has been commented on by Jacob who attributes the four symbols to stand for the four exile nations that the Jews were subjected to—Babylonia, Persia, Greece and Rome.

Q: Which of the following is correct about the dreidel?
(a) It has its origins in ancient Babylon.
(b) It is a game played on the Jewish new year.
(c) It can be a game for both children and adults.
(d) It reflects Israel's occupation of various nations.

32. Pond is more of a misnomer in regards to seasonal ponds. A more accurate description is they are shallow depressions that contain standing water for part, if not all, of the year. The amount and length of time these ponds contain water determine the types of plants and animals that live near them. Water volume varies yearly and often produces a vibrant and diverse ecosystem. Because the water is of a somewhat temporary nature, fish cannot survive in these ponds. This makes a seasonal pond an ideal safe zone for many amphibian species. Many rare wild flowers are also found near these ponds, producing an aesthetically pleasing and natural landscape.

Q: Which of the following is correct about seasonal ponds?
(a) They often produce rich and varied communities.
(b) They are better described as deep basins.
(c) Water levels remain consistent every year.
(d) Wild flowers are rarely found in most ponds.

33. Lasagna (pronounced "la-sa-nya") has loads of melted mozzarella, Romano and parmesan cheeses oozing from its many layers of thick flat noodles and filled with Italian sausage, meatballs, mushrooms and spinach. It is a famous Italian dish with several regional varieties but usually made with a tomato sauce or Ragú. Origins of lasagna point to one of two theories, with both coming from ancient Greece. The first theory is it is named after the Greek "laganon," a flat sheet of pasta dough sliced into strips. The other theory comes from the words "lasana" or "lasanum" which mean a "stand for a pot," or "chamber pot," which the Romans adopted and made their own. Thus, lasagna took the name of the cooking vessel it was served in.

Q: What can be inferred from the passage?
(a) There are few local variations of lasagna.
(b) Greek and Roman cultures share similarities.
(c) Lasagna was the precursor of today's pizza.
(d) Ragú is a special type of tomato sauce.

34. Early this third millennium sees a rough average of twenty-four consumer electronic items in every American household according to an industry estimate. This translates into millions of devices thrown out each year, devices containing toxic heavy metals such as lead and mercury. States have begun to ban electronics in landfills for fear of contamination through leakage. They are even passing laws that set recycling quotas. While some gadgets can be refurbished and resold, the metal and plastic recovered and recycled, some companies simply ship the electronic waste elsewhere for dismantling or disposal at lower environmental standards. In effect, this shifts the problem elsewhere. Cynics might even point out that it is easier for companies to pay the fines than to actually recycle.

Q: What can be inferred from the passage?
(a) Different countries have different laws on recycling electronic waste.
(b) The penalty for not recycling electronic waste is usually substantial.
(c) Consumer electronics has a great potential for recycling and reuse.
(d) Companies are trying to design electronics to be more environmental.

35.

Dear Bill,

I am happy to inform you that tickets for the Caribbean cruise have been booked for the Labor Day weekend and will be waiting for you at the boarding dock. Remember to arrive no later than 12:30 as the ship is scheduled to set sail by 3:00. I was able to reserve first class cabin accommodations and seats for three shows. There are four pools, several game rooms, two fitness gyms and a golf practice range for the whole family to enjoy. Please wire the balance of the account to Ace Travel agency within the next two days or the tickets will be forfeited. If you have any questions regarding any details, feel free to email me back or call me. Again, thank you for your patronage and we wish you and your family a terrific Labor Day cruise!

Warmest regards,
Stan Franklin, Accounts Manager

Q: What can be inferred from the passage?
(a) Stan is anxious to close the account in the next two days.
(b) The cruise will last four days and three nights.
(c) Bill has already put a down payment on the tickets.
(d) The cruise ship will not wait for any late passengers.

36. Solar flares are explosions on the sun that release radiation that vary in wavelengths. On Valentine's Day, the first "X-class" flare was expelled from the sun in four years. An X-class flare is the strongest of the three types of flares and has been known to wreak havoc on satellite systems. The Valentine's Day solar flare was also accompanied by a coronal mass ejection of charged particles. However, it did not interrupt satellite service on Earth as the flare's orientation lined up with the Earth's, therefore aligning the magnetic fields and preventing particles from penetrating our planet's protective magnetic shield.

Q: What can be inferred from the passage?
(a) The Earth's magnetic field has been breached in the past.
(b) Solar flares are minor releases of radioactive material.
(c) The X-type solar flare is the most common of all flares.
(d) Solar flares routinely penetrate deep into the Earth's surface.

37. The average worker spends five to eight hours a day being stationary in front of his computer monitor. The long term cost of this type of behavior is unhealthy weight gain, fatigue and general lack of motivation. Introducing the Strong Stationary Desk Bike, a revolutionary exercise machine that can be fitted under any desk. Built of the highest quality alloys and aluminums, the Strong Stationary Desk Bike has 20 settings from beginner to the avid athlete. So, while you are typing up that accounting report or drafting a marketing proposal, you can also improve your cardiovascular fitness with the smart Strong Stationary Desk Bike, order now!

Q: What can be inferred from the passage?
(a) The adverse effects of working is reduced with Strong Stationary Desk Bike.
(b) Unhealthy employees lead to a significant decrease in production.
(c) The Strong Stationary Desk Bike is popular with big companies.
(d) People prefer to have desk jobs rather than to work in the field.

Part III **Questions 38—40**

Read the passage. Then identify the option that does NOT belong.

---

38. The Florida Keys were made famous in the movie *True Lies* when Harrier jets destroyed a part of one of the many bridges that connect the 4,500 islands of this archipelago. (a) The Keys start 15 miles south of Miami and extend in an arching form going south to southwest, heading to the most populated city Key West and ending at the uninhabited Dry Tortugas. (b) For automobile travel, the Keys have a 127 mile highway called the Overseas highway that runs its entire length. (c) At its most southern point, the Keys are a mere 90 miles from Cuba, which has made it a favorite hideout for drug smugglers. (d) The locals prefer a laid-back lifestyle of sun bathing, swimming and fishing.

39. Studying past occurrences of social transformation may be the key in reducing the damage caused by climate change: For instance, approximately 44 percent of all Californians smoked in 1965. Forty-five years later, that number has dropped to an amazingly low 9.3 percent, a figure unimaginable prior to actually happening. (a) Many tobacco companies are still reeling from the prolonged decrease in smoking. (b) Scientists are studying the technical aspects of reducing climate change as well as the top ten historical behavior changes. (c) These changes include smoking cessation, seat belt use, vegetarianism, drunk driving, recycling, yoga and others. (d) What these behavioral changes tell scientists is the approximate time it takes for individuals to change habits that require more resources from the planet.

40. German manufacturer Krupp revealed the world's largest earth digger, and technically the largest moving machine. (a) Standing at nearly 100 meters tall, with an unfathomable 600 meters in length, this digger weighs 45,000 tons and can move more than 76,000 cubic meters of coal, rock and earth a day. (b) Krupp's giant digger took more than 5 years of planning and over $100 million to design and manufacture. (c) It requires a special handling class license to operate that takes years to acquire. (d) The Goliath of a machine can slowly move from one location to another and has enormous digging wheels that come right out of a macabre science fiction horror film.

ACTUAL TEST 3

READING
COMPREHENSION

Part I   Questions 1—16

Read the passage. Then choose the option that best completes the passage.

1.   Standing at roughly five stories high, with a length of 170 meters and a width of 13 meters, the Ohio-class nuclear submarine is a silent killer in the waters. The U.S. Navy has 14 of these mammoth-sized stealth vehicles that stay hidden beneath the murky depths of the oceans for months on end. The only limitations they have is food supply, otherwise these submarines could stay submerged indefinitely. Each ship has fifteen officers in charge of a rotating crew of 140 submariners. This fleet of nuclear subs carries approximately 50 percent of the United States' total nuclear arsenal, which help it to serve the purpose of _____.

   (a) keeping the enemy confused at all times
   (b) being a long-distance deterrence force
   (c) dominating the major Atlantic trade zones
   (d) showing America's strength in diplomacy

2.   Blue jeans are _____, from fashionistas to your chubby plumber. Comfortable and durable, blue jeans were invented by a young Levi Strauss who moved to San Francisco during the California Gold Rush in 1853. Strauss' intentions were to open a store selling his brother's dry goods but found what the miners really needed were strong pants that could stand up to their harsh working conditions. Initially, Levi fashioned rough canvas that was originally meant for tents or wagon covers, into overalls. Although the miners approved of the durability, they complained of skin chaffing. Levi then turned to twilled cotton from Nimes, France, called "serge de Nimes," and voilá! Demin blue jeans made history.

   (a) a favorite accessory for everyone in America
   (b) popular with teens around the world
   (c) a global symbol of Western freedom
   (d) the go to apparel worldwide for everyone

3. We've all had our spotlight moments, belting out our favorite love ballad at the top of our voice. However, we usually do this in the privacy of our showers so those with discerning ears do not suffer. All that changed in 1971, when Daisuke Inoue of Kobe, Japan, invented the karaoke machine. The concept and technology of karaoke was nothing new at the time. Since the advent of the multi-track recorder, recording artists since the 60s had been laying down separate tracks songs and professional performers often sang to recordings sans vocals. Yet, the karaoke machine was the first to combine video and music, _____ the lyrics as they sang along to their favorite tunes.

(a) allowing amateur singers to read
(b) creating a multi-media depiction of
(c) paving the way for future stars to read
(d) forcing participants to pay attention to

4. Mental disorders can often be so debilitating they render the sufferer incapable of _____. On the other hand, many of history's greatest thinkers were inflicted with some sort of mental disability. No case is as true as John Forbes Nash, Jr., who suffers from paranoid schizophrenia. Despite this often very serious diagnosis, Nash has gone on to hold the post of Senior Research Mathematician at Princeton University. He is credited for his priceless contributions to many fields including game theory, market economics, evolutionary biology, artificial intelligence and even military theory. In 1994, Nash was awarded the Nobel Prize in Economic Sciences with fellow game theorists Richard Selten and John Harsanyi.

(a) holding down high-profile, lucrative positions
(b) differentiating abstract and tangible theories
(c) carrying out basic functions of everyday life
(d) recognizing their infinite physical potential

5.

> To James Simmons, Ace Cabinets,
>
> This week's shipment of oak, pine, and cedar will be delayed three days because of an unfortunate delay due to flooding at our number three and four lumber yards. As you know, in order to maintain our strict standard of quality, we never let subpar lumber leave our yards and are therefore forced to let the wood dry in our kilns longer. Even though this method of heat-treating lumber diverges from our usual practice, please do not worry about the integrity of the lumber as we will test and retest for structural defects. _____, Larry's Lumber will offer you a 10 percent discount for the delay and will split shipping costs with Ace Cabinets.
>
> Yours truly,
> Jenna Franklin

(a) In light of our long-standing relationship
(b) Because the wood may be less-than-perfect
(c) To prevent another conflict with your company
(d) After another two shipments of lumber

6.

Along with other iconic images of San Francisco such as the Golden Gate Bridge and Alcatraz, the cable car system is _____. This system runs from downtown Union Square to Fisherman's Wharf and is often ridden by commuters and tourists alike. The two types of cars in use are the single and double ended car. Single-ended cars have an open-sided front segment with seats facing outward and can carry around 60 passengers. The double-ended cars are almost identical to the single-ended, but are longer and can carry almost 70 passengers. The tolling of the cable car bells let you know you're on the hilly streets of San Francisco.

(a) an integral part of the city's rich heritage
(b) celebrated by city planners the world over
(c) praised by rail enthusiasts for its longevity
(d) duly in need of refurbishing and repair

7.   When you land in the Anchorage, Alaska airport, there stands a large, stuffed Kodiak bear that _____ of this vast, pristine wilderness. The Kodiak is like a brown bear on mega-steroids. The largest Kodiak was put down by a Forest Ranger after it had eaten a hiker. The Ranger not only unloaded his 7mm semi-automatic rifle into the beast, but had to reload, and shoot him in the head to kill him. This goliath weighed over 737 kilograms and stood 3.85 meters at shoulder height and a mouth-dropping 4.27 meters at the top of his head. That means this Kodiak could've looked in on you if you lived on the second floor. Better close those curtains!

(a) stoically conveys the wild beauty
(b) serves as a reminder of the dangers
(c) once roamed the airport grounds
(d) epitomizes the majestic grandeur

8.   The world's biggest bank heist took place in 2005 at a Brazilian Bank perpetrated by a gang of _____. With aliases like "The German, The Tortured and the Big Digger," this group of thieves spent weeks burrowing underground a block away from their artificial grass store they had set up as a front. This devious cabal got away with the equivalent of 80 million U.S. dollars and to this day, has authorities baffled about their identities. What is known is that they dug a tunnel fitted with wood supports, lighting and even air conditioning. Their piece de résistance was drilling through two meters of reinforced concrete to the bank's holding room without triggering a single alarm.

(a) well-known notorious international ex-convicts
(b) former bank employees and police officers
(c) disgruntled and desperate local shop owners
(d) highly sophisticated and colorful pilferers

9. Alzheimer's disease is named after a German psychiatrist Alois Alzheimer after he was the first to describe the affliction in 1906. It is considered the most widespread manifestation of dementia, a common term for memory loss and other incapacitating mental degradation in seniors. Alzheimer's is not a natural part of growing old and is devastating not only for the diagnosed, but for the entire family. Alzheimer's is often a long-term disease that progressively gets worse, from basic memory loss to the point where the patient is unable to communicate and react to their surroundings. Although medical science is able to lessen the patient's symptoms and improve their quality of life, there is still no cure for Alzheimer's, which is _____ in America.

(a) the sixth leading cause of death
(b) continuously being studied extensively
(c) creating social unrest and upheaval
(d) taking the lives of many young adults

10. How many restless nights will you endure plagued by the _____? With the Nature-Safe Ultrasonic mosquito repellent, you can have peace of mind and undisturbed slumber the whole night through. Mosquitoes and other pests are highly sensitive to ultrasonic waves which are inaudible to the human ear. No longer do you have to worry about harmful chemicals and the disapproving smells of traditional repellents. The Nature-Safe Ultrasonic repellent is also environment friendly by not releasing detrimental materials into the atmosphere. You'll never lose another minute of sleep with the Nature-Safe Ultrasonic mosquito repellent. Order now and we'll throw in the traveler's size mini repellent for free, the ideal accessory for camping, hiking, a day on the lake and more!

(a) foul smell and grimy feel of regular insect repellent
(b) haunting memories of a perfect day ruined by vermin
(c) incessant buzzing and painful biting of mosquitoes
(d) lack of sleep brought on by the pitter-patter of rodents

11. Whether herding cattle over the hot plains of the American heartland or trekking through the uncharted Rocky Mountains, the cowboy was never without his iconic cowboy hat. Initially there was no standard headwear for early American pioneers making their way out west until in 1865, John Batterson Stetson set the bar when he began manufacturing a broad rimmed, high-crowned felt hat called the "Boss of the plains." Cowboy hats served the important function of protecting the wearer from the punishing rays of the sun and the harsh whipping of torrential rains. Natural in color and water resistant, the cowboy hat was an immediate success with bronco-busters and became the _____.

(a) fashion hit of the cosmopolitan bourgeoisie
(b) ubiquitous image of the cowboy we know today
(c) universal symbol of American entrepreneurial spirit
(d) most sought after accoutrement of industrial America

12. If you've ever gone for a bike ride at night, you can thank your reflectors for _____. However, these reflectors are very different from a simple mirror. Where the latter reflects light on a perpendicular wave length, the former is a retroreflector and reflects light back to its source with minimal dispersion of light. What this means in plain English is that with a mirror, light can bounce back at a different angle from the source and be of little use. On the other hand, a retroreflector is like a prism of mirrors and therefore the reflection can be seen at nearly any angle from the light source ensuring motorists from almost any direction can see you.

(a) helping you see the path in front of you
(b) guaranteeing an accident-free experience
(c) differentiating you from other bicyclists
(d) warning automobilists of your presence.

13. After a long day at the beach being out in the sun too long, many of us reach for a soothing lotion to cool our sunburn. The main ingredient of these ointments is usually Aloe vera, a plant indigenous to Africa with a long and well-documented history of human use. Aloe vera is one of 299 species of Aloe and has nearly as many uses. It has abundant, broad, fleshy leaves that comprise its rosette and grows in tropical as well as arid regions. Aloe vera has proven medicinal properties and can be used both externally and internally. Not only does it _____, but it also provides a thin layer over cuts and wounds that prevents infection.

(a) give immediate relief from sunburns
(b) have great commercial potential
(c) possess a fresh appearance and aroma
(d) ease aching joints, tendons and bones

14. The hamburger has arguably become one of the world's most popular foods and _____. From 15th century minced meats, to "Hamburg steak" from Hamburg, Germany, and finally to the New World where the first hamburger was served on a bun. Incidentally, one popular fast food burger chain has actually been the focus of an economic indicator. The price of this restaurant's big hamburger is a benchmark that shows the health of the country's overall economy when compared to the American price. The closer the price is to the U.S. price, the closer that country's economy is to the United States. Who would have thought a tasty patty of beef inside a bun would become so relevant to global economics?

(a) has a long history of evolution
(b) is considered the best finger food
(c) is prepared in countless ways
(d) has a reputation of being unhealthy

15.

As bored teens, my friends and I would experiment with anything we found in the house or garage. One of our favorite experiments was the spud-gun. All you need for a spud-gun, or potato cannon, is a simple polyvinyl chloride (PVC) pipe, potatoes, and some sort of combustible propellant like hairspray. To operate the gun, just jam a potato into one end of the PVC pipe, add the propellant into the other end and then cap it. You must leave a small hole at the capped end in order to ignite it with a lighter. _____, the expansion of gases shoots the spud out at a great velocity, so be very careful where you point your potato cannon!

(a) Instead
(b) Meanwhile
(c) Ultimately
(d) Nevertheless

16.

To Beth Johnson, Humane Society,

Yesterday's broadcast on Channel 5, *Eyewitness News*, brought tears to my eyes as they reported on the unfortunate fire that razed the Humane Society. I am writing to offer not only my sympathy, but also myself as a volunteer in watching over some of the little four-legged survivors. I own a large ranch just outside of town and have the capacity to house and feed up to twenty dogs or cats until the Humane Society rebuilds. I feel as a community, our capacity to help those in need should extend beyond our fellow humans. _____, it has been said that a true measure of a society's enlightenment is seen in how they take care of their pets.

Yours truly,
Penelope Lee, Lee's Horse Ranch

(a) Conversely
(b) Moreover
(c) On the other hand
(d) Henceforth

Part II **Questions 17—37**

Read the passage and the question. Then choose the option that best answers the question.

---

17. Just about every American teenager is required to read J.D. Salinger's masterpiece, *The Catcher in the Rye*. Written in 1951, this unforgettable novel still appeals to the adolescent reader's feelings of uncertainty, anguish, estrangement and rebellion. Since its debut, *Catcher* has sold more than 65 million copies worldwide, with an average of a quarter million leaving the shelves every year. Salinger wrote *Catcher* from the subjective point of view of the main character and antagonist, Holden Caulfield. The book has stirred controversy since its initial publication because of the use of colloquial language, which includes many words that are deemed foul. Even as late as 1981, *Catcher* was the most censored and also second-most taught novel in American public schools.

Q: What is the main idea of the passage?
(a) J.D. Salinger exaggerated the attitudes of angst of his era.
(b) Readers can only get censored copies of *The Catcher in the Rye*.
(c) Public schools often forbid the teaching of *The Catcher in the Rye*.
(d) *The Catcher in the Rye* is a much challenged and studied novel.

18. Ever since Sir Isaac Newton discovered that passing white light through a prism results in its separation into all visible colors in 1666, psychologists have been studying the effects of colors on the human psyche. In general, the colors that are considered "warm," that is red, orange and yellow, typically induce a range of feelings from comfort and tenderness to anger and hostility. On the other end of the spectrum are the "cool colors" of blue, purple and green. Researchers have found these colors evoke a sense of calm, however, they can also touch our melancholy and sad sides. This may be why skilled artists are able to masterfully employ different colors to express a wide range of emotions.

Q: What is the main idea of the passage?
(a) Colors are clearest when white light flows through a prism.
(b) Human emotions have no safeguards against certain colors.
(c) Different colors predominantly stir up different feelings.
(d) The color spectrum is made up of only cold and warm hues.

19.

To Leonard Manning,

You're blog's assertion that our country's recent intervention in the civil war in East Africa is a noble cause against tyranny is just another ineffectual attempt at neo-conservative brain-washing. Many of today's netizens are way too young to remember the so-called "humanitarian" military escapades this once great nation embarked on with disastrous results. They have little knowledge of how many innocent lives have been taken by our indiscriminate bombings and other hostilities. You must not perpetuate the sense that conflicts are best solved with the sword rather than intelligent discourse. Shame on you for putting our nation's hostile aggression in a favorable light in spite of the dismal results.

Disapprovingly yours,
Jessica Goldman, DFL Chairwoman

Q: Which of the following claims is made in the blog?
(a) Military intervention is justified for liberty's sake.
(b) Today's youth is open to conservative indoctrination.
(c) Altruistic interventions are often bloody and violent.
(d) Aggressive behavior supersedes rational rhetoric.

20.   Kramer and Krantz (K&K) is seeking a Senior International Public Relations Specialist (SIPRS). K&K is the leading manufacturer and supplier of LED panels and bulbs in the Midwest and is looking to expand into the Chinese market. Qualified candidates will be at least a college graduate with a degree in public relations or related field, possess a minimum of 8 years of PR experience, be fluent in English and Chinese, and be willing to travel 50 percent of the time. The SIPRS is accountable for responding to overseas media inquiries, maintaining a close relationship with journalists, and development and distribution of K&K's overseas PR network. To apply, email a cover letter, resume, and list of references to jobs@K&KLLC.com.

Q: What is the best title of the passage?
(a) K&K's Ambitious Chinese Expansion
(b) Seeking Qualified Media Consultant
(c) Augmenting K&K's Overseas Presence
(d) Qualified PR Specialist Needed

21. Nigerian officials announced an ambitious new plan to pull the country out of its ignominious title of being one of the world's nine most illiterate countries. Nigeria's Minister of Education and her administration have proffered a staggering 60 percent increase in funding for public schooling in remote, rural areas, which has experts shaking their heads. This nation of over 155 million people has an abysmal 32 percent illiteracy rate with more than half of its populace living outside of urban areas. Combined with a weak infrastructure, this poses a serious challenge in getting the materials and teachers to the parts of the country that need them the most.

Q: What is the main purpose of the Minister of Education's plan?
(a) To better the roads and buildings in the countryside
(b) To improve the literacy rate of all Nigerian citizens
(c) To raise the budget for education to 60 percent
(d) To augment the number of educators and supplies

22. Early in his presidency, John F. Kennedy faced a military and political debacle that had serious detrimental ramifications for the U.S., while at the same time strengthening the resolve of Cuban communists. This crisis was dubbed the Bay of Pigs Invasion, a covert, CIA backed military coup of Fidel Castro's regime. In three short days, Castro's Eastern Bloc trained forces defeated the invading Cuban exiles and CIA operatives that sought to dethrone the communist government. Due to this failure, Castro saw a meteoric rise in popularity as the country swelled with new found nationalism. The botched coup was a severe embarrassment for the Kennedy administration and made Castro suspicious of any future American overtures of peace and negotiation.

Q: What is mainly discussed about the Bay of Pigs invasion?
(a) The CIA was incompetent in their training of Cuban exiles.
(b) Fidel Castro found increased support due to its failure.
(c) Kennedy had an unfavorable impression of Castro.
(d) Americans became more suspicious of U.S. interventions.

23. Without oil, the world would come to a screeching halt. Just how does all the oil get from the drills in oil fields or deep sea rigs to our gas station pump? Supertankers are gigantic ocean faring vessels averaging 350 meters in length, 60 meters in width and holding capacity of over 400,000 tons. The largest supertanker is the Norwegian owned Knock Nevis, which is over 458 meters in length and if tipped on its end, would surpass the Petronas Towers' height. Its length is the equivalent of about six and a half Boeing 747 jets, 14 blue whales, or 61 elephants. When fully laden with 564,000 tons of crude oil, it cannot pass through the English Channel.

Q: Which of the following is correct about supertankers?
(a) They provide the crude oil that fuels our planet.
(b) Their lengths do not exceed five football pitches.
(c) They cannot traverse the English Channel.
(d) They routinely come straight from the oil fields.

24. Akira Kurosawa was a prolific Japanese filmmaker with a resume of 30 films covering his 57 year career. He was posthumously named "Asian of the Century" in the "Arts, Literature and Culture" by *AsianWeek* magazine. While living, Kurasawa accepted the Academy Award for Lifetime Achievement in 1990. Perhaps his best known film is the 1954 classic *Seven Samurai* starring Toshiro Mifune, Kurasawa's leading man in over 15 of his films. Like most great storytellers, Kurasawa employed the master and disciple theme not only in the physical sense but also the spiritual in many of his films. His unique and bold cinematography style made him one of the most significant and influential filmmakers in cinema history.

Q: Which of the following is correct about Akira Kurosawa?
(a) He was strongly influenced by the Academy Awards from Hollywood.
(b) He accepted *AsianWeek* magazine's "Asian of the Century" award.
(c) He trusted in Toshiro Mifune as a proficient and talented actor.
(d) He dabbled with the mentor and student relationship in a few films.

25. The catalyst to the worst ideological experiment in the world was the Russian Revolution of 1917. This revolution took place in two stages, the first being the overthrowing of the Russian Tsar, Nicholas II, by members of the Imperial parliament. The second phase of the revolution was Lenin and the Bolshevik's (worker's party) usurping of power from the newly formed Provisional Government of St. Petersburg. Following the coup by the worker's party, the Soviet Union was formed and the Bolshevik's arbitrarily appointed themselves to positions of power and violently squashed any dissidence. The ultimate outcome of the communist's revolution has been judged by history as a period of rule by fear and repression, economic ruin, and the loss of millions of lives.

Q: Which of the following is correct about the Russian Revolution?
(a) The last ruling monarchy of Russia was deposed.
(b) Imperial parliament members overthrew the Bolshevik.
(c) An era of prosperity and equality for all was realized.
(d) It led to tolerance of differing political viewpoints.

26. The highest paid entertainer in the world from the 50's through the 70's was a pianist and showman from a small Midwest suburb by the name of Wladziu Valentino Liberace. A flamboyant but classically trained pianist, Liberace performed Liszt's Second Piano Concerto with the Chicago Symphony in 1939 at the young age of 20. In early 1940, he moved to New York where his musical style evolved from classical music to pops with a classical tinge. Although he struggled both in financial terms and popularity during this time, by the late 40's, Liberace was performing in night clubs around the U.S. and was quickly on his way to becoming an immensely successful entertainment legend.

Q: Which of the following is correct about Liberace?
(a) He was the highest paid performer in the first half of the 20th century.
(b) He was the most successful entertainer for nearly three decades.
(c) Major symphony orchestras sought him out as a concert soloist.
(d) He was born in a small rural suburb of New York City.

27. With heating and electrical costs going through the roof, the Fantastic Energy Emitting Leaf (FEEL) houseplant is the smart answer to those increasing bills. FEEL is a synthetic plant with leaves made from nickel and cobalt catalysts that efficiently and cleanly increase its energy production tenfold. Just add water! Appearing like a regular potted plant, FEEL's thirty energy producing appendages take in the sun's endless solar power and converts it into enough wattage to power the average household all day. Do your part in preserving our environment, and being fiscally responsible, buy a FEEL artificial household plant today!

Q: Which of the following is correct about FEEL?
(a) Solar energy is stored as watts in its leaves.
(b) Energy is created from solar rays, nickel and cobalt.
(c) Utility bills and pollution are sure to decrease daily.
(d) It can provide all the energy for the common man.

28. *One Hundred Years of Solitude* is considered Gabriel García Márquez's finest masterpiece. Initially published in Spanish in 1967, it has since been translated into 37 languages and has sold more than 20 million copies worldwide. As the title implies, it is a story about several generations of the Buendía family headed by its patriarch and founder Macondo, a metaphoric Columbia, José Arcadio Buendía. García Márquez masterfully employed symbolic and metaphoric literary tools to tell the story of the conquests of Latin America by Europeans. Yellow and gold are often used to represent the imperialism of the Spaniards, with gold symbolizing the search for economic opulence and yellow embodying death, change and destruction.

Q: Which of the following is correct about *One Hundred Years of Solitude*?
(a) It is a highly figurative narrative of the Spanish conquests.
(b) García Márquez wanted the whole world to be able to read it.
(c) It depicts the Buendía family as the founders of Columbia.
(d) Jose Arcadio Buendía is the main character throughout the story.

29. Every year, just before Spring Break, March Madness sweeps the United States. This is the time the National Collegiate Athletic Association sponsors the college basketball championship and starts with the sweet sixteen, the top sixteen basketball teams from universities and colleges nationwide. This month is highly televised and anticipated as fans of all ages and walks of life tune in to this amateur basketball tournament. The heat really turns up when the final four advance to the semi-finals. Winning the championship game is a prestigious honor for any school and one that gives current, former and future students something to brag about.

Q: Which of the following is correct about March Madness?
(a) It corresponds with college student's Spring Break vacation.
(b) Major networks televise it to generate interest in basketball.
(c) The best sixteen teams contend for the championship title.
(d) University students enjoy exclusive coverage of the games.

30. Imagine a shark weighing more than 100 metric tons with a length of 20 meters. This perfect predator lived approximately 1.5 to 25 million years ago. Scientists have aptly named this beast Megalodon which is Greek for "big tooth." Based on fossil records and reconstruction, Megalodon's bite force exceeded 41,000 pounds of pressure and its serrated teeth were not only good for sawing through their prey but also grabbing and shaking it ruthlessly. Megalodon was the ultimate predator that didn't stay in one location but instead adapted to live in many environments including shallow coastal waters and deep seas. It was an aggressive hunter with tremendous speed, fierce jaws, and a healthy appetite for whales and other marine life.

Q: Which of the following is correct about Megalodon?
(a) It aggressively guarded its narrow territory.
(b) Whales and other nautical animals were its quarry.
(c) Scientists speculate it was the precursor of whales.
(d) Its large mass impeded its mobility and velocity.

31.   *CSI* and its ilk have become a popular genre of television show where forensic science is the star attraction. Forensic science is often described as "applying science to law." These scientists are the investigators that pore over any physical evidence left at a crime scene. Like putting the pieces of a puzzle together, highly-trained forensic specialists take special care in preserving and collecting any leftover residue such as blood, fingerprints, hairs, fibers, and anything else that can lead them to the perpetrators of a crime. Unlike how Hollywood depicts their work, forensic science is not at all as glamorous as shows like *CSI* would have you believe but they are just as persistent in their pursuit for justice.

Q: Which of the following is correct about forensic science?
(a) It is accurately portrayed on television.
(b) All criminals leave forensic evidence.
(c) Hollywood has taken great interest in it.
(d) It is the last step in solving a crime.

32.   More and more schools in Western countries are experimenting with a "No Homework" policy. Many parents have found that the battle to force their children to do homework every night is "just not worth it." Attending a school with this policy does not mean that students do no studying or educational related activities when the school bell rings. Instead, children are encouraged to take books home, read by themselves or with their parents, and write a sentence or two about each chapter they read. Students these days are often engrossed in many other activities such as music, dance, art, swimming, soccer, etc., and parents feel their child is too exhausted to be obligated with mandatory homework.

Q: Which of the following is correct according to the passage?
(a) Western students are losing interest in traditional studies.
(b) Children at these schools with no homework take it upon themselves to study.
(c) Extracurricular activities transcend school curriculums.
(d) Teachers are becoming increasingly less tolerant of homework.

33. Friday the 13th is often associated with ill omens and bad luck as was the case for the Uruguayan Ruby team whose airplane crashed in the snowy Andes Mountains on that inauspicious day in October of 1972. Only 16 out of the 45 passengers made it back to civilization after a harrowing 72 day ordeal. Without food, water, and communication devices like radios, the survivors had to resort to cannibalism in order to stay alive long enough for some of the team members to make the arduous journey to civilization. Their tale of horror and heroics is immortalized in a book written two years later by British author Piers Paul Read which was later made into a movie.

Q: What can be inferred from the passage?
(a) Tragic events often occur on Friday the 13th.
(b) Being an athlete increased the chance for rescue.
(c) The will to survive pushes humans to great lengths.
(d) The survivor's story was inaccurately portrayed on film.

34. Underwriter's Limited (UL) is a non-profit independent safety science company whose standards are accepted worldwide. They provide expertise in vital five strategic businesses which include Product Safety, Environment, Life and Health, University, and Verification Services. UL is an icon of trust and upholds its mission of "Working for a safer world since 1894." Since its inception, the 6,921 employees consisting of scientists, engineers and others at UL have tested nearly 85,000 products with customers in 102 countries at their 68 laboratories. If your product has the UL mark, you can take pride and have confidence that it has passed a series of the most vigorous and strict safety tests.

Q: What can be inferred from the passage?
(a) UL establishes the global bar for quality testing.
(b) Only the safest products get the UL mark of approval.
(c) UL employs the smartest scientists and engineers.
(d) Profits generated at UL are passed on to the consumer.

35.   A diamond is supposed to be a girl's best friend, but not if it came at a tremendous human cost. Blood diamonds, or conflict diamonds, are rough cut diamonds that lack transparency about their place of origin. Often used to fund insurgencies or armed conflicts, blood diamonds come from the mines of war-torn countries. These countries are found mainly in Africa and include Angola, Liberia, Sierra Leone, the Ivory Coast, the Democratic Republic of Congo, and Zimbabwe. Although much concerted international effort has been put in to restrict the flow of conflict diamonds, the illegal trade continues to build up the coffers of illegitimate and oppressive regimes and warlords who use the funds to arm themselves.

Q: What can be inferred from the passage?
(a) Blood diamonds are easily identified by their place of origin.
(b) Countries in war zones have stopped producing blood diamonds.
(c) Most African nations forbid the trade of conflict diamonds.
(d) Conflict diamonds are still sold on the international markets.

36.   Researchers from NASA have a strong desire to "take another large step for mankind" by returning to our moon's surface for the reason of mining its valuable resources. Of the many attractive elements such as iron, silicon, aluminum and magnesium, none are considered as valuable as helium-3 (He-3). He-3 is nearly non-existent on Earth and aerospace engineers argue it is the perfect fuel for fusion reactors. Not only is the United States hankering to map out and claim its own territory on our celestial satellite, but so do the Russians, Chinese and Indians. This may prompt a new space race and perhaps inevitably the first extra-terrestrial real estate disputes.

Q: What can be inferred from the passage?
(a) Lunar exploration has been done by the U.S., Russia, China and India.
(b) Mining the moon will require the cooperation of many nations.
(c) Aerospace engineers are running out of energy alternatives.
(d) Large amounts of helium-3 may be the ideal energy for fusion power.

37. Kentucky Fried Chicken was founded by Colonel Sanders who began serving fried chicken in the 1930's during the Great Depression. His Sanders Court & Café was such a big hit that in 1935 the Governor of Kentucky, Ruby Laffoon, awarded Sanders the honorary title of Kentucky Colonel in honor of his contribution to the state. Having initially cooked his fried chicken in an iron skillet, Sanders changed to pressure cooking to save on time. The Colonel opened his first Kentucky Fried Chicken restaurant in 1952, and as early as 1960 his Original Recipe was being served in over 600 locations. Sanders sold his KFC franchising shares in 1964 for an amount equivalent to a paltry $14 million dollars today.

Q: What can be inferred from the passage?
(a) The Colonel foresaw the huge demand for his chicken.
(b) Sanders could have made a great deal more on his shares.
(c) Kentucky is a state known for its culinary prowess.
(d) Chicken was an unaffordable luxury during the 1930's.

Part III **Questions 38—40**

Read the passage. Then identify the option that does NOT belong.

38. Tiles are usually made of ceramic, stone, metal, or glass and often cover roofs, floors, walls, baths, showers, swimming pools, and tabletops. (a) A tiled surface is typically made up of many different colored individual pieces that when combined form a beautiful, sanitary, and easy-to-clean facade. (b) Tiles have been found dating back to 3,000 years BC in ancient Greece and spread to Europe and Asia Minor. (c) The tiles used for floor coverings have to be thicker than those used to cover walls and other surfaces. (d) Tiling is still done today using some of the same materials that have been used over the last 5 millenniums and is still considered a high-skilled craft.

39. The grapes behind Shiraz wine were once thought to have come from near the Persian city of the same name which is around 900 kilometers from modern day Tehran. (a) However, this was a chicken and egg issue as people contemplated whether the Romans brought the grapes and wine from the Rhone Valley or if they acquired the port in Shiraz itself. (b) If you are from Australia, you call the wine Shiraz but if you're from the French Avignon area, you might call it Syrah. (c) Eventually the truth was discovered through DNA testing that the production of Shiraz wine did indeed come from the Romans. (d) Although two of the world's most famous regions for Shiraz grapes are in Europe, it is Australia that has made their name with the production of Shiraz wines.

40. One of the world's longest pipelines is the Trans-Alaska Pipeline System (TAPS) which runs 1,300 kilometers from northern Alaska at the Arctic Sea to its most southern point at Valdez, Alaska. (a) It is commonly called the Pipeline but this moniker only refers to the actual pipeline. (b) TAPS was built between 1974 and 1977 and includes 11 pump stations, kilometers of feeder pipelines, and the Valdez Terminal. (c) Many environmental, legal, and political controversies have surrounded TAPS since the discovery of oil in the Arctic. (d) However, when oil shortage catastrophes arise like they did in 1973 and in current times, people tend to look more favorably on the crude oil we can get from TAPS.

ACTUAL TEST 4

TEPS

READING
COMPREHENSION

Part I   Questions 1—16

Read the passage. Then choose the option that best completes the passage.

1.   Income disparity has always been a major concern for any society's well-being. Many people complain of the rich getting richer and the poor getting poorer, but is this necessarily true? The Gini coefficient is a statistical model named after the Italian statistician Corrado Gini. It measures the distribution of wealth within a society and ranges from 0 to 1, _____. According to a recent study, the countries that had the worse income equality were Namibia (.70), South Africa (.65) and Lesotho (.63). The lowest Gini scores go to Luxembourg (.26), Norway (.25) and Sweden (.23). Not surprisingly, the United States scored (.45) which is still in the worst 33 percent worldwide.

(a) 0 being total inequality and 1 being total equality
(b) the higher the score, the better the equality
(c) 0 being total equality and 1 being total inequality
(d) determined with a handful of calculations

2.   Tired of waking up every time your spouse turns over or gets out of bed? Finding it hard to have a full night's rest? Then say goodbye to sleepless nights by switching to a Deluxe Airy Cloud Mattress. The Airy Cloud comes with dual feather-top air mattresses and twin soundless pumps. With an easy-to-read LCD display, you can set the exact softness or firmness of your air mattress. The Airy Cloud mattress also comes with dual heat settings at no extra charge to soothe those aching muscles! Call today for a free 90-day "try it, you'll like it" test period. We're sure that once you try our mattress, you'll never go back to a regular one. _____. Call today!

(a) A regular bed is the size of our twin mattress
(b) You won't even return a delivery charge
(c) Lighten your back and your wallet
(d) Don't risk another restless night

3. The ballpoint pen has its origins in 1938 with a Hungarian newspaper editor Laszlo Biro who got tired of always refilling his fountain pens and having the tip poke through the paper. He noticed the ink from the newspaper printing press did not smear and worked with his chemist brother to use that ink in pen form. Biro fitted a small metal ball at the tip of a pen to transfer ink to paper. Earlier prototypes leaked or got clogged and depended on gravity to move the ink around the metal ball. So the Biro brothers developed capillary motion for ink delivery and this made their pens better as _____.

(a) it could be given the limitations of their technology
(b) the other competing ball-point pens on the market
(c) you didn't need to hold them straight upright
(d) people didn't have to refill the pen as much

4. Many orthopedics would give feet more support in the shoe, especially if the foot was injured. Short of ordering a custom-fit shoe, the idea that a special foam can adapt to the individual shape of a foot led to special shoes. Legend has it that George B. Boedecker came up with the idea for the trendy footwear when he wore some simple foam slippers while relaxing at a spa. The first shoes were unveiled in 2002 at a boat show in Fort Lauderdale, Florida, and all 200 pairs sold out quickly. By 2007, the company had 5,300 people employed with annual sales of nearly $170 million. Today you can find these foam shoes in every corner of the planet. _____ some foam slippers at a health spa.

(a) It wouldn't be if Boedecker didn't put on
(b) This new global phenomenon started from
(c) They are inspired as Boedecker by
(d) Not bad for an invention inspired by

5. Due to the coarse nature of the food it eats, a cow has not one but four stomachs _____. Digestion starts when a cow chews the food just enough to swallow it. The food travels to the first two stomachs, the rumen and the reticulum where it is stored. After filling herself up with this process, the cow rests. Sometime later, she regurgitates the partially chewed food, now called cud, and thoroughly chews and swallows it again. Now the cud enters the third and fourth stomachs, the omasum and the abomasum, and is digested. Milk is produced when some of this digested food enters the bloodstream and into the udder.

(a) to facilitate the digestive process of plants like grass
(b) to digest the food without requiring too much chewing
(c) which the rough vegetation is processed by the animal
(d) that digests the grass or corn eaten in great quantities

6. Chilean wineries have seen a substantial increase in exportation, especially thanks to free trade agreements. Once only considered as quaint "boutique" wineries, Chilean wineries have seen a meteoric rise of over five times from 12 wineries in 1995 to over 70 by 2005. They can boast being the fifth largest exporter and ninth largest producer in the world. Interestingly, Chilean wineries can thank the phylloxera louse for some of their success. This destructive vine parasite native to the New World went to Europe and Australia onboard trading vessels in the late 18th century and _____. Chilean wineries were spared the carnage and therefore maintained their high quantity and quality.

(a) took root in select and favorable localities
(b) acclimated to the hemiepiphyte soil and ecology
(c) virtually obliterated the local vineyards
(d) facilitated the vineyards' watershed basins

7.

> Dear Editor,
>
> You posit the tepid and shallow argument that a lack of historical understanding is the cause of America's current problems. Let us not forget that nearly every historic conflict has roots in resentment and a vendetta-like mentality towards previous altercations. So to ascribe America's current involvement in armed conflicts simply on a deficiency in comprehension of history is the same Euro-centric babble that somehow seeps over the pond and onto our shores. I just always had faith that this periodical would not get swept in by trendy waves of dangerously left slanting liberal views. With this said, _____ that this magazine is on its way down that slippery slope of biased journalism.
>
> Sincerely,
>
> Victor Banian

(a) I'm overwhelmingly ecstatic it finally appears
(b) it is evident to me as a long time reader
(c) there is yet no precedents to show
(d) many readers have improperly purported

8.   Let's say a phone you want to buy is selling at $500 _____. The question is whether you would still be willing to part with your money. Many consumers may, and this kind of economic measurement is described by price elasticity of demand (PED) coined by Alfred Marshall. This index measures the sensitivity or elasticity of a product's demand based on its price. So if the $50 increase doesn't affect sales of the phone, the PED is low and inelastic. Conversely, if the price increases compared to other brands, consumers might not pay the higher price but instead switch brands. Then the PED is high and elastic.

(a) but you would also pay up to $550
(b) which increases the price to $550
(c) but the price increases to $550
(d) which will not sell much at $550

9. The Boeing B-52 Stratofortress bomber is an iconic image of the Cold War. Standing at around 40 feet with a wingspan of 185 feet, the B-52 houses a crew of five and over 70,000 pounds of mixed ordnance which includes bombs, mines, and missiles in various configurations. It served as a deterrent and counteractive to the perceived nuclear threat of the Soviet military during the Cold War. As a long-range, subsonic, jet-powered strategic bomber, the B-52 can reach _____. It has seen action in many armed conflicts from Vietnam to Desert Storm. As of February 2009, the Air Force still operated 90 out of the 744 original B-52 bombers in service.

(a) its purpose in major air-to-air combat situations
(b) the limits of any required reconnaissance mission
(c) millions of pounds of supplies in a single journey
(d) sensitive targets quickly and with deadly force

10. An international bestseller and subject for university-level studies, *Freakonomics* poses unusual economic questions and theories from its analysis of thought-provoking data. The authors Steven D. Levitt and Stephen J. Dubner bring to light interesting economic principles at work in our day-to-day lives and add credence to even disputed theories. For example, they point to the win-loss statistics of sumo wrestlers and game theory to assert the existence of match fixing. Many readers find it a worthy and enlightening read that questions their preconceptions. However, just as with most books regarding economics and society, *Freakonomics* has its share of critics who object to some of the data that they _____.

(a) deem as overly simplified but appropriate nonetheless
(b) have poured over for hours and hours
(c) view as not having been correctly interpreted
(d) argue is perfectly acceptable in the proper context

11. Although pool has long been associated with royalty as the "Noble Game of Billiards" in the 1800's, _____ since its inception in the 1500's. The game of pocket pool was actually invented nearly 300 years after billiards. Billiards was an adaptation of an outdoor game similar to croquet, with the green fabric representing the grass. The word "billiards" comes from either the French word "billart" for one of the sticks or "bille" which means ball. The word "pool" means "to ante" in a bet and stuck with the game when pool tables were installed in betting rooms to help gamblers pass the time. The game of eight-ball pocket pool was invented around 1900.

(a) commoners have been familiar with it
(b) the royalty of Europe banned it in court
(c) local magistrates provided it for small fares
(d) French aristocracy often lost to their British rivals

12. The head of the major U.S. electronics giant Sator recently lambasted one of its major overseas suppliers, Areva, for a lack of innovation in developing creative new hardware offerings. Areva is the supplier of the hardware for many of the company's hit consumer electronics but is perceived as lacking state-of-the-art designs to compete in the fast-changing field. Nevertheless, Areva is set to continue to remain the major supply partner to Sator. This isn't the first time the outspoken CEO of Sator, Redding Perot, has _____. Webia and Cogitech have for a long time written Sator's software but are still not exempt from his frequent and public tongue lashings.

(a) criticized the electronics parts conglomerate
(b) found flaws in competing companies products
(c) openly and publicly criticized his industry suppliers
(d) reprimanded his overseas chip suppliers

13.   There is a city that in the past century has hosted a national revolution, a fascist movement, and even division by a concrete wall. If this sounds interesting to you, then you must come to Berlin where the tumultuous nature of its past can still be seen today. The observation deck at Panoramapunkt is unmatched for its view of Potsdamer Platz, Daimler City, the Sony Centre, and the Beishem Centre areas. For a hip and trendy dining experience, try fusion dishes like beef bavette and sesame potatoes while lounging on a platform bed at Spindler & Klatt. Transportation is easy on one of _____·_____, the U-Bahn and S-Bahn trains, buses, and trams.

    (a) its many authentic and antique transports
    (b) the privately run and owned express services
    (c) the major rail and waterways of the city
    (d) the three major means of public transport

14.   The ancient epic poems, *The Iliad* and *The Odyssey*, were at some point in their history _____. But based on this literary evidence, the issue of whether just one author created them remains debated. Controversy still surrounding these works is collectively referred to as the "Homeric" questions. Critics of the one-author theory point to inconsistencies in *The Iliad*, for example the fact that the king of the Paphlagonians is slain but then reappears later on, mourning the loss of his son. However, proponents of the one-author theory maintain that an ancient Greek poet at the time recited all his poems, including these two very lengthy ones, by heart and so variations, changes, and even mistakes therein could occur.

    (a) only passed on orally by the ancient poets
    (b) committed to paper and then manually copied
    (c) retold and elaborated on by other Greek poets
    (d) criticized for inaccuracies in their story lines

15. With all our technological wonders and medical breakthroughs, how is it that what was once a previously eradicated disease has reemerged to become the leading infectious killer of adults over 26? There are many reasons at multiple levels for the reemergence of tuberculosis, or TB. Some physical reasons include increased travel, migration and tourism _____ social reasons such as global degradation in healthcare and incidents of TB in AIDS patients also raise the fatality numbers. Additionally, as we have seen with many other diseases, new strains of TB have developed that are immune to the currently used vaccines. All these factors make TB, an airborne contagion that often stays latent, yet again a scourge on humanity.

(a) while
(b) albeit
(c) where
(d) even

16. It has been said that the instincts that keep us alive in the jungle will kill us on the street. This is no better illustrated than during times of extreme market upheaval and unpredictability. _____ for the majority of us, we end up buying when the market's hot and selling when it's not. In essence, we buy high and sell low, rather than stick to our guns as is advised. However, even our financial planners aren't immune to this human nature. In 2009, almost 30 percent of advisers moved their clients out of the stock market and into more conservative instruments, going against the most basic tenet of market investing and costing them recuperating gains on the subsequent uptick.

(a) Conversely
(b) Unfortunately
(c) Interestingly
(d) Accordingly

Part II **Questions 17—37**

Read the passage and the question. Then choose the option that best answers the question.

17. Scientist only first began speculating on the magma ocean theory of Earth after the first moon rock samples were gathered from the Apollo missions and studied in the lab. The moon rocks revealed that at some point the moon was entirely covered in magma. This theory was based on the fact that heavier elements like iron were found deeper than the lighter materials found near the surface. Since the moon was actually a part of the Earth that was violently separated by a giant asteroid collision, scientists drew the conclusion that the Earth's core samples would be similar with the moon rocks. The results agreed with the theory as more iron was found at greater depths.

Q: What is mainly being discussed in this passage?
(a) How the Apollo missions contributed to scientific knowledge
(b) The role of the moon rocks in Earth's early history
(c) The geology of the moon based on rock samples
(d) A theory using parallels between the moon and Earth

18. Referred to as "the cradle of Chinese civilization" the Huang He or Yellow River is the sixth longest river in the world. It is considered the birthplace of China, with some of the most prosperous dynasties living on or near it. However, due to major flooding and the loss of the Xin dynasty due to floods, the river is also known as "China's Sorrow." Like other major water sources, the Yellow River is and has historically been a crucial resource for farming, hydroelectricity, fishing, transport and many others purposes. These days, pollution has unfortunately made nearly one-third of the river unusable even for irrigation and industrial purposes.

Q: What is the best title for the passage?
(a) Problems on the World's Major Waterways
(b) The Yellow River's Significance to China
(c) China and Its Yellow River Valley Civilizations
(d) The Many Blessings of the Yellow River

19.

Dear Mr. Roy Farley,

This is your third and last notice of the balance in arrears for your closed US Bank credit card ending in 4974. Payment in full is required of the $1,580.94 outstanding balance by the 21st of this month. Failure to remit the outstanding amount will result in US Bank turning over your account to a third party credit agency. Remember that every day a payment is late detrimentally affects your credit rating, so please do not delay in sending your late payment. Service specialists are available Monday through Friday from 8:00 a.m. to 8:00 p.m. Eastern Time to process over the phone payments or to answer any questions.

Sincerely,

Mark Murphy, Accounts Management

Q: What is the main purpose of the letter?
(a) To inform the client that late payments result in lower credit ratings
(b) To collect overdue money before selling off the credit account
(c) To notify the client of his credit card status and billing amount
(d) To threaten the client with a lower credit rating and closed account

20.

Globalization means more air travel and aviation experts follow this with a projected 32 percent increase in passenger levels from 2009 to 2014. This means the current number of 2.5 billion will be 3.3 billion people in the air yearly. Paradoxically, airline prices on average have fallen 60 percent, in real value, over the last 40 years. In addition, social and economic pressures call for increased spending to make air travel more environmental. Planes have become more efficient; in 1967 Boeing introduced its 737 which carried 100 passengers a distance of 2,775 kilometers. Today, a B737-800 can carry double the number of passengers using 23 percent less fuel. Still, airlines are struggling to meet or improve their bottom line.

Q: What is the main topic of the passage?
(a) How air travel has become more efficient and environmental
(b) The projected boom in air travel will increase social pressures
(c) Two factors that continue to challenge the business of airlines
(d) Benefits of government subsidies and hand outs for the airlines

21. The Whitney Senior Center will be hosting a pancake and sausage breakfast this upcoming Saturday from 7:30 in the morning to 2:30 in the afternoon. Prepaid tickets can be found online at whitneysrctr.org or at the center's front desk. Tickets at the door are $2.00 more and are first come, first serve. Remember, a donation of nonperishable goods or used toys will reduce your ticket by $1.00 per customer. All proceeds go to the St. Agnes orphanage, so come enjoy a delicious and filling pancake and sausage breakfast this Saturday and let us do the dishes!

Q: What is the main purpose of the announcement?
(a) To gather donated foods or toys for the orphanage
(b) To offer a breakfast set up to support a charitable cause
(c) To raise more operational money for the Senior Center
(d) To suggest ways for the seniors to economize on their meal

22. If you've ever wondered why people fail to cooperate even for their own best interests, then you would find the prisoner's dilemma intriguing. Originally framed by Merrill Flood and Melvin Dresher in 1950, the prisoner's dilemma is a scenario in game theory that sheds light on cooperation. There are two suspects in separate rooms. They go free if they betray the other suspect who will then receive a ten-year sentence. If they both betray each other, they both get a five-year sentence. If they both stay silent, they both serve a six-month sentence. Ideally the two prisoners should cooperate and be silent but they cannot be sure the other will not betray them and hence the prisoner's dilemma.

Q: What is the best title for the passage?
(a) Cooperation Expressed in the Prisoner's Dilemma
(b) Betrayal and Cooperation Based in Game Theory
(c) Game Theory Applied to Law Enforcement
(d) The Prisoner's Dilemma in Decision Making

23.   Agoraphobia is seen when an individual has a morbid fear of open spaces, crowds, or social conditions they have no control over. It typically results in panic attacks or a debilitating anxiety and is often triggered by being in places where previous attacks had occurred. This disorder appears in people in their early to mid-twenties and therefore is not generally thought of as having its roots in early childhood years. However, its exact cause is still unclear to experts and victims alike. Over two-thirds of sufferers are women with about 2.2 percent of Americans diagnosed with agoraphobia.

Q: Which of the following is correct according to the passage?
(a) Agoraphobia is an enigmatic social disorder.
(b) Most men have a predisposition for agoraphobia.
(c) Agoraphobia is an irrational fear of meeting friends.
(d) Sufferers of agoraphobia see symptoms from childhood.

24.   When you think about the world's best-selling toy, you probably assume it's an electronic gizmo that every child has or wants. Would it surprise you that the answer is a plastic cube? Invented in 1974 by a Hungarian sculptor and professor of architecture, Ernö Rubik, the Rubik's Cube had sold 350 million units worldwide by 2009. An ingenious three dimensional puzzle with six faces of varying colors consisting of nine smaller squares, this toy was launched by Ideal Toy Corp. in 1980 and walked away with the German Game of the Year award for Best Puzzle. Thirty years later it's still a hot seller. Competitions are still held for those who can solve it the fastest.

Q: Which of the following is correct about the Rubik's Cube?
(a) It came to market six years after its invention.
(b) It is made of six faces, six squares and six colors.
(c) It was invented by a doctorate of sculpture.
(d) It garnered several awards for Best Puzzle.

25.   Local actor Raphael Ramon is about to be swallowed up in this Friday's opening performance of *A Little Shop of Horrors* at Yu's Performing Arts Theater. Ramon, who depicted Laertes in *Hamlet* at the Barrymore Theater last year, plays geeky flower shop worker Seymour in an Asian take on this quirky cult musical by Howard Ashman and Alan Menken. The carnivorously-insatiable, man-eating plant Audrey is to be played by Cynthia Bechtold under the acclaimed director Marilyn Podawiltz. The show is the second this year for the theater with an ambitious schedule of eight productions in all. It also continues the theater's zany remaking of classic plays and musicals with an Asian spin.

Q: Which of the following is correct about *A Little Shop of Horrors*?
(a) Friday night is its encore performance.
(b) The leading man played Hamlet last year.
(c) The director is well respected nationwide.
(d) The plant is portrayed by Marilyn Podawiltz.

26.   Where else but in the frozen lands of Norway would you find the odd coupling of cross country skiing and rifle marksmanship? In 1861, the Trysil Rifle and Ski Club was formed to promote national defense even as the military had already been using skiing and marksmanship as regular exercise for its soldiers. Best known as the Winter Olympic Sport of biathlon, athletes test their endurance, stamina and shooting prowess on a 20 kilometer track. Competitors shoot four times at each shooting lane in the order of prone, standing, prone, and standing. Penalties of usually one minute are added to the biathletes final times for any missed target.

Q: What is true according to the passage?
(a) The Norwegian army utilizes skiing purely as sport.
(b) The biathlon started as a common military exercise.
(c) The modern Winter Olympics created the sport of biathlon.
(d) Biathletes must hone shooting accuracy more than skiing skills.

27.   As the use of paper increased in the 19th century, so did the demand for a paper fastener. Interestingly enough, the first stapler was a hand-crafted tool made in France for King Louis XV. Unlike today's stapler, each of king's staplers was inscribed with the royal insignia. Like many inventions, there were many contributors to the invention of the stapler. Three patents were filed in the 1860's in America and Britain for contraptions that were the precursors to today's staplers. However, Henry R. Heyl in 1877 filed a patent for the first machine that both inserted and clinched staples in one step, and thus is recognized today as the inventor of the modern stapler.

Q: Which of the following is correct about the modern stapler?
(a) It owes its existence to three famous British inventors.
(b) It has historical roots in the medieval royal courts of Europe.
(c) It has an unclear lineage up to the modern inventors of the 1860's.
(d) It saw an increase in demand in conjunction with paper's usage.

28.   Parliament's investigation into the demise of a major London brokerage house has come up against some exceptional challenges that may result in few or no criminal charges being filed against the ex-CEO, chairman and members of the board. Investigators have found glaring errors in their accusation that the former executives of the firm hid billions of euros of liabilities in its balance sheets, which made the bank appear that much more solvent. People affected by the firm's collapse are still planning further civil and criminal suits to recuperate their losses which amount to billions of euros and, for many, their entire retirement pensions.

Q: Which of the following is correct about the brokerage firm?
(a) It is experiencing difficult hurdles in their investigation.
(b) It had recently undergone a change in management.
(c) It is currently under investigation for price manipulation.
(d) People are upset with its solvency and low pension plans.

29.   There are some competing explanations behind the namesake "teddy bear." The true story by consensus is that it originates with President Theodore Roosevelt who was an avid outdoorsman and hunter. After three days on an unsuccessful bear hunting excursion, his aides tracked down an old bear and tied it to a tree for the president to shoot. Roosevelt refused to be so unsportsmanlike and a political cartoonist captured the story in a cartoon. Later, a novelty store owner put two stuffed bears on display and asked the president for permission to call them "Teddy's Bears." The touching story and catchy name stuck and a new category of children's toy was born.

Q: Which of the following is correct about the teddy bear?
(a) It is named after President Franklin Roosevelt.
(b) There are variations to the story of its origins.
(c) It was the original name of two stuffed toys.
(d) There are several derivations for the name.

30.   Many experts in the industry believe we are not too far from that moment when computers surpass humans in intelligence. Watson, the new IBM supercomputer, showed how a super computer can beat the world's best contestants on the hit show "Jeopardy." What is even more impressive is the fact that this proves how computers are now capable of learning "natural language," the process of disassembling and parsing an input of words and sentences. This is considerably more complicated than the opposite process of assembling output because input can often contain unexpected and unknown features. This is the cutting edge of artificial intelligence to date.

Q: Which of the following is correct about today's level of computer intelligence?
(a) It has attained its theoretical maximum potential.
(b) It has resulted in computers smarter than humans.
(c) It may exceed human intelligence in the near future.
(d) It can be useful for news gathering and reporting.

31. The lighter side of this dismal economy was witnessed at today's speech given by former Chase Bank CEO and current Banking Minister Franklin Torres. Comedy relief was had when he tried to explain how the economy was getting better thanks to his department's bailout interventions and interest rate cuts. When reporters complained about increasing prices for staples such as food and gas, the minister responded by saying, "you can buy a smart phone with double the power for the same price today as two years ago. Let's keep everything in perspective." Loud outbreaks of laughter and murmuring resonated the auditorium and prompted one reporter to ask rhetorically, "you can't eat a smart phone, can you?"

Q: Which of the following is correct about the minister's speech?
(a) It was given at an economic forum by the Bank Minister.
(b) The speaker's comment resulted in unexpected anger and hostility.
(c) The speaker was convincing the crowd about economic changes.
(d) Its intent was to reassure the public about an ailing economy.

32. Animal behavior researcher Josh Klein has invented a way to make money with trained crows. Klein argues that crows are some of the smartest animals, even exceeding chimpanzees and dolphins. He points out that they often use ingenious methods for getting food. For instance, crows will wait for a traffic signal to change to drop acorns or other nuts onto the street. After the nuts are run over by vehicles, they will again wait for the lights to change to retrieve their reward. Klein has cleverly designed boxes that dispense peanuts when a crow drops a coin into a slot. He hopes to gather some of the estimated $250 million in loose change lying around New York City.

Q: Which of the following is correct according to the passage?
(a) Klein has made millions with his peanut dispenser.
(b) Crows are much easier to train than chimps or dolphins.
(c) Klein has his crows collecting coins to obtain peanuts.
(d) Crows prefer eating peanuts to acorns or other nuts.

33. A longbow is ideally made from yew, although white woods such as elm, ash and hazel were often used because of their availability. It can be as tall as a man and be deadly at over 300 yards. A skilled archer could release twelve rounds in a minute whereas a crossbow can only shoot three. Many armies won battles due to their relentless showers of longbow arrows. Imagine incessant volleys of thousands of arrows descending upon your forces twelve times a minute. Today, archery survives as a sport, for hunting, and still in some cultures as a main weapon of defense.

Q: What can be inferred from the passage?
(a) Archers were not highly respected in the past.
(b) Bows has always been common as a sport.
(c) White woods have similar characteristics as yews.
(d) Militaries treated archers as only supplemental forces.

34. It was my first ice fishing excursion on a lake in the bone-chilling cold of a Minnesota winter. Jake stopped his truck and walked up to my window to tell me to follow him on the lake at least thirty feet behind his vehicle to prevent cracks due to sonic alignment. And my fears were not quelled when he said I had to keep my windows open in case I broke through the ice. Nevertheless, when we got to the fishing shack, I was pleasantly surprised. There were two beds, chairs, a propane wall-mounted heater, diesel generator and even a satellite dish. It was certainly far from the preconceived "roughing it" experience I had imagined.

Q: What can be inferred from the passage?
(a) The writer's fears of hardship did not come true.
(b) Ice fishing can often be fatal for its participants.
(c) Ice fishing is a very popular activity in Minnesota.
(d) The writer and companion were new to ice fishing.

35. Despite Brazil's stellar involvement in the global economy, its labor laws are hampering it from reaching its full potential. Imagine the case of a businessman and his partners who purchased a chain of pharmacies. Upon possession of ownership, the employees sued the businessman for back wages amounting to about half a million dollars. Without proper records, the businessman lost the suit and subsequently his ownership. Brazil's archaic labor laws are set out in 900 articles and were derived from the corporatist labor code of Mussolini's Italian era. Even when owners and employees mutually agree on a change, it is virtually impossible to go through with it because of the rigidity of these cumbersome labor laws.

Q: What can be inferred from the passage?
(a) Brazil's labor laws are a model for emerging countries.
(b) Mussolini's Italy respected owner's rights over laborer's rights.
(c) Brazil's economy could do better with labor law reform.
(d) Owners in Brazil have strong rights thanks to Mussolini.

36. It was all colorful balloons and fireworks at the groundbreaking ceremony of the new Caterpillar facility at Greenhill. Mayor Thomas Wadden dug the first hole with Jim Hanson, CEO of Northern Contractors. The new building will be a state-of-the-art green energy facility and the builders are vying for a LEED platinum certificate for green construction. Innovations such as wind mills, solar panels and rainwater-catching basins will guarantee that this building leaves a nominal carbon footprint. Locals are happy to see the return of the tractor giant after last year's F5 tornado demolished the old complex. Furthermore, the re-employment of over a hundred of the townspeople was the jolt this sleepy town's economy desperately needed.

Q: What can be inferred from the passage?
(a) Caterpillar is a major employer in the community.
(b) LEED is a consumer rights certification organization.
(c) The new facility will only consume green energy.
(d) Hundreds of townspeople will become unemployed.

37. Science fiction is becoming science fact as technology continues its exponential pace of growth. Humankind has been tinkering with machines and finding better ways to exploit them ever since the first caveman picked up a tool. However, revolutionary new work has opened the way for microchip implants in humans. Back in 1998, British scientist Kevin Warwick performed the first sub-dermal transponder implant by inserting a microchip in his hand. The microchip enabled him to open doors and turn on lights in his building. Other proposed uses for such implants are for verifying personal identification as well as providing medical information such as existing conditions, allergies, and medications being taken. This information would be useful to paramedics.

Q: What can be inferred from the passage?
(a) Microchip implants will save many lives in the future.
(b) Technology allows us to mimic science fiction movies.
(c) Kevin Warwick's test received tremendous praise.
(d) Human-machine interface has become a reality.

Part III   **Questions 38—40**

Read the passage. Then identify the option that does NOT belong.

38.   You want those fifteen minutes of fame to last a little longer? (a) Well, the first thing to do is get your foot in the door by taking a lot of risks on a reality show. (b) TV companies are always looking for people to do outlandish and wacky things on television. (c) This type of entertainment has long been the bread and butter of the major networks. (d) Once you're on a reality show, like the one where you have to live with a group of strangers, don't make friends but instead play the black sheep of the cast and you'll be guaranteed more interview talk time.

39.   Excalibur is the mythical sword of King Arthur Pendragon, son of Uther Pendragon. (a) King Arthur was recognized as the rightful heir to the throne when he pulled the magical sword from the stone. (b) He and his fearless and trustworthy Knights of the Round Table had many battles and quests, with the ultimate quest being the search for the Holy Grail. (c) Arthur and his knights ruled over all of Britain and resided within the golden walls of Camelot, their fortress city. (d) In the end, King Arthur's heart was broken by Guinevere when she had a scandalous tryst with Sir Lancelot.

40.   Dumplings are commonly thought of as some meat or vegetable filling wrapped in a dough covering and then steamed, boiled, or fried. (a) There are hundreds of different types of dumplings in many different countries, varying in their ingredients and names. (b) They are very versatile and can be enjoyed regardless of the season. (c) From a Georgian lamb and beef filled Khinkali to a Chinese shrimp stuffed Har Gow, everybody has a dumpling to choose from. (d) Some believe that the modern dumpling was invented about 500 to 600 years ago in China and from there spread throughout the world.

ACTUAL TEST 5

READING
COMPREHENSION

Part I Questions 1—16

Read the passage. Then choose the option that best completes the passage.

1. In an article called "The Role of Higher Education in Social Mobility," the authors state that while most Americans believe the notion that anyone with strong motivation and sufficient ability should successfully gain entry into America's universities, this simply isn't what the research is conveying. Income related gaps in terms of access to and success in higher education are ballooning. The pool of qualified youth is far greater than the number admitted and enrolled, meaning that it would be possible for universities to increase enrollment without _____.

   (a) blemishing their affirmative action records
   (b) targeting protected groups
   (c) creating a diluted brand
   (d) reducing the quality of the student body

2. Quotes encapsulate famous and memorable words from important and remarkable persons. Sometimes they can serve to _____. "Give me liberty or give me death" as quoted from Patrick Henry symbolizes revolutionary America's move for political autonomy. Apart from their historical context, some quotes are timeless and forever give us something to ponder about. "The unexamined life is not worth living" is cited as a lasting word of advice by Socrates. Of course, one quote alone often does not do justice to the full scope of a great person's life. And we must also be careful that so-called famous quotes are not really misinterpretations when removed from their context.

   (a) remind us of our place in history
   (b) represent an important moment in time
   (c) give a summary of a person's life
   (d) illustrate the lives of great thinkers in history

3. Although Leonardo Da Vinci and Michelangelo are known for being masterful painters, both listed their painting talents as subordinate to their other capabilities. Leonardo, while offering his services to the duke of Milan, gave primacy to his qualifications as a military and hydraulic engineer, architect, and sculptor before painter. Michelangelo also conveyed to Pope Julius II that he was first a sculptor and then a painter. Both possessed mammoth egos and contributed to the notion of a "Renaissance Man"— _____.

(a) a person of broad knowledge and skill
(b) a man of humble yet respected knowledge
(c) a slightly crazed yet brilliant mastermind
(d) a coward with issues of abandonment

4. _____ that occur every 90 to 120 minutes throughout the night. While a transitional stage exists as you fall asleep, potentially adding another stage, it doesn't repeat, therefore, excluding it from being part of the cycle. During the first three stages your body's metabolic rate and temperature decreases, endocrine glands secrete growth hormones and blood is sent to muscles to be reconditioned. However, during the fourth stage in which Rapid Eye Movement (REM) occurs, your blood pressure increases, respiration becomes erratic and your involuntary muscles become paralyzed. This is when the mind is revitalized and your emotions are being fine-tuned.

(a) Your sleep cycle consists of four repetitive stages
(b) It is often said that people have mini-dreams
(c) Many couples have snoring episodes
(d) Sleep researchers conclude people feel warm spots

5. With an ever-increasing world population, _____. In terms of decreasing losses, researchers have been engaged in bio-engineering which began with the tinkering of plant DNA, adapting them to resist pests and disease. It was first achieved by cross-pollinating plants showing the desired resistance with the target plant. Later more sophisticated techniques were developed with which researchers cut and spliced each plant's DNA. With these techniques came the extremely challenging prospect of isolating the specific genes in plants that offered the traits needed by researchers.

(a) decreasing the crops that are prone to infestation is important
(b) increasing the number crops planted has become paramount
(c) scientists have striven to increase yields and improve crop quality
(d) the use of technology has taken a back seat to crop management

6. We at Driving 101 are dedicated to _____. We provide constructive feedback after every lesson. Through many years of instruction, we have identified the best practices in training individuals who are anxious about driving. Our experienced instructors teach you the various skills needed to be a good defensive driver. We also teach parking skills. Many of our learners are very surprised at how quickly they learn to parallel-park through us. Before a road test, we give you a mock test so that you know exactly what to expect. We get you results and our success rate is very high. Read about our courses on our website www.Driving101.com.

(a) helping you to pass written examinations
(b) training you to be a competitive racer
(c) equipping you with great driving skills
(d) teaching you to drive defensively

7. Originally coached by his Canadian father Walter, Wayne Gretzky, _____, played with 20 year olds in Brantford, Ontario at the age of only 14. Upon joining the Edmonton Oilers in 1979, he rose to unprecedented fame, shattering records and winning 4 Stanley Cups in 7 years. In 1988, however, he made a drastic move, agreeing to be traded to Los Angeles. Canadians were outraged. His agent at the time, Peter Pocklington, was burned in effigy and Gretzky was considered a traitor by many Canadians. However, years later, at his last game in Canada, he was honored and cheered by all as he left the ice forever.

(a) prohibited from playing full time in the NHL
(b) a late bloomer on the professional circuit
(c) seen by many as a classic ice hockey prodigy
(d) talented businessman, but not a good player

8. In 490 B.C. the out-armed and out-numbered Athenian and Plataea armies defeated the Persians, claiming victory for the democratic way of life. King Darius of Persia had sent his army to conquer Athens as a result of Athens interceding in revolt with other Greek city-states against Persian domination. Ennobled by their participation in their democratic society, their willingness to sacrifice all was paramount to their victory. The Greek armies fought with fervor, _____ hand to hand combat, archery and in seizing their enemies' ships.

(a) back-dropped by more soldiers and weapons for
(b) their submission to their enemy coming in
(c) but the Persian army were experts in
(d) refusing to be defeated and being decisively triumphant in

9. *Harvard Business Review* blogger Ron Ashkenas is telling managers to leverage their top performers or risk losing them. Inept managers often unintentionally dampen exceptional employees, telling them to "slow down" or "research more" because they feel threatened, fearing a subordinate will steal their thunder. In contrast, however, managers should embrace a top performer, stretch him or her to their limit and offer assignments that take their careers to the next level. By doing so, the manager will be recognized for _____, in addition to having the skills to develop people for the good of the company.

    (a) having an eye for talent
    (b) targeting non-performers
    (c) profiteering on the backs of others
    (d) building solid fundamentals

10. *The Rocky Horror Picture Show* began as a stage play in London around 1973. Capturing the attention of Lou Adler, an American producer, the show was brought to the big screen by him a year later. Critics and movie-goers alike ridiculed the movie at first; however, _____ grew over the years. Today, it is the longest running theatrical movie in history and watching it with the right audience can be one of the most rewarding experiences one could hope for. As it is often shown at midnight, fans dress up like their favorite characters and scream along with the actors on the screen.

    (a) government censoring
    (b) a small cult following
    (c) funding for new movies
    (d) touring theatrical performances

11. Shakespeare's *Hamlet* _____, focusing on the quagmires stemming from love, death and betrayal. Particularly frustrating is the fact that no clear positive resolutions present themselves due to the vagueness of Hamlet's world and his all-consuming insecurity. From scene to scene, he seems certain of one thing but later doubts what he has experienced. Others in the play seem to be able to act on their thoughts whereas he simply seems dumbfounded.

(a) was a distinguished gentlemen with a penchant for hunting
(b) was a landlord of sorts
(c) is a truly ambiguous and exasperating tragedy
(d) is an enthralling journey of self-discovery

12. _____ water intoxication. It occurs when water dilutes the body's sodium levels in the bloodstream, causing an imbalance of water in the brain. Symptoms can include a feeling of nausea, excessive fatigue, and in extreme cases, hallucinations or possibly even death. Water intoxication is most likely to occur during periods of intense athletic performance when athletes try to re-hydrate too quickly. The daily recommended amount of water is eight cups per day; however, not all of this water must be consumed in the liquid form as most foods also contribute to the body's water intake.

(a) The simple addition of rum leads to
(b) Recent dehydration problems refer to
(c) Oxygen–infused water can cause
(d) Drinking too much water can lead to

13. Aaliyah _____ Madonna, Mariah Carey, Beyonce, and others. An R&B singer, dancer, fashion model and actress, she was most known for her hit songs and collaborations with other musical giants, her modeling, and her acting in two motion pictures. Upon her success as an R&B singer, she was offered to further her career in motion pictures and was slated to appear in the two sequels to *The Matrix* as a supporting actress amongst other high-profile roles. However, the budding actress and accomplished singer's life was tragically cut short in 2001 when she died in a plane crash at the age of 22.

(a) was an investor in studios and real estate with mentors such as

(b) was a key player in the early success of women in show business, like

(c) struggled to find success in her early twenties, very similar to

(d) was an aspiring professional on the cusp of joining the ranks of

14. Czar Nicholas II, planning to revoke the onerous laws of his predecessors, was overthrown and killed by the Russian working class group called the Bolsheviks who desired more rapid reforms. Though his entire family was thought to be executed, rumors of a surviving daughter began to surface. One woman, Anne Anderson, steadfastly insisted that she was his daughter. She claimed that she was rescued by soldiers, but later left destitute in Germany. Scores of the Czar's relatives, ex-servants and acquaintances grilled her, with many saying she resembled the daughter. However, it was finally decided in court that _____ so her inheritance claim was denied.

(a) there was a lack of conclusive evidence

(b) she was the Czar's daughter

(c) the Czar had her out of wedlock

(d) there was nothing remaining in the Czar's estate

15.

Dear Mr. Smith,

Thank you for the order that you have placed for the full team kit. We wish to confirm that the order will consist of 12 red and white striped jerseys (size large) and 12 white shorts (size large). We envisage that the delivery time on this order will be approximately 3 weeks from the date of this letter. _____, please be aware that we have experienced a slight delay on recent orders and there is a possibility that the order may take an additional 2 weeks beyond the expected date. Once again we thank you for your order and should there be any problems, please do not hesitate to contact me.

Kevin Song

(a) Fortunately
(b) Then
(c) However
(d) Of course

16. It is no secret to gardeners that cold and frost are the enemies of plants and vegetables. With the Age of Discovery and the industrial production of glass, greenhouses for housing tropical plants and growing fruits and vegetables have taken root especially in the colder climates of England and the Netherlands. _____ glass enclosures are rather expensive to construct and maintain, cheaper plastic coverings have made large-scale greenhouse gardening affordable. Improvements in durability have extended the life of the material to several years or even a decade, increasing the convenience and productivity of agriculture in parts of the world and extending the growing season year-round.

(a) In that
(b) Whereas
(c) As though
(d) Since

REA

Part II **Questions 17—37**

Read the passage and the question. Then choose the option that best answers the question.

17. The untrained eye may be forgiven for assuming that a piece of sheet music constitutes the final form of a musical work. What with all the clefs and key signatures, not to mention the articulation marks for pizzicatos and crescendos, the work of the performer would seem to be indubitably laid out in a clear-cut notation. And yet such is not to be the case when the original inspiration of the composer's muse precipitates onto the written medium to be read by another soul, another spirit driven by its own irrepressible sensibilities and tendencies. Then what may be recast or left unheard through the prism of accent marks and dotted notes is what is ineffable and evanescent in the music.

Q: What is the main topic of the passage?
(a) The difficulties of performing a musical work well
(b) Why any musical notation can be reinterpreted
(c) How to listen for the original intent in any music
(d) A call to reinvent today's system of scoring music

18.
Dear Ms. Dornier,

Reflecting upon my tour of your facility in Thailand last week with your delightful staff, I would like to convey my admiration for such a well-run factory. I was especially impressed with your floor arrangement and personnel. I don't believe I have ever viewed such a cost efficient and smoothly run manufacturing process. Additionally, all of your employees were extremely courteous and made a fantastic effort to explain various functions and answer my inquiries. Finally, I would be most appreciative if you would extend a special thank you to Mr. Borat from me. He was most hospitable during my visit and I really enjoyed our discussions over dinner the night before my departure.

Yours faithfully,
George Eliot
General Manager

Q: What is the main purpose of the letter?
(a) To report on an overseas factory and its current status
(b) To thank Mr. Borat for his hospitality and helpfulness
(c) To critique the facility and staff in the Thailand location
(d) To express gratitude for hosting a visit by the author

19. Heading up the Northern Renaissance in art, the Flemish artists of the 15th century such as Jan van Eyck were masters of oil painting in the tradition of northern Gothic art. A detailed naturalism and richness of color characterize their art. Their religious altarpieces as well as more secular works have remained admired for their virtuosity and realism. The style is in the tradition of verisimilitude to nature without a preoccupation with linear perspective as in some of the Italian landscape paintings of that era. It can be said that these paintings with their shallow or even ambiguous perspective are most at home in the context of the sculptural and architectural elements of a gothic cathedral setting.

Q: What is the main topic of the passage?
(a) Comparing northern and southern styles of renaissance art
(b) Characterizing the artistry of the Flemish masters
(c) Appreciating the techniques of medieval Flemish art
(d) Placing Gothic art and architecture in its historical context

20. Teaching autistic children in school requires a little extra skill and effort. Here are a few ideas to help teachers handle autistic children in their classroom. For one thing, students with autism like to have a fixed time table for the day as it helps them feel comfortable. Teachers also need to be flexible to the different learning styles of autistic students. Students with autism may also need some extra time to do their assignments. Some students with autism who struggle with group activities can be given an option of working independently for group projects. A lot of children with autism may need some additional care from teachers to be able to keep up with regular students.

Q: What is the passage mainly about?
(a) Helping autistic students get along with peers
(b) Supporting students suffering from autism with assignments
(c) Punishing autistic students that misbehave
(d) Helping teachers teach children with autism

21. The public face of the UN may be the high-profile functions of urgent international matters such as peacekeeping and international law. But the more run-of-the-mill administrative operations of the multi-national organization have been questioned as another example of runaway overhead. Given that the number of annual meetings can run in the tens of thousands and the number of reports published in the hundreds of thousands, some see redundancy and inefficiency as a concern. The yearly budget of $5 billion excludes the money spent on military operations worldwide, which, if accounted for, is estimated at closer to $20 billion.

Q: What is the best title for the passage?
(a) How to Streamline UN Operational Costs
(b) The Causes of Inefficiency in Running the UN
(c) Estimates on the Organizational Cost of the UN
(d) Concerns about the Public Image of the UN

22. The fact is your personal information is vulnerable to falling into the wrong hands. If you shop online, your personal information such as your credit card account, a bank account, a job is out there. If your information is used fraudulently, you may not find out about it for months or even longer, depending on how closely you monitor your credit report. At Identity Ensure, we help guard you against more than just credit fraud. We alert you whenever we detect your personal information being used to apply for wireless services, retail credit, utilities, check orders & reorders, and mortgage loans within our extensive network.

Q: What is the main purpose of the passage?
(a) To warn about the dangers of identity theft online
(b) To advertise a credit protection agency
(c) To inform how people have their identity stolen
(d) To criticize the system of a credit card company

23. Malcolm Gladwell in his book *Blink: The Power of Thinking Without Thinking* would put forth the case that quick judgments made based on a slice of information available can be just as good or even better than slow judgments based on extensive deliberation. The argument goes that information overload hinders and not helps the cause of reaching a decision. Compounding the problem would be subconscious biases skewing the process, or conflicting forces causing paralysis by analysis. A caveat to all this is that this near-instant analysis would have to be built on the foundation of extensive prior knowledge. Detractors may even accuse this approach of glorifying intuition.

Q: Which of the following is correct according to the passage?
(a) Prejudices can slowly worsen decision making over time.
(b) Intuition is the way to reach a carefully considered decision.
(c) Critics of the book claim that the author is inconsistent.
(d) This theory argues against too much education is useless.

24. If it is to be taken as valid that people form deep emotional bonds with their pets, then the old cliché that a pet is a part of the family could also be accepted. From a sociological point of view, a pet really does alter family dynamics in that different family members would have different relationships with the pet. People can be classified according to whether they treat a pet as merely an animal or as a family member. To put it simply, pets could become a point of contention in the family. On the other hand, pets could act as intermediaries in the way, for example, children might in keeping families together.

Q: Which of the following is correct according to the passage?
(a) Adults accept pets as part of the family more than children do.
(b) Families can possibly grow apart from owning a pet.
(c) Pets almost always lead people to form deep emotional bonds.
(d) Children and pets may fight for affection within a family.

25.

Dear Mr. Brown,

This is with reference to your letter for my conditional hire within your organization as a copy writer. I am very much delighted to get this good news from your side and I would like to thank you for providing me the chance to prove my capabilities by serving in your organization. Though I would like to join you as soon as possible, I need to clarify that, as per our discussion, I am already working in an organization and require a little time to resign from my current employment. Barring any issues, I should be available to start on Tuesday, October 8th. Thank you most sincerely for your time and consideration.

Sincerely,
James Conn

Q: Which is correct about the person receiving this letter?
(a) Since he already gets another job, he is rejecting the offer.
(b) His company wants to purchase the sender's company.
(c) The sender is supposed to send him a letter of resignation.
(d) He has hired the sender to work at his company.

26.
The boll weevil is an insect that destroys cotton plants, and has been a menace to every American state in which cotton is grown. Boll weevils eat the silky fibers in the seedpods of cotton plants and the buds of cotton flowers. Four or five times during a single season, female weevils lay their eggs inside the cotton buds, proliferating their population exponentially. The government would like to get rid of the boll weevil by spraying a powerful poison over the cotton fields, but this spraying is believed to also kill spiders and other useful insects. The one positive effect that has come from the boll weevil is that it has forced many farmers to raise alternative crops from which they have thrived.

Q: Which of the following is correct about boll weevil according to the passage?
(a) They are impervious to any chemical spray.
(b) Only the seeds of the cotton plant are eaten.
(c) They can reproduce several times a year.
(d) Spiders are their main natural enemy.

27.

The old adage that truth can be stranger than fiction still often succeeds in winning acceptance. When looking around for extrasolar planets, or exoplanets, analogous to the ones we know, the physics often turn out to baffle us once again. The Kepler "Planet Hunter" space telescope set out in 2009 to orbit the sun and look at star systems in the Northern Cross. Since then, it's been transmitting back data that has scientists going back to the drawing board. Whole collections of planets closer to their star than thought possible have heads being scratched. And with the number of possible planets detected at over 1,200, estimates say that nearly one-fifth of all stars in the universe have planets orbiting them.

Q: Which of the following is correct about extrasolar planets according to the passage?
(a) Scientists think one-fifth of them have planets in orbit.
(b) Some are detected unexpectedly close to their stars.
(c) The Northern Cross has approximately 1,200 of them.
(d) Physicists find them analogous to ones already known.

28.

Today, January 1st, I'm announcing my candidacy for mayor. Over the past five years, we have seen the deterioration of our community as the incumbent mayor has allowed our infrastructure to reach a state of disrepair with pot-holed roads, underfunded transit lines and inadequate power supply. Well, I would like to change all of that! By voting for me, you are voting for a positive change in our community. My first priority as Mayor will be to revitalize our community through a partnership with the private sector to pave new roads, improve upon transit and most importantly, increase power generation through the use of wind turbines in the Windy Hill region of our town. So, please vote for me in September and we will again build a community we can be proud of.

Kevin Jenkins,
Mayoral Candidate for Smallsville

Q: Which of the following is correct according to the passage?
(a) Wind power is promised to supplement the town's energy supply.
(b) Jenkins will begin his campaign for mayor in September.
(c) The town of Smallsville is located on Windy Hill.
(d) Upkeep of the town's infrastructure is not an election issue.

29. From the lens of two millenniums gone past, it may not be readily noticeable just how inventive an ancient and venerated work of literature is. *The Records of the Grand Historian* by the historiographer Sima Qian is at once a classic book on history as well as an innovative document. Even as the *Shiji* has been a template for many future works ever since the Han Dynasty when it was written, it departed from its precedents which mainly served to glorify their dynastic reigns. It is a monumental book which encompasses not only the standard chronicle of significant events but also has a section that portrays in vivid human detail the important personages who comprised these events.

Q: Which of the following is correct according to the passage?
(a) The history respected the point of view of rival dynasties.
(b) Every single history book since the Shiji has copied its style.
(c) Important historical figures are described in a separate section.
(d) The author Sima Qian does not glorify the dynasty he chronicles.

30. Commuter highway routes display a curious impediment to their traffic flow that doesn't have to do with highway design. In the event of a visually outstanding scene of an accident, and even if the vehicles in questions are off to the side of the road, newscasters almost obligatorily mention the gaper's delay which at times increase commute times by not a negligible amount of minutes. The sight of a spectacular crash or the flashing lights of police cruisers attract the gaping of on-lookers and their concomitant slowing down their own speeds even without any obstacle on the road. This curiosity about a car crash is perhaps inevitable. With this almost invariable delay, the best choice is often to use an alternate course.

Q: Which of the following is true according to the passage?
(a) A gaper's delay actually increases the danger of driving.
(b) More lanes on a highway can help remedy gaper's delay.
(c) Flashing police lights do not contribute to gaper's delay.
(d) Human nature is to the ultimate cause of gaper's delay.

31. Our philosophy here at Olsen Trading is to follow the exemplar tactics of the best traders. The key to their success is rather simple. Instead of believing in using complex formulas for supposedly beating the system, wise traders adhere to the firm principle of looking long-term. This is because the markets are not predictable in the short-term. When markets are erratic, an even keel can weather the storm. In fact, successful traders don't do many trades. They also make trades that may run counter to the trend. Naturally, they are humble since they know they don't beat the markets all the time. Keeping this attitude in mind, we trust that your working with us at Olsen can be mutually beneficial for all.

Q: Which of the following is recommended for making profitable trades?
(a) Look at the trends and go in the opposite direction.
(b) Resist the urge to react to sudden market fluctuations.
(c) Use simple formulas only for making many humble trades.
(d) Look to the long-term but act on the short-term.

32. Lend your company allure and show eco-consciousness by providing corporate gifts that reflect the Green trend. Environmentally-friendly corporate gifts differentiate your company, as they show you believe in a greater cause. More than adding a simple moral aspect to your business, these also make your enterprise relevant. While many suppliers have a limited selection of environment-friendly products, Branding-it-right.com has a massive array to choose from. Featured options include biodegradable items made of corn plastic and others made from recycled materials. There are organic marketing products and energy-saving corporate gifts as well.

Q: Which of the following is correct about Branding-it-right.com according to the advertisement?
(a) It uses biodegradable and recycled products in its offices.
(b) Its online inventory of items is larger than any of its competitors.
(c) Its products can help distinguish a company from the rest.
(d) It sells corporate gifts which are certified by the Green trend.

33. The Paleozoic era of geologic history begins with the Cambrian period with its seeming profusion in the diversity of life forms on Earth. This system of chronology is not accidental as the very term "Paleozoic" derives from Greek roots for "ancient" and "life." The Paleozoic saw the evolution of all the major phylum of multi-cellular organisms as we know them today, the appearance of the first fishes, insects, and reptiles dating back to around 500 million years ago. This is to say that the initial migration of life onto land happened in this era as far as the ancient and incomplete fossil records can tell us. Subsequent eras include the Mesozoic with its dinosaurs and the Cenozoic with its rise of mammals.

Q: What can be inferred about the Paleozoic era from the passage?
(a) It was so designated for its diversification of life forms.
(b) Most of the species from this era have largely died out by now.
(c) It is preceded by both the Mesozoic and Cenozoic eras.
(d) The ancient Greeks first came up with this categorization.

34. Despite the perennial doomsday predictions about population growth, the world will have seen its 7 billionth person being born sometime in 2011. The previous milestone of 6 billion was only reached at the turn of the millennium. The number in 1960 was a mere 3 billion. Current estimates foresee 8-9 billion by mid-century. Approximately 75% of the world will be living in cities with some regions becoming huge continuous urban zones. Prophesying the future has always been a risky business, but the dire prognosis of food, water, and energy shortage forever persist in relation to the issue. Although enough resources are theoretically available, adequate distribution remains only theoretical.

Q: What can be inferred from the passage?
(a) Shortages in food, water, and energy are only theoretical.
(b) The world's population explosion runs its course for now.
(c) It is difficult and pointless to predict future trends.
(d) The world will be severely overcrowded around 2050.

35.   The so-called Big Three Bailout, the federally-assisted bankruptcy and restructuring of the top three US automakers in the wake of the 2008 Credit Crisis, provided ample opportunity for finger pointing. If it wasn't for the executives with their private jets and hefty bonuses, it was the labor unions with their plush benefits and job security. Lest it be about the old head-butting between labor and management, it was reiterated time and again that the terms and conditions for the automotive unions then-existing were negotiated and agreed upon decades back by all parties involved.

Q: What opinion would the writer most likely agree with?
(a) The bailout was necessary to keep the economy stable.
(b) All sides only used the opportunity to play the blame game.
(c) Labor and management never get along and never will.
(d) People would do well to maintain historical perspective.

36.   Some might believe that winning at a game such as chess is simply a matter of using perfect logic to make the correct moves and avoid mistakes. Others might counter that beating another human player takes as much humanity as possible, cunning and illogic included. This would-be philosophical debate was put to the test when IBM's Big Blue supercomputer was pitted against the reigning world champion Garry Kasparov in a series of matches in 1996-1997. Estimated to be able to look a dozen or two moves ahead, the machine nonetheless only barely edged out its flesh-and-blood opponent.

Q: What can be inferred about the Big Blue supercomputer from the passage?
(a) It can calculate how any one move will eventually end the game.
(b) The contest with Kasparov proved that logic is all-important in chess.
(c) It won a few matches but also lost a few to its opponent.
(d) Non-logical or deceptive moves are also within its capability.

37.   As vast and empty as all of outer space may be, the zone of orbital space in which satellites and space stations can operate is predetermined by the physics of the planet we inhabit. Within this useful range of low Earth orbits there lurk not only micro-meteorites but also an increasing amount of man-made space debris. The smallest of these estimated 600,000 orbiting space particles are one reason for the metal foil coverings and other protective armor on space vehicles. The larger of a centimeter or more, though tracked to the best of our ability, today represent the greatest risk to any space mission. The International Space Station, the MIR Station, and the Space Shuttles all show the markings of collisions on panels, windows, and solar cells.

Q: What can be inferred about orbital space particles from the passage?
(a) Satellites can maneuver around them most of the time.
(b) Metal foil and armor on spacecraft protect them adequately.
(c) They are meteorites found throughout our solar system.
(d) Even small ones are a significant threat to astronauts.

Part III   Questions 38—40

Read the passage. Then identify the option that does NOT belong.

38.   Even the Caesars of ancient Rome were famously occupied with managing the already teeming capital of their far-flung empire. (a) The Eternal City over the years has done nothing if not proven that urban upkeep itself is an eternal work. (b) The ancient city center has perhaps never seen better days after the barbarians took over than today. (c) Today's millions of inhabitants are but too numerous to all find accommodations in the ruins of the original site as the medieval population had done. (d) Contemporary urban sprawl surrounds the ancient municipality and puts pressures on it.

39.   Skiing is not only one of the most popular sports in the world but is also one of the oldest modes of transportation. (a) Remains of skis that date back to 4000 B.C. have been found in Altai and Scandinavia, while ancient cave drawings in the Norwegian area depict the story of an ancient tribe if skiers from the north attacking a village over 8,000 years ago. (b) These days, skiing is a big industry that is the main source of revenue for many mountain regions. (c) Some mountain areas are remote and only accessible by skies. (d) While in the past, skiing was once an elitist sport of the rich, now it is enjoyed by a broad spectrum of society.

40.   The suburbs developed in response to several social forces. (a) The multi-lane freeways that go around the perimeter of the city spurred the development of suburban places along the city's rim. (b) Now rather than going from the suburb to the central city to work, shop, see a doctor, or enjoy a movie, suburbanites can obtain the same services by driving along the outer belt from one suburban community to another. (c) Suburban shopping malls and industrial centers have bright new facilities and ample parking. (d) Another factor has been the decentralization of jobs with manufacturing plants and distribution centers relocating to the outer rings of the city.

Read the passage. Then, identify the option that does NOT belong.

TEPS
Test of English Proficiency developed by Seoul National University

독해 Reading Comprehension

Actual Test 1

#					#					#				
1	ⓐ ⓑ ⓒ ⓓ				16	ⓐ ⓑ ⓒ ⓓ				31	ⓐ ⓑ ⓒ ⓓ			
2	ⓐ ⓑ ⓒ ⓓ				17	ⓐ ⓑ ⓒ ⓓ				32	ⓐ ⓑ ⓒ ⓓ			
3	ⓐ ⓑ ⓒ ⓓ				18	ⓐ ⓑ ⓒ ⓓ				33	ⓐ ⓑ ⓒ ⓓ			
4	ⓐ ⓑ ⓒ ⓓ				19	ⓐ ⓑ ⓒ ⓓ				34	ⓐ ⓑ ⓒ ⓓ			
5	ⓐ ⓑ ⓒ ⓓ				20	ⓐ ⓑ ⓒ ⓓ				35	ⓐ ⓑ ⓒ ⓓ			
6	ⓐ ⓑ ⓒ ⓓ				21	ⓐ ⓑ ⓒ ⓓ				36	ⓐ ⓑ ⓒ ⓓ			
7	ⓐ ⓑ ⓒ ⓓ				22	ⓐ ⓑ ⓒ ⓓ				37	ⓐ ⓑ ⓒ ⓓ			
8	ⓐ ⓑ ⓒ ⓓ				23	ⓐ ⓑ ⓒ ⓓ				38	ⓐ ⓑ ⓒ ⓓ			
9	ⓐ ⓑ ⓒ ⓓ				24	ⓐ ⓑ ⓒ ⓓ				39	ⓐ ⓑ ⓒ ⓓ			
10	ⓐ ⓑ ⓒ ⓓ				25	ⓐ ⓑ ⓒ ⓓ				40	ⓐ ⓑ ⓒ ⓓ			
11	ⓐ ⓑ ⓒ ⓓ				26	ⓐ ⓑ ⓒ ⓓ								
12	ⓐ ⓑ ⓒ ⓓ				27	ⓐ ⓑ ⓒ ⓓ								
13	ⓐ ⓑ ⓒ ⓓ				28	ⓐ ⓑ ⓒ ⓓ								
14	ⓐ ⓑ ⓒ ⓓ				29	ⓐ ⓑ ⓒ ⓓ								
15	ⓐ ⓑ ⓒ ⓓ				30	ⓐ ⓑ ⓒ ⓓ								

Actual Test 2

#					#					#				
1	ⓐ ⓑ ⓒ ⓓ				16	ⓐ ⓑ ⓒ ⓓ				31	ⓐ ⓑ ⓒ ⓓ			
2	ⓐ ⓑ ⓒ ⓓ				17	ⓐ ⓑ ⓒ ⓓ				32	ⓐ ⓑ ⓒ ⓓ			
3	ⓐ ⓑ ⓒ ⓓ				18	ⓐ ⓑ ⓒ ⓓ				33	ⓐ ⓑ ⓒ ⓓ			
4	ⓐ ⓑ ⓒ ⓓ				19	ⓐ ⓑ ⓒ ⓓ				34	ⓐ ⓑ ⓒ ⓓ			
5	ⓐ ⓑ ⓒ ⓓ				20	ⓐ ⓑ ⓒ ⓓ				35	ⓐ ⓑ ⓒ ⓓ			
6	ⓐ ⓑ ⓒ ⓓ				21	ⓐ ⓑ ⓒ ⓓ				36	ⓐ ⓑ ⓒ ⓓ			
7	ⓐ ⓑ ⓒ ⓓ				22	ⓐ ⓑ ⓒ ⓓ				37	ⓐ ⓑ ⓒ ⓓ			
8	ⓐ ⓑ ⓒ ⓓ				23	ⓐ ⓑ ⓒ ⓓ				38	ⓐ ⓑ ⓒ ⓓ			
9	ⓐ ⓑ ⓒ ⓓ				24	ⓐ ⓑ ⓒ ⓓ				39	ⓐ ⓑ ⓒ ⓓ			
10	ⓐ ⓑ ⓒ ⓓ				25	ⓐ ⓑ ⓒ ⓓ				40	ⓐ ⓑ ⓒ ⓓ			
11	ⓐ ⓑ ⓒ ⓓ				26	ⓐ ⓑ ⓒ ⓓ								
12	ⓐ ⓑ ⓒ ⓓ				27	ⓐ ⓑ ⓒ ⓓ								
13	ⓐ ⓑ ⓒ ⓓ				28	ⓐ ⓑ ⓒ ⓓ								
14	ⓐ ⓑ ⓒ ⓓ				29	ⓐ ⓑ ⓒ ⓓ								
15	ⓐ ⓑ ⓒ ⓓ				30	ⓐ ⓑ ⓒ ⓓ								

Actual Test 3

#					#					#				
1	ⓐ ⓑ ⓒ ⓓ				16	ⓐ ⓑ ⓒ ⓓ				31	ⓐ ⓑ ⓒ ⓓ			
2	ⓐ ⓑ ⓒ ⓓ				17	ⓐ ⓑ ⓒ ⓓ				32	ⓐ ⓑ ⓒ ⓓ			
3	ⓐ ⓑ ⓒ ⓓ				18	ⓐ ⓑ ⓒ ⓓ				33	ⓐ ⓑ ⓒ ⓓ			
4	ⓐ ⓑ ⓒ ⓓ				19	ⓐ ⓑ ⓒ ⓓ				34	ⓐ ⓑ ⓒ ⓓ			
5	ⓐ ⓑ ⓒ ⓓ				20	ⓐ ⓑ ⓒ ⓓ				35	ⓐ ⓑ ⓒ ⓓ			
6	ⓐ ⓑ ⓒ ⓓ				21	ⓐ ⓑ ⓒ ⓓ				36	ⓐ ⓑ ⓒ ⓓ			
7	ⓐ ⓑ ⓒ ⓓ				22	ⓐ ⓑ ⓒ ⓓ				37	ⓐ ⓑ ⓒ ⓓ			
8	ⓐ ⓑ ⓒ ⓓ				23	ⓐ ⓑ ⓒ ⓓ				38	ⓐ ⓑ ⓒ ⓓ			
9	ⓐ ⓑ ⓒ ⓓ				24	ⓐ ⓑ ⓒ ⓓ				39	ⓐ ⓑ ⓒ ⓓ			
10	ⓐ ⓑ ⓒ ⓓ				25	ⓐ ⓑ ⓒ ⓓ				40	ⓐ ⓑ ⓒ ⓓ			
11	ⓐ ⓑ ⓒ ⓓ				26	ⓐ ⓑ ⓒ ⓓ								
12	ⓐ ⓑ ⓒ ⓓ				27	ⓐ ⓑ ⓒ ⓓ								
13	ⓐ ⓑ ⓒ ⓓ				28	ⓐ ⓑ ⓒ ⓓ								
14	ⓐ ⓑ ⓒ ⓓ				29	ⓐ ⓑ ⓒ ⓓ								
15	ⓐ ⓑ ⓒ ⓓ				30	ⓐ ⓑ ⓒ ⓓ								

Actual Test 5

1	ⓐ ⓑ ⓒ ⓓ	16	ⓐ ⓑ ⓒ ⓓ	31	ⓐ ⓑ ⓒ ⓓ
2	ⓐ ⓑ ⓒ ⓓ	17	ⓐ ⓑ ⓒ ⓓ	32	ⓐ ⓑ ⓒ ⓓ
3	ⓐ ⓑ ⓒ ⓓ	18	ⓐ ⓑ ⓒ ⓓ	33	ⓐ ⓑ ⓒ ⓓ
4	ⓐ ⓑ ⓒ ⓓ	19	ⓐ ⓑ ⓒ ⓓ	34	ⓐ ⓑ ⓒ ⓓ
5	ⓐ ⓑ ⓒ ⓓ	20	ⓐ ⓑ ⓒ ⓓ	35	ⓐ ⓑ ⓒ ⓓ
6	ⓐ ⓑ ⓒ ⓓ	21	ⓐ ⓑ ⓒ ⓓ	36	ⓐ ⓑ ⓒ ⓓ
7	ⓐ ⓑ ⓒ ⓓ	22	ⓐ ⓑ ⓒ ⓓ	37	ⓐ ⓑ ⓒ ⓓ
8	ⓐ ⓑ ⓒ ⓓ	23	ⓐ ⓑ ⓒ ⓓ	38	ⓐ ⓑ ⓒ ⓓ
9	ⓐ ⓑ ⓒ ⓓ	24	ⓐ ⓑ ⓒ ⓓ	39	ⓐ ⓑ ⓒ ⓓ
10	ⓐ ⓑ ⓒ ⓓ	25	ⓐ ⓑ ⓒ ⓓ	40	ⓐ ⓑ ⓒ ⓓ
11	ⓐ ⓑ ⓒ ⓓ	26	ⓐ ⓑ ⓒ ⓓ		
12	ⓐ ⓑ ⓒ ⓓ	27	ⓐ ⓑ ⓒ ⓓ		
13	ⓐ ⓑ ⓒ ⓓ	28	ⓐ ⓑ ⓒ ⓓ		
14	ⓐ ⓑ ⓒ ⓓ	29	ⓐ ⓑ ⓒ ⓓ		
15	ⓐ ⓑ ⓒ ⓓ	30	ⓐ ⓑ ⓒ ⓓ		

Actual Test 4

1	ⓐ ⓑ ⓒ ⓓ	16	ⓐ ⓑ ⓒ ⓓ	31	ⓐ ⓑ ⓒ ⓓ
2	ⓐ ⓑ ⓒ ⓓ	17	ⓐ ⓑ ⓒ ⓓ	32	ⓐ ⓑ ⓒ ⓓ
3	ⓐ ⓑ ⓒ ⓓ	18	ⓐ ⓑ ⓒ ⓓ	33	ⓐ ⓑ ⓒ ⓓ
4	ⓐ ⓑ ⓒ ⓓ	19	ⓐ ⓑ ⓒ ⓓ	34	ⓐ ⓑ ⓒ ⓓ
5	ⓐ ⓑ ⓒ ⓓ	20	ⓐ ⓑ ⓒ ⓓ	35	ⓐ ⓑ ⓒ ⓓ
6	ⓐ ⓑ ⓒ ⓓ	21	ⓐ ⓑ ⓒ ⓓ	36	ⓐ ⓑ ⓒ ⓓ
7	ⓐ ⓑ ⓒ ⓓ	22	ⓐ ⓑ ⓒ ⓓ	37	ⓐ ⓑ ⓒ ⓓ
8	ⓐ ⓑ ⓒ ⓓ	23	ⓐ ⓑ ⓒ ⓓ	38	ⓐ ⓑ ⓒ ⓓ
9	ⓐ ⓑ ⓒ ⓓ	24	ⓐ ⓑ ⓒ ⓓ	39	ⓐ ⓑ ⓒ ⓓ
10	ⓐ ⓑ ⓒ ⓓ	25	ⓐ ⓑ ⓒ ⓓ	40	ⓐ ⓑ ⓒ ⓓ
11	ⓐ ⓑ ⓒ ⓓ	26	ⓐ ⓑ ⓒ ⓓ		
12	ⓐ ⓑ ⓒ ⓓ	27	ⓐ ⓑ ⓒ ⓓ		
13	ⓐ ⓑ ⓒ ⓓ	28	ⓐ ⓑ ⓒ ⓓ		
14	ⓐ ⓑ ⓒ ⓓ	29	ⓐ ⓑ ⓒ ⓓ		
15	ⓐ ⓑ ⓒ ⓓ	30	ⓐ ⓑ ⓒ ⓓ		

울대학교 TEPS관리위원회
번호. 02-886-3330 홈페이지. www.teps.or.kr
TEPS
Actually...
He is so friendly
When you do TEPS!
진짜 실력을 만나다, 텝스!
민간자격국가공인 영어능력검정 (제2013-10호. 1+급, 1급, 2+급, 2급에 해당)

넥서스 수준별 TEPS 맞춤 학습 프로그램

서울대 기출문제

기출·독해

서울대 텝스 관리위원회 텝스 최신기출 1200제 2017 문제집 3 | 서울대학교 TEPS관리위원회 문제 제공 | 352쪽 | 19,500원
서울대 텝스 관리위원회 텝스 최신기출 1200제 2017 해설집 3 | 서울대학교 TEPS관리위원회 문제 제공 · 넥서스 TEPS연구소 해설 | 480쪽 | 25,000원
서울대 텝스 관리위원회 텝스 최신기출 1200제 2016 문제집 2 | 서울대학교 TEPS관리위원회 문제 제공 | 352쪽 | 19,500원
서울대 텝스 관리위원회 텝스 최신기출 1200제 2016 해설집 2 | 서울대학교 TEPS관리위원회 문제 제공 · 넥서스 TEPS연구소 해설 | 480쪽 | 25,000원
서울대 텝스 관리위원회 텝스 최신기출 1200제 문제집 1 | 서울대학교 TEPS관리위원회 문제 제공 | 352쪽 | 19,500원
서울대 텝스 관리위원회 텝스 최신기출 1200제 해설집 1 | 서울대학교 TEPS관리위원회 문제 제공 · 넥서스 TEPS연구소 해설 | 480쪽 | 25,000원
서울대 텝스 관리위원회 공식기출 1000 Listening/ Grammar/ Reading | 서울대학교 TEPS관리위원회 문제 제공 | 19,000원/ 12,000원/ 16,000원
서울대 텝스 관리위원회 최신기출 1000 | 서울대학교 TEPS관리위원회 문제 제공 · 양준희 해설 | 628쪽 | 28,000원
서울대 텝스 관리위원회 최신기출 1200/SEASON 2~3 문제집 | 서울대학교 TEPS관리위원회 문제 제공 | 352쪽 | 19,500원
서울대 텝스 관리위원회 최신기출 1200/SEASON 2~3 해설집 | 서울대학교 TEPS관리위원회 문제 제공 · 넥서스 TEPS연구소 해설 | 472쪽 | 25,000원

실전 모의고사

실전·어휘

How to TEPS 영역별 끝내기 청해 | 테리 홍 지음 | 424쪽 | 19,800원
How to TEPS 영역별 끝내기 문법 | 장보금 · 써니 박 지음 | 260쪽 | 13,500원
How to TEPS 영역별 끝내기 어휘 | 양준희 지음 | 240쪽 | 13,500원
How to TEPS 영역별 끝내기 독해 | 김무룡 · 넥서스 TEPS연구소 지음 | 504쪽 | 25,000원

텝스 청해 기출 분석 실전 8회 | 넥서스 TEPS연구소 지음 | 296쪽 | 19,500원
텝스 문법 기출 분석 실전 10회 | 장보금 · 써니 박 지음 | 248쪽 | 14,000원
텝스 어휘 기출 분석 실전 10회 | 양준희 지음 | 252쪽 | 14,000원
텝스 독해 기출 분석 실전 12회 | 넥서스 TEPS연구소 지음 | 504쪽 | 25,000원

초급 (400~500점) | 중급 (600~700점)

영역별

How to TEPS intro 청해편 | 강소영 · Jane Kim 지음 | 444쪽 | 22,000원
How to TEPS intro 문법편 | 넥서스 TEPS연구소 지음 | 424쪽 | 19,000원
How to TEPS intro 어휘편 | 에릭 김 지음 | 368쪽 | 15,000원
How to TEPS intro 독해편 | 한정림 지음 | 392쪽 | 19,500원

How to TEPS 실전 600 어휘편 · 청해편 · 문법편 · 독해편 | 서울대학교 TE
관리위원회 문제 제공(어휘), 이기현(청해), 장보금 · 써니 박(문법), 황수경 · 넥서스 TE
구소(독해) 지음 | 어휘: 15,000원, 청해: 19,800원, 문법: 17,500원, 독해: 19,00
How to TEPS 실전 700 청해편 · 문법편 · 독해편 | 강소영 · 넥서스 TEPS
구소(청해), 이신영 · 넥서스 TEPS연구소(문법), 오정우 · 넥서스 TEPS연
(독해) 지음 | 청해: 16,000원, 문법: 15,000원, 독해: 19,000원

종합서

한 권으로 끝내는 텝스 스타터 | 넥서스 TEPS연구소 지음 | 584쪽 | 22,000원
How to 텝스 초급용 모의고사 10회 | 넥서스 TEPS연구소 지음 | 296쪽 | 15,000원
How to 텝스 베이직 리스닝 | 고명희 · 넥서스 TEPS연구소 지음 | 320쪽 | 18,500원
How to 텝스 베이직 리딩 | 박미영 · 넥서스 TEPS연구소 지음 | 368쪽 | 19,500원

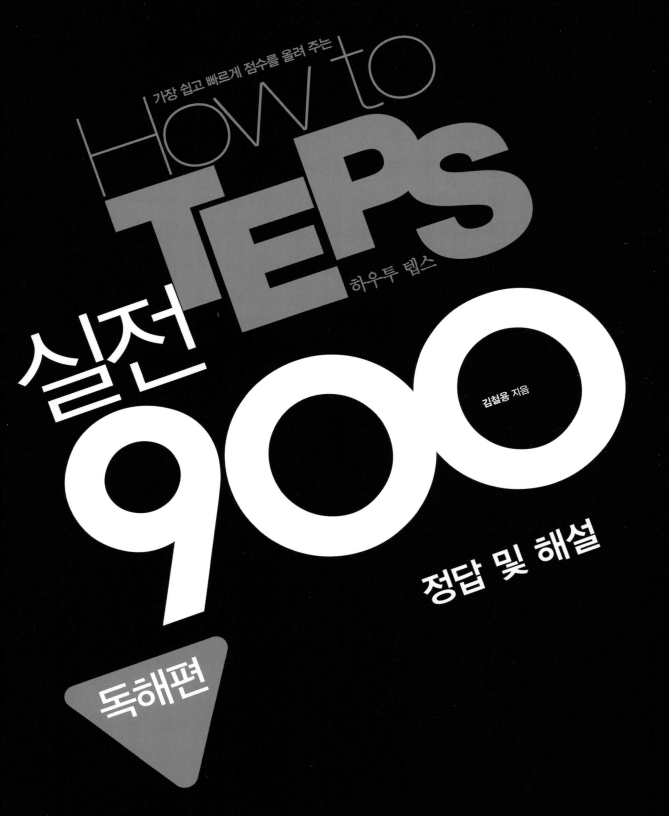

정답 및 해설

Part I

1 (b)	**2** (d)	**3** (a)	**4** (b)	**5** (a)
6 (d)	**7** (b)	**8** (d)	**9** (b)	**10** (c)
11 (a)	**12** (d)	**13** (c)	**14** (b)	**15** (c)
16 (c)				

Part II

17 (b)	**18** (a)	**19** (b)	**20** (d)	**21** (b)
22 (d)	**23** (d)	**24** (b)	**25** (a)	**26** (c)
27 (b)	**28** (b)	**29** (a)	**30** (d)	**31** (c)
32 (a)	**33** (c)	**34** (b)	**35** (c)	**36** (c)
37 (a)				

Part III

38 (a)	**39** (c)	**40** (b)

1

Almost every child grows up with crayons, those _____ used for writing, coloring or drawing. As a matter of fact, there is an army of mothers who have to clean the kitchen walls because of their toddler's artistic flair. The history of the crayon is not very clear, although the word "crayon" comes from a combination of French and Latin and was first used in 1644. The idea of using wax in combination with some sort of pigment goes back thousands of years. Ancient Egyptians developed a style of using hot beeswax with colored pigment to create a bond of color to stone known as encaustic painting. Today an approximate 5 billion crayons are made a day to keep every child occupied in their homes and classrooms.

(a) colored pencils sold in stores
(b) little sticks of colored wax
(c) famous French pastel markers
(d) evenly spaced colored lines

번역

거의 모든 아이들은 크레용을 가지고 놀면서 성장한다. 크레용은 쓰기, 색칠하기 또는 그리기에 사용되는 색이 입혀진 작은 밀랍 토막이다. 사실 아장아장 걷는 아기들의 예술적 재능 때문에 주방 벽을 닦아야 하는 많은 엄마들이 있다. '크레용'이란 단어는 프랑스어와 라틴어의 합성어에서 유래했고, 1644년 처음 사용되었지만, 크레용의 역사는 그리 명확하지 않다. 몇 가지 종류의 안료와 혼합해서 밀랍을 사용하는 발상은 수 천년 전으로 거슬러 올라간다. 고대 이집트인들은 색 안료가

든 뜨거운 밀랍을 사용해서 납화로 알려진 일단의 색채 결합을 만드는 방식을 개발했다. 모든 아이들이 가정과 교실에서 크레용을 쉴 새 없이 이용하게 하기 위해 오늘날 하루에 약 50억개가 생산되고 있다.

(a) 상점에서 판매되는 유색 연필
(b) 색이 입혀진 작은 밀랍 토막
(c) 프랑스의 유명한 파스텔 펜
(d) 균등한 간격의 색 선

해설

크레용의 역사와 쓰임새에 관한 내용으로 Ancient Egyptians developed 이하 내용 중 beeswax with colored pigment를 패러프레이징한 (b)가 빈칸에 가장 적당하다.

coloring 색칠하기 | **as a matter of fact** 사실 | **an army of** 많은 | **toddler** 걸음마를 하는 아기 | **flair** 재능 | **sort of** 어느 정도[다소] | **pigment** 안료 | **beeswax** 밀랍 | **bond** 결합 | **encaustic painting** 납화 | **occupy** ~를 바쁘게 하다

2

A remora is a brave little fish that seems to be catching a piggyback ride on much larger and dangerous sharks. The reason sharks don't eat the remora is because it actually provides a useful purpose of cleaning the shark of bacteria, while the shark provides security for the remora. This type of relationship is called symbiosis, or more specifically, they have a mutual symbiotic relationship. Scientists have classified symbiotic relationships into four categories: mutualism, where both parties benefit, commensalism, where one organism benefits and the other is neither helped nor harmed, and parasitic, where one organism feeds off the other, _____.

(a) with the goal of moving on to another soon
(b) and the other feeds off a third party
(c) providing nutrients to its young
(d) causing harm to the second party

번역

빨판상어는 훨씬 더 크고 위험한 상어를 잡아 업어 타는 것처럼 보이는 용감한 작은 물고기이다. 상어가 빨판상어를 잡아 먹지 않는 이유는 실제로 상어는 빨판상어에게 안전을 제공하는 한편 상어의 박테리아를 청소하는 유용한 용도가 되기 때문이다. 이런 유형의 관계는 공생이라 불리는데 보다 명확히 말하자면 이들은 상호 공생 관계에 있다. 과학자들은 공생 관계를 4개의 범주로 분류하는데, 양쪽이 이익을 얻는 상리 공생, 한 생명체는 이익을 얻고 다른 하나는 도움을 받지도 해를 입지도 않는 공생, 한 생물체가 다른 하나를 먹이로 삼아 상대에게 해를 입히는 기생이다.

(a) 또 다른 생명체로 곧 옮겨 가려는 목표를 가진
(b) 나머지 하나는 제삼자에게 먹이를 주는
(c) 새끼에게 영양분을 공급하는
(d) 상대에게 해를 입히는

3

One of the icons of Americana was Ansel Adams, a photographer who is _____. Ansel was born on February 20, 1920 and raised in an upper class neighborhood in San Francisco. His love for nature inspired his masterful portraits of many of the National Parks found in the western U.S., including Yosemite and Glacier. Adams' prints have been reproduced in calendars, posters, and books worldwide. Ironically, he often had money problems despite being a prolific photographer and coming from a wealthy family. However, Adams' estate reached financial independence selling his prints for an estimated total value of $25 million, with the highest price of $609,600 paid at Sotheby's New York Auction in 2006.

(a) world renowned for his classic black and white portraits
(b) well known for his charcoal and conté sketches
(c) famous for his western landscape design portraits
(d) most recognized for his urban depictions of nature

번역

미국의 우상 중 한 명인 안셀 애덤스는 고전적인 흑백 사진으로 세계적으로 유명한 사진작가이다. 안셀은 1920년 2월 20일에 태어나 샌프란시스코의 상류층이 사는 지역에서 자랐다. 자연에 대한 그의 애정이 요세미티와 글래이셔를 포함해 미국 서부의 여러 국립 공원의 거장다운 사진에 영감을 불어 넣었다. 애덤스의 사진은 달력과 포스터, 책으로 전 세계에서 재생산되고 있다. 아이러니하지만 그는 다작 사진가이고 부유한 집안 출신임에도 불구하고 종종 돈 문제가 있었다. 그러나 그의 사진은 2006년 소더비 뉴욕 경매에서 최고가인 609,600달러를 포함해 추정가 총 2,500만 달러를 판매함으로써 그의 재산은 재정적 독립을 이루었다.

(a) 고전적인 흑백 사진으로 세계적으로 유명한
(b) 목탄과 콩테 스케치로 알려진
(c) 서부 조경 디자인 사진으로 유명한
(d) 자연에 대한 도시적 묘사로 가장 인정 받는

해설

안셀은 사진작가이므로 (b)는 적절하지 않고, 그는 미국 서부 국립 공원을 묘사하는 사진을 찍었으므로 조경 설계와 도시적 묘사와도 거리가 멀다. 안셀은 경매에서 작품이 고가로 판매되므로 세계적으로 잘 알려진 사진작가임을 알 수 있다. 따라서 (a)가 정답이다.

inspire 영감을 주다 | **portrait** 사진 | **prolific** 다작의 | **estate** 재산 **conté** 콩테 (크레용의 일종) | **urban** 도시의 | **depiction** 묘사

4

You leave your office after a grueling ten hour day, but you're not going home, instead you have to pick up the groceries to prepare dinner for the family. This is a challenge that many families have, but not one you have to face if you register now at Greenfoods2U.com to become part of our exclusive internet grocery delivery service. Greenfoods2U has every product your local grocer provides plus many they may not. We guarantee 100 percent organic and fresh groceries delivered to your door within 12 hours of the order being placed. Forget the headaches of fighting for parking, struggling through check-out lanes, and _____. Sign up for Greenfoods2U.com now and leave your grocery worries to us!

(a) spending valuable time preparing meals
(b) lugging your heavy groceries home
(c) regretting you purchased inferior groceries
(d) missing precious time in your office

번역

당신은 끔찍한 10시간의 근무 뒤 사무실을 나오지만 집에 가지 않고 대신 가족을 위한 저녁 준비를 하려고 장을 봐야 합니다. 이것이 많은 가정이 갖는 어려움이지만 지금 Greenfoods2U.com에 등록해 저희 독점적인 인터넷 식료품 배달 서비스의 회원이 되시면 그런 문제에 직면하지 않아도 됩니다. Greenfoods2U는 지역 식품업자가 공급하는 모든 제품과 함께 그들이 공급하지 않을 수도 있는 제품도 많이 있습니다. 100% 유기농의 신선한 식료품이 주문한지 12시간 안에 당신의 집 앞에 배달될 것을 보장합니다. 주차하기 위해 싸우고 체크아웃 줄에서 고생하고 무거운 식료품을 집까지 끌고 가야 하는 골칫거리들은 잊으십시오. Greenfoods2U.com에 가입하고 식료품 걱정은 저희에게 맡기십시오!

(a) 식사를 준비하며 소중한 시간을 보내는
(b) 무거운 식료품을 집까지 끌고 가야 하는
(c) 질이 낮은 식료품을 구입하고 후회하는
(d) 사무실에서의 귀중한 시간을 그리워하는

해설

문맥상 장을 보면서 겪을 수 있는 골칫거리들이 예로 나와야 하므로 (b)가 적절하다.

challenge 어려움 | **face** 직면하다 | **exclusive** 독점적인 | **lug** 〈무거운 것을〉 나르다 | **inferior** 질이 낮은

5

Roughly 250 million years ago during the Paleozoic and Mesozoic periods, _____. Instead of the seven continents we know today, there was one super continent called Pangea. Yet, over the Earth's 4.6 billion year history, scientists speculate there may have been many other supercontinents. Scientists believe that Pangea split in three stages starting roughly 175 million years ago. How does the science community support the Pangea hypothesis? They have been able to identify molten glass on every continent that was caused by a tremendously violent asteroid strike in the Sahara desert. This shows that the continents were connected and is just one of the many historical clues that confirm the presence of Pangea and its subsequent split.

(a) the Earth was a totally different place
(b) our planet experienced sudden changes
(c) the sun had a sudden shift on its axis
(d) an asteroid slammed into the Earth

번역

대략 2억 5천만 년 전 고생대와 중생대의 지구는 완전히 다른 곳이었다. 우리가 오늘날 알고 있는 7개의 대륙 대신 판게아라고 부르는 하나의 거대 대륙이 있었다. 그러나 과학자들은 지구의 46억만 년의 역사에 걸쳐 다른 초대륙이 많았을 것이라고 추측한다. 과학자들은 약 1억 7천 5백만 년 전을 시작으로 판게아가 세 단계에 걸쳐 분열되었다고 믿는다. 과학계는 어떻게 판게아 가설을 입증하는가? 그들은 사하라 사막에서 매우 격렬한 소행성의 충돌로 인해 발생된 녹은 유리를 모든 대륙에서 확인할 수 있었다. 이는 대륙이 연결되어 있었음을 보여주는데, 이것은 단지 판게아의 존재와 그 후의 분리를 확인시켜주는 많은 역사적 실마리들 중 하나일 뿐이다.

(a) 지구는 완전히 다른 곳이었다
(b) 우리 행성은 갑작스런 변화를 경험했다
(c) 태양이 축에서 갑자기 변했다
(d) 소행성이 지구에 충돌했다

해설

두 번째 문장에서 7개 대륙이 아닌 판게아라고 불리는 하나의 거대 대륙이 있었다고 하므로 고생대와 중생대의 지구는 지금과 완전히 다른 모습이었다는 (a)가 문맥상 가장 자연스럽다.

Paleozoic 고생대의 | **Mesozoic** 중생대의 | **Pangea** 판게아 **speculate** 추측하다 | **supercontinent** 초대륙 | **hypothesis** 가설 **identify** 확인하다 | **molten** 녹은 | **asteroid** 소행성 | **subsequent** 차후의

6

In 2010, Christian Kandlbauer became the first European to successfully utilize a "mind-controlled" robotic arm. Kandlbauer, an Austrian, lost both his arms in a horrendous electrical accident. But today, thanks to BCI (brain-computer interface) all he has to do is think about what he wants the joints on his prosthetic arm to do, and they obey his commands. Christian is able to dress himself and is the first person to be able to drive with this type of prosthetic. BCI is promising technology not only for patients that lose their limbs, but for other handicaps such as blindness. Yet, _____ of this technology because of the non-humanitarian applications it could be used for, such as evil "terminator" type cyborgs.

(a) not every patient is a suitable candidate
(b) there is very little need to be apprehensive
(c) test have discovered many additional benefits
(d) there will always be critics and watchdogs

번역

2010년 크리스티안 칸들바우어는 생각하는 대로 움직이는 로봇 팔을 성공적으로 이용한 첫 번째 유럽인이 되었다. 오스트리아인인 칸들바우어는 끔찍한 전기 사고에서 두 팔을 모두 잃었다. 그러나 오늘날 BCI(두뇌－컴퓨터 인터페이스) 덕분에 그의 인공 팔의 관절이 할 일에 대해서 생각만 하면 관절들이 그 명령에 복종한다. 크리스티안은 혼자서 옷을 입을 수 있고 이런 종류의 인공 기관으로 운전할 수 있는 최초의 사람이다. BCI는 팔다리를 잃은 환자들뿐만 아니라 맹인과 같은 장애에도 유망한 기술이다. 하지만 사악한 '터미네이터' 타입의 사이보그 같은 비인도주의적인 용도로 사용될 수 있기 때문에 이런 기술에 대해 비판과 감시하는 눈은 항상 있을 것이다.

(a) 모든 환자가 알맞은 후보는 아니다
(b) 우려할 필요는 거의 없다
(c) 검사를 통해 추가적인 혜택을 많이 발견했다
(d) 비평과 감시하는 눈은 항상 있을 것이다

해설

마지막 문장은 터미네이터를 언급하면서 인공 기관을 이용한 BCI의 악용에 대한 우려를 나타내고 있으므로 문맥상 이에 대한 비판과 감시가 있을 것이라는 의미의 (d)가 가장 적절하다.

interface 인터페이스 | **obey** 복종하다 | **promising** 유망한 **humanitarian** 인도주의적인 | **watchdog** 감시인

7

To Kaito Yoshida, President,

I am sorry to inform you that the Better Business Bureau(BBB) has revoked Kaito Construction's membership application because of two unresolved disputes regarding contracting work at Lund's Megamall and The Hampton Hotel. However, both companies are willing to rescind their complaints to the BBB if a proper agreement is found. As you know, it is the BBB's mission to provide third party assessment of a company's business ethics and practices. Unless you are able to come to an acceptable resolution to these two rows, we will not be able to stand behind you as a BBB member. We hope you will endeavor to _____ and resubmit your application.

Sincerely,

Jennifer Keller, BBB chief auditor

(a) improve your company's image and reputation

(b) remedy these differences with the above parties

(c) increase client satisfaction by providing incentives

(d) seek the assistance of a good public relations company

번역

카이토 요시다 사장 귀하

유감입니다만, 룬즈 메가몰과 햄프턴 호텔의 도급과 관련하여 해결되지 않은 두 건의 분쟁으로 인해 거래 개선 협회는 카이토 건설의 회원 신청을 철회했음을 알려 드립니다. 그러나 두 회사는 적절한 합의점이 있다면 협회에 접수한 불만 신고를 취하할 의사가 있습니다. 아시다시피 회사의 윤리와 운영에 대한 제삼자의 평가를 제공하는 것은 거래 개선 협회의 임무입니다. 이 두 건에 대해 수용할 만한 해결책을 찾지 못한다면 귀사를 협회의 회원으로 지원할 수 없을 것입니다. 위 당사자들과의 불화를 개선하도록 하고 신청서를 다시 제출해 주시기 바랍니다.

거래 개선 협회 수석 감사관, 제니퍼 켈러

(a) 귀사의 이미지와 평판을 높이도록

(b) 위 당사자들과의 불화를 개선하도록

(c) 장려금 제공으로 고객 만족도를 높이도록

(d) 좋은 홍보 회사의 도움을 구하도록

해설

카이토 건설의 가입 신청서가 철회된 것은 다른 두 회사와 해결되지 않은 분쟁이 있기 때문이며, 해결 뒤 신청서를 다시 제출하기를 요청하고 있으므로 (b)가 적절하다.

revoke 철회하다 | **dispute** 분쟁 | **regarding** ~에 관하여 **contracting** 도급의 | **rescind** 무효로 하다 | **resolution** 해결책 **stand behind** 지지하다 | **endeavor** 노력하다 | **auditor** 감사관 **remedy** 개선하다 | **public relations** 홍보

8

Among all the branches in the U.S. military, no other unit is as _____ as the Marine Scout Sniper. This is because these specialized warriors are silent and stealthy, moving in teams of two and evading the watching eyes of their foes. Following the motto of "One shot, one kill", a qualified sniper will spend days stalking down his high valued target and then eliminate him from a mile away. The Marine Scout Sniper training course runs two months and qualified candidates come from all branches of the military. Yet, despite this fact, the training program has an attrition rate of over 50 percent. Once a candidate passes the course, he joins a brotherhood of the most elite soldiers ever.

(a) highly in demand for rear support

(b) flamboyant and visually intimidating

(c) frequently glorified in film

(d) feared and reviled by the enemy

번역

미군의 모든 부대 중 해병대 정찰병 저격수만큼 적들이 두려워하고 혐오하는 부대는 없다. 이것은 이 전문 용사들이 조용히 남의 눈을 피해 2명이 한 팀을 이루어 움직이며 경계하는 적의 눈을 피하기 때문이다. '한 방에 한 명씩'이라는 모토에 따라 숙련된 저격수는 아주 중요한 목표물을 며칠 동안 몰래 추적하고 1마일 밖에서 목표물을 제거할 것이다. 해병대 정찰병 저격수 훈련은 2개월 동안 진행되며 저격 후보자들이 모든 군부대에서 온다. 하지만 이런 사실에도 불구하고 훈련 프로그램은 50%가 넘는 자연 감소율을 보인다. 일단 후보자가 훈련 과정을 통과하면 그는 최고의 엘리트 군인들과 형제애를 맺게 된다.

(a) 후방 지원에 매우 필요한

(b) 대담하고 시각적으로 위협적인

(c) 영화에서 자주 미화되는

(d) 적들이 두려워하고 혐오하는

해설

해병대 정찰병 저격수가 잠행하고 경계하는 적의 눈을 피하여 1마일 밖에서 목표물을 제거한다고 하므로 (d)가 가장 적절하다. 대담하다는 (b)는 몰래 따라다닌다는 저격수의 특성과 맞지 않다.

scout 정찰병 | **sniper** 저격수 | **stealthy** 남의 눈을 피하는 | **evade** 피하다 | **qualified** 자격을 갖춘 | **stalk** 몰래 뒤를 밟다 | **eliminate** 제거하다 | **attrition rate** 자연 감소율 | **flamboyant** 대담한 **intimidating** 위협적인 | **glorify** 미화하다 | **revile** 매도하다

9

Five times a day, devoted Muslims _____ over the loudspeakers attached to the tall minarets of a mosque. A mosque is a Muslim house of worship characterized by its grand entryways, domes, tall minarets and prayer halls. They are often wide open spaces and can date back to the 7th century. Once only found on the Arabian Peninsula, mosques are now found in every inhabited country in the world. Just like many holy houses of worship, the mosque also serves as a community center where followers can be educated and even settle disputes.

(a) practice their formal salat, or prayers

(b) around the world are called to prayer

(c) passionately debate concepts of their faith

(d) gather in their homes to hear music

번역

전 세계의 헌신적인 이슬람교도들은 매일 5번씩 모스크의 높은 첨탑에 붙어 있는 확성기를 통해 기도하라는 부름을 받는다. 모스크는 웅대한 입구와 돔, 높은 첨탑, 기도실로 특징짓는 이슬람 예배당이다. 모스크는 보통 넓게 개방된 공간이며, 그 역사가 7세기로 거슬러 올라간다. 한때 아라비아 반도에서만 볼 수 있었던 모스크는 이제 사람이 사는 세계 모든 나라에서 볼 수 있다. 신성한 여러 예배당처럼 모스크도 신도들이 교육을 받고 분쟁 해결까지도 하는 시민 문화 회관의 역할을 한다.

(a) 그들의 공식적인 살라트, 즉 기도를 한다
(b) 전 세계적으로 기도하라는 부름을 받는다
(c) 그들의 믿음의 개념을 열정적으로 토론한다
(d) 음악을 듣기 위해 집에 모인다

해설

이슬람 모스크의 역할과 특징에 대한 글로, 헌신적인 이슬람교도들이 매일 5번씩 확성기로 기도하라는 부름을 받는다고 할 수 있다. 또한 모스크가 사람이 사는 곳이라면 전 세계에 퍼져 있다고 하므로, (b)가 적절하다. (a)는 의미상 (b)와 비슷하지만 빈칸 뒤의 문장과 자연스럽게 연결이 되지 않으므로 오답이다.

devoted 헌신적인 | **Muslim** 이슬람교도 | **minaret** 뾰족탑 | **mosque** 사원 | **worship** 예배 | **inhabited** 〈사람·동물이〉 사는 | **salat** 살라트 (이슬람교에서 하루 5번 행하는 규정된 예배)

10

Have you ever asked for a "Coke" instead of a soda? Many people refer to tissues as "Kleenex," medical adhesive bandages are better known as "Band Aids" and peanut butter is simply referred to as "Jiffy." The reason behind these "mislabels" is mass marketing's powerful effect on the public's exposure to certain products. If you are bombarded by advertisements on the radio, TV, internet, newspaper, billboard and pretty much anywhere you look, then the brand name that is being advertised can actually replace the product's name. So, _____ a "Q-tip," be sure to remember the actual product is a cotton swab.

(a) if you need a refreshing break and reach for
(b) when people tell you to protect yourself with
(c) the next time you clean your ears with
(d) if there's a sale at the hardware store for

번역

소다 대신에 '코크'를 달라고 한 적이 있는가? 많은 사람들이 휴지를 '크리넥스'라 부르고, 의료용 접착식 붕대는 '밴드에이드'로 더 잘 알려져 있으며, 땅콩버터는 간단히 '지피'로 불린다. 이런 '잘못된 명칭'은 무차별 마케팅이 특정 상품의 대중 노출에 미친 강력한 영향 때문이다. 라디오나 TV, 인터넷, 신문, 광고판 등 보이는 거의 모든 곳에 광고로 도배를 한다면, 광고 상품의 이름이 실제로 그 물건의 이름을 대신할 수

있다. 따라서 다음에 '큐팁'으로 귀를 청소할 때, 실제 그 상품의 이름이 면봉임을 기억하라.

(a) 기분 좋은 휴식이 필요하여 손을 뻗는다면
(b) 사람들이 스스로를 보호하라고 말한다면
(c) 다음에 귀를 청소할 때
(d) 철물 가게에서 세일을 한다면

해설

상품명을 대신하는 특정 브랜드가 광고의 영향 때문이라는 내용이다. 마지막 문장은 '큐팁'이 면봉을 나타내는 특정 브랜드에서 왔다는 의미이므로, 면봉이 쓰일 수 있는 상황을 생각해보면 정답은 (c)이다.

refer to 부르다 | **adhesive** 접착제 | **mislabel** 잘못된 명칭 **exposure** 노출 | **bombard** 퍼붓다 | **swab** 면봉

11

The first music video to be shown on August 1, 1981, was the appropriately entitled song "Video Killed the Radio Star" by The Buggles. This started a musical revolution all thanks to the debut of a little known channel called Music Television, or better known as MTV. This cutting-edge channel brought not only the most popular songs to our living rooms but also the singers themselves. MTV experienced a meteoric rise and expanded way beyond just music videos with live concerts, MTV unplugged, cartoons, music awards shows and many other programs. We can also thank MTV for _____ would have previously not been given the spotlight as they did with MTV.

(a) exposing us to non-mainstream music and artists who
(b) providing a variety of social and charitable programs that
(c) improving radio programs, DJs and advertisers who
(d) the attention given to television's obvious dominance it

번역

1981년 8월 1일에 선보인 첫 뮤직비디오는 제목이 딱 맞게 붙여진 버글스의 노래 '비디오가 라디오 스타를 죽였다'였다. 이 노래는 MTV로 더 잘 알려진 뮤직 텔레비전이라는 조금 밖에 알려지지 않은 채널의 등장 덕분에 음악 혁명을 일으켰다. 이 최첨단 채널은 가장 인기 있는 음악뿐만 아니라 가수들 자체를 우리 거실로 데리고 왔다. MTV는 혜성 같이 성장했고 단순히 뮤직비디오를 넘어 라이브 콘서트, MTV 언플러그드 공연, 만화, 음악 시상식 등 여러 프로그램들로 확대했다. 또한 전에는 주목 받지 못했던 비주류 음악과 가수들을 우리가 만날 수 있게 노출시켜 준 것은 MTV 덕분이라고 할 수 있다.

(a) 비주류 음악과 가수들을 우리에게 노출시켜준 것
(b) 다양한 사회적, 자선적 프로그램들을 제공해 준 것
(c) 라디오 프로그램, DJ와 광고주를 향상시킨 것
(d) 텔레비전의 명백한 우세에 대한 관심

해설

마지막 문장의 '전에는 주목을 받지 못했던'이라는 부분과 연결하여, 우리에게 그런 비주류 음악과 가수들을 소개해 준 것에 대해 고마워할 수 있다고 하는 것이 자연스러우므로 정답은 (a)이다.

appropriately 적절히 | **cutting-edge** 최첨단의 | **meteoric rise** 혜성 같은 성장 | **charitable** 자선의 | **dominance** 우세

12

_____ in human evolution. Once our ancient ancestors acquired a taste for meat, they were able to consume more protein. Not only did that protein provide more physical energy, it also supplied more nutrients for the brain. In addition, in order to catch their prey, which was generally much larger than them, hunters had to invent weapons, set traps and work together strategically. All of these factors combined to improve our reasoning and cognitive abilities as well as create social order. The better hunter you were, the more attractive you were to the clan as both a provider and leader.

(a) Many changes in dietary habits and social orders are seen
(b) Scientists to this day still argue the relevance hunting had
(c) Various geological and extra-terrestrial factors changed the direction
(d) Few people realize the importance meat-eating played

번역

인류 진화에 있어 육식의 중요성을 깨닫는 사람은 거의 없다. 우리 고대 조상들은 일단 고기의 맛을 알게 되자 좀 더 많은 단백질을 섭취할 수 있었다. 단백질은 육체적 에너지를 더 많이 제공했을 뿐만 아니라, 두뇌에도 더 많은 영양을 공급했다. 게다가 사냥꾼들은 보통 그들보다 훨씬 더 큰 먹이를 잡기 위해 무기를 발명하고 덫을 놓고 전략적으로 협동해야만 했다. 이 모든 요소들이 합쳐져 우리의 추리력과 인지 능력을 향상시키고 사회 질서를 만들어 냈다. 더 훌륭한 사냥꾼일수록 부족의 부양자이자 지도자로서 더 매력적이었다.

(a) 식습관과 사회 질서에 있어 많은 변화가 보인다
(b) 오늘날까지 여전히 과학자들은 사냥의 타당성에 대해 논쟁한다
(c) 다양한 지질학적, 외계적 요인들이 방향을 바꿨다
(d) 육식의 중요성을 깨닫는 사람은 거의 없다

해설

육식이 인류의 진화에 미친 영향에 대한 글로, 육식을 함으로써 육체적, 정신적 에너지를 얻었고, 육식을 위해 사냥을 하면서 인류의 인지 능력이 향상되고 사회 질서가 만들어졌다는 내용이다. (a)는 뒤에 인류의 식습관과 사회 질서의 변화에 대한 내용이, (b)는 사냥의 타당성에 대한 과학자들의 의견이, (c)는 지질학적, 외계적 요인들에 대한 설명이 이어질 것이다. 인류 진화에 있어서 육식이 중요하다는 전체 내용에 맞는 첫 문장으로 (d)가 가장 적절하다.

evolution 진화 | **consume** 섭취하다 | **strategically** 전략적으로 **reasoning** 추리 | **cognitive** 인식의 | **clan** 부족 | **dietary** 식사의 **relevance** 타당성 | **extra-terrestrial** 외계의

13

_____ in luxury vehicles, from the ancient palanquin, driven by man power, to today's modern day stretch limousine. The first limousine was made in 1902 and the first stretch limo in 1928 Today, limo manufacturers can modify just about any car, whether it's a Hummer, Cadillac Escalade or Rolls Royce. The process is relatively simple in theory; just cut the vehicle in half and extend it as long as desired. Limos possess all the luxurious amenities one would find in five-star hotels such as televisions, bars, dance lights, video games and more. The world's longest stretch limo reaches over 100 feet in length, requires 26 tires and boasts several beds, a heated Jacuzzi and even a helipad!

(a) Not everyone will get an opportunity to ride
(b) There are many ways to get from point A to point B
(c) For ages the wealthy and elite traveled
(d) The history of transport and travel evolved

번역

오랫동안 부유층과 엘리트들은 인력으로 움직이는 고대 1인승 가마에서부터 오늘날의 현대적 차체가 긴 리무진에 이르기까지 호화 운송 수단으로 이동했다. 최초의 리무진은 1902년에 만들어졌고 최초의 스트레치 리무진은 1928년에 만들어졌다. 오늘날 리무진 제조업체들은 허머, 캐딜락 에스컬레이드 또는 롤스로이스든 어떤 차든지 개조할 수 있다. 이론상 과정은 비교적 간단하다. 차량을 반으로 나누고 원하는 만큼 길게 연장하는 것이다. 리무진은 5성급 호텔에서 볼 수 있는 TV, 바, 무대 조명, 비디오 게임 외 많은 호화로운 편의 시설을 갖추고 있다. 세계에서 가장 긴 스트레치 리무진은 길이가 100피트가 넘고 26개의 타이어가 필요하며 침대 여러 개와 뜨거운 목욕탕, 심지어 헬리콥터 발착장을 자랑으로 한다.

(a) 모든 사람이 승차 기회를 얻지는 않을 것이다
(b) A지점에서 B지점으로 가는 데는 많은 방법이 있다
(c) 오랫동안 부유층과 엘리트들은 여행했다
(d) 교통과 이동의 역사는 진화했다

해설

스트레치 리무진이라는 고급 차량에 대한 글로 이와 연결하여 그런 고급스러운 차량을 사용할 수 있는 여유가 있는 부유층과 엘리트층을 첫 문장에 넣어 글을 시작하는 것이 자연스럽다. 따라서 (c)가 정답이다.

palanquin 1인승 가마 | **stretch limousine** 스트레치 리무진 (차체를 길게 늘린 고급 리무진) | **modify** 개조하다 | **relatively** 비교적 | **extend** 연장하다 | **amenity** 편의 시설 | **boast** 자랑하다

14

In spite of many people's belief that a rainforest and jungle are one and the same, there are distinct differences between the two. A rainforest is usually surrounded by a jungle and what sets them apart is not the amount of rainfall or climate variations. Rather, a rainforest has a very tall and thick canopy that prevents sunlight from penetrating to the ground. This in turn means there is very little plant life and vegetation due to the lack of sunlight. In contrast, a jungle has a thick undergrowth of plants. When you see images of people ＿＿＿＿＿＿＿＿＿, they are most likely in a jungle and not a rainforest.

(a) trekking under a solid covering of trees
(b) hacking their way through thick vegetation
(c) hunting in tall grasses near a body of water
(d) picking nuts and fruits from relatively tall trees

번역

열대 우림과 정글이 같다는 많은 사람들의 생각에도 불구하고 이 둘 사이에는 분명한 차이점이 있다. 열대 우림은 보통 정글로 둘러싸여 있는데, 이 둘을 갈라 놓는 것은 강수량이나 기후의 변화가 아니다. 더 정확히 말하면 열대 우림에는 햇빛이 땅으로 통과하지 못하도록 키가 크고 두터운 수관이 있다. 이것은 곧 햇빛 부족으로 식물 생명체와 초목이 거의 없다는 것을 의미한다. 이와 대조적으로 정글은 두터운 관목 식물이 있다. 두터운 초목을 잘라내고 나아가는 사람들의 이미지를 보면 그들은 아마도 열대 우림이 아니라 정글에 있는 것이다.

(a) 빽빽이 들어찬 나무숲 아래서 트레킹을 하는
(b) 두터운 초목을 잘라내고 나아가는
(c) 물 근처의 키 큰 풀밭에서 사냥을 하는
(d) 비교적 키 큰 나무에서 견과류와 과일을 따는

해설

열대 우림과 정글의 차이점에 대한 글로, 정글의 특징을 보여주며, 바로 앞서 두터운 관목 식물에 대한 내용과 자연스럽게 이어지는 (b)가 정답이다.

rainforest 열대 우림 | **distinct** 분명한 | **variation** 변화 | **canopy** 수관 (숲의 나뭇가지들이 지붕 모양으로 우거진 것) | **penetrate** 관통하다 | **vegetation** 초목 | **undergrowth** 관목 | **hack one's way through** ～을 잘라내고 나아가다

15

Still to this day, there is no definitive proof of football's origins. Some historians note a game played in China around 3,000 years ago called Tsu Chu that involved kicking a stuffed ball of animal skin through an elevated hole. Around the same time, the Japanese played a game called Kemari where participants kicked a ball through two bamboo shoots. The Romans also played a game similar to today's football and brought it to Britain. The first recorded instance of a game that resembles football is from England in 1,100, albeit that game may have better been described as an all out brawl with little to no rules. ＿＿＿＿＿＿＿＿＿ of the origins, football remains the number one game worldwide.

(a) In light
(b) As an exception
(c) In spite
(d) As a consequence

번역

아직도 오늘날까지 축구의 유래에 대한 명확한 증거는 없다. 어떤 역사가들은 3천년 전 중국에서 속이 꽉 찬 동물 가죽으로 만든 공을 지면 위에 튀어 나온 구멍으로 찼던 츠슈라고 불리는 경기를 주목한다. 거의 비슷한 시기에 일본인들은 참가자들이 두 죽순 사이로 공을 차던 게마리라는 경기를 했다. 로마인들 또한 오늘날의 축구와 비슷한 경기를 했고 영국에 가져왔다. 비록 규칙이 거의 없이 총력을 기울인 소동이라 묘사하는 게 더 나았을 것 같지만 축구와 비슷한 경기의 최초 기록은 1100년 영국에서이다. 그런 유래에도 불구하고 축구는 전 세계 제일의 경기로 남아 있다.

(a) ～을 고려하여
(b) ～의 예외로
(c) ～에도 불구하고
(d) ～의 결과로

해설

아직 정확하게 드러나지 않은 축구의 유래에 대한 글로, 선택지 중에서 그런 다양한 유래에도 불구하고 축구가 전 세계 제일의 경기라는 의미가 되는 것이 적절하다. 따라서 (c)가 정답이다.

definitive 명확한 | **origin** 유래 | **elevate** 올리다 | **participant** 참가자 | **bamboo shoot** 죽순 | **all out** 총력을 기울인 | **brawl** 소동 | **albeit** 비록 ～이기는 하나

16

It is recommended that once you receive an assignment that you begin it right away. Unfortunately, in the real world, procrastination tends to trump logic. How many times have you had to scramble to finish a task before the deadline? We have all regretted getting a late start because of our own laziness. This type of behavior is human nature, but can get us into a lot of hot water. If you start a project well before it is due, that gives you that much more time to react to any unexpected challenges. ＿＿＿＿＿＿＿＿＿, no matter how often we hear this same advice, we tend to tell ourselves we'll follow it on the next project, not this one.

(a) For instance
(b) Correspondingly
(c) Notwithstanding
(d) As an alternative

번역

과제를 받으면 바로 시작하는 것이 좋다. 불행히도 현실에서는 미루는 버릇이 논리를 이기는 경향이 있다. 마감일 전에 임무를 끝내기 위해 몇 번이나 난리를 쳤는가? 우리는 게으름 때문에 시작을 미룬 것을 후회한다. 이런 종류의 행동은 인간의 천성이며, 우리를 곤경에 빠뜨릴 수 있다. 마감 훨씬 전에 프로젝트를 시작하면 예상치 못한 어려움에 대응할 그만큼의 시간이 더 주어진다. 그럼에도 불구하고, 얼마나 자주 이와 똑같은 조언을 듣든지 상관없이 우리는 이번이 아니라 다음 과제부터 그 조언을 따라야겠다고 다짐하는 경향이 있다.

(a) 예를 들어
(b) 상응하여
(c) 그럼에도 불구하고
(d) 대안으로

해설

빈칸에는 문맥상 '그렇지만' 또는 '그럼에도 불구하고' 등이 적절하므로 (c)가 정답이다.

procrastination 미루는 버릇 | **tend to** ~하는 경향이 있다 | **trump** 이기다 | **scramble** 급히 서둘러 하다

17

Hydroblasting is a technique of removing unwanted materials off of surfaces such as dirt and rust. This method relies entirely on the energy of water striking a surface with tremendous 10,000 pounds per square inch (psi), and ultra-high, utilizing over 25,000 psi. Ultra-high hydroblasting water pressure is extremely dangerous and can sever a human limb in seconds. Unlike traditional sand and grit blasting, with hydroblasting there is no dispersal of spent abrasives or harmful chemicals into the ecosystem. Therefore, with more water–efficient hydroblasting machinery, we can be green even without toxic industrial strength cleaners.

Q: What is the main purpose of the passage?
(a) To classify the two types of hydroblasting techniques
(b) To highlight the advantages of using hydroblasting
(c) To spotlight the many uses of hydroblasting
(d) To illustrate the dangers of hydroblasting

번역

하이드로블라스팅은 먼지와 녹과 같은 불필요한 물질을 표면에서 제거하는 기술이다. 이 방법은 평방 인치(psi)당 1만 파운드로 최고 2만 5천 psi의 표면을 때리는 물 에너지에 전적으로 의존한다. 최고의 하이

드로블라스팅 수압은 극히 위험하고 인간의 팔다리를 몇 초 만에 절단할 수 있다. 전통적인 샌드블라스팅, 그릿블라스팅과 달리 하이드로블라스팅은 소모된 연마재 또는 유해한 화학 물질이 생태계로 퍼지는 일이 없다. 그러므로 좀 더 물 효율적인 하이드로블라스팅 기계를 사용하면 독성을 지닌 산업용 강력 세제를 사용할 필요가 없어 환경친화적일 수 있다.

Q: 지문의 주된 목적은?
(a) 두 종류의 하이드로블라스팅 기술을 분류하기 위해
(b) 하이드로블라스팅 기술 사용의 이점을 강조하기 위해
(c) 하이드로블라스팅의 많은 이용을 조명하기 위해
(d) 하이드로블라스팅의 위험을 설명하기 위해

해설

물을 이용한 하이드로블라스팅이라는 기술이 기존의 방법과 달리 환경친화적임을 강조하고 있으므로 (b)가 정답이다.

hydroblasting 하이드로블라스팅 (물을 이용하여 주조품 등의 표면에 붙어 있는 모래 등을 제거하는 방법) | **sever** 절단하다 | **grit** 모래 | **dispersal** 확산 | **abrasive** 연마재

18

Today's most popular type of footwear gets its name from the 1800s when a London police officer created a rubber-soled shoe so he could "sneak" up on criminals without them hearing him. This innovation sparked the birth of today's global multi-billion dollar sneaker market. Sneakers are made of flexible materials, usually with a rubber sole and leather or canvas top. Besides serving its original purpose as active footwear, the sneaker has created a whole new subculture in itself. They have been an integral part of American hip-hop culture since the 70s and really took off internationally with the growing popularity of sports like basketball.

Q: What is the best title of the passage?
(a) From Beat-Cop to Backbeat, the Story of the Sneaker
(b) The History of America's Most Expensive Footwear
(c) The Reason Behind a Multi-Million Dollar Industry
(d) How the Sneaker Changed the Music Industry

번역

오늘날 가장 인기 있는 신발의 명칭은 1800년대에서 유래하는데, 당시 런던의 한 경찰이 고무 바닥으로 된 신을 만들어 들키지 않고 범인들에게 '몰래 다가갈' 수 있었다. 이 혁신이 오늘날 전 세계적으로 수십억 달러 스니커즈 시장의 탄생의 발단이 되었다. 스니커즈는 보통 유연한 소재로 만들어지는데, 바닥은 고무로, 윗부분은 가죽이나 캔버스로 만들어진다. 활동적인 신발로서 원래의 목적에 충실한 것 이외에 스니커는 그 자체가 완전히 새로운 하위문화를 만들어 냈다. 스니커즈는 70년대 이후부터 미국 힙합 문화의 필수적인 부분이 되었고, 농구 같

은 스포츠의 인기 상승과 함께 실제 세계적으로 급격히 인기를 얻었다.

Q: 지문에 가장 잘 어울리는 제목은?

(a) 경찰에서 백비트까지, 스니커 이야기

(b) 미국의 가장 비싼 신발의 역사

(c) 수백만 달러 산업에 숨은 이유

(d) 어떻게 스니커가 음악 산업을 바꿨는가

해설

스니커라는 고무창 운동화의 유래와 그 자체로서 문화에 미치는 영향에 대해 이야기하고 있으므로 (a)가 제목으로 가장 적절하다.

sneaker 고무창 운동화 | sole 〈바닥의〉 창을 대다 | sneak up 몰래 다가가다 | spark 유발하다 | flexible 유연한 | subculture 하위문화 | integral 필수적인 | take off 급격히 인기를 얻다

19

Attention all P-Mart shoppers,

In an effort to provide the best products at the lowest prices, we are extending our popular green-light specials. For the next week, whenever a green-light flashes above any product aisle, P-Mart shoppers will be entitled to an additional 30 percent off our already low, low prices! Be sure to take advantage of this promotional offer and look for additional coupons in this Sunday's *Daily Times Newspapers*. We recognize how attractive our low prices are, but unfortunately we have to limit the number of products per customer on a product to product basis. Thank you for your continued loyalty to P-Mart, we look forward to providing you with the lowest prices for your everyday needs.

Q: What is the main purpose of the announcement?

(a) To remind customers of a purchasing limit on sale items

(b) To inform customers of a limited time sales initiative

(c) To encourage customers to read the Sunday newspapers

(d) To win over customers from a competing company

번역

P마트 고객에게 알립니다.

가장 저렴한 가격에 최고의 상품을 제공하려는 노력의 일환으로 인기 있는 초록 불 특별 할인을 연장하려 합니다. 다음 주 동안 어떤 제품 통로 위에서든 초록 불이 반짝일 때마다 P마트 고객은 아주 저렴한 가격에 30% 추가 할인을 받을 수 있습니다! 이 판촉 행사의 혜택을 꼭 받으시고 이번 주 일요일 〈데일리 타임스〉에서 추가 쿠폰을 찾으십시오. 저희의 저렴한 가격이 얼마나 매력적인지 알지만 불행히도 제품마다 고객당 제품 수를 제한해야 합니다. P마트를 계속 이용해 주셔서 감사드리며 필요한 생활용품을 여러분에게 가장 저렴한 가격으로 제공할 수 있기를 기대합니다.

Q: 안내문의 주된 목적은?

(a) 고객에게 할인 품목의 구매 제한을 상기시키기 위해

(b) 고객에게 기한이 정해진 할인의 시작을 알리기 위해

(c) 고객에게 일요 신문을 읽도록 권하기 위해

(d) 경쟁사에서 고객을 끌어오기 위해

해설

고객에게 다음주까지 연장된 '초록 불'이라는 할인 행사를 안내하기 위한 안내문이므로 정답은 (b)이다.

extend 연장하다 | special 특별 할인품 | entitle 권리를 주다 promotional 홍보의 | recognize 인식하다 | initiative 시작

20

Studies performed over a long period of time have shown clear and strong links between the clearing of vegetation and the decline of annual rainfall. This has also led to more extreme periods of drought and increased vulnerability to extreme climatic changes. Vegetation systems offer crucial feedback to mechanisms that buttress water vapor recycling in micro and meso scales. Having a variety of heterogeneous forms of vegetation can ensure an atmospheric condition suitable to precipitation and therefore, increase the resilience of agro-ecosystems to drought and extreme climates. On the other hand, if we continue to develop landscapes with our current state of mind, climate change will only be exasperated and long term hazards will be harder to suppress.

Q: Which of the following claims is made in the passage?

(a) Extreme climates occur predominantly in areas of heavy vegetation.

(b) Changing methods of land development won't slow climate change.

(c) Having diverse vegetation makes the land susceptible to drought.

(d) Vegetation density has a positive correlation to precipitation levels.

번역

장기간에 걸쳐 행해진 연구들이 초목 제거와 연간 강우량의 감소 사이에 분명하고 밀접한 연관을 보여준다. 이것은 또한 더 지독한 가뭄기와 극심한 기후 변화에 대한 취약성 증가로 이어졌다. 식물계는 마이크로 규모와 메소 규모 사이의 물의 증발 순환을 지탱하는 절차에 중요한 피드백을 준다. 다양한 종류의 식물을 기르는 것은 강수에 적합한 대기 조건을 보장해 주고, 그래서 가뭄과 극한 기후에 대한 농업 생태계의 회복력을 증가시킬 수 있다. 반면, 우리가 현재와 같은 마음 상태로 계속 주변을 개발한다면 기후 변화는 격해질 뿐이고 장기적 위험은 더 숨기기가 어려워질 것이다.

Q: 지문에서 언급된 주장은?

(a) 극한 기후는 대부분 식물이 많은 지역에서 발생한다.

(b) 육지개발 방법의 변화가 기후 변화를 늦추지는 못할 것이다.

(c) 다양한 식물을 키우면 지대가 가뭄에 민감해진다.

(d) 식물 밀도는 강수 정도와 긍정적인 상관관계가 있다.

해설

식물과 강수의 관계에 대해 설명하는 글로, 글의 중간에 다양한 종류의 식물을 키우는 것은 강수에 적합한 대기 조건을 보장하고, 그래서 가뭄과 극한 기후에 대한 농업 생태계의 회복을 증가시킬 수 있다고 하였으므로 (d)가 정답이다.

vegetation 식물 | rainfall 강수 | extreme 극심한 | vulnerability 취약성 | buttress 지지하다 | meso 중간 | heterogeneous 여러 종류로 이루어진 | precipitation 강수 | resilience 회복력 | agro-ecosystems 농업 생태계 | exasperate 화나게 하다 | predominantly 대부분

21

After World War II, America began to prosper again and young people took to gathering at their favorite soda shops or diners to hang out with their friends. Even today, teens adopt the image of the music or musicians they listen to and in essence, it defines them. Thus, an integral part of this experience was the jukebox, a freestanding, coin-operated machine that played songs a customer chose by punching in a combination of letters and numbers. Later, an individual wall-mounted jukebox could also be found at every customer's table. The term "jukebox" comes from a Gullah (African Americans living in Southeast North Carolina) word that means "rowdy, disorderly, or wicked," which amply described the hangouts of rambunctious American teens.

Q: What is the best title of the passage?

(a) Hot American Trends Post WWII

(b) The Jukebox, an American Original

(c) The Jukebox Soda Shop Revolution

(d) How the Jukebox Propelled America

번역

2차 대전 후 미국은 다시 번영하기 시작했고 젊은이들은 친구들과 어울리기 위해 좋아하는 음료 가게나 식당에 모여들었다. 오늘날에도 십대들은 그들이 듣는 음악이나 음악가의 이미지를 취하고 본질적으로 그것이 이들을 정의한다. 따라서 이런 경험의 필수적인 부분은 단독으로 세워져 동전으로 작동되는 기계인 주크박스로, 손님이 글자와 숫자의 조합을 눌러 선택한 노래를 재생한다. 후에 벽에 장착된 개개의 주크박스도 모든 손님의 테이블에서 찾아 볼 수 있었다. '주크박스'라는 용어는 걸러(노스캐롤라이나에 사는 아프리카계 미국인들)의 말에서 유래하는데, 미국 십대들의 떠들썩한 어울림을 상세히 묘사한 '소란한, 무질서한, 또는 짓궂은'이라는 의미이다.

Q: 지문에 가장 잘 어울리는 제목은?

(a) 2차 대전 후 미국의 최신 유행

(b) 미국 원조 주크박스

(c) 주크박스 음료 가게 혁명

(d) 어떻게 주크박스가 미국을 앞으로 나아가게 했는가

해설

미국에서 처음 시작된 주크박스의 유래를 설명하고 있으므로 가장 적절한 제목은 (b)이다.

prosper 번영하다 | in essence 본질적으로 | integral 필수적인 | jukebox 주크박스 (술집 등에서 동전을 넣고 음악을 틀게 되어 있는 기계) | combination 조합 | rowdy 소란스러운 | wicked 짓궂은 | amply 상세하게 | rambunctious 떠들썩한

22

Magnetic resonance imaging, or MRI, is a medical technique used in the field of radiology to visualize internal structures in detail. It offers better contrast between the various soft tissues of the body and thus, makes it ideal for imaging the brain, muscles, heart and cancers. In comparison to alternative medical imaging technology like computer tomography or X-rays, MRI does not use potentially harmful ionizing radiation. The first MRI studies performed on humans were published in 1977, long after the first X-rays on humans that were performed in 1895. Today, MRIs can give medical professionals a 3D image, which has revolutionized how certain diseases and injuries are diagnosed and treated.

Q: What is the main idea of the passage?

(a) MRI has a short but successful history in radiology.

(b) The revolutionary influence of MRIs to internal medicine

(c) MRI is an evolutionary step ahead for the medical industry.

(d) MRI offers superior and safer imaging than other methods.

번역

자기 공명 사진, 즉 MRI는 내부의 구조를 세부적으로 시각화하기 위해 방사선학 분야에서 사용되는 의료 기술이다. 이것은 몸속의 여러 가지 부드러운 조직 사이에 더 나은 대조 화면을 제공해서, 뇌와 근육, 심장, 악성 종양을 촬영하는 데 이상적이다. 컴퓨터 단층 촬영이나 X-ray와 같은 대체 의료 촬영 기술과 비교하여 MRI는 잠재적으로 유해한 전리 방사선을 사용하지 않는다. 인간에게 적용된 첫 MRI 연구는 1895년에 인간에게 행해진 첫 X-ray 이후 오랜 시간이 지난 1977년에 출판되었다. 오늘날 MRI는 3D 이미지를 전문 의료인들에게 제공할 수 있고, 이는 특정 질병과 부상을 진단하고 치료하는 방법에 혁신을 가져왔다.

Q: 지문의 주제는?

(a) MRI는 방사선학에서 짧지만 성공적인 역사를 가지고 있다.

(b) 내과에 있어서 MRI의 혁신적인 영향

(c) MRI는 의료 산업을 위한 앞선 진화적인 단계이다.

(d) MRI는 다른 방법보다 더 우수하고 안전한 촬영법을 제공한다.

컴퓨터 단층 촬영이나 엑스레이 같은 다른 촬영법과 비교하여 MRI의 우수함과 안전함을 주로 이야기하고 있으므로 정답은 (d)이다. MRI가 3D 이미지를 제공하여 특정 질병과 부상을 진단하고 치료하는 방법을 혁신시켰다고 하지만 그것이 글의 주요 내용은 아니므로 (b)나 (c)와 혼동하지 않도록 한다.

magnetic resonance imaging 자기 공명 사진 | **radiology** 방사선학 | **contrast** 대조 | **alternative** 대체적인 | **computer tomography** 컴퓨터 단층 촬영 | **ionizing radiation** 전리 방사선 | **revolutionize** 혁신시키다 | **evolutionary** 진화적인

23

Humans have always created or found sources of recreation. One unique example is sandboarding, which bears many similarities to snowboarding. A major hurdle to sandboarding is the fact that it is very difficult to build lifts in the desert. So, boarders must either take an excruciating trek back to the top of the dunes, or catch a lift on a buggy or all-terrain vehicle. Sandboarding has adherents on every continent, obviously with most of them near deserts. The Sahara desert is a favorite destination amongst boarders because it is the oldest desert on the planet, which results in sand grains that are nearly perfect polished spheres. This type of sand allows for the smoothest and fastest rides.

Q: Which of the following is correct about sandboarding?

(a) It is gaining popularity in non-desert regions.

(b) Most participants are from equatorial countries.

(c) It takes more stamina because of the heat.

(d) Lack of lifts present unique challenges.

인간은 항상 오락의 근원을 창조하거나 발견해 왔다. 하나의 독특한 예가 샌드보딩으로 스노우보딩과 비슷한 점이 많다. 샌드보딩의 큰 제약은 사막에 리프트를 짓기 어렵다는 사실이다. 그래서 보드를 타는 사람들은 몹시 괴롭게도 모래 언덕의 꼭대기로 다시 이동하거나 마차 혹은 전지형 만능차를 타야 한다. 샌드보딩은 모든 대륙에 추종자들이 있는데, 대부분 사막 근처에 눈에 띄게 있다. 사하라 사막이 보드를 타는 사람들 사이에 가장 인기 있는 곳으로, 이는 지구상 가장 오래된 사막이고 그 결과 거의 완벽하게 연마된 구형의 모래알을 가지고 있기 때문이다. 이런 종류의 모래에서 가장 부드럽고 빠른 속도로 보드를 탈 수 있다.

Q: 다음 중 샌드보딩에 대해 옳은 것은?

(a) 사막이 아닌 지역에서 인기를 얻고 있다.

(b) 참가자 대부분이 적도 근방의 국가 출신이다.

(c) 열기 때문에 더 많은 지구력을 요한다.

(d) 리프트가 없어서 독특한 어려움이 발생한다.

글의 중반에 사막에는 리프트를 짓기 어려워 보드를 타는 사람들은 모래 언덕 꼭대기에 올라가거나 마차 또는 전지형 만능차를 타야 하는 등의 독특한 어려움을 감수해야 한다고 했으므로 (d)가 정답이다. 모든 대륙에 샌드보딩의 추종자들이 있고 특히 사막 근처에 대부분이 있다고 하므로 (a)와 (b)는 옳지 않고, (c)에 대한 언급은 없다.

bear 가지다 | **similarity** 유사성 | **excruciating** 매우 고통스러운 | **dune** 모래 언덕 | **all-terrain vehicle** 전지형 만능차 | **adherent** 지지자 | **result in** 결과적으로 ~을 야기하다 | **equatorial** 적도의

24

Stretching over 2 kilometers with stacks of merchandise reaching over four stories, the fully automated warehouse of IKEA is a constant buzz of people and machines filling orders and restocking shelves. IKEA was founded in 1943 by a seventeen year old Swede by the name of Ingvar Kamprad. To fill in the rest of the acronym, "E" stands for Elmtaryd, the name of the farm Ingvar grew up in and "A" is for his home parish of Agunnard, Sweden. IKEA can be found in nearly every industrialized nation, many operating 24 hours a day. It's no wonder that in 2006, *Forbes* ranked the founder the sixth wealthiest man in the world with assets amounting over $26 billion.

Q: Which of the following is correct about IKEA?

(a) Its namesake is an acronym for the founder's name and hometown.

(b) State-of-the art mechanization is used in its enormous warehouse.

(c) Stores can be found in both developed and underdeveloped nations.

(d) Store hours differ from country to country with most closing late at night.

물품 더미로 2킬로미터 이상 뻗어 4층 이상의 높이에 닿을 수 있는 완전 자동화된 이케아의 창고는 주문을 접수하고 선반을 다시 채우는 사람들과 기계로 끊임없이 소란하다. 이케아는 1943년에 잉그바르 캄프라드라는 이름의 17세 스웨덴 청년이 설립하였다. 이케아의 머리글자의 나머지를 채워보면, 'E'는 잉그바르가 자란 농장의 이름인 엘름타드드를 나타내고, 'A'는 그의 고향 교구인 스웨덴의 아귀나르드를 나타낸다. 이케아는 거의 모든 선진국에서 볼 수 있고, 많은 이케아 상점이 하루 24시간 가동된다. 2006년 〈포브스〉가 260억 달러 이상의 자산을 가진 이 창립자를 세계에서 가장 부유한 사람 6위로 뽑은 것도 놀랄 일이 아니다.

Q: 다음 중 이케아에 대해 옳은 것은?
(a) 이케아와 동명의 이름은 창립자의 이름과 고향의 머리글자이다.
(b) 최첨단 기계화가 거대한 창고에서 사용된다.
(c) 상점들은 선진국과 후진국 모두에서 볼 수 있다.
(d) 상점의 영업 시간은 나라마다 다른데, 대부분 밤 늦게 문을 닫는다.

해설
첫 문장에서 이케아의 창고가 매우 크고 완전히 자동화되었음을 알 수 있으므로 (b)가 정답이다. 이케아라는 이름은 창립자의 이름, 창립자가 자란 농장의 이름, 고향 교구의 이름 세 가지를 합친 머리글자이고, 선진국에서 매장을 볼 수 있으며, 많은 이케아 매장이 24시간 영업을 한다고 했으므로 나머지는 글의 내용과 다르다.

merchandise 물품 | **warehouse** 창고 | **restock** 다시 채우다
acronym 머리글자 | **namesake** 이름이 같은 것 | **state-of-the art**
최첨단의 | **mechanization** 기계화

25

According to a study done by Professors William A. Luke and Patricia Hughes of St. Cloud State University, charitable giving has for a long time provided substantial amounts of funding for nonprofit organizations. However, this source of income is highly variable. The study theorizes a possible explanation for the variability that lies in the measurement of income. Furthermore, it investigates how the variability of income rises with the level of household income and varies depending on the source of income. By distinguishing types of income, permanent or transitory, the study also identifies factors in decision making by married couples. The study concludes that great variability in the flow of yearly household income has a direct negative effect on the total giving.

Q: Which of the following is correct about charitable giving?
(a) Charitable giving, although a major source of support, is inconsistent.
(b) Charitable giving is greater with married couples with transitory income.
(c) The more variable the income the greater the charitable giving.
(d) Charitable giving has been a small part of nonprofits' yearly budgets.

번역
세인트 클라우드 주립대학교의 윌리엄 A. 루크와 패트리샤 휴스 교수의 연구에 따르면, 자선 기부가 오랫동안 비영리 단체에 상당한 금액의 자금을 제공해 왔다고 한다. 그러나 이 소득의 원천은 변동이 매우 쉽다. 연구는 변동성이 소득의 측정에 대한 가능한 설명을 이론화한다. 뿐만 아니라 소득의 변동성이 어떻게 가구의 소득 수준과 상승하고 소득의

원천에 따라 달라지는지 조사한다. 연구는 소득의 유형을 영구적 또는 일시적으로 구별함으로써 결혼한 부부의 의사 결정 요인도 알아본다. 이 연구는 연간 가구 소득의 흐름에 변동이 클수록 전체 기부에 직접적이며 부정적인 영향이 있다고 결론을 내린다.

Q: 다음 중 자선 기부에 대해 옳은 것은?
(a) 자선 기부는 후원의 주요 원천이지만 일관성이 없다.
(b) 일시적 소득을 가진 결혼한 부부의 자선 기부가 더 많다.
(c) 소득의 변동이 클수록 자선 기부도 더 많다.
(d) 자선 기부는 비영리단체의 연간 예산의 작은 부분을 차지한다.

해설
글의 초반에 자선 기부가 비영리 단체에 상당한 금액의 자금을 제공해 왔으나 이 소득의 원천은 변동이 매우 심하다고 했으므로 (a)가 정답이다. 가구 소득의 흐름에 변동이 클수록 전체 기부에 직접이며 부정적인 영향이 있다고 했으므로 (b)와 (c)는 내용과 일치하지 않는다.

charitable giving 자선 기부 | **substantial** 상당한 | **variable**
변동하기 쉬운 | **source** 원천 | **income** 소득 | **distinguish** 구별하다
transitory 일시적인

26

Japanese teppanyaki-style restaurants have become a huge hit in America. Not to be confused with hibachi which is an open grill fueled by charcoal or gas, teppanyaki cooking is done on a solid griddle-type surface. Teppanyaki restaurants are known to be "where dinner is the show," with chefs being the center of attention, cooking at the table and vociferously sharing jokes. They have to be highly trained in order to juggle razor sharp cooking knives, flip grilled shrimp deftly onto customer's plates and adroitly spin uncooked eggs on a spatula. Besides having a wonderfully cooked meal, customers always leave with full stomachs and smiles on their faces because of an unforgettable experience.

Q: Which of the following is correct about teppanyaki cooking?
(a) Customers enjoy the smoky, flame-grilled steak and seafood.
(b) Chefs are typically Japanese in their soft spoken coyish ways.
(c) Customers are able to interact directly with the chefs.
(d) It is often cooked in conjunction with hibachi-style cooking.

번역
일본의 철판구이 스타일의 레스토랑이 미국에서 큰 인기를 얻고 있다. 석탄이나 가스를 연료로 때는 구멍 뚫린 석쇠인 화로와 달리, 철판구이 요리는 단단한 번철 종류의 표면에서 이루어진다. 철판구이 레스토랑은 '저녁 식사가 볼 거리인 곳'으로 알려져 있는데, 요리사들이 관심

의 중심이 되고 테이블에서 요리를 하며 큰 소리로 농담을 주고 받는다. 그들은 매우 날카로운 식칼로 곡예를 하고, 구운 새우를 솜씨 좋게 고객의 접시로 홱 뒤집어 올리고, 날계란을 주걱 위에서 능숙하게 돌리도록 많은 훈련을 받아야 한다. 훌륭하게 요리된 식사를 하는 것뿐만 아니라 잊을 수 없는 경험 때문에 고객들은 항상 든든한 배와 미소 띤 얼굴로 자리를 뜬다.

Q: 다음 중 철판구이 요리에 대해 옳은 것은?
(a) 고객은 연기가 자욱한 불에 구운 스테이크와 해산물을 즐긴다.
(b) 요리사는 대체로 조용히 수줍어하며 말하는 일본인이다.
(c) 고객은 요리사와 직접적으로 교류할 수 있다.
(d) 종종 화로 스타일의 요리와 함께 조리된다.

해설
요리사들이 테이블에서 요리를 하며 소리 높여 농담을 주고받는다고 했으므로 (c)가 정답이다. 철판구이 요리는 단단한 번철 판에서 요리를 한다고 했으므로 (a)의 내용과 다르고, (d)에 대한 언급은 없다.

griddle 번철 | **vociferously** 소리 높여 | **razor sharp** 매우 날카로운 **juggle** 곡예를 하다 | **flip** 홱 뒤집다 | **deftly** 솜씨 좋게 | **adroitly** 능숙하게 | **spatula** 주걱 | **coyish** 수줍어하는 | **in conjunction with** ~와 함께

27

During medieval times, being brought to the rack was one of the worst sentences a prisoner could face. The rack was often a raised wooden frame with two ropes attached to the top and bottom connected to a roller. Victims' arms were tied to the top ropes and legs to the bottom and a handle connected to the roller, when turned, stretched the limbs. Bones would often dislocate from their joints with a loud crack, the victims' limbs being completely ripped off their bodies in extreme cases. The purpose of the rack was to extract confessions from the victim. Failure to confess meant the torturer had permission to turn the handle more.

Q: Which of the following is correct about the rack?
(a) It was one of the most humane tools of torture.
(b) Its goal was to force admissions of guilt from prisoners.
(c) It was an unpopular interrogation technique of the time.
(d) It left prisoners with nominal physical and mental harm.

번역
중세 시대에는 고문대에 불려오는 것이 죄수들이 직면할 수 있는 최악의 형벌 중 하나였다. 고문대는 종종 높은 나무틀 위에 두 밧줄이 달려 있고 아래는 굴림대와 이어져 있었다. 희생자의 팔은 위의 밧줄에 묶이고 다리는 굴림대에 연결된 아래 부분 손잡이에 묶여서, 돌리면 팔다리를 잡아 늘렸다. 종종 크게 부서지는 소리와 함께 뼈가 관절에서 탈구

되고 심한 경우 희생자의 팔다리가 몸에서 완전히 뜯겨 나가기도 했다. 고문대의 목적은 희생자로부터 자백을 끌어내는 것이었다. 자백을 하지 않는 것은 고문자가 손잡이를 더 돌릴 수 있도록 허락한다는 것을 의미했다.

Q: 다음 중 고문대에 대해 옳은 것은?
(a) 가장 인간적인 고문 도구 중 하나였다.
(b) 죄수들이 죄를 자백하도록 강제하는 것이 목표였다.
(c) 그 당시 평판이 좋지 않은 심문 기술이었다.
(d) 죄수들에게 아주 적은 육체적, 정신적 피해를 남겼다.

해설
고문대의 목적은 희생자로부터 자백을 끌어내는 것이었다고 했으므로 (b)가 정답이다. 고문대의 평판에 대한 언급이 없는데, 잔인한 수법으로 죄수들은 원하지 않았겠지만 고문하는 사람의 입장에서는 효율적인 방법이라고 생각할 수 있으므로 (c)는 정답이 아니다.

medieval 중세의 | **rack** 고문대 | **sentence** 형벌 | **attach** 붙이다 **limb** 팔다리 | **dislocate** 탈구시키다 | **rip off** 떼어내다 | **extract** 끌어내다 | **confession** 자백 | **humane** 인간적인 | **interrogation** 심문 | **nominal** 아주 적은

28

Notice: Beginning next Monday, the Humanities Building will close the top two floors for three weeks in order to remove asbestos. This means students attending art classes on the fourth and fifth floors will be relocated to the basement level. Assigned classrooms will be posted at both the main and rear entrances of the Humanities building. As you should know, asbestos is an older insulating material that has been found to be carcinogenic. Of course all safety precautions will be in place, including, but not limited to, increased ventilation, industrial strength plastic curtains and dust free disposal. Please take note of the changes and we apologize for the inconvenience.

Sincerely,
Jeanette Torres,
University Building and Maintenance

Q: Which of the following is correct about the Humanities Building?
(a) It will be closed for the next three weeks.
(b) Asbestos removal will take under a month.
(c) Art classes will be relocated to the first floor.
(d) Additional fire safety measures will be installed.

번역
공지: 다음 주 월요일을 시작으로 석면 제거를 위해 인문대 건물의 맨 위 두 층을 3주 동안 폐쇄합니다. 따라서 4층과 5층에서 교양 과목 수업을 듣는 학생들은 지하층으로 이전 시킬 것입니다. 배정된 교실은 인문대 건물의 정문과 후문에 공지할 것입니다. 알다시피 석면은 발암성인 것으로 알려진 오래된 단열 자재입니다. 당연히 환기를 증가시키고,

고성능 비닐 막과 먼지 없는 처리를 할 것이며, 여기에 국한하지 않고 모든 안전 예방 조치를 준수할 것입니다. 변동 사항에 주의하길 바라며 불편을 끼쳐 죄송합니다.

대학 건물 유지 보수 담당자, 자넷 토레스

Q: 다음 중 인문대 건물에 대해 옳은 것은?

(a) 앞으로 3주 동안 폐쇄될 것이다.

(b) 석면 제거는 한 달 미만이 걸릴 것이다.

(c) 교양 과목 수업은 1층으로 이전될 것이다.

(d) 추가적인 화재 안전 수단이 설치될 것이다.

해설
석면 제거를 위해 인문대 건물의 4층과 5층이 3주 동안 폐쇄된다고 하므로 정답은 (b)이다.

art 교양 과목 | **asbestos** 석면 | **relocate** 이전하다 | **insulating** 단열의 | **carcinogenic** 발암성의 | **precaution** 예방 조치 | **ventilation** 환기 | **disposal** 처리 | **take note of** ~에 주의하다

29

Who would have thought that America's longest running sitcom would be a satirical cartoon? *The Simpsons* debuted on December 17, 1989 after having a few shorts run on the *Tracy Ullman Show* on Fox and hasn't stopped poking fun at modern day society. The creator, Matt Groening, based the characters of Homer, Marge, Bart, Lisa and Maggie on his real-life parents and family. *The Simpsons* is aired in over 60 countries worldwide and has had a notable impact on real life as evidenced in the many universities that teach classes based on the cartoon. As a matter of fact, at the University of California, Berkeley, *The Simpsons* has made it onto the syllabus of one of their philosophy classes.

Q: Which of the following is correct about *The Simpsons*?

(a) It started as a cameo filler to another Fox show.

(b) It is a sardonic lampoon of the working elite.

(c) It has garnered a limited cult following in the U.S.

(d) It has attracted the attention of academics worldwide.

번역
미국의 가장 오래 방영된 시트콤이 풍자 만화가 될 것이라고 누가 생각이나 했겠는가? 〈심슨 가족〉은 폭스사의 〈트레이시 울먼 쇼〉에 단편 몇 편이 방영된 후 1989년 12월 17일 시작했고, 그 후 끊임없이 현대 사회를 조롱하고 있다. 제작자인 맷 그레이닝은 호머, 마지, 바트, 리사, 매기의 캐릭터를 그의 실제 부모님과 가족에서 따왔다. 〈심슨 가족〉은 세계적으로 60여 개 국가에서 방송되고, 만화에 기초한 수업을 가르치는 많은 대학에서 증명되었듯이 실생활에 두드러진 영향을 끼친 만화이다. 사실은 캘리포니아 버클리대에서 〈심슨 가족〉이 철학 수업 중 하

나의 강의 계획서에 있다.

Q: 다음 중 〈심슨 가족〉에 대해 옳은 것은?

(a) 폭스사의 다른 쇼의 짧은 채우기용 단편 영화로 시작했다.

(b) 일하는 엘리트에 대한 냉소적인 풍자이다.

(c) 미국에서 제한적인 숭배 집단을 얻었다.

(d) 전 세계적으로 학술적 주목을 받았다.

해설
〈심슨 가족〉은 데뷔 전 폭스사의 〈트레이시 울먼 쇼〉에 단편으로 방영되었다고 하므로 (a)와 일치한다. 현대 사회를 조롱하며, 60여개 국가에서 방송되고 있으므로 (b)와 (c)는 옳지 않다.

satirical 풍자적인 | **short** 단편 영화 | **poke fun at** ~을 조롱하다 | **notable** 두드러진 | **syllabus** 강의 계획서 | **filler** 〈시간을 채우기 위한〉 단편 영화 | **sardonic** 냉소적인 | **lampoon** 풍자 | **garner** 얻다 | **cult** 숭배자 집단

30

Racing down the fresh powder covered hills, curving like a pro, you're ready to hit that jump but all of a sudden, your goggles fog up! CRASH! This is a skier or snowboarder's worst nightmare, but it doesn't have to be for you. Introducing Cat's Eyes X-treme lens cleaner with their patented anti-fog veneer. With a clean, non-abrasive cloth, gently rub a pea-size amount on your goggles for a cleaner and fog-free skiing and snowboarding experience. No more do you have to worry about losing your sight as you fly down your favorite hill!

Q: Which of the following is correct about Cat's Eyes X-treme?

(a) It improves a winter sports enthusiast's proficiency.

(b) It can make you stand out amongst all others.

(c) It requires a bit of work to apply but is worth it.

(d) It leaves a revolutionary anti-fog covering on goggles.

번역
신선한 가루로 뒤덮인 언덕을 달려 내려오며 프로처럼 곡선을 그려 점프를 할 준비가 되어 있는데 고글에 김이 서린다! 쿵! 이것은 스키나 스노보드를 타는 사람들의 최악의 악몽이지만 여러분은 그럴 필요는 없습니다. 특허 받은 김 서림 방지 겉면이 있는 캣츠 아이 익스트림 렌즈 클리너를 소개합니다. 더 깨끗하고 김이 서리지 않는 스키와 스노보드 경험을 위해 깨끗하고 마멸을 일으키지 않는 천으로 고글에 콩알 만한 크기의 양으로 부드럽게 문지르세요. 가장 좋아하는 언덕을 날아 내려가며 시야를 잃을까 봐 더 이상 걱정할 필요가 없습니다.

Q: 다음 중 캣츠 아이 익스트림에 대해 옳은 것은?

(a) 열렬한 겨울 스포츠 지지자들의 능숙도를 향상시킨다.

(b) 사람들 사이에서 당신을 돋보이게 할 수 있다.

(c) 쓰는 데 약간의 노력이 필요하지만 그럴 가치가 있다.

(d) 고글에 혁신적인 김 서림 방지 막을 남긴다.

캣츠 아이 익스트림이라는 제품이 스노우보다가 쓰는 고글에 김 방지 표면을 만드는 특허를 받은 렌즈 클리너라고 하므로 (d)가 정답이다.

fog up 김이 서리다 | **patented** 특허 받은 | **anti-fog** 김 서림 방지
veneer 베니어판(얇게 켠 널빤지) | **non-abrasive** 마멸을 일으키지 않는
enthusiast 열렬한 지지자 | **proficiency** 능숙 | **stand out** 눈에 띄다
revolutionary 혁신적인

31

With the increase in working hours, more consideration has been put into making sure that employees have both the right equipment and environment. This concern has led to the development of ergonomics, the study of designs that best fit the human body. Spending hours in front of a computer monitor and typing repetitively can lead to repetitive stress disorders. Ergonomics in the workplace involves making sure the computer monitor is at eye level, to prevent neck strain, placing an ergonomic keyboard at the right level, and making sure the office chair is straight and at the right height. With these safeguards in place, the worker will be more productive and will be less susceptible to mental and physical strain.

Q: Which of the following is correct about ergonomics?
(a) It can reduce employee retention if used properly.
(b) It is a standard that all employees strive to achieve.
(c) It concentrates on human interactions with equipment.
(d) It hasn't attracted many followers and practitioners.

번역

노동 시간이 길어지면서 직원들이 알맞은 장비와 환경 모두를 확실히 갖도록 하기 위해 신중한 고려를 해왔다. 이런 고민이 인체에 꼭 맞는 디자인에 대한 연구인 인체 공학의 발달을 가져왔다. 컴퓨터 화면 앞에서 몇 시간을 보내는 것과 반복적으로 타이핑하는 것은 반복 스트레스 장애를 가져올 수 있다. 직장에서의 인체 공학이란 목의 부담을 방지하기 위해 컴퓨터 화면이 반드시 눈높이에 있도록 하고, 인체 공학적 자판을 알맞은 위치에 놓고, 사무실 의자는 반드시 똑바로 알맞은 높이에 있도록 하는 것이다. 이런 안전장치들을 제대로 배치함으로써 일하는 사람은 좀 더 생산적이 될 것이며, 정신적·육체적 압박에 덜 예민할 것이다.

Q: 다음 중 인체 공학에 대해 옳은 것은?
(a) 적절히 사용되면 직원 유지비를 줄일 수 있다.
(b) 모든 직원이 성취하기 위해 애써야 하는 기준이다.
(c) 인간과 장비의 상호작용에 집중한다.
(d) 추종자와 참여자를 많이 끌어들이지 못했다.

해설

인체 공학은 인간의 신체에 가장 적합하고 편안한 디자인에 대한 연구이며, 직장에서 직원과 주변 물건과의 관계라는 예를 들고 있다. 따라서 (c)가 정답이다.

make sure 반드시 ~하다 | **repetitively** 반복적으로 | **disorder** 장애
ergonomics 인체 공학 | **strain** 부담 | **safeguard** 안전장치
susceptible 예민한 | **retention** 유지비 | **strive** 애쓰다 | **practitioner** 실천하는 사람

32

The Very Large Array, or VLA, is a set of 27 radio antennae that are 10 stories high with a 25 meter diameter parabola dish. The individual antennae are arranged in a Y pattern and are moved four times in a 16 month period. The reason behind the routine relocation of the antennae is to change the resolution of the images captured, kind of like the zoom on your camera. VLA is highly valued because unlike conventional telescopes, radio waves can penetrate gases and clouds that can block the view of a telescope. Contrary to popular belief originating from showing VLA in movies such as *Contact* and *Independence Day*, VLA is not used to search for extra-terrestrials.

Q: Which of the following is correct about the passage?
(a) VLA is superior to telescope observatories.
(b) VLA has inspired many movies about aliens.
(c) VLA is the largest set of stationary radio antennae.
(d) VLA is like a camera and can quickly zoom in and out.

번역

전파 망원경망, 즉 VLA는 27개의 라디오 안테나 세트로, 10층 건물 높이에 직경 25미터 포물선형 접시가 달려 있다. 개개의 안테나는 Y자 형태로 배열되었고 16개월 동안 4번 움직인다. 이 정기적인 안테나 이동은 카메라의 줌 렌즈처럼 포착한 이미지의 해상도를 바꾸기 위해서다. VLA는 평범한 망원경과 달리 망원경의 시야를 방해하는 가스와 구름을 전파가 뚫고 지나갈 수 있기 때문에 그 가치가 매우 높다. 〈콘택트〉와 〈인디펜던스 데이〉와 같은 영화에서 VLA가 등장해서 알고 있는 대중적인 생각과 달리 VLA는 외계인을 찾는 데는 사용되지 않는다.

Q: 다음 중 옳은 것은?
(a) VLA는 망원경 전망대보다 더 우수하다.
(b) VLA는 외계인에 대한 여러 영화에 영감을 주었다.
(c) VLA는 움직이지 않는 가장 큰 라디오 안테나 세트이다.
(d) VLA는 카메라와 같아 줌 렌즈를 재빨리 확대·축소할 수 있다.

해설

VLA는 평범한 망원경과 달리 망원경의 시야를 막는 가스와 구름을 전파가 뚫고 지나갈 수 있기 때문에 가치가 매우 높다고 했으므로 (a)가 정답이다. VLA는 이미지의 해상도를 바꾸기 위해 16개월에 4번 움직인다고 했으므로 (c)와 (d)는 틀리다. 외계인에 대한 영화에 등장은 했지만, 영화에 영감을 주었는지는 알 수 없으므로 (b)도 옳지 않다.

diameter 직경 | parabola 포물선 | resolution 해상도
conventional 진부한 | radio wave 전파 | penetrate 침투하다
observatory 전망대 | stationary 움직이지 않는

Lent 사순절 | penitential 참회의 | discipline 훈련 | devotion 헌신
Mardi Gras 참회 화요일 | hurrah 만찬 | transpire 일어나다
indulgence 마음대로 하게 함 | reveler 신난 사람 | descend upon
갑자기 덮치다 | devotee (광신적) 신자 | debauchery 방탕

33

Lent is the Catholic penitential time leading up to Easter and is a period marked with sacrifice and self-discipline to show your devotion to God. Mardi Gras, on the other hand, is a last hurrah before the solemn Lenten season, which begins on Ash Wednesday. French for "Fat Tuesday," Mardi Gras is celebrated in New Orleans, Louisiana, and transpires during the same time as other Carnival festivals like in Rio de Janeiro, Brazil. This period is marked by an over-indulgence of fatty and rich foods, alcohol and dancing. Revelers tend to dress up in exotic costumes and are known to party for many nights on end.

Q: What can be inferred from the passage?
(a) Mardi Gras pales in size and length compared to Carnival in Brazil.
(b) New Orleans is a peaceful city until Mardi Gras fans descend upon it.
(c) **Mardi Gras allows devotees a last chance for debauchery before Lent.**
(d) Costumes worn during Mardi Gras are symbolic of Christ's sacrifice.

번역

사순절은 부활절까지 이르는 천주교에서 참회의 시간이고 신에 대한 헌신을 보여주기 위해 희생과 자기 수련을 나타내는 기간이다. 반면 참회 화요일은 재의 수요일에 시작하는 엄숙한 사순절 기간 전의 마지막 만찬이다. 프랑스어로 '살찐 화요일'인 참회 화요일은 루이지애나의 뉴올리언즈에서 기념되고 동시에 브라질의 리우데자네이루에서도 다른 카니발 축제로 일어난다. 이 기간에는 기름지고 영양가가 높은 음식을 마음껏 먹고, 술을 많이 마시며 춤을 추면서 기념한다. 신난 사람들은 이국적인 복장으로 차려입고 쉬지 않고 며칠 밤 동안 파티를 하는 것으로 알려져 있다.

Q: 지문을 통해 유추할 수 있는 것은?
(a) 참회 화요일은 브라질의 카니발에 비하면 규모나 기간에 있어 약하다.
(b) 참회 화요일 추종자들이 급습할 때까지 뉴올리언즈는 평화로운 도시이다.
(c) **참회 화요일은 열성 신자들에게 사순절 전 마지막 방탕의 기회를 준다.**
(d) 참회 화요일 동안 입는 복장은 예수의 희생을 상징한다.

해설

참회 화요일은 엄숙한 사순절 전의 마지막 만찬으로, 기름지며 영양이 많은 음식과 술을 마음껏 먹고 춤을 추면서 축하한다고 하므로 (c)를 유추할 수 있다.

34

Since the advent of the automobile, over 20 million fatalities have been recorded. Even as late as the 1950's, car manufacturers stood by the claim that it was impossible to make vehicles any safer than they were because the physical forces of a crash were too great to overcome. At the same time, after testing with cadavers, the first crash test dummy was unveiled. A crash test dummy is a full-scale anthropomorphic test device (ATD) that resembles the human body in weight, proportions, and movement. Today's dummies are equipped with sensitive high-tech sensors that provide vital crash test data. Thanks to these silent heroes, humans have the greatest chances of surviving fatal accidents than they have ever had.

Q: What can be inferred from the passage?
(a) **Cadavers provided important feedback on automobile crashes.**
(b) Auto manufacturers in the 50's just worried about making money.
(c) Crash test dummies aren't acknowledged enough for their contributions.
(d) Understanding of physics in the 50's was much less than today.

번역

자동차의 출현 이래 2천만 명 이상의 사망자가 기록되었다. 1950년대에조차 자동차 제조업자들은 자동차 충돌의 물리적 힘은 이겨내기에는 너무 강해서 그 당시의 자동차들보다 더 안전하게 만드는 것은 불가능하다고 주장하는 편이었다. 동시에 해부용 시체를 이용해 시험한 후 최초의 시험용 인체 모형이 공개되었다. 충돌 시험용 인체 모형은 무게 비율과 움직임에 있어 인체와 비슷한 실물 크기로 의인화한 시험용 장치이다. 오늘날의 인체 모형은 생명에 관한 충돌 시험 자료를 제공하는 민감한 첨단 기술 감지기를 갖추었다. 이 조용한 영웅 덕에 인간은 어느 때보다 치명적인 사고에서도 살아남을 가장 높은 가능성을 가지고 있다.

Q: 지문을 통해 유추할 수 있는 것은?
(a) **해부용 시체는 자동차 충돌에 관한 중요한 피드백을 제공했다.**
(b) 50년대의 자동차 제조업체들은 그저 돈을 버는 것에 대해서만 걱정했다.
(c) 충돌 시험용 인체 모형은 기여하는 바에 대해 충분한 인정을 받지 못한다.
(d) 50년대에는 물리학에 대한 이해가 오늘날보다 훨씬 적었다.

해설

해부용 시체를 이용한 시험 뒤 최초의 시험용 인체 모형이 나왔다고 하므로 시체를 이용한 시험이 중요한 자료를 제공했을 것이라는 것을 유추할 수 있다. 따라서 (a)가 정답이다. (b)는 지나친 확대 해석이고, 마지막 문장을 통해 인체 모형이 공헌한 점이 인정됨을 알 수 있으므로 (c)는 옳지 않다.

advent 출현 | **fatality** 사망자 | **cadaver** 해부용 시체 | **dummy** 인체 모형 | **unveil** 공개하다 | **full-scale** 실물 크기의 **anthropomorphic** 의인화된 | **proportion** 비율 | **vital** 생명에 관한

35

The best horror films always involve a demonic spirit possessing a poor, innocent victim. The possessed is transformed into the evil spirit and acts violently, speaking in tongues and scaring those around them. Every culture around the world has a similar tale of spirit possession as well as a cure for the possessed. Often referred to as an exorcism, a priest or spiritual healer uses prayers, religious symbols, gestures, etc. to remove the haunting spirit from the possessed body. The possessed is not considered evil themselves, rather just a hapless victim. Therefore, the exorcism in itself is considered a cure rather than a punishment. Exorcism rites can be found in Judaism, Christianity and Islam as well as in Buddhism.

Q: What can be inferred from the passage?

(a) The major religions practice the same rituals to cure the possessed.

(b) Evil spirits prey on the weak of mind and feeble of heart.

(c) Exorcisms have been practiced for hundreds of years.

(d) Spiritual healers have supernatural powers to expunge evil spirits.

번역

최고의 공포 영화에는 항상 불쌍하고 죄 없는 희생자를 홀리는 악령이 있다. 악령에 홀린 사람들은 사악한 영혼으로 바뀌고, 폭력적으로 행동하고 방언을 하며 주변 사람들을 위협한다. 세계의 모든 문화에는 악령에 홀린 사람들의 치료뿐만 아니라 영혼 소유에 관한 비슷한 이야기가 있다. 흔히 악령 쫓기 의식으로 불리는데, 목사나 영적 치료자가 악령에 홀린 사람의 몸에 늘 따라다니는 영혼을 떼기 위해 기도나 종교적 상징물, 몸짓 등을 이용한다. 홀린 사람 자체는 악하다고 여겨지지 않고, 오히려 불운한 피해자로 여겨진다. 그래서 악령 쫓기 의식 그 자체가 처벌이라기보다는 치료로 여겨진다. 악령 쫓기 의식은 불교뿐만 아니라 유대교, 기독교, 이슬람교에서도 볼 수 있다.

Q: 지문을 통해 유추할 수 있는 것은?

(a) 주요 종교들은 악령에 홀린 이들을 치료하기 위해 동일한 의식을 행한다.

(b) 악령은 정신이 약하고 마음이 약한 자들을 먹이로 삼는다.

(c) 악령 쫓기 의식은 수백 년간 행해지고 있다.

(d) 영적 치료자는 악령을 없애는 초자연적 힘을 가지고 있다.

해설

세계의 모든 문화에 영혼 소유와 홀린 사람들의 치료에 관한 비슷한 이야기가 있고, 악령을 쫓는 의식은 유대교, 기독교, 이슬람교와 불교에서도 발견된다고 했으므로 (c)를 유추할 수 있다. 악령을 쫓는 의식이 주요 종교에서 발견되기는 하지만 모두 같은 의식 절차를 행한다고는 할 수 없으므로 (a)는 적절하지 않다.

demonic 악마의 | **spirit** 정신, 영혼 | **possess** 홀리다 | **speak in tongues** 방언을 하다 | **rite** 의식 | **exorcism** 악령 쫓기 의식 **hapless** 불운한 | **ritual** 의식 | **feeble** 허약한 | **expunge** 지우다

36

Paul Bunyan and his companion Babe the Blue Ox are mythical figures whose origins are still in dispute. Some claim the myths originated with French Canadians who spun the yarns during their rebellion against the Queen of England. Others claim the legends were a marketing ploy by the lumber industry. In the folklores, Paul Bunyan is a giant of a lumberjack and Babe the Blue Ox is equally as large. The stories give credit to Paul Bunyan for creating the Grand Canyon by dragging his axe behind him, digging the Great Lakes as a watering hole for Babe, and forming Mount Hood by piling rocks on top of his campfire to extinguish it. Now that's a tall tale!

Q: What can be inferred from the passage?

(a) Paul Bunyan is a favorite tale told in the southern regions of America.

(b) Paul Bunyan was a myth conceived by lumberjacks in North America.

(c) Both Americans and Canadians stack claims to the invention of Paul Bunyan.

(d) Babe the Blue Ox is responsible for the creation of many geological sites.

번역

폴 버니언과 그의 친구 파란 황소 베이브는 그 유래가 아직도 논쟁 중인 신화 속 인물들이다. 어떤 이들은 이 신화가 영국 여왕에 대한 반란 중에 프랑스계 캐나다인이 늘어놓은 꾸며낸 이야기에서 유래한다고 주장한다. 다른 이들은 이 전설이 벌목업계의 홍보 술책이라고 주장한다. 민간 전승에 의하면 폴 버니언은 거인 나무꾼이고 파란 황소 베이브도 그만큼 크다. 이야기들은 폴 버니언이 도끼를 질질 끌고 가서 그랜드 캐니언을 만들고, 베이브를 위한 물구덩이로 오대호를 파고 모닥불을 끄기 위해 위에 돌을 쌓아 후드산을 만들어 낸 것으로 나온다. 지금은 믿기 어려운 이야기이다!

Q: 지문을 통해 유추할 수 있는 것은?

(a) 폴 버니언은 아메리카 대륙의 남쪽 지역서 가장 인기 있는 이야기이다.

(b) 폴 버니언은 북미의 나무꾼들이 상상한 신화적 인물이다.
(c) 미국인과 캐나다인 모두 폴 버니언을 고안했다고 주장한다.
(d) 파란색 황소는 많은 지질학적 장소의 형성에 일조를 했다.

첫 문장에서 그 이야기의 기원이 아직도 논쟁 중이라고 하며, 폴 버니언 신화를 캐나다인이 만들었다는 얘기도 있고 이 거인 나무꾼이 미국의 유명한 곳을 만들었다는 주장도 있는 것으로 보아 (c)가 정답이다.

companion 친구 | **yarn** 꾸며낸 이야기 | **rebellion** 반란 | **ploy** 술책
folklore 민간 전승 | **lumberjack** 나무꾼 | **give credit to** ~을 믿다
extinguish 끄다 | **tall tale** 믿기 힘든 이야기 | **conceive** 상상하다
geological 지질학적인

37

To Caroline Schoenberg, HR Director,

I want to thank you again for the opportunity to interview with your firm. Working for Brandon& Partners has been a goal of mine since I entered the field of intellectual property rights. Over my eight year career representing inventors across our state I have established a fantastic network of inventors. I have won over 16 cases for my clients, the most notable being Jesper Hassan, the inventor of America's most popular anti-snoring treatment, Snore-no-more facemask. I know that I can be a highly valuable asset to Brandon&Partners. Thank you again for your time and I look forward to hearing from you soon.

Sincerely yours,

Jeff Johnson

Q: What can be inferred from the passage?
(a) Jeff can bring many clients to Brandon&Partners.
(b) Caroline is an intellectual property rights lawyer.
(c) Brandon&Partners is the largest patent law firm.
(d) Jeff has more wins than losses for his clients.

인사부장 캐롤라인 쇤버그 씨께

귀사에 면접을 볼 기회를 주셔서 다시 한번 감사 드리고 싶습니다. 지적 소유권 분야에 발을 들인 후 브랜든앤파트너스에서 일하는 것이 저의 목표였습니다. 주 전체에 걸쳐 발명가들을 대표한 8년의 경력을 통해 발명가들과 좋은 관계를 형성했습니다. 제 고객들을 위해 16건 이상 승소하였고, 가장 주목할 만한 것은 미국의 가장 인기 있는 코골이 방지책인 스노어노모어 마스크 발명가 제스퍼 하산입니다. 제가 브랜든앤파트너스에 매우 소중한 자산이 될 것을 확신합니다. 시간을 내 주셔서 다시 한번 감사 드리며 곧 연락 주시기를 기대합니다.

제프 존슨

Q: 지문을 통해 유추할 수 있는 것은?
(a) 제프는 브랜든앤파트너스에 많은 고객을 데려올 수 있다.
(b) 캐롤라인은 지적 재산권 변호사이다.

(c) 브랜든앤파트너스는 가장 큰 특허 법률 회사이다.
(d) 제프는 고객을 위한 승소가 패소보다 더 많다.

브랜든앤파트너스로 이직을 원하는 제프 존슨이 면접 후 쓴 편지이다. 8년의 경력을 통해 발명가들과 좋은 관계를 형성했다는 부분에서 그가 브랜든앤파트너스에서 일하게 되면 그 고객들을 데려올 수 있을 것이라는 것을 유추할 수 있으므로 (a)가 정답이다.

HR 인사부 (Human Resources) | **intellectual property rights**
지적 재산권 | **network** 관계 | **notable** 주목할 만한 | **snore** 코를 골다
asset 자산 | **patent** 특허

38

Tattoos have become a popular fashion trend these days with over 25% of Americans sporting at least one. **(a) For a long time Westerners thought only sailors and criminals got tattoos.** (b)However, evidence of tattooing dates back about 5000 B.C. as evidenced in the discovery of Ötzi the iceman who was found in the Ötz valley in the Alps and had an estimated 57 carbon tattoos. (c) Tattooing has also been found on Egyptian mummies dating around the end of the second millennium B.C. and Japanese tattooing is believed to date nearly 10,000 years ago. (d) Western tattooing comes from Polynesia and when 18th century explorers were first exposed to tattoos, it became instantly popular with the sailors.

문신은 미국인의 25% 이상이 최소한 하나는 자랑삼아 보이는 대중적인 패션 유행이 되었다. **(a) 오랫동안 서양인들은 오직 선원이나 범죄자들만이 문신을 한다고 생각했다.** (b) 그러나 알프스의 외츠 계곡에서 발견돼 약 57개의 탄소 문신을 가진 외치 얼음 인간의 발견에서 증명됐다시피 문신의 증거는 기원전 5000년경으로 거슬러 올라간다. (c) 기원전 2000년 말 이집트의 미라에서도 문신이 발견되었고 일본의 문신은 약 1만년 전으로 여겨진다. (d) 서양 문신은 폴리네시아에서 유래해 18세기 탐험가들이 처음 문신을 접했을 때 선원들 사이에 바로 인기를 얻었다.

문신의 역사와 유래에 대한 글로, 첫 문장에서 미국인의 상당수가 자랑삼아 보이는 대중적인 유행이 되었다는 문장과 (a)는 어울리지 않는다.

sport 자랑삼아 보이다 | **date back** 〈시간을〉 거슬러 올라가다
expose 접하게 하다 | **instantly** 즉시

39

One of history's first incredibly dramatic the footage came on May 6, 1937, when the German passenger airship LZ 129 Hindenburg was engulfed in flames over Lakehurst, New Jersey. (a) The Hindenburg was a hydrogen-filled airship with 97 crew and passengers. (b) Its initial landing was delayed because of thunderstorms but was cleared later that day. **(c) During the time the Hindenburg was waiting to land, it made its way towards Manhattan, which caused quite the stir as people scrambled to get a glimpse of the floating silver ship.** (d) At approximately 7:25 p.m., the Hindenburg suddenly went up in flames, which prompted Herbert Morrison to exclaim the historical words, "Oh the humanity!" during his WLS radio broadcast.

번역

역사상 최초의 믿을 수 없을 정도로 극적인 장면 하나는 1937년 5월 6일 독일 여객 비행선 LZ 129 힌덴버그가 뉴저지의 레이크허스트 상공에서 불길에 휩싸인 사건이었다. (a) 힌덴버그는 수소로 채워진 비행선으로, 97명의 승무원과 승객을 태우고 있었다. (b) 비행선의 첫 착륙이 뇌우로 인해 지연되었지만 그날 나중에 허가를 받았다. (c) 힌덴버그가 착륙하기 위해 기다리는 동안 맨해튼을 향하고 있었는데, 사람들이 이 떠다니는 은색 배를 보기 위해 서로 다투자 상당한 혼란을 일으켰다. (d) 오후 약 7시 25분에 힌덴버그는 갑자기 불길에 타올랐고, 이로 인해 WLS 라디오 방송 중에 허버트 모리슨은 '오 인류여'라는 역사적인 말을 외쳤다.

해설

힌덴버그라는 비행선이 화염에 휩싸인 사고에 대한 글로, 상공에서 불이 난 사건의 경위에 대해 서술하고 있으며, (c)는 사건에서 가장 벗어난 이야기이다.

incredibly 믿을 수 없을 정도로 | **footage** 장면 | **engulf** 완전히 뒤덮다 | **hydrogen** 수소 | **stir** 혼란 | **go up in flames** 타오르다 | **exclaim** 외치다

40

Life for the blind was forever changed for the better after a blind Frenchman by the name of Louis Braille invented the Braille system for reading and writing. (a) Braille characters, or cells, are constructed of a six dot position system, arranged in a rectangle with two columns containing three raised dots each. **(b) Not everyone was excited for the innovation Braille had created, but it still became the standard for the blind.** (c) Braille came from a method of communication created for Napoleon who demanded a silent way for soldiers to communicate on the field without light. (d) Although this system was originally rejected because of its complexity, the blind around the world hail it as a godsend.

번역

루이 브라유라는 이름의 프랑스 맹인이 읽기와 쓰기를 위한 브라유 체계를 개발한 이후 맹인의 인생이 보다 나은 쪽으로 영원히 바뀌었다. (a) 브라유 문자 또는 구멍은 6개의 점을 위치시키는 체계로 구성되는데, 각각 3개의 볼록 점이 있는 세로줄 2개가 직사각형으로 배열된다. **(b) 모든 사람들이 브라유가 만든 제도에 열광적이지는 않았지만 여전히 맹인들을 위한 표준이 되었다.** (c) 브라유 점자는 병사들이 전장에서 빛 없이 의사소통을 할 수 있는 소리 없는 방식을 원했던 나폴레옹을 위해 만들어진 의사소통법에서 유래했다. (d) 이 체계는 그 복잡함 때문에 처음에는 받아들여지지 않았지만 전 세계의 맹인들은 하나님이 주신 선물이라고 높이 평가한다.

해설

브라유 점자를 소개하며 그 유래와 의의를 이야기하고 있는데, (b)는 결론으로 볼 수 있는 문장으로, 유래를 설명하고 있는 글의 중간에서는 어색하다.

character 문자 | **construct** 구성하다 | **contain** 포함하다 | **innovation** 제도 | **complexity** 복잡성 | **hail** 칭찬하다 | **godsend** 하나님이 주신 선물

Part I

1 (b)	**2** (d)	**3** (a)	**4** (c)	**5** (d)
6 (b)	**7** (c)	**8** (b)	**9** (a)	**10** (c)
11 (b)	**12** (d)	**13** (a)	**14** (c)	**15** (c)
16 (a)				

Part II

17 (d)	**18** (b)	**19** (d)	**20** (c)	**21** (a)
22 (c)	**23** (b)	**24** (b)	**25** (a)	**26** (b)
27 (c)	**28** (c)	**29** (d)	**30** (b)	**31** (c)
32 (a)	**33** (b)	**34** (a)	**35** (c)	**36** (a)
37 (b)				

Part III

38 (d)	**39** (a)	**40** (c)

우아한 자태로 물 위로 떠오르는 것으로 알려져 있다. 혹등고래의 가장 놀라운 행동 중 하나는 매년 하와이로 이주하는 것이다. 혹등고래는 세 개 지역에서 이동하는데 일부는 멕시코의 바자에서, 일부는 일본 근처에서, 약 60%가는 알래스카에서부터 3,500마일을 집단 이주한다. 하와이는 어린 새끼에게 안전한 피난처가 되기 때문에 혹등고래는 하와이로 이동한다. 대부분은 작은 물고기 떼와 크릴 새우가 풍부한 물에서 먹고 살기 위해 알래스카로 돌아가는데, 하와이의 바다에는 이런 작은 생물체들이 없다.

(a) 할리우드에서 막 나온 거대한 괴물을 상상한다
(b) 보통 곡예를 하는 괴물이 떠오르지는 않는다
(c) 거대한 바다 동물에 대해 생각할지도 모른다
(d) 이런 목록에 맞는 현존 생물체가 없다

해설

Yet으로 연결된 두 번째 문장에서 혹등고래가 피겨 스케이팅 선수가 부러워할 정도의 우아한 자태로 물 위로 떠오르는 것으로 알려져 있다고 하므로 이와 상대적인 내용인 (b)가 빈칸에 가장 적절하다.

humpback whale 혹등고래 | **breach** 〈고래가〉 물 위로 떠오르다
green with envy 몹시 샘을 내는 | **migrate** 이동하다 | **haven** 피난처
school 떼 | **krill** 크릴 새우 | **envision** 상상하다 | **acrobatic** 곡예의
leviathan 거대한 바다짐승 | **bill** 목록

1

When you think of a 12-16 meter long mammal weighing approximately 36,000 kilograms, _____. Yet, this describes the humpback whale, which is known to breach the water in a graceful display that would make any figure skater green with envy. One of the most amazing behaviors of the humpback whale is its yearly migration to Hawaii. Humpbacks migrate from three areas; some from Baja, Mexico, others from near Japan, and about 60 percent make the 3,500 mile trek from Alaska. Humpbacks migrate to Hawaii because it provides a safe haven for the young pups. The majority return to Alaska to feed on the small fish schools and krill rich waters, whereas Hawaii's waters are free of these smaller organisms.

(a) you envision a giant monster straight out of Hollywood
(b) an acrobatic leviathan usually doesn't come to mind
(c) you probably are thinking about an enormous sea animal
(d) there is no present day organism that can fit this bill

번역

12~16미터 길이에 약 36,000킬로그램의 무게가 나가는 포유류를 상상할 때 보통 곡예를 하는 괴물이 떠오르지는 않는다. 그러나 이것은 혹등고래를 묘사하는데 이는 피겨 스케이팅 선수가 부러워할 정도의

2

Dear Mr. McGraw,

As per our discussion regarding the new marketing initiative, _____ the mailings by next month. Our target market was determined by zip codes of the upper 10 percent income earning households. These are "at risk" clients because they have no field agents or planners and are thus considered home office accounts. The cost of this campaign is a little over the budget for this fiscal year, but we have reserve funds which will compensate for next year. Please take the time to review the numbers and the marketing materials to make sure they are in compliance. Please email me with any questions, thank you again for your time!

Sincerely,
Aaron Flanagan, Marketing and Research

(a) our accounting department should expect
(b) this firm's biggest competitor will distribute
(c) television and radio stations will send
(d) we need your final approval to launch

번역

맥그로우 씨께

새로운 마케팅 계획에 대한 양사간 논의와 관련해서 다음 달까지 진행될 우편물 발송을 시작하기 위해서 귀사의 최종 승인이 필요합니다. 당사의 표적 시장은 수입 상위 10%인 가정이며, 해당 주소지

로 우편물 발송이 결정되었습니다. 그들에게는 현장 대리점이나 계획 플래너가 없기 때문에 그들은 손실 위험이 있는 고객이며, 따라서 본사 고객으로 간주됩니다. 이번 캠페인 비용은 올해 회계 연도의 예산을 약간 상회하지만, 당사는 내년에 충당할 수 있는 유보 자금이 있습니다. 재정에 관한 자료와 마케팅 자료가 맞는지 시간을 내서 검토해 주십시오. 질문이 있으시면 제게 이메일을 보내 주세요. 시간을 내주셔서 다시 한번 감사 드립니다.

마케팅 및 조사 담당, 애런 플래내건

(a) 당사의 경리부가 기대하다
(b) 당사의 최대 경쟁사가 배포하다
(c) TV 및 라디오 방송국이 발송하려 하다
(d) 시작하기 위해서 귀사의 최종 승인이 필요하다

회사가 고객에게 메일을 보내는 마케팅 활동을 위해서 사업 파트너에게 재정 자료와 마케팅 자료를 보내면서 검토를 요청하는 내용이다. 빈칸은 이와 관련해서 서신을 보내는 목적이 무엇인지 들어가는 것이 자연스러우므로 (d)가 정답이다.

as per ~에 따라서 | **initiative** 계획 | **mailing** 메일 발송 | **target market** 표적 시장 | **zip code** 우편 번호 | **at risk** 손실 위험이 있는 | **field agent** 현장 대리인 | **home office** 본사 | **account** 고객 | **launch** 착수하다

3

Around 79 A.D. the city of Pompeii and its sister city of Herculaneum were completely obliterated by the eruption of Mount Vesuvius. It wasn't until over 1,500 years later that the two ancient cities were accidentally rediscovered under 4 to 6 meters of pumice and ash. Because of the volcanic debris, Pompeii gives us a remarkably clear glimpse into the lives of the Roman people at the height of the empire. The excavated town gives us a snapshot of Roman life such as the forums, the baths, numerous houses, and some out of town villas. Today Pompeii is one of _____ over 2.5 million visitors a year.

(a) Italy's most frequently visited tourist spots with
(b) the Renaissance's best preserved cities for
(c) Romania's most valued and remarkable cities with
(d) the world's most active volcanic spectacles

서기 79년 경 폼페이 시와 자매 도시인 헤르쿨라네움은 베수비오 화산 폭발로 인해서 완전히 사라졌다. 이 두 개 고대 도시가 4~6m 의 부석과 화산 잔해 아래에서 우연히 다시 발견된 것은 그로부터 1,500년이 훨씬 지나서였다. 화산 잔해를 통해 폼페이는 제국 전성기 시절 로마인의 생활을 놀라울 정도로 명확하게 보여준다. 발굴된 도심에서 공개 토론장, 목욕탕, 수많은 집, 몇몇 도시 근교 빌라와 같은 로마인들의 생활을 엿볼 수 있다. 오늘날 폼페이는 매년 250만 명 이상이 방문하는, 이태리에서 사람들이 가장 자주 찾는 관광지 중 하나이다.

(a) 이태리에서 사람들이 가장 자주 찾는 관광지
(b) 르네상스 시대의 가장 잘 보존된 도시
(c) 루마니아에서 가장 소중하고 주목할 만한 도시
(d) 세계에서 가장 활동적인 화산 경관

화산재에 묻혔던 폼페이는 화산 폭발 당시의 모습을 그대로 간직했기 때문에, 당시 로마인들의 생활을 엿볼 수 있어서 매년 250만 명 이상이 방문하고 있다는 내용이다. (b)는 르네상스 시대를 말하고 있고, (c)의 Romania는 오늘날의 루마니아이며, (d)는 오늘날 가장 활발하게 활동하는 화산의 장관이라는 내용으로 내용상 거리가 멀다. 따라서 정답은 (a)이다.

sister city 자매도시 | **obliterate** 사라지다 | **eruption** 폭발, 분출 | **pumice** 부석 | **volcanic debris** 화산 파편 | **at the height of** ~의 절정에, ~이 한창일 때에 | **excavate** 발굴하다 | **forum** 공개 토론장 | **spot** 장소 | **spectacle** 광경

4

It's a hot muggy one out there today and by the look of things from the News 5 Eye in the Sky helicopter, many people are _____. We got two cars pulled over on the westbound interstate highway 15 at mile post 164, but after that things are clear sailing. Over on the beltline heading to Santa Cruz there's a car pulled over with its hood up, looks like overheating problems there. Traffic's a little packed behind the overheated car, it looks like too many people are more interested in the broken-down car than on the freeway. Other than that, doesn't look to bad out there in the greater metropolis.

(a) seeking shelter under the highway over passes
(b) bundling up and putting on more layers
(c) trying to flee the city to head to the beach
(d) queuing up at the gas station and car washes

오늘은 몹시 무더우며, 스카이 헬리콥터의 News 5 Eye로 촬영한 바에 의하면, 많은 사람들이 도시를 벗어나서 해변으로 향하고 있습니다. 서쪽으로 가는 15번 주간 고속 도로의 164번 이정표에 두 대의 차가 도로 옆으로 세워져 있지만, 그 다음부터는 흐름이 순탄합니다. 산타쿠르즈로 향하는 순환 도로에는 차 한 대가 후드가 열린 채로 세워져 있는데, 과열 문제 같아 보입니다. 과열된 차 뒤로 교통이 약간 정체되고 있으며, 꽤 많은 사람들이 고속 도로를 달리는 것보다 고장 난 차에 많은 관심이 있는 듯 합니다. 그밖에 이 대도시에서 문제점은 전혀 없어 보입니다.

(a) 고속 도로의 지나친 통행량으로 쉴 곳을 찾고 있는
(b) 옷을 더 두둑하게 껴입고 있는
(c) 도시를 벗어나서 해변으로 향하고 있는
(d) 주유소 및 세차장에서 대기하고 있는

무덥고 찌는 날씨에 도시의 고속 도로 교통 상황을 방송국 헬기의 카메라로 중계하는 내용이다. (a)처럼 지나친 정체 상황은 아니고, (b)는 더운 날씨와 무관하며 (d)역시 고속 도로 상의 교통 상황과 무관한 내용이다. 무덥고 찌는 날씨를 감안하면 정답은 (c)이다.

muggy 무더운 | pulled over 차가 도로 옆에 세워져 있는
westbound 서쪽으로 가는 | interstate 각 주간의 | beltline 순환 도로
hood 〈자동차의〉 앞덮개, 후드 | overheating 과열 | metropolis 주요
도시 | bundle up 옷을 두둑하게 입다

5

For millenniums, the sword determined who ruled the land. Interestingly enough, the sword developed from the dagger and the oldest sword-like weapon dates back to 3300 B.C. in Turkey. However, this weapon is considered more of an extended dagger than an actual sword. It wasn't until stronger alloys such as steel and better heat treatment processes were developed that swords longer than 60 centimeters were produced. This is because the tensile strength of bronze decreases tremendously the longer the weapon is and thus bends easily. Perhaps it is more accurate that _____ for thousands of years.

(a) swords were more popular than pens
(b) the bronze age was defined by the dagger
(c) swords and daggers were treasured by men
(d) the sword was mightier than the pen

수천 년 동안 검이 대지의 지배자를 결정했다. 흥미롭게도 검은 단검에서 발전했고, 가장 오래된 검과 같은 무기의 기원은 기원전 3300년의 터키로 거슬러 올라간다. 하지만 이 무기는 실제 검이라기보다는 단지 단검을 늘린 것으로 여겨진다. 강철과 같은 더 강한 합금과 더 우수한 열처리 공정이 개발된 이후에 길이 60cm가 넘는 검이 생산되었다. 무기의 길이가 길수록 청동의 인장 강도가 엄청 감소하여 쉽게 휘기 때문이다. 아마도 수천 년 동안 검이 펜보다 더 강했다는 표현이 더 정확하다.

(a) 검이 펜보다 더 유행했다
(b) 청동기 시대는 단검으로 정의되었다
(c) 남자들은 검과 단검을 소중히 여겼다
(d) 검이 펜보다 더 강했다

지문의 요지는 수천 년 동안 검이 대지의 지배자를 결정했다는 첫 번째 문장이다. 빈칸은 지문의 요지와 문맥상 일관성 있는 부분을 찾는 문제이다. (a), (b) 및 (c)는 요지와 무관하며 정답은 (d)이다.

millennium 천년 | sword 검 | dagger 단검 | alloy 합금 | heat
treatment processes 열처리 공정 | tensile strength 인장 강도
bronze 청동

6

Tired of pulling out that garden hose and all the other pool cleaning equipment to _____ your pool every week? With the Solar Breeze robotic pool cleaner, you no longer have that worrisome headache. Unlike other pool cleaners that make you wait until debris sinks to the bottom of the pool and clogs the pipes, the Solar Breeze lightly skims the surface automatically picking up floating particles there may be. Leaves, bugs and other debris usually float on the top of the water for over three hours, the whole time leeching contaminants into your pool. At only $500, the Solar Breeze is a worthy investment that is not only convenient and safe, but also environmentally friendly, order now!

(a) make your tool shed clean and neat
(b) keep the litter and debris out of
(c) moisten and maintain water temperature in
(d) thoroughly preserve the water quality of

매주 수영장에서 쓰레기와 부스러기를 제거하기 위해서 정원용 호스와 다른 수영장 청소 장비를 끌어내느라 지쳤나요? 솔라 브리즈 로봇 수영장 청소기를 사용하면 더 이상 골머리를 썩히지 않으셔도 됩니다. 부스러기가 수영장 바닥에 가라 앉아 배관을 막을 때까지 기다려야 하는 다른 수영장 청소기와 달리 솔라 브리즈는 떠다닐지도 모르는 부스러기를 자동으로 집어서 수면에서 가볍게 걷어냅니다. 나뭇잎, 곤충, 기타 찌꺼기는 보통 3시간 이상 물 위를 떠다니는데, 이는 오염물이 수영장에 들러붙는 시간입니다. 솔라 브리즈는 단 500달러만으로 가능한 편리하고 안전할 뿐만 아니라 환경친화적인 투자입니다. 지금 주문하세요.

(a) 공구 보관 창고를 깨끗하게 정돈하다
(b) 쓰레기와 부스러기를 제거하다
(c) 촉촉하게 하고 수온을 유지하다
(d) 철저히 수질을 유지하다

이 지문은 수영장 청소 장비를 광고하는 내용이며, 빈칸은 무슨 목적으로 호스와 수영장 청소 장비를 끌어내는지 묻고 있으므로 정답은 (b)이다.

equipment 장비 | debris 부스러기 | sink 가라앉다 | clog 막다
skim 걷어내다 | float 떠다니다 | leech 들러붙다 | contaminant
오염 물질 | environmentally friendly 환경친화적인 | shed ~을 보관
하는 곳, 광

7

Imagine a competition involving running a track of 253.3 meters over two wet and dry obstacles while carrying another competitor who has to weigh at least 49 kilograms with a goal of winning your own weight in beer. Every year in Finland and the states of Wisconsin and Michigan, the Wife Carrying competition is held. Legend has it that this unusual game originated in Finland at the end of the 18th century, inspired by a man named Herkko Rosvo-Ronkanien who was a leader of a gang of thieves notorious for stealing not only goods from towns, but women as well. Today _____ and certainly can make or break a marriage depending on if you drop your spouse or not.

(a) the race is highly regarded in all circles
(b) competitors rigorously train year round
(c) this spectacle has become world-renowned
(d) racers can be found in all shapes and sizes

번역

맥주에 취한 상태에서 자신의 몸무게를 능가하고자 체중이 최소 49kg인 경쟁자를 들쳐 메고 두 개의 젖고 마른 장애물 위로 253.3m의 트랙을 달려야 하는 시합을 상상해보자. 매년 핀란드와 위스콘신 주, 미시간 주에서는 부인을 들쳐 메고 달리는 시합이 열린다. 전설에 의하면 이 특이한 경기는 마을에서 물건뿐 아니라 여자들도 훔친 것으로 악명이 높았던 도둑떼 두목인 헤르코 로스보 론카니엔에게 영감을 받아 18세기 말 핀란드에서 유래했다. 오늘날 이 구경거리는 세계적으로 유명해졌고 배우자를 떨어뜨리는지 그렇지 않은지 여부에 따라서 성혼 또는 파혼을 확실히 결정짓게 된다.

(a) 경주는 모든 사회에서 높게 평가된다
(b) 경쟁자들은 1년 내내 혹독한 훈련을 받는다
(c) 이 구경거리는 세계적으로 유명해졌다
(d) 경주 참가자들은 모습과 체격이 다양하다

해설

앞뒤 문맥만을 가지고 정답을 고르기가 쉽지 않은 문제이다. 하지만 매년 핀란드와 위스콘신 주, 미시간 주에서 이 시합이 열린다는 내용으로부터 세계적으로 유명해졌다는 (c)를 짐작할 수 있다.

competition 시합 | **obstacle** 장애물 | **in beer** 맥주에 취해서 | **unusual** 특이한 | **originate** 유래하다 | **inspired** 영감을 받은 | **notorious** 악명이 높은 | **depend on** ~에 따라서 | **spouse** 배우자 | **circles** 집단, 사회

8

Dr. Martin Cooper is considered the inventor of the first portable telephone and the one to _____. A former general manager for the systems division in Motorola, Dr. Cooper revealed the cell phone in April of 1983, calling his rival at Dell laboratories in a gesture akin to sticking one's tongue. Motorola's DynaTAC was a 9x5x1.75 inches, weighed a whopping 2.5 pounds and had a talk time of only 35 minutes. That pales in comparison to today's smart phones that are only 4.5x2.31x0.37 inches, weighing as little as 4.8 ounces with features such as text messaging, internet browsing, video phone, talk times of up to 14 hours and much more.

(a) bring it out of the military and into the public
(b) place the first cellular call in history
(c) market it effectively in Europe and Asia
(d) breathe life into a flagging industry

번역

마틴 쿠퍼 박사는 최초로 휴대용 전화기를 발명하여 역사상 최초로 휴대용 전화기로 통화한 사람으로 여겨지고 있다. 모토로라 시스템부의 부장이었던 쿠퍼 박사는 델 연구소에 근무하는 경쟁자에게 전화해서 약을 올리는 듯한 표현으로 1983년 4월 휴대 전화의 실체를 드러냈다. 모토로라 다이나택의 규격은 9X5X1.75인치이고 2.5파운드의 엄청난 무게였으며 통화 시간은 35분에 불과했다. 이 제품은 규격이 단지 4.5X2.31X0.37인치이고, 문자 메시지 보내기, 인터넷 검색, 비디오 폰 기능을 갖춘 상태에서 무게가 4.8온스에 불과하고 최장 통화 시간이 14시간이며, 많은 기능을 가지고 있는 오늘날의 스마트폰에 비하면 아무것도 아니다.

(a) 군사용에서 대중이 사용할 수 있도록 하다
(b) 역사상 최초로 휴대용 전화기로 통화하다
(c) 유럽과 아시아에서 효과적으로 판매하다
(d) 침체된 산업에 생명을 불어넣다

해설

빈칸 앞의 문장 마틴 쿠퍼 박사가 최초로 휴대용 전화기를 발명했다는 내용과, 빈칸 뒤의 문장인 쿠퍼 박사가 델 연구소에 근무하는 경쟁자에게 전화해서 1983년 4월 휴대 전화의 실체가 드러났다는 내용으로 미루어 정답은 (b)이다.

inventor 발명가 | **portable** 휴대의 | **former** 전직 | **division** 부, 국 | **in a gesture** ~의 몸짓[표현]으로 | **akin** ~와 유사한 | **whopping** 엄청 큰 | **pale in comparison to** ~에 비하면 아무것도 아니다 | **browse** 〈웹 등의 정보를〉 검색하다 | **talk time** 통화 시간

9

With fewer and fewer couples marrying in developed nations, many sociologists, psychologists and other experts have been fretting over declining birthrates. What is it in our society today that is either keeping people from marrying or leading them so easily to divorce? Some argue our everyday workload has increased significantly, especially in the last 20 years. Couple that with an accompanying rise in communications and electronic devices, which ironically should assist us in having closer relationships but unfortunately often has the opposite effect. We need to prioritize our lives and determine what is really important to us. So instead of browsing your social networks soon as you get home, try doing some face to face interaction, _____.

(a) you'll find it just as or even more rewarding

(b) via video phone or video chatting online

(c) rather than logging on and surfing the internet

(d) it may help you with your job and career

결혼하는 남녀가 점점 줄어드는 선진국에서 많은 사회학자, 심리학자, 기타 전문가들이 출생률 감소에 대해서 노심초사하고 있다. 오늘날 우리 사회에서 결혼에 장애가 되거나 그렇게 쉽게 이혼을 하도록 하는 것은? 어떤 사람들은 하루 업무량이 특히 최근 20년간 상당히 증가했다고 주장한다. 역설적이게도 사람들이 더 밀접한 관계를 가지는 데 도움이 되어야겠지만, 불행히도 종종 반대 효과를 내는 통신 및 전자 장비의 증가와 이것을 연관시켜 보자. 우리는 생활의 우선순위를 매기고 우리에게 정말 중요한 것을 결정해야 한다. 그러니 집에 도착하자마자 소셜 네트워크를 돌아다니는 대신 얼굴을 맞대고 상호 교류한다면 그것이 매우 보람 있는 일이란 것을 알게 될 것이다.

(a) 그것이 매우 보람 있는 일이란 것을 알게 될 것이다

(b) 비디오 폰이나 온라인 화상 채팅을 통해서

(c) 인터넷에 접속해서 서핑을 하기 보다는

(d) 일과 경력에 도움이 될 수 있다

통신 및 전자 장비의 증가로 인해서 사람들의 관계가 소원해지고, 결국 결혼하는 커플 수가 감소하고 있다는 내용으로 빈칸은 사람들이 인터넷이 아니라 직접 얼굴을 맞대고 교류한다면 어떤 결과가 나타날 것인가를 묻는 내용이 들어가야 자연스럽다. 따라서 정답은 (a)이다. (b)와 (c)는 지문의 요지와 반대 내용이고 (d)의 경우 인간관계와 관련성이 없다.

developed nation 선진국 | sociologist 사회학자 | psychologist 심리학자 | fret 노심초사하다 | birthrate 출생률 | keep from ~을 참다 workload 업무량 | couple 연결하다 | prioritize 우선순위를 매기다 interaction 상호 교류

10

Nearly everyone knows of Walt Disney and his enormous Disney enterprise, but what people tend to forget is that if it weren't for two brothers from Germany, _____. The Brothers Grimm are Jakob and Wilhelm Grimm born at the end of the 1700's and died around the mid 1800's. The two collected German folktales and are credited for re-introducing now classic fairytales such as Cinderella, The Frog Prince, Hansel and Gretel, Sleeping Beauty, Snow White and many more. The Brothers Grimm published a manuscript containing several dozen fairytales in 1810. It has been rumored that they only collected stories by word of mouth from peasants, but in reality, many of the storytellers were middle-class or aristocrats that heard the stories from their servants.

(a) Disney would have settled into the newspaper industry

(b) Mickey and Minnie Mouse may not have been born

(c) Disney may never have been such a success

(d) Disneyworld and Pixar would never have existed

거의 모든 사람들이 월트 디즈니와 그의 거대한 디즈니 기업에 대해서 알고 있지만, 독일 출신의 두 형제가 없었다면 디즈니가 결코 그러한 성공을 거두지 못했을 것이라는 것은 쉽게 잊는다. 그림 형제는 1700년대 말에 태어나서 1800년대 중반 무렵에 죽은 야코프 그림과 빌헬름 그림이다. 두 사람은 독일의 설화를 수집했고 〈신데렐라〉, 〈개구리 왕자〉, 〈헨젤과 그레텔〉, 〈잠자는 숲속의 공주〉, 〈백설공주〉 등 많은 고전 동화를 새롭게 소개한 것으로 인정을 받고 있다. 그림 형제는 1810년 수십 편의 동화가 실린 한 권의 필사본을 발행했다. 그들은 소작농이 구전한 동화만을 수집했다는 소문이 있지만, 실제로는 하인들에게서 이야기를 들은 많은 중산층이나 귀족이 이야기꾼이 되었다.

(a) 디즈니는 신문업에 자리를 잡았을 것이다

(b) 미키와 미니 마우스는 탄생하지 않았을 수도 있었다

(c) 디즈니가 결코 그러한 성공을 거두지 못했을 것이다

(d) 디즈니 월드와 픽사가 결코 존재하지 않았을 것이다

지문 도입부에서 거대한 디즈니 기업과 지문 중반부의 그림 형제가 소개한 많은 고전 동화와의 관련성을 생각해 보면, 빈칸은 그림 형제가 없었다면 디즈니가 어떻게 되었을 것인가를 묻는 문제임을 짐작할 수 있다. 따라서 정답은 (c)이다.

enterprise 기업 | if it weren't for ~이 없었다면 | collect 수집하다 be credited for ~으로 인정받다 | fairytale 동화 | manuscript 필사본 | contain ~이 들어있다 | peasant 소작농 | middle-class 중산층 | aristocrat 귀족

11

Dear Gabby,

Recently my 16-year-old daughter has been nagging me _____ her driver's license and I am a little worried. I know today's cars are much safer than when we grew up, but I also know that today's kids have mobile phones which makes it that much more dangerous for them to drive. My daughter keeps saying that her friends have cars so why can't she? She won't see the logical reasoning I give her to wait until college to have a car and we haven't talked to each other in almost a week. I just don't know what to do!

Desperate in Arizona,
Susan Kraemer

(a) to take her to a private tutor for

(b) for a new car but she just got
(c) to pay for the annual renewal of
(d) for a greater weekly allowance and

보세요. 간단하지만 매우 효과적인 이 골프 도우미는 클럽 헤드에 부착되어 공을 날리고자 하는 지점을 지적해 줍니다. 골프 팰 자기 포인터로 일주일만 연습하면 골프 성적이 5타나 줄어듭니다! 지금 주문하시면 저렴한 프로모션 가격인 49.99달러에 드리며, 많은 골프 공을 잃어버리지 않게 되어 본전을 뽑을 뿐 아니라 골프장에서 부러움의 대상이 될 겁니다.

(a) 골프 핸디캡을 개선함으로써
(b) 지역의 다양한 골프 경기에서
(c) 2인용 골프 시즌비를 내기 위해
(d) 많은 골프 공을 잃어버리지 않게 되어

번역

개비 씨께

열여섯 살 먹은 제 딸이 최근 새 차를 사달라고 저를 성가시게 하고 있습니다. 하지만 그 아이는 운전면허를 딴 지 얼마 되지 않아서 조금 걱정이 됩니다. 요즘 차들은 우리가 자랄 때보다 훨씬 더 안전하다는 것을 알지만 요즘 애들은 휴대 전화 때문에 운전하기가 훨씬 더 위험해서 말입니다. 딸 아이는 자기 친구들은 차를 가지고 있는데 왜 자기는 안되냐고 합니다. 딸 아이는 차를 가지려면 대학생이 될 때까지 기다리라는 저의 타당한 이유를 이해하지 못할 것이며, 우리는 거의 일주일이 지나도록 말을 안 했습니다. 어떻게 해야 할지 모르겠습니다.

애리조나에서 수전 크레머가 조언을 간절히 바라며

(a) 개인 교습을 받게 해 달라고
(b) 새 차를 사달라고 하지만 막 딴
(c) 매년 하는 운전면허 갱신 비용을 납부해달라고
(d) 매주 주는 용돈을 올려 달라고

해설

16세의 딸이 있는 어머니가 딸의 요구 사항과 관련해서 조언을 구하는 편지이다. 아이는 차를 운전하고 싶어하고 어머니는 아직은 위험하니 대학생이 될 때까지 기다리라고 하면서 갈등을 빚는 내용이 나오므로 (b)가 빈칸에 들어 갈 내용으로 적절하다.

nag 성가시게 굴다 | **driver's license** 운전면허 | **logical** 사리에 맞는 **reasoning** 추론 | **desperate** 간절히 바라는

해설

초보자를 대상으로 골프 도우미 장비를 광고하는 내용이다. 빈칸은 장비가 비용 만큼의 가치가 있는지와 관련된 내용이며, (a), (b), (c)는 초보자가 일주일 연습해서 할 수 있기에는 능력 밖의 일이다. 공 구입 비용이 절약되어 장비 구입비가 회수될 수 있다는 내용인 (d)가 가장 적절하다.

errant 잘못된 | **slice** 〈골프 타법〉 슬라이스 | **effortlessly** 노력하지 않고, 쉽게 | **swing** 스윙 동작 | **aid** 도우미 | **attach** 부착하다 | **stroke** 타 | **envy** 부러움의 대상 | **single** 〈골프〉 2인 경기

12

Tired of spending hours searching for an errant tee shot? Have your golf buddies stopped calling you because of your terrible slice? Then improve your swing quickly and effortlessly with the new Golf-Pal magnetic pointer. This simple, yet highly effective golf aid attaches to your club head and points to where you want your ball to fly. After only one week of practicing with the Golf-Pal magnetic pointer, your golf score will go down five strokes! Order now for the low introductory rate of $49.99 and not only will you make your money back _____, but you'll also be the envy of the golf course!

(a) by improving your golf handicap
(b) in various local golf tournaments
(c) to pay for a single golf season
(d) by not losing so many golf balls

번역

잘못된 티샷에 대한 연구로 몇 시간을 보내는 게 지겨우신가요? 형편없는 슬라이스 때문에 골프 친구들이 더 이상 찾아주지 않나요? 그렇다면 새로운 골프 팰 자기 포인터로 빠르고 쉽게 스윙 동작을 개선해

13

One of the world's most revolutionary building materials is concrete. During the Roman Empire, concrete was widely utilized and spawned the Roman Architectural Revolution. Originally made from quicklime, pozzolana and an aggregate of pumice, concrete freed the Romans from the restrictive chains of bricks and stones. Concrete allowed for innovation and a marked increase in architectural complexity for Roman architects, with examples such as the Roman Pantheon, still the world's largest unreinforced concrete dome. Today's concrete structures use a different mixture of materials as well as iron or steel reinforcement. Furthermore, modern concrete has allowed us to keep pushing the envelope _____.

(a) for the tallest structures in the world
(b) to better ways of constructing domes
(c) of human ingenuity and competence
(d) for building green and eco-friendly

번역

세계에서 가장 혁신적인 건축 자재 중 하나는 콘크리트이다. 로마 제국 시대에 콘크리트는 널리 사용되었고, 로마의 건축 혁명을 낳았다. 원래 생석회, 화산회, 부석 골재로 만든 콘크리트는 벽돌과 돌이라는 제약적인 사슬에서 로마인을 자유롭게 했다. 콘크리트는 로마의 건축가들이 건축물의 복잡함에 있어 혁신과 두드러진 증가를 가능하게 했다. 그 예로 철근으로 보강하지 않은 여전히 세계에서 가장 큰 콘크리트 돔 건축물인 로마의 판테온 신전을 들 수 있다. 오늘날의 콘크리트 건축물에

는 철이나 강철 보강재뿐만 아니라 자재가 다양하게 혼합되어 사용된다. 더욱이 현대에 들어와서 콘크리트를 사용함으로써 세계에서 가장 높은 건축물에 대한 한계치가 계속 초월되고 있다.

(a) 세계에서 가장 높은 구조물에 대한
(b) 돔 건축물 건설을 위한 더 나은 방향으로
(c) 인간의 독창성과 능력에 대한
(d) 환경 및 자연 친화적인 건축을 위한

해설
지문은 건축 혁신에 있어서 콘크리트가 기여한 내용을 기능적인 면에서 소개하고 있다. 빈칸은 근대에 들어서 철근 콘크리트와 자재의 다양한 혼합을 통해 어떤 면에서 구조물의 한계를 초월해 가고 있는가를 묻는 내용으로 (a)가 문맥상 가장 어울린다.

revolutionary 혁신적인 | **building material** 건축 자재 | **spawn** ~을 낳다 | **quicklime** 생석회 | **pozzolana** 화산회 | **restrictive** 제약적인 | **complexity** 복잡성 | **push the envelope** 한계를 도전하다

14

Baseball as we know it today requires some specialized equipment, none more so than _____. Interestingly enough, the early players of this game didn't wear gloves. It wasn't until 1875 that a St. Louis outfielder Charles Waitt sported a pair of fleshed-colored gloves. The concept slowly caught on with other players as they experimented with different types of gloves. The early gloves were most suitable for picking up ground balls and did not include the webbing between the first finger and thumb as we see in today's modern baseball glove.

(a) the unique ball and bat combination itself
(b) other sports such as soccer or football
(c) the baseball glove with its unique design
(d) the baseball diamond the game is played on

번역
우리가 오늘날 알고 있는 야구는 독특한 디자인의 야구 글로브 같은 특수 장비가 필요하다. 흥미롭게도 초기의 야구 선수들은 글러브를 끼지 않았다. 1875년이 되어서야 세인트루이스의 외야수인 찰스 웨이트가 색이 있는 두툼한 한 쌍의 장갑을 처음 착용했다. 다른 선수들이 여러 가지 형태의 글러브를 시험 삼아 착용하면서 이러한 개념은 서서히 선수들에게 대중화되었다. 초기 글러브는 땅볼을 잡기에 가장 적합했고, 우리가 요즘 야구 글러브에서 보는 것과 같은 엄지와 집게손가락 사이의 가죽끈은 없었다.

(a) 독특한 볼과 배트의 조합
(b) 축구나 미식축구 같은 다른 스포츠
(c) 독특한 디자인의 야구 글로브
(d) 경기가 진행되는 야구 경기장

해설
야구 경기에는 특수 장비가 필요하다고 말하며 빈칸 뒤에 야구 글로브의 탄생에 대해 언급하고 있으므로 정답은 (c)이다.

pastime 여가 활동 | **outfielder** 외야수 | **sport** 자랑스럽게 입다 | **fleshed** 두툼한 | **catch on with** 대중화되다 | **webbing** 〈야구 글러브의 손가락을 잇는〉 가죽끈 | **first finger** 집게손가락

15

Long before we had sprawling mega malls to find every item we may need or want, there was the bazaar. The word, bazaar, originated in ancient Persia and represented a permanent area to sell merchandise. Characterized by their lively atmosphere and plethora of products, today's modern bazaars do not differ that greatly from ancient ones and have flourished globally. _____, bazaars are found in countries near the Middle East such as Azerbaijan as well as in distant countries like Ireland and China.

(a) In the end
(b) At the same time
(c) Consequently
(d) Notwithstanding

번역
필요하거나 원하는 모든 품목을 찾을 수 있는 메가몰이 퍼지기 오래 전에 바자가 있었다. 바자는 고대 페르시아에서 유래되었고 상품을 판매하는 영구적인 구역을 나타낸다. 활기찬 분위기와 넘쳐나는 상품이 특징인 오늘날의 현대식 상점가는 고대의 시장 거리와 그리 크게 다르지 않으며 세계적으로 번창했다. 따라서 아일랜드나 중국과 같은 멀리 떨어진 나라뿐만 아니라 아제르바이잔과 같은 중동 근방의 국가에서도 발견된다.

(a) 결국
(b) 동시에
(c) 따라서
(d) 그럼에도 불구하고

해설
빈칸 앞뒤의 내용을 적절하게 연결하는 접속사를 찾는 문제이다. 오늘날의 시장은 전 세계적으로 번창했다는 내용과 현대식 상점가는 중동 근방 국가와 중동에서 멀리 떨어진 나라에서도 볼 수 있다는 내용을 이어주는 가장 적절한 접속사는 (c) Consequently이다.

mega mall 메가몰 | **bazaar** 바자, 시장 거리 | **originate** 유래하다 | **represent** 나타내다 | **merchandise** 상품 | **atmosphere** 분위기 | **plethora** 과다, 과잉 | **flourish** 번창하다

16

Life-giving water is a figure of speech on several levels. We need water itself to sustain our lives but seas and rivers also provide food. This is one of the reasons civilizations have sprung up around bodies of water or rivers. Ancient Egyptians and Chinese were using fishing rods, hooks and lines as early as 2000

B.C. even though a majority of fishermen used simple handlines. Early fishing lures were made of bone or bronze, the latter being strong but very thin and not easily visible to the fish. It wasn't until the 1900's that an American company started manufacturing lures for commercial use, _____ lures were made by individual craftsmen for private use.

(a) prior to that
(b) instead of when
(c) where
(d) even though

생명을 주는 물은 여러 가지 측면에서 담화의 주제가 된다. 생명을 유지하기 위해서 물 자체가 필요하기도 하지만 그밖에 바다나 강은 먹거리도 제공한다. 이것이 수역 주변이나 강가에서 문명이 싹튼 이유 중 하나이다. 대부분의 어부들은 간단히 손 낚싯줄을 사용했지만 고대 이집트인과 중국인들은 기원전 2000년 경에 이미 낚싯대, 바늘, 낚싯줄을 사용하고 있었다. 초기의 미끼는 뼈나 청동으로 만들어졌고, 청동 미끼는 강하고 매우 얇았으며 물고기들이 쉽게 알아차리지 못했다. 한 미국 회사가 상업적 용도로 미끼를 제작하기 시작한 것은 1900년대에 들어와서였다. 그 전까지는 공예가들이 개인적인 용도로 미끼를 만들었다.

(a) ~전에
(b) ~한 때 대신
(c) ~한 곳
(d) ~했음에도 불구하고

문맥상 미끼의 제작 용도에 관한 가장 자연스러운 연결어는 (a)가 된다.

civilization 문명 | spring up 싹트다 | bodies of water 수역
fishing rod 낚싯대 | handline 손 낚싯줄 | lure 미끼 | visible 볼 수 있는 | commercial use 상업적인 용도 | craftsman 공예가

17

Residents of Grand Rapids awoke to a thunderous explosion as Becker's Grain and Feed grain silo 14 exploded around six in the morning Tuesday. The explosion was a result of a perfect storm of dry conditions followed by an unseasonal electrical storm. Any finely ground organic material is highly flammable; especially flour which is what was being stored at Becker's farm. Silo 14 and two nearby grain elevators were completely destroyed. Fire fighters worked past noon to keep the blaze under control and prevent it from spreading to other nearby farm structures. Fortunately no human injuries were reported, although some livestock had to be treated for minor burns.

Q: What is mainly discussed in the news passage?
(a) The devastating effects of an electric shock
(b) The dangers of using elevators to store grain
(c) A grain elevator explosion at a local farm
(d) The effects of a detrimental situation on a grain farm

화요일 아침 6시경 베커의 그레인 앤 피드 곡물 농장의 14번 곡류 저장고가 폭발하면서 그랜드 래피즈의 주민들은 우레와 같은 폭발 소리에 잠을 깼습니다. 폭발은 곡물이 건조된 후, 때 아닌 심한 뇌우에 잇따른, 더 할 수 없이 나쁜 상황의 결과였습니다. 곱게 빻은 유기물은 어떤 것이라도 인화성이 매우 크며, 특히 베커 농장에 저장되어 있던 밀가루가 그랬습니다. 14번 곡류 저장고 근처에 있는 두 대의 곡물 운반 승강기가 완전히 파손되었습니다. 소방수들이 불길을 잡고 인근 다른 농장의 구조물로 번지는 것을 막기 위해 정오가 지나도록 작업했습니다. 몇몇 가축은 가벼운 화상으로 인해서 치료를 받아야 했지만 다행스럽게도 다친 사람은 보고되지 않았습니다.

Q: 뉴스 지문에서 주로 논의되는 것은?
(a) 감전의 대단히 파괴적인 효과
(b) 곡물 저장을 위해서 승강기를 사용하는 것에 대한 위험성
(c) 지역의 농장에서 곡물 승강기의 폭발
(d) 안 좋은 일이 겹친 상황이 곡물 농장에 끼친 영향

곡물이 건조된 후, 계절에 안 맞는 심한 뇌우가 쳐서 곡물저장 탱크가 폭발하면서 농장에 발생한 피해를 보도하는 뉴스 내용이다. (b)와 (c)는 지문에 없는 내용이고, (a)의 경우라도 곡물이 마르지 않았거나 우기였다면 피해가 덜 했을 것이다. 최악의 나쁜 상황인 건조된 곡물 가루와 때 아닌 심한 뇌우가 농장에 큰 피해를 초래했으므로 (d)가 정답이다.

explosion 폭발 | silo 곡류 저장소 | perfect storm 더할 수 없이 나쁜 상황 | followed by 뒤이어, 잇달아 | electrical storm 심한 뇌우 flammable 인화성의 | blaze 불길 | burn 화상 | devastating 엄청난 detrimental 해로운

18

It's the little things in life that have made the biggest impact on our civilization. A great example of this is the peppercorn, or black pepper. Not to be confused with the long pepper fruit, black pepper is derived from the spherical peppercorn and has been used in India since at least 2000 B.C. In early times, all pepper found in Europe came from India and the surrounding areas. Pepper became so popular that it was even used as collateral or even currency. Pepper and other spices from India led the Portuguese and other European countries to find a quicker route to India. This in turn led to the discovery and colonization of the Americas and has forever changed world history.

Q: What is the best title of the passage?
(a) How the Pepper Found Its Way to India
(b) How the Pepper Changed Civilization
(c) Pepper, the Spice of the Silk Road
(d) How the Pepper Divided the East from the West

번역

인류 문명에 가장 큰 충격을 주는 것은 생활에 있어서 사소한 것들이다. 이에 대한 하나의 좋은 예가 후추 열매 혹은 후추이다. 긴 후추 열매와 혼동이 되지 않도록 후추(black pepper)란 단어는 구형의 후추(spherical peppercorn)에서 유래했고, 최소한 기원전 2천년 전부터 인도에서 사용되었다. 먼 옛날, 유럽에서 볼 수 있었던 후추는 모두 인도와 그 주변 지역에서 온 것이다. 후추는 큰 인기를 얻어 담보물이나 통화로도 사용되었다. 후추 및 기타 인도산 향신료로 인해서 포르투갈과 여타 유럽 국가는 인도로 가는 보다 빠른 경로를 찾게 되었다. 이는 결국 아메리카의 발견과 식민지화로 이어졌고 세계 역사를 영구적으로 바꾸었다.

Q: 지문에 가장 잘 어울리는 제목은?
(a) 후추가 어떻게 인도에 전래되었는가
(b) 후추가 문명을 어떻게 바꾸었가
(c) 실크로드의 향신료인 후추
(d) 후추가 어떻게 서양에서 동양을 분리시켰는가

해설

후추로 인한 남북 아메리카의 발견과 식민지화, 세계 역사의 영구적인 변화를 언급하고 있다. (a), (c) 및 (d)는 지문과 관계 없는 내용이다. 따라서 정답은 (b)이다.

impact 충격 | **peppercorn[black pepper]** 후추 | **derive from** 나오다[파생되다] | **spherical** 구형의 | **collateral** 담보(물) | **currency** 통화 | **route** 경로 | **in turn** 결국[결과적으로] | **colonization** 식민지화

19

The other day I was walking to the campus library when I bumped into Jenny, a friend of a high school classmate. We never really talked much and I really didn't have a good first impression of her at the homecoming football game. When asked where I was going, I told her that I had a paper due and was heading to the library. She asked what class it was for, and I told her the paper was for my poli sci 211 class with Professor Adkins and it was already a day late. Jenny offered to help since she had remarkably had that same professor the previous semester. I was shocked at her willingness to help me, a virtual stranger. Guess it proves you can't judge a book by its cover!

Q: What is the main topic of the passage?
(a) It's impossible to make a first impression again.
(b) People's perception is their reality.
(c) Friends can appear suddenly out of thin air.
(d) First impressions aren't necessarily correct.

번역

일전에 대학 도서관으로 걸어가다가 고등학교 때 같은 반이었던 제니와 마주쳤습니다. 우리는 실제로 많은 대화를 한 적이 전혀 없었고, 동창회 미식축구 시합에서도 그녀에 대한 첫인상이 좋지 않았습니다. 어디로 가는 중이냐는 질문을 받았을 때. 나는 제출해야 할 과제물이 있어서 도서관에 가는 중이라고 말했습니다. 그녀는 어떤 수업 과제물이냐고 물었고, 애드킨즈 교수의 정치학 221 수업에 관한 것이며, 이미 제출 기한이 하루 늦었다고 대답했습니다. 제니는 지난 학기에 그 교수님 강의를 들었기 때문에 도와주겠다고 제의했습니다. 저는 낯선 사람이나 다름없는 제게 기꺼이 도움을 주는 그녀의 마음에 충격을 받았습니다. 뭐든지 겉만 보고 판단할 수 없다는 것이 증명되었습니다.

Q: 지문의 주제는?
(a) 첫인상을 다시 만드는 것은 불가능하다.
(b) 선입견은 현실이다.
(c) 친구는 난데없이 나타날 수 있다.
(d) 첫인상이 반드시 정확하지는 않다.

해설

고교 시절 가졌던 급우에 대한 첫인상이 대학에 들어와서 바뀐 상황을 설명하고 있으므로 (d)가 가장 적절한 주제이다.

bump into ～와 마주치다 | **homecoming** 동창회 | **paper** 과제물 **due** 제출해야 하는 | **poli sci** 정치학 (political science) | **willingness** 기꺼이 하고자 하는 마음

20

Dear valued customer,

You have received this email as a nationwide customer outreach program and this is not an advertisement. MBH Incorporated has recognized your continued patronage of our open source operating system and want to invite you to continue adding your valuable contents and comments. We have vastly improved the response time and eradicated many glitches due to your feedback. In honor of your service to MBH Inc., we would like to do a profile spotlight on you with your permission. Please respond at your earliest convenience to this email or on the website at www.mbh.com.

With gratitude,
Christine Sayers, Customer Response Team

Q: What is mainly discussed in the letter?
(a) The value of open source content and comments
(b) An invitation to subscribe to the profile spotlight page
(c) Acknowledging a customer's contribution to the company
(d) Recognizing the flaws in open source content

(c) Drug manufacturers' manipulation of protein molecules

(d) The difficulty with current methods of combining drugs with proteins

번역

인체의 일반 세포는 약 7천 개의 각기 다른 단백질 분자를 갖고 있다. 단백질 분자의 일부는 물질이 세포를 들락거리는 것을 제어한다. 다른 단백질 분자는 세포 외부에서 내부로 신호를 보낸다. 시판되는 약품 중 절반 이상이 이러한 단백질과 함께 효과를 내거나 상호작용을 하기 때문에 단백질 분자는 보통 제약사의 연구 목표가 된다. 하지만, 과거에는 중요한 다른 요소를 단백질에서 제거해서 잘게 썰지 않고는 단백질과 함께 약의 효능을 연구하기가 어려웠다. 단백질 자체를 건드리거나 변경시키지 않고도 레이저를 이용해서 이러한 단백질 분자를 연구하는 새로운 방법이 발견되었다. 모든 환자가 어떤 약에도 동일한 반응을 보이지 않기 때문에 이 기법은 연구 및 치료에 있어 좋은 조짐을 내포한다.

Q: 지문에서 주로 논의되는 것은?

(a) 단백질 분자를 이용해서 약의 효과를 연구하는 데 있어서의 돌파구

(b) 인체에 있어서 단백질 분자의 두 가지 중요한 용도

(c) 제약사에 의한 단백질 분자의 조작

(d) 약과 단백질을 결합하는 현재의 방법과 관련된 어려움

해설

인체 세포에서 중요한 역할을 하는 단백질 분자는 제약사의 연구 목표이다. 과거에는 단백질과 함께 약의 효능을 연구하기가 어려웠지만, 레이저를 이용한 새로운 방법이 발견되어 연구 및 치료에 있어서 조짐이 좋다는 내용이다. 따라서 정답은 (a)이다.

protein 단백질 | **molecule** 분자 | **manufacturer** 제조사 | **efficacy** 효능 | **chop up** 잘게 썰다 | **alter** 변경시키다 | **promising** 조짐이 좋은 | **potential** 가능성 | **react** 반응하다 | **breakthrough** 돌파구

22

An announcement of a less than friendly M&A between two of the largest telecommunications giants has many business leaders in the U.S. apprehensive. Moreover, if the merger is approved by Congress, then there will only be three companies to choose from. This could have major implications for businesses who make operating systems for smartphones and provide apps. Unnamed company sources say they are concerned that the merger will make the purchasing company powerful enough that they could control the environment around smartphones and their accessories. Furthermore, the merger could mean that the biggest player will also unfairly determine price.

Q: What is the best title of the passage?

(a) Imminent M&A Will Test America's Resolve

(b) Major Telecom Merger to be Mulled on Wall Street

(c) Deal for Telecom Takeover Raises Concerns

번역

친애하는 고객님

전국적인 고객 지원 프로그램의 일환으로 고객님께 이메일을 보내고 있으며 이것은 광고가 아닙니다. MBH 주식회사는 고객님께서 당사의 오픈 소스 운영 체계의 지속적인 후원자임을 인식하고 고객님의 소중한 콘텐츠 제공과 지속적으로 의견을 주실 것을 청하는 바입니다. 당사는 고객님의 정보와 의견 덕분에 응답 시간을 광범위하게 개선했고 많은 결함을 뿌리 뽑았습니다. MBH 주식회사에 대한 고객님의 기여에 경의를 표하며 당사는 고객님이 허락하신다면 고객님의 프로필을 집중 조명하려고 합니다. 편하실 때 본 이메일에 회신을 하시거나 웹사이트 www.mbh.com을 통해 회신 부탁드립니다. 감사합니다.

고객 대응팀, 크리스틴 세이어스

Q: 편지에서 주로 논의되는 것은?

(a) 오픈 소스 콘텐츠와 의견의 가치

(b) 프로필 집중 조명 페이지로 가입 초대

(c) 회사에 대한 고객의 기여를 인정함

(d) 오픈 소스 콘텐츠의 결함을 인식함

해설

회사에서 오픈 소스 운영 체계에 대한 고객의 기여를 인정하고, 콘텐츠와 의견의 제공을 요청하면서 회사에 고객의 서비스에 대한 감사 표시로 고객의 이력을 집중 조명해 주겠다고 제의하는 내용이다. 따라서 정답은 (c)이다.

nationwide 전국적인 | **outreach** 지원 활동 | **patronage** 후원 **open source** 오픈 소스 | **operating system** 운영 체계 | **eradicate** 근절하다 | **glitch** 결함 | **flaw** 결함

21

The human body has about 7,000 different types of protein molecules in the average cell. Some of these protein molecules control the movement of materials in and out of the cell. Others send signals from the outside of the cell to the inside. Protein molecules are often the target of drug manufacturers with over half the drugs on the market working and interacting with these proteins. However, in the past it has been difficult to study the efficacy of these drugs with the proteins without depriving the proteins of other crucial elements and chopping them up. A new method for studying these protein molecules has been discovered using a laser without disturbing or altering the proteins themselves. This technique has promising potential for both research and treatment as not all patients react the same to certain drugs.

Q: What is mainly discussed in the passage?

(a) A breakthrough in studying drugs effects with protein molecules

(b) The two main uses of protein molecules in the human body

(d) Business Leaders Agree About M&A

번역

최대 통신 업체 두 회사 간에 결코 우호적이지 않은 인수 합병 발표로 인해서 미국의 많은 기업 지도자들이 불안해 하고 있다. 더욱이 국회가 합병을 승인하는 경우, 선택 대상인 회사는 세 개만 남는다. 이는 스마트폰을 위한 운영 체제를 만들고 응용 프로그램을 제공하는 기업들에 중대한 영향을 미칠 수 있다. 익명의 회사 소식통은 합병으로 인해서 매수 회사가 스마트폰과 폰 액세서리를 둘러싼 환경을 통제할 수 있을 만큼 강력해질 것이 우려된다고 말한다. 더욱이 합병은 최대 규모의 회사가 불공정한 방식으로 가격을 결정할 것이라는 것을 의미한다.

Q: 지문에 가장 잘 어울리는 제목은?
(a) 임박한 인수 합병으로 미국의 의지 시험대에 오르다
(b) 월가에서 심사숙고하는 주요 통신회사 합병
(c) 통신 회사 인수건으로 인한 우려 고조
(d) 기업 지도자들 인수 합병의 찬성

해설

통신 업체 중 가장 큰 규모의 두 회사 간에 이루어지는 적대적 인수 합병 발표로 인하여 많은 기업 지도자들이 매수 회사가 기업 환경을 통제할 수 있을 만큼 강력해지고 불공정한 방식으로 가격을 결정할 것에 대한 우려를 나타내고 있다는 내용이다. 따라서 정답은 (c)이다.

M&A 인수 합병 (merger and acquisition) | **telecommunication** 통신 | **apprehensive** 우려하는 | **implication** 영향 | **unnamed** 익명의 **source** 소식통 | **imminent** 임박한 | **resolve** 결의, 의지

23

The word scuba is an acronym for "self-contained underwater breathing apparatus" and is commonly thought of having been invented by an Australian by the name of Ted Eldred who improved on Jacques-Yves Cousteau's aqualung invention. Prior to the self-contained tank, divers relied on oxygen to be pumped to them from the surface through a long hose. This was incredibly dangerous as divers were helpless if any mechanical problems arose during their dive. Early problems of oxygen toxicity were experienced with Cousteau's aqualung rebreather system but are now remedied with modern scuba equipment.

Q: Which of the following is correct about scuba diving?
(a) It was originally developed by Jacques-Yves Cousteau.
(b) It was a great improvement from previous diving methods.
(c) It requires hours of training and certification courses.
(d) It is the safest way to experience underwater sight seeing.

번역

스쿠버란 단어는 '자급식 잠수용 수중 호흡 장치'의 약어이며 자크 이브 쿠스토의 잠수용 호흡기를 개량했던 테트 엘드레드라는 한 호주인이 발명한 것으로 흔히 여겨진다. 자급식 탱크 이전에 잠수부는 긴 호스를 통해 수면에서 펌프로 공급되는 산소에 의존했다. 이는 잠수하는 동안 기계상의 문제가 발생하는 경우 잠수부들은 속수무책이기 때문에 이것은 대단히 위험했다. 쿠스토의 잠수용 호흡기의 경우 초기 산소 중독이라는 문제가 발생했지만, 이 문제는 이제 현대식 스쿠버 장비로 해결되었다.

Q: 스쿠버 다이빙에 대해서 다음 중 옳은 것은?
(a) 자크 이브 쿠스토가 개발했다.
(b) 이전 잠수 방법을 상당히 개선했다.
(c) 수시간 동안의 훈련 및 인증 과정이 필요하다.
(d) 수중 관광을 맛보기 위한 가장 안전한 방법이다.

해설

테드 엘드레드가 자크 이브 쿠스토보다 먼저 잠수용 호흡기를 개발했기 때문에 (a)는 오답이며, (c)는 지문에 없는 내용이고, (d) 스쿠버 다이빙이 관광의 대상이 되기에는 위험하기 때문에 모두 정답에서 제외된다. 초기의 산소 중독 문제가 현대식 스쿠버 장비로 해결되었다는 내용으로 보아 정답은 (b)이다.

self-contained 자급방식의 | **breathing apparatus** 호흡 장비 **aqualung** 잠수용 호흡기 | **helpless** 속수무책인 | **toxicity** 중독 **rebreather** 수중 호흡기 | **remedy** 해결하다 | **equipment** 장비

24

Forming a musical band really is not as difficult as it may seem. All you need is some like minded friends with the same tastes in music as you. Ideally, these friends should have some formal musical training, but as history has proved, it is not absolutely necessary. Many self-taught musicians have made it big. One guitar legend comes to mind, and that is Eric Clapton. Clapton taught himself how to play the guitar at a young age and was known to lock himself in his room for hours listening to music over and over and copying it. He has been a headliner for over four decades as an internationally acclaimed blues and R&B guitarist and singer. Pretty good for a do-it-yourselfer!

Q: Which of the following is correct about Eric Clapton?
(a) He started playing the guitar in high school.
(b) He has been highly sought for over forty years.
(c) He had little formal training in grade school.
(d) His style of music originated in Europe.

번역

음악 밴드를 구성하는 것은 보기보다 실제로 어렵지 않다. 자신과 음악 취향이 같고 생각이 비슷한 친구 몇몇만 있으면 충분하다. 친구들이

어느 정도 정식 음악 교육을 받아야 하는 것이 이상적으로 여겨지겠지만, 역사적으로 증명되었듯이 음악 교육이 반드시 필요한 것은 아니다. 독학한 많은 음악가들이 큰 성공을 거두었다. 한 기타의 전설이 생각나는데 그는 바로 에릭 크랩튼이다. 크랩튼은 어린 나이에 기타 연주법을 독학했고, 방에 처박혀 몇 시간 동안 음악을 듣고 또 듣고 따라 한 것으로 알려져 있다. 그는 전 세계적으로 환호를 받는 블루스 및 R&B 기타리스트 겸 가수로 40년 이상 스타의 자리를 지켰다. 독학으로 배운 사람으로써는 놀라운 일이다!

Q: 다음 중 에릭 크랩튼에 대해 옳은 것은?
(a) 고등학교 시절에 기타를 연주하기 시작했다.
(b) 40년 이상 많은 인기를 얻었다.
(c) 초등학교에서 정식 교육을 거의 받지 않았다.
(d) 그의 음악 스타일은 유럽에서 유래했다.

해설

(a), (c) 및 (d)는 지문에 없는 내용이며, He has been a headliner 이하에서 크랩튼이 40년 이상 스타의 자리에 있었음을 알 수 있으므로 정답은 (b)이다.

like minded 생각이 비슷한 | tastes in music 음악적 취향
self-taught 독학의 | make it big 큰 성공을 거두다 | headliner
저명인사 | acclaimed 환호를 받는 | do-it-yourselfer 손수 만드는 사람,
혼자 하는 사람 | grade school 초등학교

25

Many cultures originated from nomadic tribes that never settled in any particular area permanently. Referred to as "itinerants" in society today, surprisingly there are still approximately 30-40 million nomads around the world. Nomads fall into one of three categories based on their economic specialization. The first group is by far the oldest of the three and is known as the hunting and gathering nomads. This group drives and follows wild game and plant life according to the seasons. The second category is pastoral nomads who raise livestock and drive and move with them in patterns to maintain pasture sustainability. The last group is the peripatetic nomads who contribute specialized skills and crafts to their society and are most commonly found in industrialized nations.

Q: Which of the following is correct about nomads?
(a) Some follow the seasonal migration of their prey.
(b) Many eventually settle in industrialized nations.
(c) Pastoral nomads are the most common today.
(d) Nomadic life has triggered environmental hazards.

번역

많은 문화가 특정 장소에 결코 영구 정착하지 않았던 유목민 종족으로부터 유래되었다. 오늘날 사회에서 '떠돌이'라고 불리고 있는, 놀랍게도

전 세계적으로 아직도 약 3~4천만 명의 유목민이 존재한다. 유목민은 경제적인 전문 영역을 근거로 세가지 중 하나의 범주에 속한다. 제1집단은 단연코 세 개 집단 중 가장 오래되었고, 사냥과 채취를 하는 유목민이다. 이 집단은 계절에 따라서 야생 사냥감과 식물을 따라간다. 제2집단은 가축을 기르면서 목초지를 유지시키기 위해서 정형화된 방식으로 가축을 몰고 이동하는 목축 유목민이다. 마지막 집단은 자신이 속한 사회에 전문적인 기술과 솜씨를 제공하며 산업화된 나라에서 가장 일반적으로 볼 수 있는 일을 하러 이동해 다니는 유목민이다.

Q: 다음 중 유목민에 대해 옳은 것은?
(a) 일부는 사냥감을 찾아 계절에 따라 다른 지역으로 이동한다.
(b) 결국 많은 유목민이 산업화된 나라에서 정착한다.
(c) 목축 유목민이 오늘날 가장 일반적이다.
(d) 유목 생활은 환경적인 위험을 초래했다.

해설

(b)는 지문의 내용만으로는 알 수 없고, 일을 하러 돌아 다니는 유목민이 가장 일반적이라고 했으므로 (c)도 정답에서 제외된다. 목축 유목민은 목초지를 유지시키기 위해서 가축을 몰고 이동하므로 (d)도 정답에서 제외된다. (a)가 사냥과 채취를 하는 제1집단 유목민에 관한 내용이므로 정답이다.

nomadic 유목의 | tribe 종족 | itinerant 떠돌이 | specialization
전문 영역, 전공 | game 사냥감 | pastoral 목축 | sustainability
지속가능성 | peripatetic 이동해 다니는

26

Nearly everyone dreams of striking it rich by winning the lottery. Ironically, how many of these people actually buy lottery tickets? The largest prize ever won with a single lottery ticket in the United States was a whopping $177,270,519.67, split amongst eight co-workers at a Nebraska meat processing plant in 2006. The actual amount before taxes was $365 million and the workers wisely chose the lump sum cash payout rather than a lifetime payout that in the end pays you much less. Surprisingly enough, all eight workers said they would continue on with the jobs as usual. However, this golden pot at the end of the rainbow doesn't always guarantee a fairy story ending. As a matter of fact, nearly three out of every five lottery winner files for bankruptcy within five years of their winning.

Q: Which of the following is correct about the lottery?
(a) Only one person can claim a winning ticket.
(b) Choosing the right payout is crucial for value.
(c) Winnings are received free of state and federal tax.
(d) Lottery winners usually stay at their jobs.

번역

거의 모든 사람들이 복권에 당첨되어 벼락부자가 되는 꿈을 꾼다. 역설적으로 이들 중 얼마나 많은 사람들이 실제로 복권을 구입할까? 미

국에서 여태까지 복권 한 장으로 받은 최고 당첨금은 2006년 네브라스카의 육류 가공 공장에서 일하는 8명의 직장 동료에게 나누어 지급된 엄청난 금액인 177,270,519.67달러였다. 실제 세금 공제 전 금액은 3억 6천 5백만 달러였고, 그들은 결국 훨씬 적게 지급되는 평생 지급 방식이 아닌 현명하게도 일시불 현금 지급을 선택했다. 놀랍게도 8명의 동료들은 모두 평소대로 계속 일을 하겠다고 말했다. 하지만 무지개 끝에 걸린 황금 냄비가 항상 행복한 결말을 보장해주는 것은 아니다. 전체 복권 당첨자 5명 중 거의 3명은 당첨 후 5년 내에 파산을 신청하게 된다.

Q: 다음 중 복권에 대해 옳은 것은?

(a) 한 사람만 당첨될 수 있다.

(b) 올바른 지급 방식을 선택하는 것이 가치로 봤을 때 중요하다.

(c) 주세 및 연방세를 면제받고 당첨금을 받는다.

(d) 보통 복권 당첨자들은 하던 일을 그대로 한다.

최고의 복권 당첨금을 받게 된 8명의 근로자가 현명하게 일시불을 선택하고 계속 일을 했지만 통계적으로 많은 당첨자들이 결국 파산한다는 내용으로 보아 정답은 (b)가 된다.

strike it rich 벼락부자가 되다 | **prize** 당첨금 | **whopping** 엄청 큰 | **meat processing plant** 육류 가공 공장 | **before tax** 세금 공제 전 | **lump sum** 일시불 | **payout** 지불금 | **file for** 신청하다 | **bankruptcy** 파산

27

Rare earth metals, contrary to their namesake, are actually quite common on the planet, but not usually in highly concentrated amounts like other minerals and ore. Uses for rare earth metals range from rare microwave filters to lasers and X-ray machines. They are also crucial for many other electronic components such as batteries for laptops and mobile phones and camera lenses. Mining rare earth metals can pose some serious environmental risks including radioactive slurry and other toxic elements seeping into the groundwater or escaping into the air. The Burik Merah mine in Malaysia is currently under a $100 million clean-up effort after many residents blamed the refinery for birth defects and cases of leukemia.

Q: Which of the following is correct about rare earth metals?

(a) Only a few industries depend on them for essential components.

(b) They may soon be traded at equal or greater value than gold.

(c) There are many hazards in mining, refining and storing the waste.

(d) They are expensive because they are not commonly found on the planet.

이름과는 달리 희토류 금속은 실제로 지구에 상당수 존재하지만 다른 광물이나 광석과 같이 일반적으로 고농축된 양은 아니다. 희토류 금속의 용도는 보기 드문 마이크로파 필터에서 레이저 및 엑스선 기계에 이른다. 희토류 금속은 노트북 컴퓨터와 휴대 전화 전지, 카메라 렌즈와 같은 다른 많은 전자 부품에도 매우 중요하다. 희토류 금속 채굴로 지표수에 스며들거나 대기 중으로 빠져나가는 방사능 슬러리 및 기타 독성 요소를 포함해서 몇 가지 심각한 환경 위험이 제기될 수 있다. 말레이시아의 부릭 메라 광산의 경우 많은 주민들이 선천적 결손증과 백혈병을 이유로 제련소를 탓한 이후 현재 1억 달러의 비용을 들여 정화 사업이 진행 중이다.

Q: 다음 중 희토류 금속에 대해 옳은 것은?

(a) 몇몇 산업만이 필수 부품과 관련해서 희토류 금속에 의존한다.

(b) 희토류 금속은 곧 금 이상의 가격으로 거래될 것이다.

(c) 희토류 금속의 채굴, 제련 및 폐기물 보관에 있어서 많은 위험이 도사리고 있다.

(d) 희토류 금속은 지구에서 흔히 발견되지 않기 때문에 비싸다.

지문에 의하면 희토류 금속은 저농축 상태로 지구에 상당량 존재하며 많은 산업에서 이용되고 있다. 따라서 (a)와 (d)는 정답에서 제외되고 (b)는 지문에 없는 내용이다. 희토류 금속 채굴로 몇 가지 심각한 환경 위험이 야기될 수 있고 말레이시아의 부릭 메라 광산의 제련소로 인해서 선천적 결손증과 백혈병이 발생했다는 내용이 있으므로 정답은 (c)이다.

rare-earth metal 희토류 금속 | **ore** 광석 | **microwave** 마이크로파 | **electronic component** 전자 부품 | **pose** 제기하다 | **radioactive slurry** 방사능 슬러리 | **seep** 스며들다 | **groundwater** 지표수 | **birth defect** 선천적 결손증 | **leukemia** 백혈병

28

Various sausages are produced the world over, but none may beat the uniqueness of haggis. This dish is often attributed to Scotland in spite of the first written recipe coming from Lancashire in North West England in 1430. The traditional way to prepare haggis is to stuff a sheep's stomach with its 'pluck,' that is heart, liver and lungs, minced onions, oatmeal and other spices. The filling is also mixed with a stock, and left to simmer for about three hours. Many people consider haggis as a sausage or even a pudding. Although one might at first think haggis sounds unappetizing, it has legions of fans around the world.

Q: Which of the following is correct about haggis?

(a) It has its origins in North West Wales.

(b) It is not considered a type of sausage.

(c) It utilizes the major organs of the sheep.

(d) It is a quick and easy dish to prepare.

(d) It is an example of neoclassical Italian Renaissance design.

번역

미국독립선언서의 주요 저자이자 제3대 미국 대통령인 토머스 제퍼슨은 비범한 건축가이기도 했다. 인근의 버지니아대학교 외에 제퍼슨은 자신의 웅장한 소유지인 몬티셀로를 설계했다. 제퍼슨은 집 설계의 기초를 이태리 르네상스 시대의 건축가인 안드레이 팔라디오가 저술한 책에 쓰여진 신고전주의 원리에 두었다. 몬티셀로의 이미지는 2달러짜리 지폐와 1956년의 우표에 등장할 뿐 아니라, 1938년 이후 5센트짜리 동전의 뒷면을 장식하고 있다. 제퍼슨은 주프랑스 미국 공사로 7년을 보낸 후 돌아와서 몬티셀로를 리모델링했고 책에서 읽기만 했던 건물을 직접 볼 수 있는 기회를 얻었다.

Q: 다음 중 몬티셀로에 대해 옳은 것은?
(a) 유명한 이태리 건축가가 설계했다.
(b) 통화와 우표 디자인에 대혁신을 일으켰다.
(c) 제퍼슨이 영국에서 돌아온 후 리모델링 되었다.
(d) 이태리 르네상스 시대의 신고전주의 설계의 한 예이다.

해설

제퍼슨이 이태리 르네상스 시대의 건축가가 저술한 책의 신고전주의 원리에 기초해서 몬티셀로를 설계했고, 그가 프랑스에서 돌아온 후 리모델링 되었으므로 (a)와 (c)는 정답에서 제외되며 (d)가 정답이 된다. 또한, 몬티셀로의 이미지가 2달러짜리 지폐와 1956년의 우표 및 5센트짜리 동전에 나와 있지만 통화와 우표 디자인에 영향을 끼쳤다는 내용은 없으므로 (b)도 정답이 아니다.

Declaration of Independence 미국독립선언서 | **extraordinary** 비범한 | **architect** 건축가 | **estate** 소유지 | **principle** 원리, 원칙 | **adorn** 장식하다 | **nickel** 5센트짜리 동전 | **postage stamp** 우표 | **remodel** 리모델링하다 | **in person** 직접 몸소 | **currency** 통화

번역

전 세계적으로 다양한 소시지가 생산되지만, 어떤 소시지도 해기스의 독특함에 미치지는 못할 것이다. 1430년 잉글랜드 북서부의 랭커셔에서 요리법이 처음 쓰여졌음에도 불구하고 이 요리는 보통 스코틀랜드 음식으로 여겨지고 있다. 해기스를 만드는 전통 방식은 양의 위를 심장, 간, 허파, 다진 양파, 오트밀, 기타 향신료 등으로 이루어진 플럭으로 채워 넣는 것이다. 내용물을 육수로 섞고 약 3시간 동안 끓도록 둔다. 많은 사람들이 해기스를 소시지 혹은 심지어는 푸딩이라고 생각한다. 처음에는 해기스가 맛이 없을 것으로 생각했지만, 해기스는 전 세계적으로 많은 팬들이 있다.

Q: 다음 중 해기스에 대해 옳은 것은?
(a) 웨일즈 북서부에서 유래했다.
(b) 소시지 한 종류로 간주되지 않는다.
(c) 양의 주요 장기를 사용해서 만든다.
(d) 빠르고 쉽게 만들 수 있는 요리이다.

해설

잉글랜드 북서부의 랭커셔에서 유래한 해기스는 양의 내장 부위와 다진 양파, 오트밀, 향신료를 섞어 양의 위에 채워 넣고 3시간 동안 끓여서 만드는 손이 많이 가는 음식으로 많은 사람들이 해기스를 소시지 또는 푸딩이라고 생각하고 있다는 내용이다. 따라서 (a), (b) 및 (d)는 지문의 내용과 다르며 정답은 (c)이다.

uniqueness 독특함 | **attribute** ~의 것으로 여기다 | **stuff** 채우다 **stomach** 위 | **liver** 간 | **mince** 다지다 | **filling** 내용물 | **stock** 육수 **simmer** 끓이다 | **unappetizing** 맛이 없는 | **legion** 많은 사람들 **utilize** 이용하다

29

Besides being the principal author of the Declaration of Independence and the third president of the United States, Thomas Jefferson was also an extraordinary architect. In addition to the nearby University of Virginia, Jefferson also designed his magnificent estate "Monticello." Jefferson based the house design on the neoclassical principles written in the book by the Italian Renaissance architect Andrea Palladio. Its image has adorned the back side of the U.S. nickel since 1938 as well as appearing on the two dollar bill and a 1956 postage stamp. Jefferson remodeled Monticello after he returned from spending seven years as the Minister of the U.S. to France and had the opportunity to see in person the building he had only read about.

Q: Which of the following is correct about Monticello?
(a) It was designed by a famous Italian architect.
(b) It revolutionized currency and postage stamps design.
(c) It was remodeled after Jefferson returned from England.

30

Have you ever daydreamed about inventing that next hit product? In 2009, there were 4,548,072 patents granted worldwide. Not all inventions of course are a big hit, for example the "toilet snorkel," a patent granted in 1983 for a tube that allows a person to utilize the fresh air found at the back of a toilet when faced with a house fire. Also part of the "not so practical" invention category is the "cheese filtered" cigarette patented in 1966, as if smoking wasn't disgusting enough without adding the mellow flavor of a Gouda or sharp tang of cheddar. Last on the list is the "bulletproof desk" patent that was granted in 2001. This school desk has a clear bulletproof glass top with a handle that allows the terrorized student to hide behind the protective glass. Needless to say, public schools and universities around the country have not yet taken a shine to this desk.

Q: Which of the following is correct about patents?

(a) Criteria for patent grants have become stricter.

(b) Millions of patent applications are filed every year.

(c) Patents are only granted for inventions deemed useful.

(d) Inventors have a limit for the number of patents a year.

번역

다음 번 히트 상품 발명에 대해서 꿈꿔본 적이 있나요? 2009년 전 세계적으로 4,548,072건의 특허가 승인되었습니다. 물론 모든 발명품이 대성공을 거둔 것은 아닙니다. 예를 들어 집에 불이 났을 때 변기 뒷부분의 신선한 공기를 이용할 수 있도록 해주는 튜브에 대해서 1983년 특허가 인정된 '변기 스노클'이 있습니다. 또한 '별로 실용적이지 않은' 발명의 범주에 드는 것으로는 1966년 특허가 승인된 '치즈 필터' 담배가 있으며 고다 치즈의 부드러운 풍미나 체다 치즈의 톡 쏘는 맛을 첨가하지 않고도 흡연이 그렇게 역겹지 않은 듯 느껴집니다. 마지막으로 2011년에 승인된 '방탄 책상' 특허가 있습니다. 이 학교용 책상은 윗부분에 투명한 방탄유리가 있고, 테러를 당한 학생이 보호 유리 뒤에 숨을 수 있도록 손잡이가 달려 있습니다. 물론 전국적으로 이 책상에 반한 공립학교와 대학교는 아직 없습니다.

Q: 다음 중 특허에 대해 옳은 것은?
(a) 특허 인정 기준이 더욱 엄격해졌다.
(b) 매년 수백만 건의 특허 신청이 접수된다.
(c) 유용한 것으로 여겨지는 발명에 대해서만 특허가 인정된다.
(d) 발명가가 1년에 받을 수 있는 특허 수에는 제한이 있다.

해설

(a)와 (d)는 지문에 없는 내용이고, 실용성 여부에 관계없이 특허가 주어진 몇 가지 예가 지문 중 있으므로 (c)도 정답이 아니다. 2009년 전 세계적으로 4,548,072건의 특허가 인정된 것으로 보아 정답은 (b)이다.

daydream 공상하다 | **grant** 승인하다 | **patent** 특허 | **flavor** 풍미
sharp tang 톡 쏘는 | **bulletproof** 방탄 | **take a shine to** ~에 반하다 | **grant** 승인하다 | **deem** 여기다

31

For every holiday, there are always accompanying games. The dreidel is a spinning top with four-sides played during the Jewish holiday of Hanukkah. Each side has a symbol that forms an acronym that stands for "a great miracle happened here," the miracle referring to what is once happened in Israel. For adults, the four symbols stand for the rules of a gambling game. The symbolism of the dreidel has been commented on by Jacob who attributes the four symbols to stand for the four exile nations that the Jews were subjected to—Babylonia, Persia, Greece and Rome.

Q: Which of the following is correct about the dreidel?
(a) It has its origins in ancient Babylon.

(b) It is a game played on the Jewish new year.

(c) It can be a game for both children and adults.

(d) It reflects Israel's occupation of various nations.

번역

휴일마다 항상 벌어지는 시합이 있다. 드레이들은 유태인의 명절인 하누카에 갖고 노는 사각형의 말이다. 각 면에는 '이곳에서 발생한 위대한 기적'을 의미하는 약어로 구성된 하나의 상징이 있는데 그것은 이스라엘 땅에 일어났던 기적을 말한다. 어른들에게 있어서 네 가지 상징은 도박 게임의 규칙을 의미한다. 야곱이 드레이들의 상징성을 언급했는데, 네 가지 상징은 유태인이 지배당했던 네 개의 망명국인 바빌론, 페르시아, 그리스 및 로마를 의미하는 것으로 보고 있다.

Q: 다음 중 드레이들에 대해 옳은 것은?
(a) 고대 바빌론에 기원을 두고 있다.
(b) 유태인이 새해에 하는 게임이다.
(c) 아이와 어른이 할 수 있는 게임이다.
(d) 이스라엘이 여러 국가를 점령한 것을 반영한다.

해설

(a), (b), (d)는 지문에 없는 내용이다. 어른에게 있어서 네 개의 상징은 도박 게임의 규칙을 의미한다라는 내용으로 보아, 아이들도 하는 게임임을 알 수 있다. 따라서 정답은 (c)이다.

accompanying 수반하는 | **dreidel** 사각형의 말 | **spinning top** 팽이
form 구성하다 | **acronym** 약어 | **stand for** 의미하다 | **symbolism** 상징성 | **exile nation** 망명국 | **subject** 지배하다 | **occupation** 점령

32

Pond is more of a misnomer in regards to seasonal ponds. A more accurate description is they are shallow depressions that contain standing water for part, if not all, of the year. The amount and length of time these ponds contain water determine the types of plants and animals that live near them. Water volume varies yearly and often produces a vibrant and diverse ecosystem. Because the water is of a somewhat temporary nature, fish cannot survive in these ponds. This makes a seasonal pond an ideal safe zone for many amphibian species. Many rare wild flowers are also found near these ponds, producing an aesthetically pleasing and natural landscape.

Q: Which of the following is correct about seasonal ponds?

(a) They often produce rich and varied communities.

(b) They are better described as deep basins.

(c) Water levels remain consistent every year.

(d) Wild flowers are rarely found in most ponds.

번역

연못이란 명칭은 계절 연못에 관해서는 오히려 부적절하다. 더 정확하게 기술하자면 연못은 일 년 내내는 아닐지라도 일부 기간 동안 고인

물을 담고 있는 움푹하고 얕은 곳이다. 연못에 물이 고여 있는 양과 기간에 따라 근처에 사는 동식물의 종류가 결정된다. 매년 수량은 변하고 종종 활기차고 다양한 생태계를 형성한다. 물은 어느 정도 일시적 성질의 것이기 때문에 이러한 연못에서는 물고기가 생존할 수 없다. 따라서 계절 연못은 많은 양서류에게 이상적으로 안전한 지역이 된다. 연못 부근에서 찾아볼 수 있는 많은 희귀 야생화가 미적으로 즐겁고 자연스러운 풍경을 자아낸다.

Q: 다음 중 계절 연못에 대해 옳은 것은?
(a) 보통 풍부하고 다양한 군락을 형성한다.
(b) 깊은 웅덩이라고 기술하는 것이 더 정확하다.
(c) 매년 수위가 한결 같다.
(d) 대부분의 연못에서 야생화를 거의 찾아 볼 수 없다.

해설
지문은 계절 연못은 어느 기간 동안 물이 고여 있는 움푹하고 얕은 곳으로, 매년 수량이 변하고 종종 활기차고 다양한 생태계를 형성하며, 근처에 많은 희귀 야생화들이 자라고 있는 내용이다. 따라서 (b), (c), (d)는 틀린 내용이고 (a)가 정답이다.

more of 오히려 | **misnomer** 부적절한 명칭 | **shallow** 얕은 **depression** 움푹 패인 곳 | **standing water** 고인 물 | **vibrant** 활기찬 **ecosystem** 생태계 | **amphibian species** 양서류 | **aesthetically** 미적으로 | **landscape** 풍경 | **basin** 웅덩이

33

Lasagna (pronounced "la-sa-nya") has loads of melted mozzarella, Romano and parmesan cheeses oozing from its many layers of thick flat noodles and filled with Italian sausage, meatballs, mushrooms and spinach. It is a famous Italian dish with several regional varieties but usually made with a tomato sauce or Ragú. Origins of lasagna point to one of two theories, with both coming from ancient Greece. The first theory is it is named after the Greek "laganon," a flat sheet of pasta dough sliced into strips. The other theory comes from the words "lasana" or "lasanum" which mean a "stand for a pot," or "chamber pot," which the Romans adopted and made their own. Thus, lasagna took the name of the cooking vessel it was served in.

Q: What can be inferred from the passage?
(a) There are few local variations of lasagna.
(b) **Greek and Roman cultures share similarities.**
(c) Lasagna was the precursor of today's pizza.
(d) Ragú is a special type of tomato sauce.

번역
라자냐는 여러 겹의 두툼하고 평평한 국수에서 흘러 내리는 녹은 모짜렐라 치즈, 로마노 치즈, 파르메산 치즈를 얹은 것으로 이태리 소시지, 미트볼, 버섯 및 시금치로 채워진다. 라자냐는 지역에 따라서 몇 가지 종류가 있는 유명한 이태리 요리지만, 대개 토마토 소스인 라구로 만

든다. 라자냐의 기원은 고대 그리스에서 유래한 두 가지 이론이 하나로 모아지고 있다. 첫 번째 이론은 그리스어로 띠 모양으로 얇게 썬 넙적한 판 형태의 파스타 반죽이라는 의미의 라가논에서 이름을 따서 명명했다는 것이다. 두 번째 이론은 냄비용 스탠드 또는 요강을 의미하는 라자냐 또는 라자넘이라는 단어에서 유래했고, 이것을 로마인들이 취해서 자기들 것으로 만들었다는 것이다. 이와 같이 라자냐는 음식을 내는 조리 용기의 명칭을 딴 것이다.

Q: 지문을 통해 유추할 수 있는 것은?
(a) 지역마다 라자냐의 종류는 다양하지 않다.
(b) 그리스와 로마의 문화는 닮은 점이 있다.
(c) 라자냐는 오늘날 피자의 선구자였다.
(d) 라구는 특수한 종류의 토마토 소스이다.

해설
라자냐는 지역에 따라서 몇 가지 종류가 있다고 하므로 (a)는 정답에서 제외되고, 라구가 특별한 토마토 소스라는 내용이 지문에 없으므로 (d)도 제외된다. (c) 역시 지문에 없는 내용이다. 라자냐의 기원에 관한 두 가지 이론 모두 고대 그리스에서 유래하고, 그 중 하나의 이론을 로마인들이 취해서 자기들 것으로 만들었다는 내용으로 보아 두 문화는 닮은 점이 있다고 유추할 수 있다. 따라서 정답은 (b)이다.

ooze 흘러 내리다 | **spinach** 시금치 | **variety** 종류 | **Ragú** 볼로네제 [고기로 만든] 소스 | **name after** ~의 이름을 따서 명명하다 | **adopt** 취하다 | **vessel** 용기 | **variation** 변형 | **precursor** 선도자

34

Early this third millennium sees a rough average of twenty-four consumer electronic items in every American household according to an industry estimate. This translates into millions of devices thrown out each year, devices containing toxic heavy metals such as lead and mercury. States have begun to ban electronics in landfills for fear of contamination through leakage. They are even passing laws that set recycling quotas. While some gadgets can be refurbished and resold, the metal and plastic recovered and recycled, some companies simply ship the electronic waste elsewhere for dismantling or disposal at lower environmental standards. In effect, this shifts the problem elsewhere. Cynics might even point out that it is easier for companies to pay the fines than to actually recycle.

Q: What can be inferred from the passage?
(a) **Different countries have different laws on recycling electronic waste.**
(b) The penalty for not recycling electronic waste is usually substantial.
(c) Consumer electronics has a great potential for recycling and reuse.
(d) Companies are trying to design electronics to be more environmental.

업계 추정에 따르면 2000년대 초, 모든 미국 가정에는 평균 약 24개의 가전제품이 있는 것으로 나타났다. 이는 매년 폐기되는 수백만 개의 제품이 납과 수은 같은 독성이 있는 중금속을 함유하고 있음을 의미한다. 주 정부들은 중금속 누출로 인한 오염의 두려움 때문에 전자 기기를 매립지에 버리는 것을 금지하기 시작했다. 주 정부들은 심지어 재활용 할당량을 지정하는 법안을 통과시키고 있다. 몇몇 장치는 재설비하고 재판매할 수 있으며, 금속과 플라스틱은 재생하고 재활용할 수 있지만, 일부 기업은 전자 폐기물을 분해하거나 환경 기준이 낮은 곳에서 처리하기 위해 다른 곳으로 수송해 버린다. 사실 이런 처리는 다른 곳에 문제를 떠넘기는 것이다. 냉소적인 사람들은 회사가 재활용을 하는 것보다 벌금을 내는 것이 더 쉽다고 지적할지도 모른다.

Q: 지문을 통해 유추할 수 있는 것은?

(a) 전자 폐기물 재활용에 있어서 국가들 간에는 서로 다른 법안이 있다.
(b) 전자 폐기물을 재활용하지 않는 것에 대한 벌금은 보통 상당하다.
(c) 소비 가전은 재활용과 재사용에 있어 뛰어난 가능성이 있다.
(d) 기업들은 보다 친환경적인 전자 제품을 디자인하려고 노력하고 있다.

유해 중금속을 포함하고 있는 전자 폐기물을 재활용하는 법안에 대해 일부 주 정부들이 관련 법안을 마련하고 있고, 기업에 따라 폐기물 처리 방법이 다르다고 하는 것으로 보아 (a)를 유추할 수 있다.

consumer electronic item 가전제품 | toxic 독성의 | lead 납 | mercury 수은 | landfill (쓰레기) 매립지 | contamination 오염 | leakage 누출 quota 할당(량) | gadget 기기 | refurbish 재설비하다 | dismantle 분해하다 | disposal 처리 | cynic 부정적인 사람 | substantial 상당한

35

Dear Bill,

I am happy to inform you that tickets for the Caribbean cruise have been booked for the Labor Day weekend and will be waiting for you at the boarding dock. Remember to arrive no later than 12:30 as the ship is scheduled to set sail by 3:00. I was able to reserve first class cabin accommodations and seats for three shows. There are four pools, several game rooms, two fitness gyms and a golf practice range for the whole family to enjoy. Please wire the balance of the account to Ace Travel agency within the next two days or the tickets will be forfeited. If you have any questions regarding any details, feel free to email me back or call me. Again, thank you for your patronage and we wish you and your family a terrific Labor Day cruise!

Warmest regards,
Stan Franklin, Accounts Manager

Q: What can be inferred from the passage?

(a) Stan is anxious to close the account in the next two days.

(b) The cruise will last four days and three nights.
(c) Bill has already put a down payment on the tickets.
(d) The cruise ship will not wait for any late passengers.

빌 씨께

노동절 주말 카리브 해 유람선 여행권이 예약되었음을 알려 드립니다. 저는 승선 부두에서 기다리겠습니다. 배가 3시에 출항할 예정이니 늦어도 12시 30분까지 도착해야 한다는 것을 명심하십시오. 1등 선실과 3개의 쇼를 관람할 수 있는 좌석을 예약하였습니다. 배에는 가족 전체가 즐길 수 있는 수영장 네 곳, 게임방 몇 개, 헬스클럽 두 곳, 골프 연습장이 있습니다. 앞으로 이틀 이내에 잔금을 에이스 트래블 사로 송금해 주십시오. 그렇지 않으면 예약이 취소됩니다. 어떤 내용이든 질문이 있다면 이메일이나 전화 주십시오. 다시 한번 애용해 주셔서 감사 드리며 고객님과 가족분들이 노동절 동안 멋진 유람선 여행을 하시기를 기원합니다.

경리과장, 스탠 플랭클린

Q: 지문을 통해 유추할 수 있는 것은?
(a) 스탠은 앞으로 이틀 후 접수를 마감하려고 한다.
(b) 유람선 여행 기간은 3박 4일이다.
(c) 빌은 이미 여행권 구입을 위한 계약금을 지불했다.
(d) 유람선은 늦게 오는 승객을 기다리지 않을 것이다.

여행사 직원이 빌에게 노동절 주말 동안의 유람선 여행권이 예약되었음을 이메일로 알리는 내용으로 12시 30분까지 도착할 것을 요청하고 있으나, 배가 3시에 출발한다고 하니 (b), (d)는 정답에서 제외되며, (a)는 지문에 없는 내용이다. 잔금을 송금하라는 내용으로 보아 빌이 계약금을 이미 지불했음을 유추할 수 있으므로 (c)가 정답이다.

cruise 유람선 여행 | boarding dock 승선 부두 | no later than 늦어도 ~까지 | set sail 출항하다 | cabin 선실 | wire 송금하다 balance 잔금 | forfeit 박탈하다 | patronage 애용

36

Solar flares are explosions on the sun that release radiation that vary in wavelengths. On Valentine's Day, the first "X-class" flare was expelled from the sun in four years. An X-class flare is the strongest of the three types of flares and has been known to wreak havoc on satellite systems. The Valentine's Day solar flare was also accompanied by a coronal mass ejection of charged particles. However, it did not interrupt satellite service on Earth as the flare's orientation lined up with the Earth's, therefore aligning the magnetic fields and preventing particles from penetrating our planet's protective magnetic shield.

Q: What can be inferred from the passage?

(a) The Earth's magnetic field has been breached in the past.

(b) Solar flares are minor releases of radioactive material.
(c) The X-type solar flare is the most common of all flares.
(d) Solar flares routinely penetrate deep into the Earth's surface.

태양 플레어는 파장이 다른 방사선을 방출하는 폭발이다. 발렌타인 데이에 첫 번째 X-등급 플레어가 4년만에 방출되었다. X-등급 플레어는 3가지 종류의 플레어 중에서 가장 강력하며 위성 시스템에 엄청난 피해를 입히는 것으로 알려져 있다. 또한 발렌타인 데이에 있었던 태양 플레어 역시 하전 입자의 코로나 물질 방출이 있었다. 하지만 플레어의 방향이 지구와 나란했기 때문에 자기장을 일직선으로 정렬하고 입자가 지구의 자기 차폐막을 침투하는 것을 막았기 때문에 지구의 위성 서비스가 방해 받지 않았다.

Q: 지문을 통해 유추할 수 있는 것은?
(a) 과거에 지구 자기장이 파괴되었다.
(b) 태양 플레어는 방사능 물질을 소량 방출한다.
(c) X-등급 태양 플레어는 모든 플레어 중에서 가장 일반적이다.
(d) 태양 플레어는 일상적으로 지구 표면 깊숙히 침투한다.

태양 플레어가 위성 체계에 엄청난 피해를 입히는 것으로 보아 많은 방사능 물질이 배출되는 것으로 보이며, X-등급 플레어는 모든 플레어 중에서 가장 강력하다. 또한 플레어는 태양 표면 폭발 시 지구의 표면이 아니라 지구의 자기 차폐막을 침투한다. 발렌타인 데이에 있었던 태양 플레어의 방향이 지구 자기장과 나란했기 때문에 위성 서비스가 방해 받지 않았다는 내용으로 보아 (a)가 정답이다.

solar flare 태양 플레어 (태양 표면의 폭발) | release 방출하다 | radiation 방사선 | wavelength 파장 | wreak havoc on ~에 엄청난 피해를 입히다 | coronal mass ejection 코로나 물질 방출 | charged particle 하전 입자 | orientation 방향 | align 일직선으로 하다 | penetrate 관통하다 | magnetic shield 자기 차폐막 | breach 구멍을 뚫다

37

The average worker spends five to eight hours a day being stationary in front of his computer monitor. The long term cost of this type of behavior is unhealthy weight gain, fatigue and general lack of motivation. Introducing the Strong Stationary Desk Bike, a revolutionary exercise machine that can be fitted under any desk. Built of the highest quality alloys and aluminums, the Strong Stationary Desk Bike has 20 settings from beginner to the avid athlete. So, while you are typing up that accounting report or drafting a marketing proposal, you can also improve your cardiovascular fitness with the smart Strong Stationary Desk Bike, order now!

Q: What can be inferred from the passage?

(a) The adverse effects of working is reduced with Strong Stationary Desk Bike.
(b) Unhealthy employees lead to a significant decrease in production.
(c) The Strong Stationary Desk Bike is popular with big companies.
(d) People prefer to have desk jobs rather than to work in the field.

일반 근로자는 컴퓨터 모니터 앞에서 움직이지 않는 상태로 하루에 5~8시간을 보냅니다. 이러한 행동 방식을 장기간 취하면 건강에 좋지 않은 체중 증가, 피로, 일반적인 의욕 부진이 따르게 됩니다. 어떤 책상 아래에도 설치할 수 있는 혁신적인 운동 기구인 스트롱 스테이셔너리 데스크 바이크를 소개합니다. 최고 품질의 합금과 알루미늄으로 제작된 스트롱 스테이셔너리 데스크 바이크는 초보용부터 열심히 운동하는 선수용까지 20단계로 설정이 가능합니다. 따라서 회계 보고서를 타이핑하거나 영업 제안서를 작성하면서 이 멋진 스트롱 스테이셔너리 데스크 바이크로 심혈관 건강을 증진시킬 수 있습니다. 지금 주문하십시오.

Q: 지문을 통해 유추할 수 있는 것은?
(a) 스트롱 스테이셔너리 데스크 바이크로 일의 부작용을 줄일 수 있다.
(b) 건강이 나쁜 직원은 생산성이 상당히 떨어진다.
(c) 스트롱 스테이셔너리 데스크 바이크는 대기업에서 인기가 있다.
(d) 사람들은 현장근무보다는 책상에서 일하는 직업을 좋아한다.

사무실 근무자는 보통 움직이지 않는 상태로 하루에 5~8시간을 일하기 때문에 장기적으로 건강에 좋지 않고, 전반적으로 의욕이 떨어지니 스트롱 스테이셔너리 데스크 바이크를 책상 아래 설치해서 운동을 하면 심혈관 건강이 좋아진다고 광고하는 내용이다. 지문에 의하면 스트롱 스테이셔너리 데스크 바이크는 일의 부작용을 줄이는 것이 아니라 심혈관을 개선한다는 내용이며, (c)와 (d)는 지문에 없는 내용이다. 따라서 정답은 (b)이다.

stationary 움직이지 않는 | weight gain 체중 증가 | motivation 의욕 | revolutionary 혁신적인 | alloy 합금 | avid 열심인 | accounting 회계 | proposal 제안서 | cardiovascular fitness 심혈관 건강

38

The Florida Keys were made famous in the movie *True Lies* when Harrier jets destroyed a part of one of the many bridges that connect the 4,500 islands of this archipelago. (a) The Keys start 15 miles south of Miami and extend in an arching form going south to southwest, heading to the most populated city Key West and ending at the uninhabited Dry Tortugas. (b) For automobile travel, the Keys have a 127 mile highway called the Overseas highway that runs its entire length. (c) At its most southern point, the Keys are a mere 90 miles from Cuba, which has made it a favorite hideout for drug smugglers. **(d) The**

locals prefer a laid-back lifestyle of sun bathing, swimming and fishing.

[번역]

플로리다 키스는 영화 〈트루 라이즈〉에서 해리어 전투기들이 군도에 있는 4,500개의 섬을 연결하는 많은 교량 중 하나의 교량 일부를 파괴하면서 유명해졌다. (a) 키스는 마이애미 남부에서 15마일 떨어진 지점에서 시작해서 남쪽에서 남서쪽으로 가면서 아치 형태로 뻗어 있고, 인구가 가장 많은 도시인 키웨스트를 향하고 사람이 살지 않는 드라이 토르투가스에서 끝난다. (b) 키스 전체를 지나는 오버시즈라고 불리는 127마일의 자동차 여행용 고속 도로가 있다. (c) 최남단 지점은 쿠바에서 단지 90마일 떨어져 있기 때문에 마약 밀수범들이 매우 좋아하는 도피처가 되었다. **(d) 지역 주민들은 일광욕, 수영 및 낚시와 같은 느긋한 생활 방식을 좋아한다.**

[해설]

(a), (b), (c)는 모두 키스의 지리적인 조건에 관한 내용이고 (d)는 지역 주민의 생활 방식에 관한 내용이다. 따라서 정답은 (d)이다.

Harrier jet 해리어 전투기 | **archipelago** 군도 | **head to** ~로 향하다 | **uninhabited** 사람이 살지 않는 | **hideout** 도피처 | **smuggler** 밀수범 | **laid-back** 느긋한

39

Studying past occurrences of social transformation may be the key in reducing the damage caused by climate change: For instance, approximately 44 percent of all Californians smoked in 1965. Forty-five years later, that number has dropped to an amazingly low 9.3 percent, a figure unimaginable prior to actually happening. **(a) Many tobacco companies are still reeling from the prolonged decrease in smoking.** (b) Scientists are studying the technical aspects of reducing climate change as well as the top ten historical behavior changes. (c) These changes include smoking cessation, seat belt use, vegetarianism, drunk driving, recycling, yoga and others. (d) What these behavioral changes tell scientists is the approximate time it takes for individuals to change habits that require more resources from the planet.

[번역]

과거에 일어났던 사회 변화에 대한 연구는 기후 변화로 인한 피해를 줄이는 실마리가 될 수 있다. 예를 들어 1965년에는 모든 캘리포니아 주민의 약 44%가 흡연을 했다. 45년 후, 그 수가 놀랍게도 낮아져 9.3%로 감소했는데, 이것은 실제로 일어나기 전까지는 상상하기 어려운 수치이다. **(a) 장기적인 흡연 감소로 인하여 아직도 담배 회사들이 휘청거리고 있다.** (b) 과학자들은 역사상 최대 10위까지의 행동 변화뿐만 아니라 기후 변화를 감소시키는 기술적인 면에 대해서 연구하고 있다. (c) 이러한 변화로는 금연, 안전벨트 착용, 채식주의, 음주 운전, 재활용,

요가 등이 있다. (d) 이러한 행동 변화가 과학자들에게 시사하는 바는 개인이 더 많은 지구 자원을 필요로 하는 습관을 바꾸는 데 걸린 대략적인 기간이다.

[해설]

사회 변화에 대한 연구를 통해서 기후 변화로 인한 피해를 줄일 수 있다는 것이 요지이다. (b), (c), (d)는 모두 기후 변화와 기후 변화로 인한 사람들의 행동 변화에 관한 내용이지만, (a)는 흡연자의 감소로 담배 회사들이 곤경에 처했다는 내용이므로 정답은 (a)이다.

social transformation 사회 변화 | **figure** 수치 | **unimaginable** 상상할 수 없는 | **reel** 휘청거리다 | **prolonged** 장기적인 | **cessation** 중단 | **vegetarianism** 채식주의

40

German manufacturer Krupp revealed the world's largest earth digger, and technically the largest moving machine. (a) Standing at nearly 100 meters tall, with an unfathomable 600 meters in length, this digger weighs 45,000 tons and can move more than 76,000 cubic meters of coal, rock and earth a day. (b) Krupp's giant digger took more than 5 years of planning and over $100 million to design and manufacture. **(c) It requires a special handling class license to operate that takes years to acquire.** (d) The Goliath of a machine can slowly move from one location to another and has enormous digging wheels that come right out of a macabre science fiction horror film.

[번역]

독일 제조업체인 크루프는 세계 최대의 굴착기를 선보였는데, 이것은 기술적으로 가장 큰 움직이는 기계이다. (a) 길이가 가늠이 불가능할 정도인 600m이고, 높이가 거의 100m인 이 굴착기의 무게는 45,000톤이고 하루에 76,000세제곱미터 이상의 석탄과 바위, 흙을 운반할 수 있다. (b) 크루프 거대 굴착기는 기획에 5년 이상이 걸렸고, 설계 및 제작에 1억 달러 이상이 소요되었다. **(c) 이 장비를 운전하려면 면허를 따는 데 몇 년이 걸리는 특수 조작 면허가 필요하다.** (d) 이 장비의 골리앗 기중기는 한 위치에서 다른 위치로 서서히 이동할 수 있으며, 섬뜩한 공상 과학 공포 영화에서 막 가져온 것 같은 엄청난 굴착 바퀴를 가지고 있다.

[해설]

독일의 제조업체인 크루프 사의 굴착기를 소개하는 내용으로 (a), (b) 및 (d)는 장비의 규격, 성능 및 설계, 제작 기간과 비용에 관한 내용이다. 반면 (c)는 장비를 운전하는 데 필요한 면허에 관한 내용이므로 정답이 된다.

manufacturer 제조업체 | **digger** 굴착기 | **unfathomable** 가늠이 불가능한 | **cubic meters** 세제곱미터 | **license** 면허 | **macabre** 섬뜩한

Part I

1 (b)	**2** (d)	**3** (a)	**4** (c)	**5** (a)
6 (a)	**7** (b)	**8** (d)	**9** (a)	**10** (c)
11 (b)	**12** (d)	**13** (a)	**14** (a)	**15** (c)
16 (b)				

Part II

17 (d)	**18** (c)	**19** (a)	**20** (d)	**21** (b)
22 (b)	**23** (a)	**24** (c)	**25** (a)	**26** (b)
27 (c)	**28** (a)	**29** (c)	**30** (b)	**31** (c)
32 (b)	**33** (c)	**34** (a)	**35** (d)	**36** (d)
37 (b)				

Part III

38 (c)	**39** (b)	**40** (a)

1

Standing at roughly five stories high, with a length of 170 meters and a width of 13 meters, the Ohio-class nuclear submarine is a silent killer in the waters. The U.S. Navy has 14 of these mammoth-sized stealth vehicles that stay hidden beneath the murky depths of the oceans for months on end. The only limitations they have is food supply, otherwise these submarines could stay submerged indefinitely. Each ship has fifteen officers in charge·of a rotating crew of 140 submariners. This fleet of nuclear subs carries approximately 50 percent of the United States' total nuclear arsenal, which help it to serve the purpose of _____.

(a) keeping the enemy confused at all times
(b) being a long distance deterrence force
(c) dominating the major Atlantic trade zones
(d) showing America's strength in diplomacy

번역

길이가 170m, 폭이 13m인 약 5층 건물 높이의 오하이오급 핵잠수함은 물속의 조용한 살인마이다. 미국 해군은 몇 달이고 계속해서 해양의 어두운 심해에 숨어 있는 거대한 크기의 이러한 잠함급을 14대 보유하고 있다. 이 잠수함의 유일한 제약은 식량 공급인데, 그렇지 않으면 무기한 잠수할 수 있다. 각 잠수함에는 교대 근무하는 140명의 잠수함 승무원을 담당하는 15명의 장교가 있다. 핵잠수함 함대는 미국의 전체 핵무기의 약 50%를 싣고 있으며, 이것이 장기적으로 전쟁 억제 영향력이라는 목적을 수행하는 데 도움이 되고 있다.

(a) 적을 항상 혼란스럽게 하는

(b) 장기적으로 전쟁 억제 영향력이라는
(c) 대서양의 주요 무역 지대를 지배하는
(d) 외교에 있어서 미국의 힘을 보여주는

해설

세계 강대국들이 핵을 보유하고 있는 것은 상호 견제를 통해 전쟁이 일어나지 않게 하기 위해서이므로 가장 적절한 것은 (b)이다.

Ohio-class 오하이오급 | **submarine** 잠수함 | **stealth** 스텔스 (레이더에 잘 포착되지 않게 만든 것) | **murky** 어두운 | **on end** 계속하여 **arsenal** 무기 | **deterrence** 전쟁 억제

2

Blue jeans are _____, from fashionistas to your chubby plumber. Comfortable and durable, blue jeans were invented by a young Levi Strauss who moved to San Francisco during the California Gold Rush in 1853. Strauss' intentions were to open a store selling his brother's dry goods but found what the miners really needed were strong pants that could stand up to their harsh working conditions. Initially, Levi fashioned rough canvas that was originally meant for tents or wagon covers, into overalls. Although the miners approved of the durability, they complained of skin chaffing. Levi then turned to twilled cotton from Nimes, France, called "serge de Nimes," and voilá! Demin blue jeans made history.

(a) a favorite accessory for everyone in America
(b) popular with teens around the world
(c) a global symbol of Western freedom
(d) the go to apparel worldwide for everyone

번역

청바지는 패션 리더에서부터 통통한 배관공에 이르기까지 전 세계적으로 모든 사람이 애용하는 의류이다. 편안하고 튼튼한 청바지는 1853년 캘리포니아 골드러시 때 샌프란시스코로 이주한 청년 리바이 스트라우스가 고안했다. 스트라우스는 형의 포목을 파는 상점을 열려는 의도였지만 광부들이 정말 필요로 하는 것은 혹독한 작업 환경에 견딜 수 있는 튼튼한 바지라는 것을 알았다. 처음에 리바이는 원래 텐트나 4륜마차 덮개용으로 사용되었던 거친 캔버스 천으로 오버롤을 만들었다. 광부들은 내구성에 대해서는 인정을 했지만 피부가 쓸린다며 불평했다. 그러자 리바이는 프랑스의 님에서 생산된 능직으로 짠 면인 '세르주 데 님'으로 바꾸었고, 잔! 데님 청바지는 역사를 만들었다.

(a) 미국의 모든 사람들이 좋아하는 장신구
(b) 전 세계적으로 10대에게 인기 있는
(c) 서구의 자유에 대한 세계적인 상징
(d) 전 세계적으로 모든 사람이 애용하는 의류

해설

오늘날 청바지는 편리하고 실용적이라 많은 사람이 입는 의류이며, 데님 청바지가 역사를 만들었다는 마지막 문장으로 보아 청바지가 인기가 있다는 내용이 자연스럽다. 따라서 가장 적절한 것은 (d)이다.

fashionista 패션 리더 | plumber 배관공 | dry goods 포목 | fashion
만들어 내다 | canvas 천 | overalls 오버롤 (상하가 하나로 이어진 작업복)
durability 내구성 | chaff 썰다 | twilled 능직으로 짠 | the go 유행

3

We've all had our spotlight moments, belting out our
favorite love ballad at the top of our voice. However,
we usually do this in the privacy of our showers so
those with discerning ears do not suffer. All that
changed in 1971, when Daisuke Inoue of Kobe,
Japan, invented the karaoke machine. The concept
and technology of karaoke was nothing new at the
time. Since the advent of the multi-track recorder,
recording artists since the 60s had been laying down
separate tracks songs and professional performers
often sang to recordings sans vocals. Yet, the
karaoke machine was the first to combine video and
music, _____ the lyrics as they sang
along to their favorite tunes.

(a) allowing amateur singers to read
(b) creating a multi-media depiction of
(c) paving the way for future stars to read
(d) forcing participants to pay attention to

번역

우리 모두 좋아하는 러브 발라드를 목청껏 노래하며 주목 받는 순간
이 있었다. 하지만 우리는 보통 샤워 속에서 하기 때문에 분별력이 있
는 귀를 가진 사람은 시달림을 받지 않는다. 이 모든 것은 1971년 일
본 고베의 다이스케 이노우에가 가라오케 기계를 발명하면서 바뀌었다.
가라오케의 개념과 기술은 그 당시 새로운 것이 아니었다. 다중 트랙
리코더가 등장한 때부터, 1960년대 이래 녹음 아티스트들은 트랙곡을
분리하여 저장하고 있었으며, 직업 가수들은 종종 음성 없이 녹음했다.
하지만 가라오케 기계는 처음으로 영상과 음악을 조합해 아마추어 가
수들이 가장 좋아하는 곡조를 따라 노래하면서 가사를 읽을 수 있도록
했다.

(a) 아마추어 가수들이 가사를 읽을 수 있도록 하는
(b) 멀티미디어의 묘사를 창작하는
(c) 장래의 스타들이 읽을 수 있도록 길을 열어주는
(d) 참가자들이 주목을 하지 않을 수 없도록 만드는

해설

빈칸은 가라오케가 영상과 음악을 조합하여 노래를 부르면서 노래 가
사로 무엇을 하였는가를 묻는 문제이다. 비디오와 음악의 조합에 주목
하면 가장 적절한 것은 (a)임을 알 수 있다.

belt out 힘차게 노래하다 | **at the top of one's voice** 목청껏 소리를
질러 | **discerning** 분별력이 있는 | **concept** 개념 | **advent** 등장
lay down 저장하다 | **sans** ~없이 | **vocal** 음성 | **lyric** 가사
pave the way for ~을 위해 길을 열다

4

Mental disorders can often be so debilitating they
render the sufferer incapable of _____.
On the other hand, many of history's greatest thinkers
were inflicted with some sort of mental disability.
No case is as true as John Forbes Nash, Jr., who
suffers from paranoid schizophrenia. Despite this
often very serious diagnosis, Nash has gone on to
hold the post of Senior Research Mathematician at
Princeton University. He is credited for his priceless
contributions to many fields including game theory,
market economics, evolutionary biology, artificial
intelligence and even military theory. In 1994, Nash
was awarded the Nobel Prize in Economic Sciences
with fellow game theorists Richard Selten and John
Harsanyi.

(a) holding down high-profile, lucrative positions
(b) differentiating abstract and tangible theories
(c) carrying out basic functions of everyday life
(d) recognizing their infinite physical potential

번역

정신 장애는 종종 환자의 심신을 쇠약하게 해서 일상생활의 기본적인
기능을 수행할 수 없게 한다. 한편, 역사적으로 가장 위대했던 많은 사
상가들은 일종의 정신 장애로 고통을 겪었다. 망상형 정신 분열증을 앓
고 있는 존 내쉬가 바로 그런 경우이다. 일반적으로 매우 심각한 이런
진단에도 불구하고 내쉬는 프린스턴대학교에서 수학 연구원직을 계속
맡고 있다. 그는 게임 이론, 시장 경제학, 진화 생물학, 인공 지능 및 군
사 이론까지 많은 분야에 아주 중요한 기여를 한 것으로 평가 받고 있
다. 1994년 내쉬는 동료 게임 이론가인 리차드 젤텐과 존 하사니와 함
께 노벨 경제학상을 수상했다.

(a) 수익성이 매우 좋은 지위를 유지하고 있는
(b) 추상적인 이론과 유형의 이론을 구별하고 있는
(c) 일상생활의 기본적인 기능을 수행하는
(d) 그들의 무한한 신체적 잠재력을 인식하는

해설

빈칸은 심신이 쇠약해지는 정신 장애자들이 어떠한 능력을 가지지 못
하는가를 묻는 문제이다. 뒤이어 그 반대의 예로 존 내쉬는 장애에도
불구하고 직분을 수행하고 있다는 내용이 이어지므로 가장 적절한 것
은 (c)이다.

disorder 장애 | **debilitating** 심신을 쇠약하게 하는 | **inflict** 괴롭히다
paranoid schizophrenia 망상형 정신 분열증 | **credit** ~의 공으로
여기다 | **high-profile** 세간의 이목을 끄는 | **lucrative** 수익성이 좋은
differentiate 구별하다 | **tangible** 유형의

5

To James Simmons, Ace Cabinets,

This week's shipment of oak, pine, and cedar will be

delayed three days because of an unfortunate delay due to flooding at our number three and four lumber yards. As you know, in order to maintain our strict standard of quality, we never let subpar lumber leave our yards and are therefore forced to let the wood dry in our kilns longer. Even though this method of heat-treating lumber diverges from our usual practice, please do not worry about the integrity of the lumber as we will test and retest for structural defects. _____, Larry's Lumber will offer you a 10 percent discount for the delay and will split shipping costs with Ace Cabinets.

Yours truly,
Jenna Franklin

(a) In light of our long-standing relationship
(b) Because the wood may be less-than-perfect
(c) To prevent another conflict with your company
(d) After another two shipments of lumber

번역

에이스 캐비닛 사의 제임스 시몬스 씨께

당사의 세 번째와 네 번째 재목 저장소의 홍수로 인한, 불운한 작업 지연으로 인해 금주의 오크, 소나무 및 삼나무 선적이 3일 지연될 것입니다. 아시다시피 당사는 엄격한 품질 기준을 유지하기 위해 수준 이하의 목재를 절대 작업장에서 출하하지 않기 때문에 가마에서 목재를 더 오래 건조하지 않을 수 없습니다. 이러한 목재 열처리 방법은 평상시 관행과 다르지만 구조적인 결함에 대한 검사 및 재검사를 할 것이기 때문에 목재의 보전에 대해서는 걱정하지 마십시오. 양사간의 오랜 관계를 고려해 래리스 럼버 사는 납품 지연에 대해 10% 할인을 제공할 것이며 에이스 캐비닛 사와 배송비를 분담할 것입니다.

제나 프랭클린

(a) 양사간의 오랜 관계를 고려해
(b) 목재의 품질이 완벽하지 못하므로
(c) 귀사와 또 다른 분쟁이 생기지 않도록
(d) 목재를 앞으로 2회 더 선적한 뒤

해설

목재 공급 회사가 바이어에게 선적 지연을 통지하는 편지로 납품 지연에 대해 10% 할인을 제의하고 있으며, 빈칸에는 그 이유나 배경이 들어가야 한다. 지문에는 목재의 품질에 대해 걱정하지 말라는 내용이 있으므로 (b)는 틀리다. 지연으로 분쟁이 발생했었다는 내용이 없고, 이미 목재가 선적되었다는 내용도 없으므로 (a)가 가장 적절하다.

shipment 선적 | cedar 삼나무 | lumber yard 재목 저장소 | subpar 수준 이하의 | kiln 가마 | diverge 벗어나다 | integrity 보전 | in light of ~을 고려하여 | long-standing 오래 계속되는

6

Along with other iconic images of San Francisco such as the Golden Gate Bridge and Alcatraz, the cable car system is _____. This system runs from downtown Union Square to Fisherman's Wharf and is often ridden by commuters and tourists alike. The two types of cars in use are the single and double ended car. Single-ended cars have an open-sided front segment with seats facing outward and can carry around 60 passengers. The double-ended cars are almost identical to the single-ended, but are longer and can carry almost 70 passengers. The tolling of the cable car bells let you know you're on the hilly streets of San Francisco.

(a) an integral part of the city's rich heritage
(b) celebrated by city planners the world over
(c) praised by rail enthusiasts for its longevity
(d) duly in need of refurbishing and repair

번역

골든게이트와 앨커트래즈와 같은 샌프란시스코의 다른 상징적인 이미지와 함께 케이블카 시스템은 도시의 여러 전통의 필수적인 부분입니다. 이 시스템은 도심지인 유니언 스퀘어에서 피셔맨스 워프까지 운행하며 보통 통근자들과 관광객들 모두가 이용합니다. 사용 중인 전차 두 종류는 편면 전차와 양면 전차입니다. 편면 동력 전차는 앞부분이 개방되었고 좌석은 바깥을 향해 있으며 약 60명의 승객을 태울 수 있습니다. 양면 동력 전차는 편면 동력 전차와 거의 똑같지만 길이가 더 길고 약 70명의 승객을 태울 수 있습니다. 케이블카의 종이 울리면 여러분이 샌프란시스코의 언덕길을 지나고 있다는 것입니다.

(a) 도시의 여러 전통의 필수적인 부분
(b) 전 세계의 도시 계획자들이 기념하는
(c) 열광적인 철도팬들이 그 오랜 역사를 칭송하는
(d) 재단장과 수리를 적당히 필요로 하는

해설

샌프란시스코의 케이블카를 소개하고 있으며, 빈칸은 이것이 샌프란시스코의 여타 상징적인 이미지와 함께 무엇인지 묻는 문제이다. 따라서 가장 적절한 것은 (a)이다.

iconic 상징적인 | downtown 도심지 | segment 부분 | identical 똑같은 | toll 〈종·시계가〉 치다 | hilly 언덕이 많은 | heritage 전통 | duly 적당히

7

When you land in the Anchorage, Alaska airport, there stands a large, stuffed Kodiak bear that _____ of this vast, pristine wilderness. The Kodiak is like a brown bear on mega-steroids. The largest Kodiak was put down by a Forest Ranger after it had eaten a hiker. The Ranger not only unloaded his 7mm semi-automatic rifle into the beast, but had to reload, and shoot him in the head to kill him. This goliath weighed over 737 kilograms and stood 3.85 meters at shoulder height and a mouth-dropping 4.27 meters at the top of his head. That means this Kodiak could've looked in on you if you lived on the second floor. Better close those curtains!

(a) stoically conveys the wild beauty
(b) serves as a reminder of the dangers
(c) once roamed the airport grounds
(d) epitomizes the majestic grandeur

알래스카의 앵커리지 공항에 내리면, 이 광대하고 자연 그대로의 야생의 위험을 상기시키는 박제된 커다란 코디액 불곰이 있습니다. 코디액 불곰은 스테로이드를 맞은 엄청나게 큰 갈색곰 같습니다. 가장 큰 코디액 불곰은 하이커를 잡아먹은 뒤 삼림 관리원에 의해 사살되었습니다. 관리원은 7mm 반자동 소총을 짐승에게 쏘았을 뿐 아니라 탄환을 다시 장전해서 머리를 쏘아 죽였습니다. 이 골리앗은 체중이 737kg가 넘고, 서면 어깨까지 높이가 3.85m이며 머리 끝까지는 4.27m인 입이 딱 벌어지는 몸집이었습니다. 이 말은 당신이 2층에 산다면 코디액 불곰이 집 내부를 들여다 볼 수 있었다는 것을 의미합니다. 커튼을 치는 것이 좋겠군요!

(a) 야생의 아름다움을 냉정하게 전하는
(b) 위험을 상기시키는 역할을 하는
(c) 이전에 공항 비행장을 배회했던
(d) 장엄한 광경의 전형인

빈칸은 하이커를 잡아먹은 뒤 사살된 엄청난 크기의 박제 코디액 불곰이 앵커리지 공항에 설치된 이유를 묻는 문제이며, 야생 곰의 무시무시함에 대해 이야기하므로 가장 적절한 것은 (b)이다.

stuffed 박제의 | **pristine** 자연 그대로의 | **put down** 죽이다 | **forest ranger** 삼림 관리원 | **unload** 총알을 빼내다 | **stoically** 냉정하게 | **epitomize** ~의 전형이다

8

The world's biggest bank heist took place in 2005 at a Brazilian Bank perpetrated by a gang of _____. With aliases like "The German, The Tortured and the Big Digger," this group of thieves spent weeks burrowing underground a block away from their artificial grass store they had set up as a front. This devious cabal got away with the equivalent of 80 million U.S. dollars and to this day, has authorities baffled about their identities. What is known is that they dug a tunnel fitted with wood supports, lighting and even air conditioning. Their piece de résistance was drilling through two meters of reinforced concrete to the bank's holding room without triggering a single alarm.

(a) well-known notorious international ex-convicts
(b) former bank employees and police officers
(c) disgruntled and desperate local shop owners

(d) highly sophisticated and colorful pilferers

2005년 매우 지적이고 다양한 좀도둑들로 구성된 한 갱단이 침투한 브라질 은행에서 세계 최대의 은행 강도 사건이 일어났다. 일명 '독일인, 고문 당한 사람, 대단한 광부'로 불리는 이 도둑 집단은 위장으로 차린 인공 잔디 상점에서부터 1블록의 거리의 지하를 몇 주간 팠다. 이 기만적인 음모단은 8천만 달러 상당을 훔쳐 달아났고, 지금까지도 당국은 그들의 신분을 전혀 알아내지 못하고 있다. 알려진 것은 그들이 목재 받침, 조명과 에어컨 시설까지 된 굴을 팠다는 것이다. 가장 인상적인 것은 경보장치 하나 작동시키지 않고 은행의 접견실까지 2m 두께의 철근 콘크리트 벽에 구멍을 뚫은 것이었다.

(a) 잘 알려진 악명 높은 국제 전과자들
(b) 전직 은행 직원들과 경찰관들
(c) 불만이 있고 필사적인 지방 상점 주인들
(d) 매우 지적이고 다양한 좀도둑들

범행이 매우 치밀하고 토목 및 건설 (굴착) 및 전기(조명)을 동원해 기술적으로 범행을 한 것으로 보아 정답은 (d)이다.

heist 강도 | **perpetrate** 〈나쁜 짓을〉 범하다, 저지르다 | **sophisticated** 지적인 | **pilferer** 좀도둑 | **authority** 당국 | **surmise** 추측하다 | **front** 위장 사업 | **devious** 기만적인 | **cabal** 음모단 | **baffle** 허우적거리다 | **identity** 정체 | **piece de resistance** 가장 인상적인 것 | **ex-convict** 전과자 | **disgruntled** 불만인

9

Alzheimer's disease is named after a German psychiatrist Alois Alzheimer after he was the first to describe the affliction in 1906. It is considered the most widespread manifestation of dementia, a common term for memory loss and other incapacitating mental degradation in seniors. Alzheimer's is not a natural part of growing old and is devastating not only for the diagnosed, but for the entire family. Alzheimer's is often a long-term disease that progressively gets worse, from basic memory loss to the point where the patient is unable to communicate and react to their surroundings. Although medical science is able to lessen the patient's symptoms and improve their quality of life, there is still no cure for Alzheimer's, which is _____ in America.

(a) the sixth leading cause of death
(b) continuously being studied extensively
(c) creating social unrest and upheaval
(d) taking the lives of many young adults

알츠하이머병은 독일의 정신과 의사인 알로이스 알츠하이머가 1906년 처음으로 이 고통의 원인을 기술한 뒤 그의 이름을 따서 명명되었

다. 이 병은 노인들 사이에 기억 상실 및 여타 정상적인 생활을 못하게 하는 정신 퇴화를 가리키는 일반적인 용어이며, 가장 광범위한 치매의 증상으로 여겨진다. 알츠하이머 병은 노화에서 자연적인 부분이 아니며, 환자뿐만 아니라 온 가족에게도 충격적이다. 알츠하이머 병은 점차적으로 악화되는 장기적인 질병으로, 기본적인 기억 상실에서부터 환자가 의사소통을 못하고 주변 상황에 대응하지 못할 정도에 이른다. 의학이 환자의 증상을 줄이고 삶의 질을 향상시킬 수 있지만, 알츠하이머 병에 대한 치료법이 없으며 미국에서는 사망 원인 6위로 뽑히는 병이다.

(a) 사망 원인 6위로 뽑히는 병
(b) 계속 광범위하게 연구되는
(c) 사회적인 불안과 격변을 초래하는
(d) 많은 청년들의 목숨을 앗아가는

해설

지문은 노인에게 발병하는 알츠하이머 병에 관한 내용이다. 빈칸 앞에 '아직도 알츠하이머 병에 대한 치료법이 없다'는 말에 비추어 (a)가 가장 적절하다.

psychiatrist 정신과 의사 | **affliction** 고통의 원인 | **manifestation** 증상 | **dementia** 치매 | **incapacitate** 무능력하게 하다 | **degradation** 퇴화 | **surrounding** 주변(의 상황) | **upheaval** 격변

습니다. 모기와 해충은 사람의 귀에는 들리지 않는 초음파에 매우 민감합니다. 전통적인 방충제의 해로운 화학 약품과 못마땅한 냄새를 더 이상 걱정할 필요가 없습니다. 네이처 세이프 초음파 모기 퇴치기는 해로운 물질을 공기 중으로 방출하지 않기 때문에 환경친화적입니다. 네이처 세이프 초음파 모기 퇴치기를 사용하면 1분이라도 더 잠을 자지 못하는 일은 결코 없을 것입니다. 지금 주문하시면 여행자용 규격의 소형 퇴치기를 덤으로 드립니다. 이것은 캠핑이나 하이킹을 하거나 호수에서 하루를 보내는 용도 등으로 이상적인 부속품입니다!

(a) 일반적인 해충 방충제의 악취와 더러운 느낌
(b) 기생충으로 인해 망가진 완벽한 하루에 대한 잊을 수 없는 기억
(c) 모기의 끊임없는 윙윙거림과 고통스럽게 물어댐
(d) 쥐들이 뛰는 소리로 인한 수면 부족

해설

환경친화적인 초음파 모기 퇴치기를 광고하는 내용으로 빈칸은 무엇 때문에 괴롭힘을 당하고 잠을 자지 못하는지 묻고 있다. 따라서 가장 적절한 것은 (c)이다.

plague 괴롭히다 | **repellent** 퇴치기 | **slumber** 잠 | **sensitive** 민감한 | **detrimental** 해로운 | **throw in** ~을 덤으로 거저 주다 | **grimy** 더러운 | **incessant** 끊임없는 | **pitter-patter** 후다닥 소리 | **rodent** 설치 동물

10

How many restless nights will you endure plagued by the _____? With the Nature-Safe Ultrasonic mosquito repellent, you can have peace of mind and undisturbed slumber the whole night through. Mosquitoes and other pests are highly sensitive to ultrasonic waves which are inaudible to the human ear. No longer do you have to worry about harmful chemicals and the disapproving smells of traditional repellents. The Nature-Safe Ultrasonic repellent is also environment friendly by not releasing detrimental materials into the atmosphere. You'll never lose another minute of sleep with the Nature-Safe Ultrasonic mosquito repellent. Order now and we'll throw in the traveler's size mini repellent for free, the ideal accessory for camping, hiking, a day on the lake and more!

(a) foul smell and grimy feel of regular insect repellent
(b) haunting memories of a perfect day ruined by vermin
(c) incessant buzzing and painful biting of mosquitoes
(d) lack of sleep brought on by the pitter-patter of rodents

번역

끊임없이 윙윙거리고 고통스럽게 물어대는 모기로 인한 괴롭힘을 당하면서 얼마나 많은 밤을 견디실 겁니까? 네이처 세이프 초음파 모기 퇴치기로 마음의 평안을 얻고 밤새 방해 받지 않고 숙면을 취할 수 있

11

Whether herding cattle over the hot plains of the American heartland or trekking through the uncharted Rocky Mountains, the cowboy was never without his iconic cowboy hat. Initially there was no standard headwear for early American pioneers making their way out west until in 1865, John Batterson Stetson set the bar when he began manufacturing a broad rimmed, high-crowned felt hat called the "Boss of the plains." Cowboy hats served the important function of protecting the wearer from the punishing rays of the sun and the harsh whipping of torrential rains. Natural in color and water resistant, the cowboy hat was an immediate success with bronco-busters and became the _____.

(a) fashion hit of the cosmopolitan bourgeoisie
(b) ubiquitous image of the cowboy we know today
(c) universal symbol of American entrepreneurial spirit
(d) most sought after accoutrement of industrial America

번역

미국 심장부의 뜨거운 평원에서 소떼를 몰든지 미지의 로키 산맥을 지나 이동하든지, 카우보이라면 상징적인 카우보이 모자를 반드시 썼다. 1865년 존 배터슨 스테트슨이 챙이 넓고 높은 '평원의 두목'이라 부르는 중절모를 제작해 기준을 정하기 전까지 처음엔 서부로 가는 초기 미국 개척자들을 위한 표준적인 모자가 없었다. 카우보이 모자는 살인적인 태양 광선과 세차게 내리치는 폭우로부터 착용자를 보호하는 중

요한 기능을 수행했다. 색상이 자연스럽고 방수가 되는 카우보이 모자는 야생마를 길들이는 카우보이와 더불어 즉시 성공을 거두었고 오늘날 우리가 알고 있는 카우보이의 아주 흔한 이미지가 되었다.

(a) 국제적인 중산층의 패션 히트 상품
(b) 우리가 알고 있는 카우보이의 아주 흔한 이미지
(c) 미국 기업가 정신의 일반적인 상징
(d) 산업국인 미국에서 사람들이 가장 많이 찾았던 장신구

해설

빈칸은 카우보이 모자가 야생마 길들이는 카우보이로 즉각적인 성공을 거두어서 어떻게 되었는가를 묻고 있다. 따라서 정답은 (b)이다.

herd 무리를 지어 가다 | **trek** 이동하다 | **uncharted** 미지의 | **set the bar** 기준을 세우다 | **rim** 둘러싸다 | **high-crowned** 〈모자의〉 층이 높은 | **felt hat** 중절모 | **punishing** 살인적인 | **torrential rain** 폭우 | **bronco-buster** 야생마를 길들이는 카우보이 | **ubiquitous** 어디에나 있는 | **accoutrement** 장신구

12

If you've ever gone for a bike ride at night, you can thank your reflectors for _____. However, these reflectors are very different from a simple mirror. Where the latter reflects light on a perpendicular wave length, the former is a retroreflector and reflects light back to its source with minimal dispersion of light. What this means in plain English is that with a mirror, light can bounce back at a different angle from the source and be of little use. On the other hand, a retroreflector is like a prism of mirrors and therefore the reflection can be seen at nearly any angle from the light source ensuring motorists from almost any direction can see you.

(a) helping you see the path in front of you
(b) guaranteeing an accident-free experience
(c) differentiating you from other bicyclists
(d) warning automobilists of your presence

번역

밤에 자전거를 타러 간 적이 있다면, 자동차 운전자에게 당신이 있음을 경고해 주는 반사경의 덕을 볼 수 있습니다. 하지만 이 반사경은 단순한 거울과는 아주 다릅니다. 후자는 수직 파장으로 빛을 반사하는 반면, 전자는 역반사체이며 빛을 최소한 분산시켜 광원으로 다시 반사합니다. 쉬운 말로, 거울의 경우 광원과 다른 각도로 빛이 반사되어 밤에 거의 소용이 없다는 것을 의미합니다. 반면, 역반사체는 거울의 프리즘과 같아서 광원의 거의 모든 각도에서 반사광을 볼 수 있기 때문에, 자동차 운전자들이 거의 모든 방향에서 당신을 볼 수 있습니다.

(a) 당신 앞의 길을 보도록 도와주는
(b) 사고 없는 경험을 보장해 주는
(c) 자전거를 타는 다른 사람을 당신과 구분하는
(d) 자동차 운전자에게 당신이 있음을 경고하는

해설

지문의 요지는 자전거 반사경 덕택에 밤에 자동차 운전자들이 거의 모든 방향에서 자전거를 탄 사람을 볼 수 있다는 내용이다. 빈칸은 무슨 이유 때문에 반사경의 덕을 볼 수 있는지 묻고 있으므로 (d)가 정답이다.

reflector 반사경 | **perpendicular** 수직의 | **wave length** 파장 | **dispersion** 분산 | **reflection** 반사광 | **light source** 광원

13

After a long day at the beach being out in the sun too long, many of us reach for a soothing lotion to cool our sunburn. The main ingredient of these ointments is usually Aloe vera, a plant indigenous to Africa with a long and well-documented history of human use. Aloe vera is one of 299 species of Aloe and has nearly as many uses. It has abundant, broad, fleshy leaves that comprise its rosette and grows in tropical as well as arid regions. Aloe vera has proven medicinal properties and can be used both externally and internally. Not only does it _____, but it also provides a thin layer over cuts and wounds that prevents infection.

(a) give immediate relief from sunburns
(b) have great commercial potential
(c) possess a fresh appearance and aroma
(d) ease aching joints, tendons and bones

번역

긴 하루 해변에서 태양에 너무 오래 노출되고 나면 많은 사람들이 햇빛으로 인한 그을림을 진정시키기 위해 수딩 로션을 집어 든다. 이 크림의 주성분은 보통 아프리카 원산지인 알로에 베라인데, 인간이 알로에 베라를 사용한 역사가 오래전에 잘 기록되었다. 알로에 베라는 299종의 알로에 중 하나이고 여러 용도가 있다. 풍부하게 달린 알로에 베라의 넓은 다즙 잎은 로제트 모양으로 퍼지며 건조 지역은 물론 열대 지방에서도 자란다. 알로에 베라는 입증된 의약적 성질을 가지고 있고 내복용과 피부용으로 사용이 가능하다. 알로에 베라는 햇빛으로 인한 그을림을 즉시 완화시킬 뿐 아니라 베거나 상처를 입은 부위에 얇은 층을 형성해 감염을 예방한다.

(a) 햇빛으로 인한 그을림을 즉시 완화시키는
(b) 상업적으로 대단한 잠재력을 가지고 있는
(c) 신선한 외양과 향기가 있는
(d) 관절, 힘줄 및 뼈의 통증을 완화시키는

해설

알로에 베라의 용도에 관한 것이다. 빈칸은 알로에 베라가 베거나 상처를 입은 부위의 감염을 방지하는 것 외에 어떤 용도가 있는지 묻고 있다. 지문 첫 문장에 나와 있는 대로 정답은 (a)이다.

sunburn 햇빛으로 인한 그을림 | **ointment** 화장용 크림 | **indigenous** 원산의 | **fleshy** 다육질의 | **rosette** 로제트 (잎 등이 여러 겹 서로 겹쳐져 방사상으로 나와 있는 모양) | **arid** 건조한 | **tendon** 힘줄

14

The hamburger has arguably become one of the world's most popular foods and _____. From 15th century minced meats, to "Hamburg steak" from Hamburg, Germany, and finally to the New World where the first hamburger was served on a bun. Incidentally, one popular fast food burger chain has actually been the focus of an economic indicator. The price of this restaurant's big hamburger is a benchmark that shows the health of the country's overall economy when compared to the American price. The closer the price is to the U.S. price, the closer that country's economy is to the United States. Who would have thought a tasty patty of beef inside a bun would become so relevant to global economics?

(a) has a long history of evolution
(b) is considered the best finger food
(c) is prepared in countless ways
(d) has a reputation of being unhealthy

번역

햄버거는 이론의 여지는 있지만 세계에서 가장 인기 있는 식품 중 하나가 되었으며, 오랜 진화의 역사를 가지고 있다. 15세기 다진 고기에서 시작해 독일 함부르크 지방에서 온 '함박스테이크'가 되었고, 마침내 신세계로 전파되어 최초의 햄버거가 둥근 빵에 얹혀서 처음으로 제공되었다. 덧붙여 말하자면 유명 패스트푸드 버거 체인 하나는 현재 경제 지표의 중심이 되었다. 이 식당의 큰 햄버거 가격은 미국의 가격과 비교하여 그 나라 경제 전반의 안정성을 보여주는 기준이다. 가격이 미국의 가격과 비슷할수록 이 나라의 경제는 미국과 근접하다. 둥근 빵 조각 사이의 맛있는 소고기 패티가 세계 경제와 그렇게 관련이 있게 될 것이라고 생각이나 했을까?

(a) 오랜 진화의 역사를 가지고 있는
(b) 손으로 집어 먹는 최고의 음식으로 여겨지는
(c) 수많은 방식으로 조리되는
(d) 건강에 좋지 않은 것으로 유명한

해설

빈칸 뒤에는 햄버거의 변천 과정이 나오며, 하나의 경제 지표가 될 정도라고 하므로, 가장 적절한 것은 (a)이다. 조리 방법이나 건강 식품에 대한 언급은 없다.

arguably 이론의 여지는 있지만 | **minced** 다진 | **bun** 둥근 빵
indicator 지표 | **benchmark** 기준 | **overall** 전반적인
relevant to ~와 관련이 있는

15

As bored teens, my friends and I would experiment with anything we found in the house or garage. One of our favorite experiments was the spud-gun. All you need for a spud-gun, or potato cannon, is a simple polyvinyl chloride (PVC) pipe, potatoes, and some sort of combustible propellant like hairspray. To operate the gun, just jam a potato into one end of the PVC pipe, add the propellant into the other end and then cap it. You must leave a small hole at the capped end in order to ignite it with a lighter. _____, the expansion of gases shoots the spud out at a great velocity, so be very careful where you point your potato cannon!

(a) Instead
(b) Meanwhile
(c) Ultimately
(d) Nevertheless

번역

따분해 하는 십대인 내 친구와 나는 집이나 차고에서 보이는 것은 무엇이든지 실험을 하려 했다. 우리가 가장 좋아하는 실험 중 하나는 감자 총이었다. 감자 총 또는 감자 대포를 위해 필요한 것은 간단한 폴리염화비닐관 (PVC관), 감자, 헤어 스프레이 같은 일종의 연소성 추진제이다. 총을 작동시키려면 PVC관 한쪽 끝에 감자를 쑤셔 넣고 다른 한쪽에는 추진제를 넣고 뚜껑을 닫는다. 뚜껑으로 막은 끝부분에 반드시 작은 구멍을 남겨두어서 라이터로 점화할 수 있도록 해야 한다. 결국 가스가 팽창해서 굉장한 속도로 감자가 발사된다. 따라서 감자 대포를 어디에 가리키는지에 대해 매우 주의해야 한다!

(a) 대신
(b) 한편
(c) 결국
(d) 그럼에도 불구하고

해설

빈칸의 접속사 앞은 감자 대포로 모든 발사 준비를 마치고 불을 붙인다는 내용이고, 빈칸 뒤에는 감자가 발사된다는 감자 대포 놀이의 순서에 대한 내용이므로 가장 적절한 것은 (c)이다.

spud 감자 | **polyvinyl chloride** 폴리염화비닐 (PVC) | **combustible** 연소성의 | **propellant** 추진제 | **jam** 쑤셔 넣다 | **ignite** 점화하다
expansion 팽창 | **velocity** 속도

16

To Beth Johnson, Humane Society,

Yesterday's broadcast on Channel 5, *Eyewitness News*, brought tears to my eyes as they reported on the unfortunate fire that razed the Humane Society. I am writing to offer not only my sympathy, but also myself as a volunteer in watching over some of the little four-legged survivors. I own a large ranch just outside of town and have the capacity to house and feed up to twenty dogs or cats until the Humane Society rebuilds. I feel as a community, our capacity to help those in need should extend beyond our fellow humans. _____, it has been said that a true measure of a society's enlightenment is seen in how they take care of their pets.

Yours truly,

Penelope Lee, Lee's Horse Ranch

(a) Conversely
(b) Moreover
(c) On the other hand
(d) Henceforth

동물 애호회의 베스 존슨 씨께

어제 방송된 5번 채널 〈목격자 뉴스〉에서 동물 애호회 건물을 완전히 파괴한 불운한 화재에 대한 보도를 보고 눈물이 났습니다. 저는 연민이 들기도 하지만, 네 다리의 작은 생존 동물 몇 마리를 보살피는 자원봉사자로서 지원하기 위해 이 편지를 보냅니다. 도시를 벗어나면 제 소유의 대목장이 바로 있으며 동물 애호회 건물이 다시 지어질 때까지 개나 고양이 20마리까지는 재우고 먹일 수 있는 수용력이 있습니다. 저는 주민으로서 어려움에 처한 대상을 돕는 우리의 역할을 같은 인간을 초월해서 확장해야 한다고 생각합니다. 더욱이 사회의 깨우침에 대한 진정한 척도는 사람들이 애완동물을 어떻게 돌보는가에서 판단된다는 말이 있습니다.

리 씨네 목장의 페넬로페 리

(a) 반대로
(b) 더욱이
(c) 반면
(d) 앞으로

화재가 난 동물 애호회에 생존 동물을 돌보는 자원봉사에 지원하기 위해 쓴 편지다. 빈칸 뒤의 문장은 앞의 '인간의 역할이 같은 인간을 초월해서 확장되어야 한다'는 말을 강조하므로 알맞은 접속사는 (b)이다.

Humane Society 동물 애호회 | **raze** 완전히 파괴하다 | **sympathy** 연민 | **ranch** 목장 | **capacity** 수용력 | **community** 주민 **enlightenment** 깨달음

17

Just about every American teenager is required to read J.D. Salinger's masterpiece, *The Catcher in the Rye*. Written in 1951, this unforgettable novel still appeals to the adolescent reader's feelings of uncertainty, anguish, estrangement and rebellion. Since its debut, *Catcher* has sold more than 65 million copies worldwide, with an average of a quarter million leaving the shelves every year. Salinger wrote *Catcher* from the subjective point of view of the main character and antagonist, Holden Caulfield. The book has stirred controversy since its initial publication because of the use of colloquial language, which includes many words that are deemed foul. Even as late as 1981, *Catcher* was the most censored and also second-most taught novel in American public schools.

Q: What is the main idea of the passage?
(a) J.D. Salinger exaggerated the attitudes of angst of his era.
(b) Readers can only get censored copies of *The Catcher in the Rye*.
(c) Public schools often forbid the teaching of *The Catcher in the Rye*.
(d) *The Catcher in the Rye* is a much challenged and studied novel.

거의 모든 미국의 10대는 제롬 데이비드 샐린저의 걸작 〈호밀밭의 파수꾼〉을 읽어야 한다. 1951년에 쓰인 이 잊지 못할 소설은 아직도 불안정, 고뇌, 불화, 반항에 대한 청소년 독자의 감정에 호소력을 가지고 있다. 처음 출간된 이후 〈호밀밭의 파수꾼〉은 전 세계적으로 6천 5백만부 이상, 평균 25만권이 매년 판매되었다. 샐린저는 주인공이자 적인 홀든 콜필드에 대한 주관적인 관점으로 〈호밀밭의 파수꾼〉을 썼다. 책은 불결하다고 생각되는 단어를 다수 포함한 구어를 사용했기 때문에 첫 출판된 이후 논란을 불러일으켰다. 심지어 바로 1981년에 〈호밀밭의 파수꾼〉은 미국의 공립 학교에서 가장 검열을 많이 받고 두 번째로 가장 많이 가르치는 소설이 되었다.

Q: 지문의 요지는?
(a) 제롬 데이비드 샐린저는 자기 시대의 고뇌하는 자세를 과장했다.
(b) 독자들은 검열을 거친 〈호밀밭의 파수꾼〉만을 구할 수 있다.
(c) 공립 학교에서는 종종 〈호밀밭의 파수꾼〉을 가르치는 것을 금한다.
(d) 〈호밀밭의 파수꾼〉은 많은 이의가 제기되고 공부하는 소설이다.

샐린저의 〈호밀밭의 파수꾼〉에 대한 글로, 미국 공립 학교에서 가장 많이 검열되고 두 번째로 가장 많이 교육하는 소설이라는 마지막 문장이 지문의 핵심이다. 따라서 정답은 (d)이다.

adolescent 청소년기의 | **estrangement** 불화 | **rebellion** 반항 **subjective** 주관적인 | **antagonist** 적 | **stir** 유발하다 | **initial** 처음의 **colloquial language** 구어 | **censor** 검열하다 | **angst** 고뇌

18

Ever since Sir Isaac Newton discovered that passing white light through a prism results in its separation into all visible colors in 1666, psychologists have been studying the effects of colors on the human psyche. In general, the colors that are considered "warm", that is red, orange and yellow, typically induce a range of feelings from comfort and tenderness to anger and hostility. On the other end of the spectrum are the "cool colors" of blue, purple and green. Researchers have found these colors evoke a sense of calm, however, they can also touch our melancholy and sad sides. This may be why skilled artists are able to masterfully employ different colors to express a wide range of emotions.

Q: What is the main idea of the passage?
(a) Colors are clearest when white light flows through a prism.
(b) Human emotions have no safeguards against certain colors.
(c) Different colors predominantly stir up different feelings.
(d) The color spectrum is made up of only cold and warm hues.

번역

1666년 아이작 뉴턴 경이 프리즘을 통과하는 백색광은 모든 가시 색상으로 분리된다는 것을 발견한 이후로 심리학자들은 인간의 심리에 미치는 색의 효과에 대해 연구했다. 보통 빨간색, 오렌지색, 노란색과 같이 '따뜻하다'고 여겨지는 색상은 대체로 안락과 애정에서부터 분노와 적개심에 이르는 감정을 일으킨다. 스펙트럼의 다른 한쪽 끝은 파란색, 자주색, 초록색과 같은 '시원한 색상'이다. 연구원들은 이러한 색상이 차분한 느낌을 자아내지만, 우리의 우울함과 슬픈 측면에 작용할 수 있다는 것을 알아냈다. 그래서 숙련된 미술가는 다양한 범위의 감정을 표현하기 위해 여러 가지 색을 능수능란하게 사용할 수 있는 것일 수도 있다.

Q: 지문의 요지는?
(a) 백색광이 프리즘을 통과할 때 색이 가장 선명하다.
(b) 인간의 감정은 어떤 색들에 대해서는 보호 수단이 없다.
(c) 다른 색은 대개 다른 감정을 불러일으킨다.
(d) 색의 스펙트럼은 차고 따뜻한 색조들로만 구성된다.

해설

지문에서는 따스한 느낌과 서늘한 느낌을 주는 색상을 예로 들면서 색상이 인간의 감정에 미치는 효과를 설명하고 있다. 따라서 가장 적절한 것은 (c)이다.

visible 가시의 | **psyche** 마음 | **induce** 일으키다 | **hostility** 적개심 **touch** 작용하다 | **melancholy** 우울 | **masterfully** 능수능란하게 **employ** 이용하다 | **predominantly** 대게

19

To Leonard Manning,

You're blog's assertion that our country's recent intervention in the civil war in East Africa is a noble cause against tyranny is just another ineffectual attempt at neo-conservative brain-washing. Many of today's netizens are way too young to remember the so-called "humanitarian" military escapades this once great nation embarked on with disastrous results. They have little knowledge of how many innocent lives have been taken by our indiscriminate bombings and other hostilities. You must not perpetuate the

sense that conflicts are best solved with the sword rather than intelligent discourse. Shame on you for putting our nation's hostile aggression in a favorable light in spite of the dismal results.

Disapprovingly yours,
Jessica Goldman, DFL Chairwoman

Q: Which of the following claims is made in the blog?
(a) Military intervention is justified for liberty's sake.
(b) Today's youth is open to conservative indoctrination.
(c) Altruistic interventions are often bloody and violent.
(d) Aggressive behavior supersedes rational rhetoric.

번역

레너드 매닝 씨께

동아프리카의 내전에 최근 우리나라가 개입한 것이 전제 정치에 대항한 숭고한 대의라는 당신 블로그의 주장은 또 하나의 헛된 신보수주의적 세뇌시키기에 불과합니다. 오늘날의 많은 네티즌들은 한때 위대한 국가였던 이 나라가 착수했다가 처참한 결과를 초래했던 소위 '인도주의적' 군사적 무모 행위를 기억하기에 너무 어립니다. 그들은 얼마나 많은 무고한 생명들이 우리나라의 무차별적인 폭격과 여타 교전으로 인해 희생되었는지 거의 알지 못합니다. 당신은 갈등이 지적인 담론보다는 무력으로 가장 잘 해결된다는 인식을 결코 영속시켜서는 안됩니다. 당신은 형편없는 결과에도 불구하고 우리나라의 적대적인 공격을 호의적으로 평가하는 것에 대해 부끄러운 줄 알아야 합니다.

DFL 회장, 제시카 골드만

Q: 블로그에서 언급된 주장은?
(a) 자유를 위해 군사 개입이 정당화된다.
(b) 오늘날의 젊은이들은 보수주의적 가르침에 노출되어 있다.
(c) 이타적인 개입은 종종 피비린내 나고 폭력적이다.
(d) 공격적인 행동은 이성적인 수사법을 대신한다.

해설

지문은 국가의 동아프리카 내전에 대한 군사 개입을 호의적으로 평가한 블로거에게 보내는 서신으로, 인도주의를 명분으로 시도하는 군사적 무모 행위를 옹호한 것에 대해 비난하고 있다. 따라서 블로그에서 주장하는 내용으로 가장 적절한 것은 (a)이다.

assertion 주장 | **intervention** 개입 | **civil war** 내전 **brain-washing** 세뇌 | **escapade** 무모 행위 | **indiscriminate** 무차별적인 | **perpetuate** 영속시키다 | **discourse** 담론 | **dismal** 형편없는 | **indoctrination** 주입, 가르침 | **altruistic** 이타적인 **supersede** 대신하다 | **rhetoric** 수사법

20

Kramer and Krantz (K&K) is seeking a Senior International Public Relations Specialist (SIPRS). K&K is the leading manufacturer and supplier of LED panels and bulbs in the Midwest and is looking to expand into the Chinese market. Qualified candidates will be at least a college graduate with a degree in public relations or related field, possess a minimum of 8 years of PR experience, be fluent in English and Chinese, and be willing to travel 50 percent of the time. The SIPRS is accountable for responding to overseas media inquiries, maintaining a close relationship with journalists, and development and distribution of K&K's overseas PR network. To apply, email a cover letter, resume, and list of references to jobs@K&KLLC.com.

Q: What is the best title of the passage?
(a) K&K's Ambitious Chinese Expansion
(b) Seeking Qualified Media Consultant
(c) Augmenting K&K's Overseas Presence
(d) Qualified PR Specialist Needed

크레이머 앤 크란츠(K&K)는 선임 국제 홍보 전문가(SIPRS)를 찾고 있습니다. K&K는 선도하는 미국 중서부의 LED 패널과 전구 제조업체이자 공급업체이며, 중국 시장 진출을 고려하고 있습니다. 자격이 있는 지원자는 적어도 홍보 또는 관련 분야 학위 소지자로 대졸 이상의 학력과 최소 8년 이상의 홍보 경력이 있어야 하고, 영어와 중국어에 유창하며, 자신의 시간 중 반을 기꺼이 여행에 할애할 수 있어야 합니다. SIPRS는 해외 대중 매체의 문의에 답변하고, 기자들과 긴밀한 관계를 유지하며, K&K의 해외 홍보망을 개발하고 확장하는 책임이 있습니다. 신청자는 자기 소개서, 이력서 및 신원 보증인 명단을 이메일 jobs@K&KLLC.com으로 보내 주십시오.

Q: 제목으로 가장 적절한 것은?
(a) K&K의 야심찬 중국 시장 확장
(b) 실력 있는 대중매체 컨설턴트 구함
(c) K&K의 해외 시설 증대
(d) 자격 있는 홍보 전문가 구함

중국 시장 진출을 고려하고 있는 K&K사가 국제 홍보 전문가를 구한다는 구인 광고이다. 따라서 정답은 (d)이다.

public relations 홍보 | **look to** 고려하다 | **candidate** 지원자
accountable 책임을 맡는 | **reference** 신원 보증인
augment 증가시키다

21

Nigerian officials announced an ambitious new plan to pull the country out of its ignominious title of being one of the world's nine most illiterate countries. Nigeria's Minister of Education and her administration have proffered a staggering 60 percent increase in funding for public schooling in remote, rural areas, which has experts shaking their heads. This nation of over 155 million people has an abysmal 32 percent illiteracy rate with more than half of its populace living outside of urban areas. Combined with a weak infrastructure, this poses a serious challenge in getting the materials and teachers to the parts of the country that need them the most.

Q: What is the main purpose of the Minister of Education's plan?
(a) To better the roads and buildings in the countryside
(b) To improve the literacy rate of all Nigerian citizens
(c) To raise the budget for education to 60 percent
(d) To augment the number of educators and supplies

나이지리아 정부는 문맹률이 가장 높은 세계 아홉 개 국가 중 하나라는 수치스런 타이틀에서 벗어나기 위한 야심 찬 새 계획을 발표했다. 나이지리아 교육부 장관과 행정부는 외진 농촌 지역의 공립 학교에 압도적인 60퍼센트의 지원금 인상을 제안했는데, 전문가들은 고개를 젓는다. 1억5천 5백만 인구의 이 나라는 인구의 절반 이상이 도시 밖에 거주하며 32퍼센트의 높은 문맹률을 보인다. 약한 사회 기반 시설과 결부되어 교구와 교사를 가장 필요로 하는 지역으로 보내는데 있어 이것은 심각한 어려움을 내포하고 있다.

Q: 교육부 계획의 주요 목적은?
(a) 시골의 도로와 건물을 향상시키기 위해
(b) 모든 나이지리아 국민의 식자율을 높이기 위해
(c) 교육 예산을 60퍼센트로 높이기 위해
(d) 교육자와 보급품의 수를 늘리기 위해

나이지리아의 높은 문맹률에 대한 교육부의 계획과 실현의 어려움에 대한 내용으로, 식자율을 높이기 위한 계획임을 알 수 있다. 따라서 정답은 (b)이다.

ignominious 수치스러운 | **illiterate** 문맹의 | **proffer** 권하다
staggering 압도적인 | **abysmal** 최저의 | **populace** 서민들
combined with ~와 결부되어 | **infrastructure** 사회기반시설 | **pose** 내포하다 | **literacy** 글을 읽고 쓸 수 있는 능력

22

Early in his presidency, John F. Kennedy faced a military and political debacle that had serious detrimental ramifications for the U.S., while at the same time strengthening the resolve of Cuban communists. This crisis was dubbed the Bay of Pigs Invasion, a covert, CIA backed military coup of Fidel Castro's regime. In three short days, Castro's Eastern Bloc trained forces defeated the invading Cuban exiles and CIA operatives that sought to dethrone the communist government. Due to this failure, Castro saw a meteoric rise in popularity as the country swelled with new found nationalism. The botched coup was a severe embarrassment for the Kennedy administration and made Castro suspicious of any future American overtures of peace and negotiation.

Q: What is mainly discussed about the Bay of Pigs invasion?
(a) The CIA was incompetent in their training of Cuban exiles.
(b) Fidel Castro found increased support due to its failure.
(c) Kennedy had an unfavorable impression of Castro.
(d) Americans became more suspicious of U.S. interventions.

존 F. 케네디는 임기 초기 미국에 해로운 결과를 가져다 주는 한편 동시에 쿠바 공산주의자의 결의를 강화시키는 군사적·정치적 낭패에 직면했다. 이 위기는 피그만 침공 사건이라고 불리는데, CIA가 지원한 피델 카스트로 정권의 은밀한 군사 쿠데타였다. 3일이라는 짧은 시간 동안 카스트로의 훈련된 동부 연합 세력은 침략하는 쿠바의 망명자들과 공산 정부를 무너뜨리려는 CIA 공작원들을 물리쳤다. 이 침공의 실패로 인해 새로 나타난 민족주의가 팽배해짐에 따라 카스트로는 갑자기 혜성같이 인기가 상승했다. 실패한 쿠데타는 케네디 정부로는 심한 굴욕이었고, 그 후 카스트로는 평화와 협상을 위한 미국의 어떤 교섭도 의심하였다.

Q: 피그만 침공 사건에 대해 주로 논의된 것은?
(a) CIA가 쿠바 망명자들을 훈련시키는 데 무능했다.
(b) 실패하여 피델 카스트로의 지지가 상승했다.
(c) 케네디는 카스트로에 대해 좋지 않은 인상을 가졌다.
(d) 미국인들은 미국의 개입에 대해 더 의심했다.

해설

케네디 정부의 피그만 침공의 실패로 미국은 군사적·정치적 낭패를 맛보았고, 쿠바의 민족주의가 팽배해짐에 따라 카스트로의 인기는 급상승했다는 내용이므로 (b)가 정답이다.

debacle 낭패 | **detrimental** 해로운 | **ramification** 결과 | **resolve** 결의 | **dub** ~라고 부르다 | **covert** 은밀한 | **military coup** 군사 쿠데타 **exile** 망명자 | **dethrone** 퇴위시키다 | **operative** 첩보 요원 | **swell with** ~으로 팽배하다 | **botch** 망쳐 놓다 | **overture** 제안 | **intervention** 개입

23

Without oil, the world would come to a screeching halt. Just how does all the oil get from the drills in oil fields or deep sea rigs to our gas station pump? Supertankers are gigantic ocean faring vessels averaging 350 meters in length, 60 meters in width and holding capacity of over 400,000 tons. The largest supertanker is the Norwegian owned Knock Nevis, which is over 458 meters in length and if tipped on its end, would surpass the Petronas Towers' height. Its length is the equivalent of about six and a half Boeing 747 jets, 14 blue whales, or 61 elephants. When fully laden with 564,000 tons of crude oil, it cannot pass through the English Channel.

Q: Which of the following is correct about supertankers?
(a) They provide the crude oil that fuels our planet.
(b) Their lengths do not exceed five football pitches.
(c) They cannot traverse the English Channel.
(d) They routinely come straight from the oil fields.

기름이 없다면 세계는 끽 소리를 내며 정지할 것이다. 기름은 어떻게 유전이나 심해의 굴착 장치에서 주유소 펌프에 도달할까? 초대형 유조선은 거대한 해양 선박으로, 평균 길이가 350미터에 넓이가 60미터이고 40만 톤 이상의 용적을 가진다. 가장 큰 초대형 유조선은 노르웨이의 녹 네비스인데, 길이가 458미터가 넘고 만약 배 끝으로 세워지면 높이가 페트로나스 타워를 능가한다. 그 길이는 보잉 747 제트기 약 6개 반, 흰긴수염고래 14마리, 또는 코끼리 61마리에 해당한다. 배가 원유 564,000톤으로 가득 차면 영국 해협을 지날 수 없다.

Q: 다음 중 초대형 유조선에 대해 옳은 것은?
(a) 세계에 연료를 보급하는 원유를 제공한다.
(b) 길이가 축구장 5개를 넘지 않는다.
(c) 영국 해협을 횡단할 수 없다.
(d) 정기적으로 유전에서 직접 온다.

해설

세상이 돌아가기 위해서는 석유가 필요하고 그것을 유전이나 심해의 굴착 장치에서 주유소까지 도달하게 도와주는 것이 초대형 유조선임을 알 수 있으므로 정답은 (a)이다.

screeching 끽 소리를 내는 | **halt** 정지 | **oil field** 유전 | **rig** 굴착 장치 **holding capacity** 용적 | **supertanker** 초대형 유조선 | **surpass** 능가하다 | **equivalent** 동등한 | **traverse** 횡단하다

24

Akira Kurosawa was a prolific Japanese filmmaker with a resume of 30 films covering his 57 year career. He was posthumously named "Asian of the Century" in the "Arts, Literature and Culture" by *AsianWeek* magazine. While living, Kurasawa accepted the Academy Award for Lifetime Achievement in 1990. Perhaps his best known film is the 1954 classic *Seven Samurai* starring Toshiro Mifune, Kurasawa's leading man in over 15 of his films. Like most great storytellers, Kurasawa employed the master and disciple theme not only in the physical sense but also the spiritual in many of his films. His unique and bold cinematography style made him one of the most significant and influential filmmakers in cinema history.

Q: Which of the following is correct about Akira Kurosawa?

(a) He was strongly influenced by the Academy Awards from Hollywood.

(b) He accepted *AsianWeek* magazine's "Asian of the Century" award.

(c) He trusted in Toshiro Mifune as a proficient and talented actor.

(d) He dabbled with the mentor and student relationship in a few films.

구로사와 아키라는 57년의 경력에 30편의 영화를 제작한 이력을 가진 다작을 하는 일본의 영화 제작자이다. 그는 사후 〈아시안 위크〉라는 잡지의 '예술, 문학 그리고 문화' 기사에서 '세기의 아시아인'이라고 이름 붙여졌다. 생전에 구로사와는 1990년 아카데미 평생 공로상을 받았다. 아마도 가장 잘 알려진 그의 영화는 1954년 고전인 〈7인의 사무라이〉일 것이며, 15편이 넘는 구로사와의 영화에서 주인공을 맡은 토시로 미푸네가 출연했다. 대부분의 위대한 작가들처럼 구로사와도 많은 영화에서 물리적인 면뿐만 아니라 정신적인 면의 스승과 제자라는 주제를 적용했다. 그의 독특하고 대담한 영화 스타일은 영화 역사상 그를 가장 중요하고 영향력 있는 영화 제작자 중 하나로 만들었다.

Q: 구로사와 아키라에 대해 다음 중 옳은 것은?
(a) 헐리우드의 아카데미상에서 강한 영향을 받았다.
(b) 〈아시안 위크〉라는 잡지의 '세기의 아시아인' 상을 받았다.
(c) 토시로 미푸네를 능숙하고 재능 있는 배우로 신임했다.
(d) 소수 영화에서 스승과 학생의 관계를 조금 다루었다.

지문의 중반에 구로사와가 15편이 넘는 영화에 토시로 미푸네를 주인공으로 썼다는 부분에서 구로사와가 그 배우의 능력과 재능을 믿었음을 알 수 있으므로 (c)가 정답이다.

prolific 다작을 하는 | **posthumously** 사후에 | **disciple** 제자
cinematography 영화 예술 | **influential** 영향력 있는 | **proficient** 능숙한 | **dabble** 조금 해보다

25

The catalyst to the worst ideological experiment in the world was the Russian Revolution of 1917. This revolution took place in two stages, the first being the overthrowing of the Russian Tsar, Nicholas II, by members of the Imperial parliament. The second phase of the revolution was Lenin and the Bolshevik's (worker's party) usurping of power from the newly formed Provisional Government of St. Petersburg. Following the coup by the worker's party, the Soviet Union was formed and the Bolshevik's arbitrarily appointed themselves to positions of power and violently squashed any dissidence. The ultimate outcome of the communist's revolution has been judged by history as a period of rule by fear and repression, economic ruin, and the loss of millions of lives.

Q: Which of the following is correct about the Russian Revolution?

(a) The last ruling monarchy of Russia was deposed.

(b) Imperial parliament members overthrew the Bolshevik.

(c) An era of prosperity and equality for all was realized.

(d) It led to tolerance of differing political viewpoints.

세계 최악의 이데올로기 실험에 대한 기폭제는 1917년 러시아 혁명이었다. 이 혁명은 두 단계에 걸쳐 일어났는데, 첫 번째는 제정 러시아 의회 의원들의 황제 니콜라스 2세를 타도였다. 혁명의 두 번째 단계는 레닌과 볼셰비키의 노동당이 새로 형성된 상트페테르부르크의 임시 정부로부터 권력을 찬탈하는 것이었다. 노동당의 쿠데타에 이어 소비에트 연방이 형성되었고 볼셰비키는 독단적으로 스스로 권력의 자리에 올랐고 모든 반체제를 폭력으로 진압했다. 공산주의 혁명의 궁극적인 결과는 공포와 억압, 경제의 몰락, 수백만 인명이 손실되는 통치 기간으로 역사의 심판을 받았다.

Q: 러시아 혁명에 다음 중 옳은 것은?
(a) 러시아의 마지막 통치 군주는 퇴위되었다.
(b) 제정 러시아의 의원들은 볼셰비키를 타도했다.
(c) 모든 이를 위한 번영과 평등의 시대가 실현되었다.
(d) 다른 정치적 시각에 대한 관용을 이끌었다.

러시아 혁명의 첫 단계에서 제정 러시아의 의원들이 러시아 황제 니콜라스 2세를 타도하였다고 했으므로 (a)가 정답이다.

catalyst 기폭제 | **overthrow** 타도하다 | **tsar** 황제 | **usurp** 빼앗다
provisional 임시의 | **arbitrarily** 독단적으로 | **squash** 진압하다
dissidence 반체제 | **repression** 억압 | **monarchy** 군주제 | **depose** 퇴위시키다

26

The highest paid entertainer in the world from the 50's through the 70's was a pianist and showman from a small Midwest suburb by the name of Wladziu Valentino Liberace. A flamboyant, but classically trained pianist, Liberace performed Liszt's Second Piano Concerto with the Chicago Symphony in 1939 at the young age of 20. In early 1940, he moved to New York where his musical style evolved from classical music to pops with a classical tinge. Although he struggled both in financial terms and popularity during this time, by the late 40's, Liberace was performing in night clubs around the U.S. and was quickly on his way to becoming an immensely successful entertainment legend.

Q: Which of the following is correct about Liberace?
(a) He was the highest paid performer in the first half

of the 20th century.

(b) **He was the most successful entertainer for nearly three decades.**

(c) Major symphony orchestras sought him out as a concert soloist.

(d) He was born in a small rural suburb of New York City.

번역

1950~1970년대까지 세계에서 가장 돈을 많이 받은 연예인은 블라주 발렌티노 리버라치라는 작은 중서부 교외 출신의 피아니스트이자 쇼맨이었다. 화려하나 고전적으로 훈련된 피아니스트인 리버라치는 1939년 20살이라는 어린 나이에 시카고 교향악단과 리스트의 피아노 협주곡 2번을 연주했다. 1940년 초 그는 뉴욕으로 옮겨가면서 음악 스타일이 고전 음악에서 고전적인 느낌이 가미된 대중음악으로 변화되었다. 이 시기에 재정적인 면과 인기 면에서 모두 고전했지만, 40년대 후반 미국 전역의 나이트 클럽에서 연주를 하면서 빠르게 대성공한 연예계의 전설이 되었다.

Q: 리버라치에 대해 다음 중 옳은 것은?
(a) 20세기 초반에 가장 돈을 많이 받는 연주가였다.
(b) **거의 30년 동안 가장 성공한 연예인이었다.**
(c) 주요 교향악단들이 음악회 단독 연주자로 그를 찾았다.
(d) 뉴욕의 작은 농촌 근교에서 태어났다.

해설

첫 문장에서 리버라치가 1950~1970년대까지 세계에서 가장 돈을 많이 받는 연예인이었다고 하였으므로 정답은 (b)이다.

flamboyant 화려한 | **tinge** 기미, 느낌 | **immensely** 대단히

27

With heating and electrical costs going through the roof, the Fantastic Energy Emitting Leaf (FEEL) houseplant is the smart answer to those increasing bills. FEEL is a synthetic plant with leaves made from nickel and cobalt catalysts that efficiently and cleanly increase its energy production tenfold. Just add water! Appearing like a regular potted plant, FEEL's thirty energy producing appendages take in the sun's endless solar power and converts it into enough wattage to power the average household all day. Do your part in preserving our environment and, being fiscally responsible, buy a FEEL artificial household plant today!

Q: Which of the following is correct about FEEL?
(a) Solar energy is stored as watts in its leaves.
(b) Energy is created from solar rays, nickel and cobalt.
(c) **Utility bills and pollution are sure to decrease daily.**
(d) It can provide all the energy for the common man.

번역

난방과 전기 비용이 천정부지로 치솟음에 따라. 환상적인 에너지 방출 잎사귀 (FEEL) 가정용 화초가 늘어나는 비용에 대한 지혜로운 해답이 됩니다. FEEL은 효율적이고 깨끗하게 에너지 생산을 10배로 증가시키는 니켈과 코발트 촉매제로 만들어진 잎이 달린 합성 식물로, 물만 주면 됩니다! 일반 화분 식물처럼 보이는 FEEL에 달린 30개의 에너지 생산 부속물이 무한한 태양열을 흡수하여 하루 종일 평균 가정에 전력을 공급할 만큼의 충분한 전력으로 전환합니다. 우리 환경을 보존하는데 일조하십시오. 재정적으로 책임을 다하면서 오늘 FEEL 인공 가정용 화초를 사십시오!

Q: FEEL에 대해 다음 중 옳은 것은?
(a) 잎사귀에 태양에너지를 와트로 보관한다.
(b) 태양광선. 니켈과 청록색으로부터 에너지가 만들어진다.
(c) **분명히 공과금과 오염이 매일 감소한다.**
(d) 일반 시민을 위한 모든 에너지를 공급할 수 있다.

해설

FEEL화초가 늘어나는 고지서에 대한 똑똑한 해답이고 태양열을 이용하여 효율적이고 깨끗하게 에너지를 생산한다고 하였으니 (c)가 답으로 적당하다. 마지막 문장 또한 문제에 대한 힌트를 제공한다. 그러나 FEEL의 잎이 태양 에너지를 취하여 전환한다고 하였지 보관하는 것이 아니고, 에너지를 전환하는 것이지 만드는 것이 아니므로 (a)와 (b)는 오답이다.

go through the roof 치솟다 | **synthetic** 합성의 | **efficiently** 효율적으로 | **tenfold** 10배 | **appendage** 부속물 | **convert** 전환하다 **household** 가정 | **fiscally** 재정적으로 | **artificial** 인조의 | **utility bill** 공과금

28

One Hundred Years of Solitude is considered Gabriel García Márquez's finest masterpiece. Initially published in Spanish in 1967, it has since been translated into 37 languages and has sold more than 20 million copies worldwide. As the title implies, it is a story about several generations of the Buendía family headed by its patriarch and founder Macondo, a metaphoric Columbia, José Arcadio Buendía. García Márquez masterfully employed symbolic and metaphoric literary tools to tell the story of the conquests of Latin America by Europeans. Yellow and gold are often used to represent the imperialism of the Spaniards, with gold symbolizing the search for economic opulence and yellow embodying death, change and destruction.

Q: Which of the following is correct about *One Hundred Years of Solitude*?

(a) **It is a highly figurative narrative of the Spanish conquests.**

(b) García Márquez wanted the whole world to be able to read it.

(c) It depicts the Buendía family as the founders of Columbia.

(d) Jose Arcadio Buendía is the main character throughout the story.

번역

〈백 년 동안의 고독〉은 가브리엘 가르시아 마르케스의 최고 명작이다. 1967년 스페인에서 처음 출판된 이후 37개 언어로 번역되었고 전 세계적으로 2천만 권 이상 팔렸다. 제목이 암시하듯, 이 책은 콜롬비아의 은유인 마꼰도의 설립자인 가장 호세 아르까디오 부엔디아가 이끄는 부엔디아 가의 몇 세대에 관한 이야기이다. 마르케스는 유럽인의 남미 정복에 대해 이야기하기 위해 상징적이고 비유적인 문학적 도구들을 능숙하게 이용했다. 노란색과 금은 종종 스페인의 제국주의를 나타내는데, 금은 경제적 풍요에 대한 탐색을 상징하고 노란색은 죽음과 변화, 파괴를 상징한다.

Q: 〈백 년 동안의 고독〉에 대해 다음 중 옳은 것은?

(a) 스페인 정복에 대해 상당히 비유적인 이야기이다.

(b) 마르케스는 전 세계에서 그 책이 읽혀지기를 원했다.

(c) 부엔디아 가족을 콜롬비아 건립자로 묘사한다.

(d) 호세 아르까디오 부엔디아가 이야기를 통틀어 주인공이다.

해설

〈백 년 동안의 고독〉은 유럽인의 남미 정복을 이야기하고자 노란색과 금을 이용한 상징과 비유를 통해서 스페인의 제국주의를 나타냈다고 했으므로 (a)가 정답이다.

solitude 고독 | **masterpiece** 명작 | **initially** 최초로 | **imply** 암시하다 | **patriarch** 가장 | **metaphoric** 비유적인 | **opulence** 풍요 | **embody** 상징하다 | **figurative** 비유적인

29

Every year, just before Spring Break, March Madness sweeps the United States. This is the time the National Collegiate Athletic Association sponsors the college basketball championship and starts with the sweet sixteen, the top sixteen basketball teams from universities and colleges nationwide. This month is highly televised and anticipated as fans of all ages and walks of life tune in to this amateur basketball tournament. The heat really turns up when the final four advance to the semi-finals. Winning the championship game is a prestigious honor for any school and one that gives current, former and future students something to brag about.

Q: Which of the following is correct about March Madness?

(a) It corresponds with college student's Spring Break vacation.

(b) Major networks televise it to generate interest in basketball.

(c) **The best sixteen teams contend for the championship title.**

(d) University students enjoy exclusive coverage of the games.

번역

매년 봄 방학 바로 전에 3월의 광란이 미국을 휩쓴다. 이때가 전국 대학 체육 협회가 대학 농구 대회를 후원하고 전국 종합 대학과 단과 대학에서 16개의 최고 농구팀인 스위트 식스틴 (16강)을 시작하는 때이다. 모든 연령과 각계 각층의 팬들이 이 아마추어 농구 토너먼트를 시청함에 따라 3월은 가장 방송이 많이 되고 기대되는 달이다. 마지막 4개 팀이 준결승에 진출하면 그 열기가 최고조로 치솟는다. 챔피언십에서 우승을 하는 것은 어떤 학교에든지 특별한 영광이고, 재학생과 졸업생, 예비생에게 자랑거리가 된다.

Q: 3월의 광란에 대해 다음 중 옳은 것은?

(a) 대학의 봄 방학과 동시에 있다.

(b) 주요 방송사들은 농구에 대한 관심을 일으키기 위해 방송한다.

(c) **최고의 16개 팀이 챔피언 자리를 놓고 경쟁한다.**

(d) 대학생들은 경기 독점 방송을 즐긴다.

해설

3월의 광란에서 전국 종합 대학과 단과 대학의 16개 최고 농구팀이 토너먼트 경기를 시작한다고 했으므로 정답은 (c)이다.

sweep 휩쓸다 | **sponsor** 후원하다 | **televise** 방송하다 | **anticipate** 기대하다 | **all walks of life** 각계 각층 | **tune in** 시청하다 | **brag** 자랑하다 | **generate** 발생시키다 | **contend** 경쟁하다

30

Imagine a shark weighing more than 100 metric tons with a length of 20 meters. This perfect predator lived approximately 1.5 to 25 million years ago. Scientists have aptly named this beast Megalodon which is Greek for "big tooth." Based on fossil records and reconstruction, Megalodon's bite force exceeded 41,000 pounds of pressure and its serrated teeth were not only good for sawing through their prey but also grabbing and shaking it ruthlessly. Megalodon was the ultimate predator that didn't stay in one location but instead adapted to live in many environments including shallow coastal waters and deep seas. It was an aggressive hunter with tremendous speed, fierce jaws, and a healthy appetite for whales and other marine life.

Q: Which of the following is correct about Megalodon?

(a) It aggressively guarded its narrow territory.

(b) **Whales and other nautical animals were its quarry.**

(c) Scientists speculate it was the precursor of whales.

(d) Its large mass impeded its mobility and velocity.

번역

무게가 100톤 이상 나가고 길이가 20미터인 상어를 상상해 보라. 이 완벽한 포식자는 약 150만 년에서 2,500만 년 전에 살았다. 과학자들은 이 괴물을 메갈로돈이라고 적절히 이름 붙였는데 그리스어로 '큰 이빨'이라는 뜻이다. 화석 기록과 복원에 기초하여 메갈로돈이 무는 힘은 4만 1천 파운드의 압력을 초과하고 톱니 모양의 이빨은 먹잇감을 자르는 데 뿐만 아니라 무자비하게 잡아채서 흔들기에도 좋았다. 메갈로돈은 최후의 포식자로서 한 곳에 머무르지 않고 않았으며, 낮은 연안해나 심해를 포함한 여러 환경에서 두루 살도록 적응하였다. 메갈로돈은 엄청난 속도와 사나운 턱, 그리고 고래와 다른 해양 생물에 대한 왕성한 식욕을 가진 공격적 사냥꾼이었다.

Q: 메갈로돈에 대해 다음 중 옳은 것은?

(a) 공격적으로 좁은 영토를 지켰다.

(b) 고래와 다른 해양 동물이 사냥감이었다.

(c) 과학자들은 그것이 고래의 전형이었다고 추정한다.

(d) 커다란 몸집이 기동력과 속력을 방해했다.

해설

마지막 문장에서 메갈로돈이 고래와 다른 해양 생물에 대한 왕성한 식욕을 가졌다고 했으므로 (b)가 정답이다.

predator 포식자 | **aptly** 적절히 | **exceed** 초과하다 | **serrated** 톱니 모양의 | **adapt** 적응하다 | **tremendous** 엄청난 | **territory** 영역 **nautical** 해양의 | **quarry** 사냥감 | **speculate** 추정하다 | **precursor** 선구자 | **impede** 방해하다

31

CSI and its ilk have become a popular genre of television show where forensic science is the star attraction. Forensic science is often described as "applying science to law." These scientists are the investigators that pore over any physical evidence left at a crime scene. Like putting the pieces of a puzzle together, highly-trained forensic specialists take special care in preserving and collecting any leftover residue such as blood, fingerprints, hairs, fibers, and anything else that can lead them to the perpetrators of a crime. Unlike how Hollywood depicts their work, forensic science is not at all as glamorous as shows like *CSI* would have you believe but they are just as persistent in their pursuit for justice.

Q: Which of the following is correct about forensic science?

(a) It is accurately portrayed on television.

(b) All criminals leave forensic evidence.

(c) Hollywood has taken great interest in it.

(d) It is the last step in solving a crime.

번역

〈CSI〉와 같은 류의 법의학 드라마가 텔레비전의 쇼의 가장 인기 있는 한 장르가 되었다. 법의학은 종종 '과학을 법에 응용하는 것'으로 묘사

된다. 과학자들은 범죄 현장에 남은 모든 물리적 증거를 자세히 조사하는 수사관들이다. 퍼즐의 조각들을 맞추듯 고도로 훈련된 법의학 전문가들이 혈액, 지문, 머리카락, 섬유 등과 범인을 찾게 해주는 그 밖의 모든 잔여물을 보존하고 수집하는 데 신중을 기한다. 할리우드가 그들의 작업을 묘사하는 방법과는 달리 법의학은 〈CSI〉와 같은 쇼가 믿게 만드는 것처럼 모든 것이 화려한 것은 아니지만, 그들은 정의 추구에 있어 집요하다.

Q: 법의학에 대해 다음 중 옳은 것은?

(a) 텔레비전에서 정확하게 묘사된다.

(b) 모든 범죄자들은 법의학적 증거를 남긴다.

(c) 할리우드가 법의학에 지대한 관심을 보인다.

(d) 범죄를 해결하는 마지막 단계이다.

해설

첫 문장에서 〈CSI〉나 그런 종류의 볼거리가 텔레비전 쇼의 인기 있는 장르가 되었다고 하므로 (c)가 정답이다. 법의학자들의 일이 쇼에서 보여지는 것처럼 모두 화려하지는 않다고 하므로 (a)는 틀리며, (b), (d)에 관련된 언급은 없다.

ilk 동류 | **forensic science** 법의학 | **pore over** 자세히 조사하다 **preserve** 보존하다 | **leftover** 잔재 | **residue** 잔여물 | **perpetrator** 범인 | **glamorous** 화려한 | **persistent** 집요한

32

More and more schools in Western countries are experimenting with a "No Homework" policy. Many parents have found that the battle to force their children to do homework every night is "just not worth it." Attending a school with this policy does not mean that students do no studying or educational related activities when the school bell rings. Instead, children are encouraged to take books home, read by themselves or with their parents, and write a sentence or two about each chapter they read. Students these days are often engrossed in many other activities such as music, dance, art, swimming, soccer, etc., and parents feel their child is too exhausted to be obligated with mandatory homework.

Q: Which of the following is correct according to the passage?

(a) Western students are losing interest in traditional studies.

(b) Children at these schools with no homework take it upon themselves to study.

(c) Extracurricular activities transcend school curriculums.

(d) Teachers are becoming increasingly less tolerant of homework.

번역

서구의 점점 더 많은 학교가 '숙제 내지 않기' 정책을 시험하고 있다.

많은 부모들이 밤마다 자녀들에게 숙제를 하도록 강요하는 싸움이 '그럴 가치 없음'임을 발견했다. 이런 정책을 가진 학교에 다니는 것은 학교 종이 치면 학생들이 공부를 안 하거나 교육 관련 활동들을 하지 않는 것을 의미하지는 않는다. 대신 아이들은 책을 집에 가져가서 혼자서 또는 부모님과 읽고, 읽은 각 장에 대해 한 두 문장을 쓰도록 권장 받는다. 요즘 학생들은 종종 음악, 춤, 미술, 수영, 축구 등과 같은 많은 다른 활동에 빠져 있고, 부모가 자녀에게 의무적으로 숙제를 강요하기에는 아이들이 너무 지쳐있다고 느낀다.

Q: 지문에 따르면 다음 중 옳은 것은?
(a) 서구의 학생들이 전통적인 학습에 대한 흥미를 잃고 있다.
(b) 숙제가 없는 이런 학교에 다니는 학생들은 스스로 공부한다.
(c) 정규 교과 이외의 활동들이 학교의 교과 과정을 초월한다.
(d) 교사는 숙제에 대해 점점 덜 관대해지고 있다.

숙제를 내지 않는다는 정책을 가진 학교에 다니는 아이들은 책을 집에 가져가 스스로 읽고 읽은 부분에 대해 한 두 문장을 써보도록 장려된다고 했으므로, 학생들이 스스로 공부한다는 것을 알 수 있다. 따라서 (b)가 정답이다.

force 강요하다 | **worth** 가치가 있는 | **encourage** 장려하다 | **engross** 몰두하게 만들다 | **obligate** 의무를 지우다 | **transcend** 초월하다

33

Friday the 13th is often associated with ill omens and bad luck as was the case for the Uruguayan Ruby team whose airplane crashed in the snowy Andes Mountains on that inauspicious day in October of 1972. Only 16 out of the 45 passengers made it back to civilization after a harrowing 72 day ordeal. Without food, water, and communication devices like radios, the survivors had to resort to cannibalism in order to stay alive long enough for some of the team members to make the arduous journey to civilization. Their tale of horror and heroics is immortalized in a book written two years later by British author Piers Paul Read which was later made into a movie.

Q: What can be inferred from the passage?
(a) Tragic events often occur on Friday the 13th.
(b) Being an athlete increased the chance for rescue.
(c) The will to survive pushes humans to great lengths.
(d) The survivor's story was inaccurately portrayed on film.

13일의 금요일은 종종 나쁜 징조나 불운과 연관되는데, 1972년 10월 그 불길한 날 눈 덮인 안데스 산맥에 추락한 우루과이 럭비팀의 비행기 사고의 경우도 그러하다. 45명의 승객 중 오직 16명만이 72일간의 시련을 견딘 후 문명사회로 돌아왔다. 먹을 것과 물 그리고 라디오 같은 통신 장치 없이 생존한 팀원 몇몇은 몹시 힘들게 문명사회로 돌아올

때까지 살아남기 위해 인육을 먹는 것에 의존해야만 했다. 그들의 공포와 용기 있는 행동에 대한 이야기는 2년 후 영국의 작가 피어스 폴 리드가 쓴 책에 영구히 전해지게 되었고, 후에 이것은 영화로 만들어졌다.

Q: 지문을 통해 유추할 수 있는 것은?
(a) 비극적인 일들이 종종 13일의 금요일에 일어난다.
(b) 운동선수인 것이 구조의 가능성을 증가시켰다.
(c) 생존하려는 의지가 인간으로 하여금 무엇이든 하게 만든다.
(d) 생존자의 이야기가 영화에 부정확하게 묘사되었다.

안데스 산맥의 오지에 추락한 후 살아남기 위해 생존자들이 인육까지 먹게 되었다는 부분에서 (c)를 유추할 수 있다. 추락 사고가 13일의 금요일에 발생했지만 비극적인 일들이 종종 13일의 금요일에 발생한다는 것은 지문을 통해 유추할 수 없으므로 (a)는 정답이 아니다.

associate 연관 짓다 | **omen** 징조 | **inauspicious** 불길한 **harrowing** 끔찍한 | **ordeal** 시련 | **resort to** 기대다 | **cannibalism** 인육을 먹는 풍습 | **arduous** 고된 | **heroics** 영웅적인 행동 **immortalize** 불멸하게 되다

34

Underwriter's Limited (UL) is a non-profit independent safety science company whose standards are accepted worldwide. They provide expertise in vital five strategic businesses which include Product Safety, Environment, Life and Health, University, and Verification Services. UL is an icon of trust and upholds its mission of "Working for a safer world since 1894." Since its inception, the 6,921 employees consisting of scientists, engineers and others at UL have tested nearly 85,000 products with customers in 102 countries at their 68 laboratories. If your product has the UL mark, you can take pride and have confidence that it has passed a series of the most vigorous and strict safety tests.

Q: What can be inferred from the passage?
(a) UL establishes the global bar for quality testing.
(b) Only the safest products get the UL mark of approval.
(c) UL employs the smartest scientists and engineers.
(d) Profits generated at UL are passed on to the consumer.

미국 보험업자 단체 시험소 (UL)는 그 기준을 세계적으로 인정받는 독립적 비영리 안전 과학 회사이다. 회사는 상품 안전성, 환경, 생명과 건강, 대학, 검증 서비스를 포함한 5개의 필수 전략 사업에 대해 전문 지식을 제공한다. UL은 신용의 상징이고 '1894년 이후 좀 더 안전한 세상을 위해 일한다'는 사명을 지킨다. 창설 이후 과학자와 공학자 등으로 구성된 6,921명의 UL 직원은 68개 실험실에서 102개 국가의 고객과 함께 거의 8만 5천 개의 제품을 시험했다. 만약 당신의 제품에

UL 마크가 있다면, 그 제품이 일련의 가장 강력하고 엄격한 시험들을 통과했다는 자부심과 믿음을 가져도 된다.

Q: 지문을 통해 유추할 수 있는 것은?
(a) UL인증이 품질 검사의 세계 기준을 수립한다.
(b) 가장 안전한 제품만이 UL 마크의 승인을 받는다.
(c) UL은 가장 똑똑한 과학자와 공학자만을 고용한다.
(d) UL에서 발생한 이윤은 소비자에게 전해진다.

해설
첫 문장에서 UL의 기준이 세계적으로 인정받는다고 했으므로 세계 기준을 수립한다고 유추할 수 있다. 따라서 정답은 (a)이다. UL 마크를 받은 제품은 안전성을 통과했지만, 가장 안전한 제품이 UL 마크를 받는다고는 할 수 없으므로 (b)는 정답이 아니다.

underwriter 보험사 | non-profit 비영리의 | expertise 전문 지식
vital 필수적인 | strategic 전략적인 | verification 검증 | uphold
유지하다 | inception 창립 | vigorous 강력한

35

A diamond is supposed to be a girl's best friend, but not if it came at a tremendous human cost. Blood diamonds, or conflict diamonds, are rough cut diamonds that lack transparency about their place of origin. Often used to fund insurgencies or armed conflicts, blood diamonds come from the mines of war-torn countries. These countries are found mainly in Africa and include Angola, Liberia, Sierra Leone, the Ivory Coast, the Democratic Republic of Congo, and Zimbabwe. Although much concerted international effort has been put in to restrict the flow of conflict diamonds, the illegal trade continues to build up the coffers of illegitimate and oppressive regimes and warlords who use the funds to arm themselves.

Q: What can be inferred from the passage?
(a) Blood diamonds are easily identified by their place of origin.
(b) Countries in war zones have stopped producing blood diamonds.
(c) Most African nations forbid the trade of conflict diamonds.
(d) Conflict diamonds are still sold on the international markets.

번역
다이아몬드는 여자의 가장 친한 친구로 여겨지지만, 만약 엄청난 인건비가 들었다면 그렇지 않을 것이다. 피의 다이아몬드 또는 분쟁의 다이아몬드는 출처의 투명성이 부족한 다듬어지지 않은 다이아몬드이다. 종종 내란이나 무력 분쟁에 자금을 대는 데 쓰이는 피의 다이아몬드는 전쟁으로 피폐해진 나라의 광산에서 나온다. 이런 나라는 주로 아프리카에 있는데, 앙골라, 리베리아, 시에라리온, 아이보리 코스트, 콩고 민

주공화국과 짐바브웨가 있다. 분쟁의 다이아몬드의 공급을 제한하기 위해 국제 협력이 많이 취해졌지만, 불법적이고 억압적인 정권과 스스로를 무장하는 데 자금을 써버리는 군의 지도자들의 재원 증강을 위해 불법적 거래는 계속되고 있다.

Q: 지문을 통해 유추할 수 있는 것은?
(a) 피의 다이아몬드는 그 출처를 쉽게 알아낼 수 있다.
(b) 전쟁 지역의 국가들은 피의 다이아몬드 생산을 중단했다.
(c) 대부분의 아프리카 국가가 분쟁의 다이아몬드의 거래를 금지한다.
(d) 분쟁의 다이아몬드는 여전히 국제 시장에서 팔린다.

해설
지문의 마지막에 피의 다이아몬드의 공급을 제한하기 위한 국제 협력의 노력에도 불구하고 정권과 군 지휘자들의 재원을 위해 불법적 거래가 계속된다고 하므로 아직도 피의 다이아몬드가 팔린다는 것을 유추할 수 있다. 따라서 (d)가 정답이다.

tremendous 엄청난 | conflict 분쟁 | transparency 투명성
insurgency 내란 | concerted 합의된 | restrict 제한하다 | flow
흐름, 공급 | coffer 금고 | illegitimate 불법적인 | oppressive
억압적인 | regime 정권 | warlord 군 지도자

36

Researchers from NASA have a strong desire to "take another large step for mankind" by returning to our moon's surface for the reason of mining its valuable resources. Of the many attractive elements such as iron, silicon, aluminum and magnesium, none are considered as valuable as helium-3 (He-3). He-3 is nearly non-existent on Earth and aerospace engineers argue it is the perfect fuel for fusion reactors. Not only is the United States hankering to map out and claim its own territory on our celestial satellite, but so do the Russians, Chinese and Indians. This may prompt a new space race and perhaps inevitably the first extra-terrestrial real estate disputes.

Q: What can be inferred from the passage?
(a) Lunar exploration has been done by the U.S., Russia, China and India.
(b) Mining the moon will require the cooperation of many nations.
(c) Aerospace engineers are running out of energy alternatives.
(d) Large amounts of helium-3 may be the ideal energy for fusion power.

번역
NASA의 연구원들은 중요 자원을 채굴하려는 이유로 달의 표면으로 돌아가 '인류를 위한 또 다른 큰 걸음을 내딛고자'하는 강한 열망을 가지고 있다. 철, 실리콘, 알루미늄, 마그네슘과 같은 많은 흥미를 끄는 원소들 중에서 헬륨-3만큼 귀하게 여겨지는 것은 없다. 헬륨-3는 지구에 거의 존재하지 않는 자원이며, 항공 우주 공학자들은 핵융합로에 완

벽한 연료라고 주장한다. 미국만이 우리의 천체 위성에 설계하고 영역을 주장하고자 갈망하고 있는 것이 아니라 러시아와 중국, 인도도 마찬가지이다. 이는 새로운 우주 경쟁과 함께 최초의 외계 영토 분쟁을 불가피하게 일으킬 수 있다.

Q: 지문을 통해 유추할 수 있는 것은?

(a) 달 탐험은 미국, 러시아, 중국 그리고 인도에 의해 이루어져 왔다.

(b) 달의 채굴은 많은 국가들의 협조를 필요로 할 것이다.

(c) 항공 우주공학자들은 대체 에너지가 떨어지고 있다.

(d) 많은 양의 헬륨-3가 아마도 핵융합력의 이상적인 에너지일 것이다.

해설

항공 우주 공학자들이 헬륨-3가 핵융합로를 위한 완벽한 연료라고 주장한다고 하였으므로 (d)가 정답이다.

mine 채굴하다 | **valuable** 귀중한 | **aerospace engineer** 항공 우주 공학자 | **fusion reactor** 핵융합로 | **hankering** 갈망하는 | **map out** 설계하다 | **celestial** 천체의

37

Kentucky Fried Chicken was founded by Colonel Sanders who began serving fried chicken in the 1930's during the Great Depression. His Sanders Court & Café was such a big hit that in 1935 the Governor of Kentucky, Ruby Laffoon, awarded Sanders the honorary title of Kentucky Colonel in honor of his contribution to the state. Having initially cooked his fried chicken in an iron skillet, Sanders changed to pressure cooking to save on time. The Colonel opened his first Kentucky Fried Chicken restaurant in 1952, and as early as 1960, his Original Recipe was being served in over 600 locations. Sanders sold his KFC franchising shares in 1964 for an amount equivalent to a paltry $14 million dollars today.

Q: What can be inferred from the passage?

(a) The Colonel foresaw the huge demand for his chicken.

(b) Sanders could have made a great deal more on his shares.

(c) Kentucky is a state known for its culinary prowess.

(d) Chicken was an unaffordable luxury during the 1930's.

번역

켄터키 프라이드 치킨은 1930년대 대공황기에 튀긴 닭을 내놓기 시작한 샌더스 대령이 설립하였다. 샌더스 코트 앤 카페는 선풍적인 인기를 끌자 1935년 켄터키 주지사 루비 라푼은 샌더스가 주에 공헌한 것에 경의를 표하기 위해 켄터키 대령이라는 명예 직함을 주었다. 처음에 샌더스는 철 냄비로 튀긴 닭을 요리했으나 시간을 절약하기 위해 가압 조리로 바꿨다. 대령은 1952년에 첫 번째 켄터키 프라이드 치킨 레스토랑을 열었고, 1960년 초에는 대령의 오리지널 레시피가 600개의

지점에 공급되고 있었다. 1964년 샌더스는 KFC 프랜차이즈 지분을 오늘날 1,400만 달러에 상응하는 보잘것없는 금액에 팔았다.

Q: 지문을 통해 유추할 수 있는 것은?

(a) 대령은 자신의 닭에 대한 엄청난 수요를 예측했다.

(b) 샌더스는 자신의 지분에 대해 좀더 나은 거래를 할 수도 있었다.

(c) 켄터키는 요리 솜씨로 유명한 주이다.

(d) 1930년대에 닭은 감당하기 힘든 사치였다.

해설

샌더스가 오늘날로 따지면 낮은 가격에 프랜차이즈 지분을 팔았다고 했는데, 대령이라는 직함을 받고 지점이 600개가 있을 정도면 그 가격보다 좀 더 높은 값을 받았을 수도 있었다는 유추 가능하므로 (b)가 정답이다.

honorary 영예의 | **contribution** 공헌 | **skillet** 냄비 | **paltry** 시시한 **foresee** 예측하다 | **culinary** 요리 | **prowess** 솜씨

38

Tiles are usually made of ceramic, stone, metal, or glass and often cover roofs, floors, walls, baths, showers, swimming pools, and tabletops. (a) A tiled surface is typically made up of many different colored individual pieces that when combined form a beautiful, sanitary, and easy-to-clean facade. (b) Tiles have been found dating back to 3,000 years BC in ancient Greece and spread to Europe and Asia Minor. **(c) The tiles used for floor coverings have to be thicker than those used to cover walls and other surfaces.** (d) Tiling is still done today using some of the same materials that have been used over the last 5 millenniums and is still considered a high skilled craft.

번역

타일은 보통 세라믹, 돌, 금속 또는 유리로 만들어지고 종종 지붕, 바닥, 벽, 욕조, 샤워, 수영장 그리고 테이블 윗면을 덮는다. (a) 타일을 덮은 표면은 보통 조합되었을 때 아름답고 위생적이며 청소하기 쉬운 표면을 만드는 많은 다양한 색의 개개의 조각들로 만들어진다. (b) 타일은 기원전 3,000년으로 거슬러 올라가 고대 그리스에서 발견되었고 유럽과 소아시아로 퍼져 나갔다. (c) 바닥을 덮기 위해 사용되는 타일은 벽이나 다른 표면을 덮을 때 쓰이는 타일보다 더 두꺼워야 한다. (d) 타일을 까는 데 오늘 날에도 여전히 지난 5천 년 동안 사용되어 온 것과 동일한 재료가 이용되고 아직도 매우 숙련된 기술로 여겨진다.

해설

지문에서 (b)와 (d)는 타일의 역사에 대해 이야기하고 있는데, (c)의 경우 특히 바닥에 사용되는 타일에 대해 언급하고 있어 문맥상 어울리지 않는다.

sanitary 위생적인 | **facade** 표면 | **date back** 역사가 ~나 되다 **craft** 기술

39

The grapes behind Shiraz wine were once thought to have come from near the Persian city of the same name which is around 900 kilometers from modern day Tehran. (a) However, this was a chicken and egg issue as people contemplated whether the Romans brought the grapes and wine from the Rhone Valley or if they acquired the port in Shiraz itself. **(b) If you are from Australia, you call the wine Shiraz but if you're from the French Avignon area, you might call it Syrah.** (c) Eventually the truth was discovered through DNA testing that the production of Shiraz wine did indeed come from the Romans. (d) Although two of the world's most famous regions for Shiraz grapes are in Europe, it is Australia that has made their name with the production of Shiraz wines.

번역

한 때 시라즈 와인을 만드는 포도는 오늘날의 테헤란에서 900킬로미터 정도 떨어진 같은 이름의 페르시아 도시에서 왔다고 여겨졌다. (a) 그러나, 사람들은 로마인들이 포도와 와인을 론 계곡에서 가져왔는지, 또는 그들이 시라즈에서 포트와인 자체를 획득했는지를 심사 숙고함에 따라 이것은 닭과 달걀의 문제가 되었다. **(b) 만약 네가 호주 출신이라면 그 와인을 시라즈라고 부르고, 만약 프랑스의 아비뇽 출신이라면 사이러라고 부를지도 모른다.** (c) 결국 DNA 시험을 거쳐 시라즈 와인의 생산은 정말로 로마인들에게서 전수되었다는 진실이 밝혀졌다. (d) 시라즈 포도로 세계에서 가장 유명한 지역 중 두 곳이 유럽에 있지만, 시라즈 와인의 생산으로 이름을 알린 것은 호주이다.

해설

시라즈 와인의 유래와 역사에 대해 주로 이야기하고 있는데, (b)는 와인 이름에 대한 것으로 전체 문맥에 어울리지 않는다.

contemplate 심사 숙고하다 | **port** 포트와인 (단맛이 나는 포르투갈산 적포도주)

40

One of the world's longest pipelines is the Trans-Alaska Pipeline System (TAPS) which runs 1,300 kilometers from northern Alaska at the Arctic Sea to its most southern point at Valdez, Alaska. **(a) It is commonly called the Pipeline but this moniker only refers to the actual pipeline.** (b) TAPS was built between 1974 and 1977 and includes 11 pump stations, kilometers of feeder pipelines, and the Valdez Terminal. (c) Many environmental, legal, and political controversies have surrounded TAPS since the discovery of oil in the Arctic. (d) However, when oil shortage catastrophes arise like they did in 1973 and in current times, people tend to look more favorably on the crude oil we can get from TAPS.

번역

세계에서 가장 긴 파이프 라인 중 하나는 북극해의 알래스카 북부에서 가장 남쪽 지점인 알래스카 발데즈까지 연결된 트랜스-알래스카 파이프라인 시스템 (TAPS)이다. **(a) 흔히 파이프라인이라고 부르지만 이것은 실제 파이프라인만을 일컫는 명칭이다.** (b) TAPS는 1974년에서 1977년 사이에 건설되었고, 11개의 펌프장과 수 킬로미터의 진입 파이프라인, 발데즈 터미널이 있다. (c) 북극해의 원유 발견 이후 TAPS를 둘러싸고 환경적, 법적, 정치적 논쟁이 많다. (d) 그러나 1973년에 그랬고 현재에도 그런 것처럼 석유 부족 참사가 일어나면 사람들은 TAPS에서 얻을 수 있는 원유를 더 호의적으로 보는 경향이 있다.

해설

TAPS에 대해 설명하며 TAPS를 둘러싼 논쟁에 대해 언급하고 있다. (a)는 파이프라인이라는 TAPS의 명칭에 관한 것으로 지문의 전반적인 흐름과 연관성이 없다.

moniker 별명 | **controversy** 논쟁 | **oil shortage** 석유 부족
catastrophe 참사 | **crude oil** 원유

Part I

1 (c)	**2** (d)	**3** (c)	**4** (d)	**5** (a)
6 (c)	**7** (b)	**8** (c)	**9** (d)	**10** (c)
11 (a)	**12** (c)	**13** (d)	**14** (b)	**15** (a)
16 (b)				

Part II

17 (d)	**18** (b)	**19** (b)	**20** (c)	**21** (b)
22 (d)	**23** (a)	**24** (a)	**25** (c)	**26** (b)
27 (d)	**28** (b)	**29** (b)	**30** (c)	**31** (d)
32 (c)	**33** (c)	**34** (a)	**35** (c)	**36** (a)
37 (d)				

Part III

38 (c)	**39** (d)	**40** (b)

1

Income disparity has always been a major concern for any society's well-being. Many people complain of the rich getting richer and the poor getting poorer, but is this necessarily true? The Gini coefficient is a statistical model named after the Italian statistician Corrado Gini. It measures the distribution of wealth within a society and ranges from 0 to 1, _____. According to a recent study, the countries that had the worse income equality were Namibia (.70), South Africa (.65) and Lesotho (.63). The lowest Gini scores go to Luxembourg (.26), Norway (.25) and Sweden (.23). Not surprisingly, the United States scored (.45) which is still in the worst 33 percent worldwide.

(a) 0 being total inequality and 1 being total equality
(b) the higher the score, the better the equality
(c) 0 being total equality and 1 being total inequality
(d) determined with a handful of calculations

번역

수입 불균형은 어떤 사회든 복지와 관련해 항상 주요 관심사였다. 많은 사람들은 부자는 더 부자가 되고 빈자는 더 가난해지는 것에 대해 불평하지만 이것이 반드시 사실인 것일까? 지니 계수는 이태리 통계학자 코라도 지니의 이름을 딴 통계 모델이다. 이것은 한 사회 내에서 부의 분배를 측정하며 범위가 0부터 1 사이이며 0은 완전 평등, 1은 완전 불평등을 의미한다. 최근 연구에 의하면 심한 소득 균등을 보였던 국가들은 나미비아(.70), 남아프리카공화국(.65), 레소토(.63)이다. 가장 낮은 지니 점수를 기록한 국가는 룩셈부르크(.26), 노르웨이(.25), 스웨덴

(.23)이다. 놀랄 것도 없이 미국은 0.45점을 얻어 세계적으로 여전히 최악의 불균형 국가 33% 안에 든다.

(a) 0은 완전 불평등, 1은 완전 평등을 의미한다
(b) 점수가 높을수록 균등성이 높다
(c) 0은 완전 평등, 1은 완전 불평등을 의미한다
(d) 소수의 계산 결과로 결정된다

해설

사회 복지 제도가 잘된 나라의 지니 점수는 낮고, 사회 복지 제도가 미미한 나라나 빈국의 지니 점수가 높은 것으로 미루어 (c)가 가장 적절하다.

disparity 불균형 | **well-being** 복지 | **Gini coefficient** 지니 계수 | **statistical** 통계적인 | **distribution** 분배 | **equality** 균등성 | **a handful of** 조금의

2

Tired of waking up every time your spouse turns over or gets out of bed? Finding it hard to have a full night's rest? Then say goodbye to sleepless nights by switching to a Deluxe Airy Cloud Mattress. The Airy Cloud comes with dual feather-top air mattresses and twin soundless pumps. With an easy-to-read LCD display, you can set the exact softness or firmness of your air mattress. The Airy Cloud mattress also comes with dual heat settings at no extra charge to soothe those aching muscles! Call today for a free 90-day "try it, you'll like it" test period. We're sure that once you try our mattress, you'll never go back to a regular one. _____. Call today!

(a) A regular bed is the size of our twin mattress
(b) You won't even return a delivery charge
(c) Lighten your back and your wallet
(d) Don't risk another restless night

번역

배우자가 뒤척거리거나 잠자리에서 일어날 때마다 잠을 깨는 일에 지쳤습니까? 하룻밤을 푹 쉬기가 어렵습니까? 그렇다면 딜럭스 에어리 클라우드 매트리스로 바꾸고 잠 못 이루는 밤과 작별 인사를 하십시오. 에어리 클라우드는 윗부분이 깃털로 된 이중 에어 매트리스와 무소음 펌프 한 쌍으로 이루어집니다. 읽기 쉬운 LCD 화면으로 에어 매트리스의 푹신함 또는 딱딱한 정도를 정확하게 설정할 수 있습니다. 또한 에어리 클라우드 매트리스에는 근육 통증을 덜어주는 이중 열 설정 장치가 추가 비용 없이 설치됩니다! 오늘 전화하셔서 90일간 무료로 시험 사용해 보십시오. 저희 매트리스를 사용해 보시면 절대 일반 제품을 다시 사용하지 않을 거라고 확신합니다. 또 다시 잠 못 이루는 밤을 보내지 마십시오. 오늘 전화하세요!

(a) 보통 침대가 당사의 트윈 매트리스 규격입니다
(b) 귀하는 배송비조차 반환하지 않을 겁니다
(c) 귀하의 등과 지갑을 가볍게 하십시오
(d) 또 다시 잠 못 이루는 밤을 보내지 마십시오

밤에 잠을 제대로 자지 못하는 사람들을 대상으로 숙면을 도와주는 침대를 광고하는 내용으로, 문맥과 가장 일관성 있는 문장은 (d)이다.

turn over 몸을 뒤집다 | **extra charge** 추가 비용 | **soothe** 덜어주다 **restless** 제대로 잠들지 못하는

3

The ballpoint pen has its origins in 1938 with a Hungarian newspaper editor Laszlo Biro who got tired of always refilling his fountain pens and having the tip poke through the paper. He noticed the ink from the newspaper printing press did not smear and worked with his chemist brother to use that ink in pen form. Biro fitted a small metal ball at the tip of a pen to transfer ink to paper. Earlier prototypes leaked or got clogged and depended on gravity to move the ink around the metal ball. So the Biro brothers developed capillary motion for ink delivery and this made their pens better as _____.

(a) it could be given the limitations of their technology
(b) the other competing ballpoint pens on the market
(c) you didn't need to hold them straight upright
(d) people didn't have to refill the pen as much

번역

볼펜은 1938년 헝가리 신문 편집장이었던 라즐로 비로가 항상 만년필 잉크를 다시 채워야 하고 펜 끝이 종이에 구멍을 내는 것에 지친 것으로부터 유래한다. 그는 신문 인쇄기에서 나오는 잉크가 번지지 않는 것을 알아채고, 그 잉크를 펜 형태로 사용하기 위해 화학자인 동생과 함께 작업을 했다. 비로는 잉크를 종이로 전달하기 위해 펜 끝에 작은 금속 공을 장착했다. 초기의 원형 제품은 새거나 막혔으며, 중력에 의해 잉크가 금속 공 주위를 돌았다. 그래서 비로 형제는 잉크를 전달하기 위해 모세관 운동을 개발했고 이것은 볼펜을 똑바로 세워서 잡지 않아도 될 만큼 성능이 개선되었다.

(a) 그들의 기술에 제약이 있을 수 있었다
(b) 시장에서 경쟁하는 다른 볼펜
(c) 볼펜을 똑바로 세워서 잡지 않아도 되었다
(d) 사람들이 그만큼 펜을 채우지 않아도 되었다

해설

빈칸은 새거나 막혔던 초기의 볼펜이 나중에 잉크를 전달하기 위해 모세관 운동의 개발로 성능이 개선된 이유를 묻는 문제이다. (a), (b), (d)는 문맥과 관련이 없고 잉크를 전달하는 것이 볼펜 성능의 관건이 된 것으로 미루어 (c)가 가장 적절하다.

smear 번지다 | **prototype** 원형 | **capillary** 모세관의 | **upright** 똑바로 세워 둔

4

Many orthopedics would give feet more support in the shoe, especially if the foot was injured. Short of ordering a custom-fit shoe, the idea that a special foam can adapt to the individual shape of a foot led to special shoes. Legend has it that George B. Boedecker came up with the idea for the trendy footwear when he wore some simple foam slippers while relaxing at a spa. The first shoes were unveiled in 2002 at a boat show in Fort Lauderdale, Florida, and all 200 pairs sold out quickly. By 2007, the company had 5,300 people employed with annual sales of nearly $170 million. Today you can find these foam shoes in every corner of the planet. _____ some foam slippers at a health spa.

(a) It wouldn't be if Boedecker didn't put on
(b) This new global phenomenon started from
(c) They are inspired as Boedecker by
(d) Not bad for an invention inspired by

번역

여러 정형술로 인해서 특히 발이 부상 당했을 경우라면 신발 속의 발을 더 지탱할 것이다. 주문 제작 신발을 주문하는 방법 외에도 특수 발 포체가 개개의 발 모양에 맞춰 개조할 수 있다는 아이디어가 특수 신발로 이어졌다. 전하는 이야기에 따르면 조지 베덱커는 온천에서 휴식을 취하는 동안 단순한 발포성 슬리퍼를 신고 있었는데 그때 최신 유행의 신발에 대한 아이디어가 떠올랐다고 한다. 그 최초의 신발은 플로리다 포트 로더데일에서 열린 보트 쇼에서 2002년 처음 선보였고, 200켤레가 모두 빠르게 품절되었다. 2007년에는 회사 직원 5,300명에 연 매출액은 약 1억 7천만 달러였다. 오늘날 세계 곳곳에서 이런 발포성 신발을 볼 수 있다. 휴양 온천에서의 발포성 슬리퍼에 의해 영감을 받은 발명품치고는 꽤 괜찮은 결과이다.

(a) 베덱커가 신지 않았다면 그렇지 않을 것이다
(b) 새로운 현상이 전 세계적으로 일어났다
(c) 그들은 베덱커처럼 영감을 받았다
(d) 영감을 받은 발명품치고는 꽤 괜찮은 결과이다

해설

조지 베덱커가 온천에서 휴식을 취하는 동안 떠오른 신발 아이디어가 상품이 되고 전 세계적으로 인기를 얻어 큰 성공을 거뒀다는 내용이므로 문맥상 영감 하나의 결과가 꽤 괜찮았다는 (d)가 가장 적절하다.

orthopedics 정형술 | **short of** ~을 제외하고 | **adapt** 〈용도에 맞추어〉 개조하다 | **legend has it** 전하는 이야기에 따르면 | **foam** 발포 고무 | **unveil** 발표하다

5

Due to the coarse nature of the food it eats, a cow has not one but four stomachs _____. Digestion starts when a cow chews the food just enough to swallow it. The food travels to the first two stomachs, the rumen and the reticulum where it is stored. After filling herself up with this process, the cow rests. Sometime later, she regurgitates the partially chewed food, now called cud, and thoroughly chews and swallows it again. Now the cud enters the third and fourth stomachs, the omasum and the abomasum, and is digested. Milk is produced when some of this digested food enters the bloodstream and into the udder.

(a) to facilitate the digestive process of plants like grass

(b) to digest the food without requiring too much chewing

(c) which the rough vegetation is processed by the animal

(d) that digests the grass or corn eaten in great quantities

번역

먹이가 거친 특성 때문에 소는 풀과 같은 식물의 소화 과정을 촉진시키도록 위가 하나가 아닌 4개이다. 소가 삼킬 수 있을 정도로 먹이를 씹으면 소화가 시작된다. 먹이는 처음 2개의 위인, 반추위와 벌집위로 이동해 저장된다. 이러한 과정으로 배를 충분히 채운 소는 휴식을 취한다. 얼마 뒤 소는 이제 새김질감이라고 불리는 일부분만 씹은 먹이를 역류시키고, 꼭꼭 씹어서 다시 삼킨다. 이제 새김질감은 제3 및 제4의 위인 겹주름위와 주름위로 들어가 소화된다. 우유는 이렇게 소화된 먹이 중 일부가 혈류와 유방으로 들어가 생산된다.

(a) 풀과 같은 식물의 소화 과정을 촉진시키도록

(b) 너무 많이 씹지 않고 먹이를 소화시키기 위해

(c) 동물이 거친 식물을 처리하는

(d) 다량으로 먹은 풀이나 옥수수를 소화하는

해설

위가 네 개이고 되새김질을 하는 소의 소화 과정을 기술하고 있다. 빈칸은 거친 먹이를 먹는 소가 왜 위장이 네 개인가를 묻는 문제로 (a)가 가장 적절하다.

coarse 성긴 | **digestion** 소화 | **chew** 씹다 | **swallow** 삼키다 | **rumen** 반추위 | **reticulum** 벌집위 | **regurgitate** 역류시키다 | **cud** 새김질감 | **omasum** 겹주름위 | **abomasum** 주름위 | **udder** 〈소 · 염소 등의〉 유방

6

Chilean wineries have seen a substantial increase in exportation, especially thanks to free trade agreements. Once only considered as quaint "boutique" wineries, Chilean wineries have seen a meteoric rise of over five times from 12 wineries in 1995 to over 70 by 2005. They can boast being the fifth largest exporter and ninth largest producer in the world. Interestingly, Chilean wineries can thank the phylloxera louse for some of their success. This destructive vine parasite native to the New World went to Europe and Australia onboard trading vessels in the late 18th century and _____. Chilean wineries were spared the carnage and therefore maintained their high quantity and quality.

(a) took root in select and favorable localities

(b) acclimated to the hemiepiphyte soil and ecology

(c) virtually obliterated the local vineyards

(d) facilitated the vineyards' watershed basins

번역

칠레의 포도주 양조장은 수출이 상당히 증가했는데, 특히 이것은 자유 무역 협정 덕분이다. 전에 예스러운 '부티크' 양조장으로만 여겨졌던 칠레의 포도주 양조장은 1995년 12곳에서 2005년까지 70곳 이상으로 일약 5배 이상 증가했다. 칠레의 포도주 양조장은 수출이 세계 5위이고 생산량은 세계 9위로 자랑할 만하다. 흥미롭게도 칠레의 포도주 양조장의 성공은 포도나무뿌리 진디의 덕을 어느 정도 보았다고 할 수 있다. 이 파괴적인 신세계에서 난 포도나무 기생충은 18세기 말에 무역선에 의해 유럽과 호주로 이동해 그 지역의 포도밭을 사실상 없앴다. 칠레의 포도주 양조장은 이러한 대학살을 면했기 때문에 대량 생산과 고급 품질을 유지했다.

(a) 엄선된 좋은 지역에 뿌리를 내렸다

(b) 반착생 토양과 자연 환경에 순응했다

(c) 지역의 포도밭을 사실상 없앴다

(d) 포도밭의 분수령 유역 이용을 용이하게 했다

해설

파괴적인 포도나무뿌리 진디의 덕택으로 칠레의 포도주 양조산업이 수출 세계 5위로 급성장했고, 이 벌레가 무역선에 의해 유럽과 호주로 이동했으며, 칠레의 포도주 양조산업은 이 벌레에 의한 대학살을 모면했기 때문에 고급 품질 포도주의 대량 생산을 유지했다는 내용과 빈칸을 연관지으면, (c)가 가장 적절하다.

winery 포도주 양조장 | **free trade agreement** 자유 무역 협정 | **quaint** 예스러운 | **meteoric** 일약 ~한 | **parasite** 기생충 | **carnage** 대학살 | **take root** 뿌리를 내리다 | **ecology** 자연 환경 | **acclimate** 순응시키다 | **hemiepiphyte** 반착생식물 | **obliterate** 없애다

7

Dear Editor,

You posit the tepid and shallow argument that a lack of historical understanding is the cause of America's current problems. Let us not forget that nearly every historic conflict has roots in resentment and a vendetta-like mentality towards previous altercations. So to ascribe America's current involvement in armed conflicts simply on a deficiency in comprehension of history is the same Euro-centric babble that somehow seeps over the pond and onto our shores. I just always had faith that this periodical would not get swept in by trendy waves of dangerously left slanting liberal views. With this said, _____ that this magazine is on its way down that slippery slope of biased journalism.

Sincerely,

Victor Banian

(a) I'm overwhelmingly ecstatic it finally appears
(b) it is evident to me as a long time reader
(c) there is yet no precedents to show
(d) many readers have improperly purported

편집자님께

귀하는 미국이 현재 당면한 문제가 역사적 이해의 부족 때문이라는 미온적이고 피상적인 주장을 하고 있습니다. 거의 모든 역사적인 갈등의 뿌리가 이전의 격론에 대한 분노와 상호 복수와 비슷한 심리에 뿌리를 두고 있다는 것을 잊어서는 안됩니다. 따라서 무력 분쟁에 미국이 현재 개입하고 있는 것을 단순히 역사에 대한 이해 부족의 탓으로 돌리는 것은, 어떻든 연못에서 스며 나와 우리 해안으로 스며드는 유럽 중심적인 주절거림과 똑같습니다. 저는 이 잡지가 위험스럽게 남아있는 편향된 진보적인 견해의 시류에 휩쓸리지 않을 것이라는 믿음을 항상 가지고 있었습니다. 더불어 이 잡지가 편향된 저널리즘이라는 파멸의 길을 가고 있다는 것이 오랜 독자인 제게 분명해 보입니다.

빅토르 바니앙

(a) 마침내 나타나니 매우 황홀합니다
(b) 오랜 독자인 제게 분명해 보입니다
(c) 보여줄 전례가 아직 없습니다
(d) 많은 독자들이 부적절하게 주장했습니다

잡지의 기사에 대해 반박하는 편지다. 서신을 보낸 사람은 잡지 기사를 읽은 독자라고 보는 것이 가장 적절하므로 (b)가 정답이다.

tepid 미온적인 | **shallow** 피상적인 | **resentment** 분노 | **mentality** 심리 | **altercation** 격론 | **ascribe** ~의 탓으로 돌리다 | **deficiency** 부족 | **liberal** 진보적인 | **purport** 의미하다

8

Let's say a phone you want to buy is selling at $500 _____. The question is whether you would still be willing to part with your money. Many consumers may, and this kind of economic measurement is described by price elasticity of demand (PED) coined by Alfred Marshall. This index measures the sensitivity or elasticity of a product's demand based on its price. So if the $50 increase doesn't affect sales of the phone, the PED is low and inelastic. Conversely, if the price increases compared to other brands, consumers might not pay the higher price but instead switch brands. Then the PED is high and elastic.

(a) but you would also pay up to $550
(b) which increases the price to $550
(c) but the price increases to $550
(d) which will not sell much at $550

당신이 사고 싶은 전화기가 500달러에 판매되다가 550달러로 오른다고 하자. 문제는 아직도 당신이 기꺼이 돈을 지불할 것인가이다. 많은 고객은 돈을 지불할 것이며, 이런 종류의 경제 치수는 알프레드 마샬이 만든 수요에 대한 가격 탄력성(PED)으로 설명한다. 이 지수는 가격을 기준으로 제품의 수요에 대한 민감성 또는 탄력성을 측정한다. 따라서 50달러의 가격 인상이 전화기 판매에 영향을 미치지 않는다면 PED는 탄력성이 낮아서 비탄력적이다. 반대로 다른 브랜드에 비해 가격이 오르면 고객들은 더 비싼 가격을 지불하지 않는 대신 브랜드를 바꿀 것이다. 이 경우 PED는 높고 탄력적이다.

(a) 하지만 당신은 또한 550달러까지 지불할 것이다
(b) 가격을 550달러로 인상시키는
(c) 하지만 가격이 550달러로 오른다
(d) 550달러에는 많이 팔리지 않는

가격 인상에 대한 수요의 탄력성에 대한 글이다. 빈칸 문장은 글의 전제가 되는 부분으로, 빈칸 뒤에서 아직도 돈을 지불할 용의가 있는지에 대해 문제를 제기하므로 가격이 오른다는 (c)가 가장 적절하다.

part with money 돈을 (마지못해) 내놓다 | **measurement** 치수 **elasticity** 탄력성 | **coin** 만들어 내다 | **sensitivity** 민감성 | **inelastic** 비탄력적인

9

The Boeing B-52 Stratofortress bomber is an iconic image of the Cold War. Standing at around 40 feet with a wingspan of 185 feet, the B-52 houses a crew of five and over 70,000 pounds of mixed ordnance which includes bombs, mines, and missiles in various configurations. It served as a deterrent and counteractive to the perceived nuclear threat of the Soviet military during the Cold War. As a long-range, subsonic, jet-powered strategic bomber, the B-52 can reach _____. It has seen action in many armed conflicts from Vietnam to Desert Storm. As of February 2009, the Air Force still operated 90 out of the 744 original B-52 bombers in service.

(a) its purpose in major air-to-air combat situations
(b) the limits of any required reconnaissance mission
(c) millions of pounds of supplies in a single journey
(d) sensitive targets quickly and with deadly force

하늘을 나는 요새인 보잉의 B-52 폭격기는 냉전의 상징적 이미지다. 높이 약 40피트이고 날개 폭 185피트인 B-52에는 5명의 승무원이 탑승하고 다양하게 구성된 폭탄, 지뢰, 미사일을 포함해 7만 파운드 이

상의 혼합 군수품을 수용한다. B-52는 냉전 시대에 감지된 소련군부의 핵 위협에 대한 억지력 및 반작용물로서 역할을 수행했다. 제트 추진 방식의 장거리 아음속 전략 폭격기로서 B-52는 치명적인 힘을 가지고 민감한 목표물에 신속하게 도달할 수 있다. B-52는 베트남 전쟁에서 사막의 폭풍 작전에 이르기까지 많은 무력 분쟁에서 활약했다. 공군은 처음 가동됐던 744대의 B-52 폭격기 중 2009년 2월 당시 90대를 계속 운용했다.

(a) 중요한 공중전에서 그 목적을 수행하는
(b) 필요한 모든 정찰 임무의 한계에 도달하는
(c) 1회 비행으로 수백만 파운드의 물자를 내려주는
(d) 치명적인 힘을 가지고 민감한 목표물에 신속하게 도달하는

해설

앞서 '제트 추진 방식의 장거리 아음속 전략 폭격기'라는 언급 후에는 폭격기의 수행 능력이 이어지는 것이 자연스럽다. (a)는 전투기, (b)는 정찰기, (c)는 수송기의 임무이며, (d)가 폭격기가 수행하는 역할이므로 가장 적절하다.

Stratofortress 하늘을 나는 요새 | **ordnance** 군수품 | **mine** 지뢰 | **deterrent** (전쟁) 억지력 | **counteractive** 반작용제 | **subsonic** 아음속의 (음속보다 약간 느린 속도) | **strategic** 전략의 | **armed conflict** 무력 분쟁 | **in service** 취역 중인 | **reconnaissance** 정찰

10

An international bestseller and subject for university-level studies, *Freakonomics* poses unusual economic questions and theories from its analysis of thought-provoking data. The authors Steven D. Levitt and Stephen J. Dubner bring to light interesting economic principles at work in our day-to-day lives and add credence to even disputed theories. For example, they point to the win-loss statistics of sumo wrestlers and game theory to assert the existence of match fixing. Many readers find it a worthy and enlightening read that questions their preconceptions. However, just as with most books regarding economics and society, *Freakonomics* has its share of critics who object to some of the data that they _____.

(a) deem as overly simplified but appropriate nonetheless
(b) have poured over for hours and hours
(c) view as not having been correctly interpreted
(d) argue is perfectly acceptable in the proper context

번역

세계적인 베스트셀러이고 대학교 수준의 연구인 〈괴짜 경제학〉은 생각을 자극하는 자료 분석으로 범상치 않은 경제학적인 질문과 이론을 제기한다. 저자인 스티븐 레빗과 스티븐 더브너는 우리의 일상적인 삶에서 흥미로운 경제 원리를 조명하고 논쟁의 여지가 있는 이론에도 신빙성을 주고 있다. 예를 들면, 저자들은 스모 선수들의 승패 통계와 게임 이론을 지적해 승부 조작을 주장한다. 많은 독자들은 이 책이 자신의 선입견에 이의를 제기하는 가치 있고 계몽적인 읽을거리라고 생각한다. 하지만 경제학과 사회에 관한 대부분의 책처럼, 〈괴짜 경제학〉은 정확한 해석이 아닌 것으로 보는 일부 자료에 반박하는 비평가적 몫이 있다.

(a) 지나치게 단순화되었으나 그럼에도 적절한
(b) 여러 시간 동안 쏟아 부은
(c) 정확하게 해석되지 않은 것으로 보는
(d) 그들의 주장이 적절한 문맥으로 완벽하게 수용될 수 있는

해설

비평가가 이 범상치 않은 경제학 책에 관해 취할 수 있는 일을 생각해보면 (c)가 가장 적절하다.

pose 제기하다 | **thought-provoking** 생각을 자극하는 | **credence** 믿음 | **match fixing** 승부 조작 | **preconception** 선입견

11

Although pool has long been associated with royalty as the "Noble Game of Billiards" in the 1800's, _____ since its inception in the 1500's. The game of pocket pool was actually invented nearly 300 years after billiards. Billiards was an adaptation of an outdoor game similar to croquet, with the green fabric representing the grass. The word "billiards" comes from either the French word "billart" for one of the sticks or "bille" which means ball. The word "pool" means "to ante" in a bet and stuck with the game when pool tables were installed in betting rooms to help gamblers pass the time. The game of eight-ball pocket pool was invented around 1900.

(a) commoners have been familiar with it
(b) the royalty of Europe banned it in court
(c) local magistrates provided it for small fares
(d) French aristocracy often lost to their British rivals

번역

포켓볼은 1800년대 '상류층의 당구 게임'으로서 오랫동안 왕족과 관련이 있었지만, 당구가 1500년대에 시작된 이후 평민에게 친숙한 경기였다. 사실 포켓볼 게임은 당구가 생긴지 300년 뒤에 생겨난 것이다. 당구는 크로켓과 유사한 야외 게임을 변형한 것인데, 녹색 천은 잔디를 의미한다. '당구'란 단어는 막대기 중 하나라는 프랑스 단어 'billart' 또는 공을 의미하는 'bille'에서 유래한다. 'pool'이란 단어는 내기에서 '돈을 걸다'를 의미하고, 도박장에 당구대가 설치될 때 도박꾼들이 시간을 보내도록 하기 위해 진행되었다. 8개의 공으로 하는 포켓볼 게임은 1900년 경에 만들어졌다.

(a) 평민에게 친숙한 경기였다
(b) 유럽의 왕족들은 법정에서 그것을 금지했다
(c) 지방 치안 판사들이 소액을 받고 제공했다
(d) 프랑스 귀족은 종종 경쟁국 영국에 패배했다

빈칸 앞은 포켓볼이 1800년대 상류층의 당구 게임으로서 왕족과 관련 있었지만, 1500년대에는 어떠했는지 묻는 문제이다. 바로 다음 문장에서 포켓볼이 있기 300년 전에 당구가 있었다고 나오므로 (a)가 가장 적절하다.

pool 포켓볼 | **royalty** 왕족 | **inception** 시작 | **ante** 돈을 걸다 | **stick with** ~와 함께 하다 | **magistrate** 치안 판사

12

The head of the major U.S. electronics giant Sator recently lambasted one of its major overseas suppliers, Areva, for a lack of innovation in developing creative new hardware offerings. Areva is the supplier of the hardware for many of the company's hit consumer electronics but is perceived as lacking state-of-the-art designs to compete in the fast-changing field. Nevertheless, Areva is set to continue to remain the major supply partner to Sator. This isn't the first time the outspoken CEO of Sator, Redding Perot, has _____. Webia and Cogitech have for a long time written Sator's software but are still not exempt from his frequent and public tongue lashings.

(a) criticized the electronics parts conglomerate
(b) found flaws in competing companies products
(c) openly and publicly criticized his industry suppliers
(d) reprimanded his overseas chip suppliers

번역

미국의 주요 거대 전자 업체인 세이터의 회장은 최근 중요한 해외 공급업체 중 하나인 아레바를 창의적인 새 하드웨어 제품을 제안하는 데 혁신이 부족하다고 비난했다. 아레바는 세이터의 여러 소비자 히트 전자제품용 하드웨어를 공급하는 업체이지만 빠르게 변하는 분야에서 경쟁하기 위한 최신의 설계가 부족한 것으로 인식된다. 그럼에도 불구하고, 아레바는 세이터의 주요 공급 파트너로 계속 남을 예정이다. 노골적인 세이터의 최고 경영자 레딩 패롯이 공공연히 공개적으로 자사 공급업체들을 비난한 것은 이번이 처음이 아니다. 웨비아와 코지텍은 오랫동안 세이터의 소프트웨어를 제작하고 있지만 아직도 그의 빈번하고 공공연한 꾸짖음에서는 벗어나지 못하고 있다.

(a) 전자 부품을 생산하는 대기업을 비난했다
(b) 경쟁사의 제품에서 결점을 발견했다
(c) 공공연히 공개적으로 자사 공급업체들을 비난했다
(d) 자사의 해외 칩 공급업체를 질책했다

해설

세이터의 최고 경영자가 자사의 소비자 전자제품용 하드웨어 아레바를 호되게 비난 했음에도 아레바가 계속 세이터의 중요 공급 파트너로 남아있을 예정이고, 세이터의 소프트웨어 제작사인 웨비아와 코지텍 역시 그의 잦고 공공연한 꾸짖음에서 벗어나지 못하고 있다는 내용으로

미루어 그가 공급업체들을 비난하는 것이 이번이 처음이 아니라는 것을 알 수 있다. 따라서 (c)가 가장 적절하다.

lambast 비난하다 | **outspoken** 노골적인 | **exempt** 면제되다
tongue lash 호되게 꾸짖다

13

There is a city that in the past century has hosted a national revolution, a fascist movement, and even division by a concrete wall. If this sounds interesting to you, then you must come to Berlin where the tumultuous nature of its past can still be seen today. The observation deck at Panoramapunkt is unmatched for its view of Potsdamer Platz, Daimler City, the Sony Centre, and the Beishem Centre areas. For a hip and trendy dining experience, try fusion dishes like beef bavette and sesame potatoes while lounging on a platform bed at Spindler & Klatt. Transportation is easy on one of _____, the U-Bahn and S-Bahn trains, buses, and trams.

(a) its many authentic and antique transports
(b) the privately run and owned express services
(c) the major rail and waterways of the city
(d) the three major means of public transport

번역

지난 세기 국가적 혁명과 파시스트 운동이 일어났고 심지어 콘크리트 장벽으로 분할되었던 도시가 있습니다. 이 말이 흥미롭다면 그 격동적인 과거를 오늘날 아직도 볼 수 있는 도시인 베를린에 반드시 가봐야 합니다. 파라노마풍크트의 전망대는 포츠다머 플라츠, 다임러, 소니센터, 바이셈 센터 지역을 볼 수 있어 타의 추종을 불허하는 장소입니다. 최근 유행하는 식사를 하려면 스핀들러 앤 클랫의 플랫폼 침대에 느긋하게 앉아 소고기 바베트나 참깨 감자 같은 퓨전 요리를 먹어보세요. 세 가지 주요 대중교통 수단인 U지하철과 S지하철, 버스, 전차 중 하나를 이용하면 교통이 편리합니다.

(a) 예전의 형태 그대로인
(b) 민간업체가 운영 및 소유하는 급행 서비스
(c) 도시의 주요 철도 및 수로
(d) 세 가지 주요 대중교통 수단

해설

빈칸은 U지하철, S지하철, 버스, 전차와 동격으로, 이들은 고풍스러운 것이 아니므로 (a)는 제외하고, (b)는 베를린을 소개하는 글의 분위기에 어울리지 않으며 U지하철은 국철이다. (c)는 글에 언급되지 않은 '수로'가 있어 제외한다. 운송수단이 주요 대중교통 수단 세 가지이므로 (d)가 가장 적절하다.

division 분할 | **tumultuous** 격동의 | **observation deck** 전망대
unmatched 비길 데 없는 | **hip and trendy** 최신 유행의 | **tram** 전차
authentic 진짜인 | **waterway** 수로

14

The ancient epic poems, *The Iliad* and *The Odyssey*, were at some point in their history _____. But based on this literary evidence, the issue of whether just one author created them remains debated. Controversy still surrounding these works is collectively referred to as the "Homeric" questions. Critics of the one-author theory point to inconsistencies in *The Iliad*, for example the fact that the king of the Paphlagonians is slain but then reappears later on, mourning the loss of his son. However, proponents of the one-author theory maintain that an ancient Greek poet at the time recited all his poems, including these two very lengthy ones, by heart and so variations, changes, and even mistakes therein could occur.

(a) only passed on orally by the ancient poets
(b) committed to paper and then manually copied
(c) retold and elaborated on by other Greek poets
(d) criticized for inaccuracies in their story lines

번역

고대 서사시인 〈일리아드〉와 〈오디세이〉는 역사의 어떤 시점에 종이에 기록된 다음 수기로 복사되었다. 하지만 이 문학적인 증거를 바탕으로 단지 한 명의 작가가 창작했는가 하는 문제는 논쟁거리로 남아있다. 아직도 이 작품을 둘러싸고 있는 논란을 집합적으로 '호머의' 질문이라고 부른다. 1인 저자 가설에 대한 비판들은 〈일리아드〉의 모순, 예를 들면 파플라고니아의 왕은 살해되지만 아들을 잃은 것을 슬퍼하며 다시 등장한다는 사실을 지적한다. 하지만 1인 저자 가설 지지자들은 당시의 고대 그리스 시인이 바로 이 두 편의 아주 긴 시를 포함해 자신의 모든 시를 암송했기 때문에, 그 점에 있어서 변화와 차이 그리고 실수도 생길 수 있다고 주장한다.

(a) 고대 시인들에 의해 단지 구전되었다
(b) 종이에 기록된 다음 수기로 복사되었다
(c) 다른 그리스 시인들에 의해 다시 전해지면서 정교해졌다
(d) 줄거리가 정확하지 않다고 비난 받았다

해설

지문의 요지는 〈일리아드〉와 〈오디세이〉의 저자가 한 사람인가 아닌가 이다. 아직 논쟁의 여지가 있는 부분이므로 (a)와 (c)는 정답이 될 수 없다. 또한 줄거리가 부정확하다는 것은 기억에 의한 암송으로 발생한 문제이므로 (d)도 정답에서 벗어난다. 논쟁적인 본론에 들어가기 전 객관적인 사실을 전달하는 (b)가 가장 적절하다.

epic poem 서사시 | **commit to paper** 종이에 쓰다 | **controversy** 논란 | **inconsistency** 모순 | **mourn** 애도하다 | **proponent** 지지자 | **by heart** 외워서 | **manually** 손으로 | **elaborate** 정교하게 만들어 내다

15

With all our technological wonders and medical breakthroughs, how is it that what was once a previously eradicated disease has reemerged to become the leading infectious killer of adults over 26? There are many reasons at multiple levels for the reemergence of tuberculosis, or TB. Some physical reasons include increased travel, migration and tourism _____ social reasons such as global degradation in healthcare and incidents of TB in AIDS patients also raise the fatality numbers. Additionally, as we have seen with many other diseases, new strains of TB have developed that are immune to the currently used vaccines. All these factors make TB, an airborne contagion that often stays latent, yet again a scourge on humanity.

(a) while
(b) albeit
(c) where
(d) even

번역

인류의 모든 기술적인 경이로움과 의학적 발견에도 불구하고 과거에 박멸되었던 질병이 다시 나타나 26세 이상 성인을 죽이는 주요 전염성 살인자가 된다면 어떻게 될까요? 결핵, 즉 TB가 다시 나타난다는 여러 가지 관점의 근거가 많이 있습니다. 몇 가지 물리적 이유로는 이동, 이주, 관광 여행의 증가인 한편 사회적인 이유로는 세계적으로 건강 관리 하락과 후천성 면역 결핍증 환자의 결핵 발생도 사망자의 수를 늘립니다. 또한 다른 많은 질병에서 보았듯이 현재 사용되는 백신에 면역성이 있는 새로운 변종 결핵이 발생하고 있습니다. 이러한 모든 요인으로 보통 잠복 상태로 있으며 공기로 전염되는 전염병인 결핵이 다시 인류의 재앙이 되고 있습니다.

(a) 한편
(b) 비록 ~일지라도
(c) 거기서
(d) ~조차

해설

빈칸은 결핵이 재발하는 두 가지 이유, 즉 사회적인 이유와 물리적인 이유 사이를 연결하는 접속사를 찾는 문제이다. 두 가지 종류의 이유가 비교 및 대조되고 있으므로 (a)가 가장 적절하다.

breakthrough 새 발견 | **eradicate** 박멸시키다 | **infectious** 전염성의 | **tuberculosis** 결핵 | **incident** 사건, 일 | **fatality** 사망자 | **strain** 변종 | **airborne** 공기로 전염되는 | **contagion** 전염병 | **scourge** 재앙

16

It has been said that the instincts that keep us alive in the jungle will kill us on the street. This is no better illustrated than during times of extreme market upheaval and unpredictability. _____ for the majority of us, we end up buying when the market's hot and selling when it's not. In essence, we buy high and sell low, rather than stick to our guns as is advised. However, even our financial planners aren't immune to this human nature. In 2009, almost 30 percent of advisers moved their clients out of the stock market and into more conservative instruments, going against the most basic tenet of market investing and costing them recuperating gains on the subsequent uptick.

(a) Conversely
(b) Unfortunately
(c) Interestingly
(d) Accordingly

번역

밀림에서 살 수 있는 우리의 본능이 거리에서는 우리를 죽게 할 것이라는 말이 있다. 이 말은 시장이 격변하고 예측할 수 없는 시기에 가장 잘 입증된다. 유감스럽게도 우리 대다수는 시장이 가열되면 구매하고 그렇지 않으면 매매하고 만다. 본질적으로 조언을 받은 대로 자기의 입장을 고수하지 못하고 비싸게 사고 싸게 판다. 하지만 금융 설계사들조차도 이런 인간의 본성에 영향을 받는다. 2009년에 약 30%의 상담사들이 고객을 주식 시장에서 빼내 더 보수적인 수단으로 이동시켜 시장 투자의 가장 기본적인 교의를 거슬렀고, 고객들은 뒤이은 상승 장에서의 수익으로는 손실을 만회하지 못했다.

(a) 반대로
(b) 유감스럽게도
(c) 흥미롭게도
(d) 따라서

해설

빈칸 다음은 본능적으로 주식 시장에서 오르면 사고 내리면 팔아서 손실을 보는 일반 투자자의 투자 심리에 대해 기술하고 있는데 이것은 유감스러운 일이 아닐 수 없으므로 (b)가 가장 적절하다.

upheaval 격변 | unpredictability 예측이 불가능함 | stick to one's gun 입장을 고수하다 | conservative 보수적인 | cost 잃게 하다 | recuperate 손실을 만회하다 | uptick 상승 장 | tenet 교의

17

Scientist only first began speculating on the magma ocean theory of Earth after the first moon rock samples were gathered from the Apollo missions and studied in the lab. The moon rocks revealed that at some point the moon was entirely covered in magma. This theory was based on the fact that heavier elements like iron were found deeper than the lighter materials found near the surface. Since the moon was actually a part of the Earth that was violently separated by a giant asteroid collision, scientists drew the conclusion that the Earth's core samples would be similar with the moon rocks. The results agreed with the theory as more iron was found at greater depths.

Q: What is mainly being discussed in this passage?
(a) How the Apollo missions contributed to scientific knowledge
(b) The role of the moon rocks in Earth's early history
(c) The geology of the moon based on rock samples
(d) A theory using parallels between the moon and Earth

번역

아폴로 우주 비행에서 최초로 달의 암석 샘플을 수집해서 실험실 연구가 이루어진 후에야 과학자들은 처음 지구의 용암 해양 이론에 대해 추측하기 시작했다. 달 암석은 어느 시점에 달이 완전히 마그마로 덮여 있었다는 것을 보여주었다. 이 이론은 철과 같은 무거운 원소가 지표 근처에서 발견되는 가벼운 물질보다 더 깊은 곳에서 발견되었다는 사실에 기초했다. 실제로 달은 거대한 소행성 충돌로 인해 격렬하게 분리되었던 지구의 한 부분이므로 과학자들은 지구의 핵 표본이 달 암석과 유사할 것이라는 결론을 내렸다. 깊을수록 더 많은 철이 발견되자 그 결과는 이론과 부합했다.

Q: 지문에서 주로 논의되고 있는 것은?
(a) 아폴로 우주 비행이 과학적 지식에 어떻게 기여했는가
(b) 지구의 초기 역사에 있어서 달 암석의 역할
(c) 암석 표본에 기초한 달의 지질학
(d) 달과 지구의 유사점을 이용하는 이론

해설

아폴로 달 탐사에서 수집한 달 암석에 대한 분석 결과, 과학자들은 거대한 소행성이 지구와 충돌해 달이 지구로부터 떨어져 나간 것이기 때문에 지구의 핵과 달의 암석이 유사할 것이라는 결론을 이끌어냈다는 것이 요지이다. 따라서 정답은 (d)이다.

speculate 추측하다 | element 원소 | asteroid 소행성 | core 핵 geology 지질학 | parallel 유사점

18

Referred to as "the cradle of Chinese civilization" the Huang He or Yellow River is the sixth longest river in the world. It is considered the birthplace of China, with some of the most prosperous dynasties living on or near it. However, due to major flooding and the loss of the Xin dynasty due to floods, the river is also known as "China's Sorrow." Like other major water sources, the Yellow River is and has historically been a crucial resource for farming, hydroelectricity, fishing, transport and many others purposes. These days, pollution has unfortunately made nearly one-third of the river unusable even for irrigation and industrial purposes.

Q: What is the best title for the passage?
(a) Problems on the World's Major Waterways
(b) The Yellow River's Significance to China
(c) China and Its Yellow River Valley Civilizations

(d) The Many Blessings of the Yellow River

번역

'중국 문명의 요람'으로 불리는 황허. 즉 황하는 세계에서 여섯 번째로 긴 강이다. 이 강은 가장 번영했던 몇몇 왕조가 강 위 또는 그 주변에서 자리잡았던, 중국의 태생지로 여겨진다. 하지만 대범람과 홍수로 인한 신 왕조의 멸망으로 이 강은 '중국의 슬픔'으로도 알려져 있다. 다른 주요 발원지처럼 황하는 지금도, 역사적으로도 농경, 수력 전기, 어업, 운송 및 다른 여러 목적을 위한 중대한 자원이었다. 요즘은 불행하게도 오염으로 인해 강의 약 1/3이 심지어 관개 및 공업 목적으로도 쓸 수 없게 되었다.

Q: 가장 적절한 제목은?
(a) 세계의 주요 수로가 당면한 문제
(b) 중국에 있어 황하의 중요성
(c) 중국과 황하 계곡의 문명
(d) 황하의 여러 가지 축복

해설

과거부터 오늘날까지 황하가 중국에 미친 영향과 최근의 상태에 대해 기술하고 있다. 따라서 (b)가 가장 적절하다.

cradle 요람 | **prosperous** 번영하는 | **hydroelectricity** 수력 전기 | **irrigation** 관개

19

Dear Mr. Roy Farley,

This is your third and last notice of the balance in arrears for your closed US Bank credit card ending in 4974. Payment in full is required of the $1,580.94 outstanding balance by the 21st of this month. Failure to remit the outstanding amount will result in US Bank turning over your account to a third party credit agency. Remember that every day a payment is late detrimentally affects your credit rating, so please do not delay in sending your late payment. Service specialists are available Monday through Friday from 8:00 a.m. to 8:00 p.m. Eastern Time to process over the phone payments or to answer any questions.

Sincerely,

Mark Murphy, Accounts Management

Q: What is the main purpose of the letter?
(a) To inform the client that late payments result in lower credit ratings
(b) To collect overdue money before selling off the credit account
(c) To notify the client of his credit card status and billing amount
(d) To threaten the client with a lower credit rating and closed account

번역

로이 팔리 씨께

이번이 4974로 마감된 귀하의 해지된 US 은행 신용 카드의 체납 잔금에 대한 세 번째이자 마지막 통지입니다. 이달 21일까지 미납된 1,580.94달러 전액을 지불하셔야 합니다. 미납액을 송금하지 않을 경우 US 은행은 귀하의 계정을 제3의 신용 기관에 넘길 것 입니다. 지불이 늦어지면 날마다 귀하의 신용 등급에 불리하게 작용하니 체납액 송금을 지체하지 마십시요. 동부 시간으로 월요일부터 금요일까지 오전 8시부터 오후 8시까지 서비스 담당 전문가와 통화해 전화 납부로 처리하거나 의문 사항에 대한 답변을 들을 수 있습니다.

계정 관리자, 마크 머피

Q: 편지의 주요 목적은?
(a) 고객에게 납부가 늦으면 신용 등급이 떨어진다는 것을 알리기 위해
(b) 신용 계정을 넘기기 전에 연체금을 수금하기 위해
(c) 고객에게 신용 카드 상황과 청구액을 통지하기 위해
(d) 신용 등급 하락과 계정 해지로 고객을 위협하기 위해

해설

(c)는 지문에 없는 내용이고 통지의 목적이 (d)와 같이 고객을 위협하기 위한 것은 아니다. 체납액을 내지 않으면 계정이 다른 신용 기관으로 넘어가고 신용 등급이 떨어질 것이라고 경고하는 것은 결국 연체된 금액을 수금하기 위해서이다. 따라서 정답은 (b)이다.

balance 잔금 | **in arrears** 연체되어 | **outstanding** 미결제의 | **remit** 송금하다 | **credit rating** 신용 등급 | **billing** 거래 총액

20

Globalization means more air travel and aviation experts follow this with a projected 32 percent increase in passenger levels from 2009 to 2014. This means the current number of 2.5 billion will be 3.3 billion people in the air yearly. Paradoxically, airline prices on average have fallen 60 percent, in real value, over the last 40 years. In addition, social and economic pressures call for increased spending to make air travel more environmental. Planes have become more efficient; in 1967 Boeing introduced its 737 which carried 100 passengers a distance of 2,775 kilometers. Today, a B737-800 can carry double the number of passengers using 23 percent less fuel. Still, airlines are struggling to meet or improve their bottom line.

Q: What is the main topic of the passage?
(a) How air travel has become more efficient and environmental
(b) The projected boom in air travel will increase social pressures.
(c) Two factors that continue to challenge the business of airlines
(d) Benefits of government subsidies and hand outs for the airlines

세계화는 항공 여행의 증가를 의미하고, 항공 전문가들은 2009년에서 2014년까지 승객 수준이 32% 증가할 것이라는 예상으로 세계화에 관심을 가지고 있다. 이것은 연간 비행기를 이용하는 승객 수가 현재 25억 명에서 33억 명으로 증가할 것을 의미한다. 역설적으로 평균 항공권 가격은 지난 40년 간 실제 가치로 60% 하락했다. 또한, 항공 여행이 좀 더 환경적으로 될 수 있도록 더 많은 비용을 쓰라고 요구하는 사회 및 경제적인 압력이 가해지고 있다. 항공기의 효율은 더 커졌다. 1967년 보잉이 선보인 737기는 100명의 승객을 태우고 2,775킬로미터를 날았다. 오늘날의 BT37-800은 연료를 23% 덜 쓰면서 두 배나 되는 승객을 태울 수 있다. 아직도 항공사들은 최저 손실을 맞추거나 개선하기 위해 몸부림치고 있다.

Q: 지문의 요지는?
(a) 항공 여행이 어떻게 더 효율적이고 환경적으로 되었는가
(b) 예상된 항공 여행의 인기는 사회적 압력을 높일 것이다.
(c) 항공 사업에 지속적으로 과제를 안겨주는 2가지 요인
(d) 항공사를 위한 정부 보조금과 지원금 혜택

지문에 항공 여행이 어떻게 환경적으로 되었는가에 대한 내용은 없으므로 (a)는 오답이다. (b)는 갑작스러운 항공 여행의 인기로 인해 사회적 압력이 증가한 것은 아니며, (d)는 지문에 없는 내용이다. 항공사들이 당면한 도전 과제는 환경적인 항공 여행을 위해 더 많은 비용을 쓰라는 사회 및 경제적인 압력과 최저 손실을 맞추거나 개선하는 일이다. 따라서 정답은 (c)이다.

aviation 항공 | **paradoxically** 역설적으로 | **bottom line** 손실

21

The Whitney Senior Center will be hosting a pancake and sausage breakfast this upcoming Saturday from 7:30 in the morning to 2:30 in the afternoon. Prepaid tickets can be found online at whitneysrctr.org or at the center's front desk. Tickets at the door are $2.00 more and are first come, first serve. Remember, a donation of nonperishable goods or used toys will reduce your ticket by $1.00 per customer. All proceeds go to the St. Agnes orphanage, so come enjoy a delicious and filling pancake and sausage breakfast this Saturday and let us do the dishes!

Q: What is the main purpose of the announcement?
(a) To gather donated foods or toys for the orphanage
(b) To offer a breakfast set up to support a charitable cause
(c) To raise more operational money for the Senior Center
(d) To suggest ways for the seniors to economize on their meal

다가오는 토요일 아침 7시 30분부터 오후 2시 30분까지 휘트니 노인 복지관에서 아침 식사로 팬케이크와 소시지를 제공합니다. 온라인

whitneysrctr.org나 센터의 안내 데스크에서 티켓을 미리 구입할 수 있습니다. 입구에서 구입하는 티켓은 2달러 이상이며 선착순입니다. 보존 식품이나 쓰던 장난감을 기증하시면 고객 1인당 1달러를 할인해 드린다는 것을 기억하십시오. 수익금은 전액 세인트 아그네스 고아원에 기부되니 이번 주 토요일에 오셔서 맛있고 푸짐한 팬케이크와 소시지를 즐기십시오. 설거지는 저희가 하겠습니다!

Q: 안내문의 주된 목적은?
(a) 고아원을 위해서 기증된 음식이나 장난감을 모으기 위해
(b) 자선운동을 지원하기 위해 마련된 조식 행사를 제안하기 위해
(c) 노인 복지관을 위한 운영 자금을 더 모금하기 위해
(d) 어르신들이 식사 비용을 절약할 수 있는 방법을 제안하기 위해

휘트니 노인 복지관에서 고아원에 수익금을 기부하기 위해 돈을 받고 조식을 제공하며, 보존 식품이나 쓰던 장난감을 기증하면 1인당 식사비를 1달러 감해 준다는 것을 알리는 내용이다. 따라서 정답은 (b)이다. (a)는 행사의 목적이 될 수 있다.

prepaid 선불의 | **nonperishable** 보존할 수 있는 | **proceeds** 수익금

22

If you've ever wondered why people fail to cooperate even for their own best interests, then you would find the prisoner's dilemma intriguing. Originally framed by Merrill Flood and Melvin Dresher in 1950, the prisoner's dilemma is a scenario in game theory that sheds light on cooperation. There are two suspects in separate rooms. They go free if they betray the other suspect who will then receive a ten-year sentence. If they both betray each other, they both get a five-year sentence. If they both stay silent, they both serve a six-month sentence. Ideally the two prisoners should cooperate and be silent but they cannot be sure the other will not betray them and hence the prisoner's dilemma.

Q: What is the best title for the passage?
(a) Cooperation Expressed in the Prisoner's Dilemma
(b) Betrayal and Cooperation Based in Game Theory
(c) Game Theory Applied to Law Enforcement
(d) The Prisoner's Dilemma in Decision Making

왜 사람들이 자신들에게 최선의 이익이 되는 일에 대해서도 협력하지 못하는지 궁금하다면 죄수의 딜레마가 아주 흥미롭다고 생각할 것이다. 원래 1950년 메릴 플러드와 멜빈 드레셔가 틀을 잡은 죄수의 딜레마는 협력을 설명하는 게임 이론의 시나리오이다. 2명의 용의자가 각각 다른 방에 있고, 상대방을 배신하면 풀려나지만, 그 상대방은 10년 형을 선고 받게 된다. 만일 둘 다 상대방을 배신하면 둘 다 5년 형을 받는다. 둘 다 말을 하지 않으면 둘 다 6개월 형을 선고 받는다. 이상적으로는 두 사람이 협력해서 침묵해야 하지만 그들은 상대방이 배신하지 않는다고 확신하지 못한다. 이것이 죄수의 딜레마이다.

Q: 가장 적절한 제목은?

(a) 죄수의 딜레마에서 나타난 협력

(b) 게임 이론을 기초로 한 배신과 협력

(c) 법 시행에 적용되는 게임 이론

(d) 의사 결정에서의 죄수의 딜레마

해설

죄수의 딜레마에 관한 글로, 다른 방에 있는 2명의 용의자가 어떤 결정을 내릴 때 최선의 결과를 얻을 수 있음에도 상대를 믿지 못하기 때문에 진퇴양난에 빠진다는 것이다. 따라서 정답은 (d)이다.

cooperate 협력하다 | **shed light on** ~을 해명하다 | **sentence** 선고 **betrayal** 배신

23

Agoraphobia is seen when an individual has a morbid fear of open spaces, crowds, or social conditions they have no control over. It typically results in panic attacks or a debilitating anxiety and is often triggered by being in places where previous attacks had occurred. This disorder appears in people in their early to mid-twenties and therefore is not generally thought of as having its roots in early childhood years. However, its exact cause is still unclear to experts and victims alike. Over two-thirds of sufferers are women with about 2.2 percent of Americans diagnosed with agoraphobia.

Q: Which of the following is correct according to the passage?

(a) Agoraphobia is an enigmatic social disorder.

(b) Most men have a predisposition for agoraphobia.

(c) Agoraphobia is an irrational fear of meeting friends.

(d) Sufferers of agoraphobia see symptoms from childhood.

번역

개방된 공간이나 군중 또는 자신이 통제할 수 없는 사회적 상황에 대해 병적인 두려움을 가진 개인은 광장 공포증이 있는 것으로 본다. 광장 공포증은 전형적으로 공황 발작이나 심신을 약하게 하는 불안을 일으키고 보통 이전에 발작이 일어났던 장소에 있게 되면 유발된다. 이러한 장애는 20대 초반에서 중반의 사람들에게서 나타나기 때문에 일반적으로 유년기 초기에 그 뿌리를 두고 있는 것으로 보지 않는다. 하지만 정확한 원인은 아직도 전문가와 피해자 모두 확신하지 못한다. 피해자의 2/3 이상이 여성이고 미국인 중 약 2.2%가 광장 공포증 진단을 받았다.

Q: 지문과 일치하는 것은?

(a) 광장 공포증은 불가사의한 사회적 장애이다.

(b) 대부분의 남성들은 광장 공포증에 걸리기 쉬운 소질이 있다.

(c) 광장 공포증은 친구를 만나는 것에 대한 비논리적인 두려움이다.

(d) 광장 공포증의 피해자들은 유년기부터 증상을 보인다.

해설

광장 공포증의 정확한 원인이 아직 전문가와 피해자에게 명확하게 알려지지 않았다 했으므로 정답은 (a)이다.

agoraphobia 광장 공포증 | **morbid** 병적인 | **panic attack** 공황 발작 **debilitating** 심신을 약화시키는 | **enigmatic** 불가사의한 **predisposition** 성향 | **irrational** 비논리적인

24

When you think about the world's best-selling toy, you probably assume it's an electronic gizmo that every child has or wants. Would it surprise you that the answer is a plastic cube? Invented in 1974 by a Hungarian sculptor and professor of architecture, Ernö Rubik, the Rubik's Cube had sold 350 million units worldwide by 2009. An ingenious three dimensional puzzle with six faces of varying colors consisting of nine smaller squares, this toy was launched by Ideal Toy Corp. in 1980 and walked away with the German Game of the Year award for Best Puzzle. Thirty years later it's still a hot seller. Competitions are still held for those who can solve it the fastest.

Q: Which of the following is correct about the Rubik's Cube?

(a) It came to market six years after its invention.

(b) It is made of six faces, six squares and six colors.

(c) It was invented by a doctorate of sculpture.

(d) It garnered several awards for Best Puzzle.

번역

세계에서 가장 잘 팔리는 장난감에 대해 생각해보면, 아마 모든 아이들이 가지고 있거나 원하는 전자 장치라고 생각할 것입니다. 답이 플라스틱 정육면체라면 놀랍지 않나요? 1974년 헝가리의 조각가이자 건축 교수인 에르노 루빅이 발명한 루빅스 큐브는 2009년까지 세계적으로 3억 5천만 개가 판매되었습니다. 9개의 작은 정사각형으로 구성되며 색상이 다른 6면이 있는 독창적인 3차원 퍼즐인 이 장난감은 1980년 아이디얼 토이 사가 처음 출시했고 독일의 올해 베스트 퍼즐상을 거뜬히 차지했습니다. 30년이 지나도, 이 장난감은 여전히 히트 상품입니다. 지금까지도 이 퍼즐을 가장 빨리 풀 수 있는 사람들을 위한 시합이 열리고 있습니다.

Q: 루빅스 큐브에 대해 옳은 것은?

(a) 발명 후 6년 뒤 상품으로 출시되었다.

(b) 6면, 6개의 사각형과 6가지 색상으로 이루어졌다.

(c) 조각 분야의 박사가 발명했다.

(d) 최고의 퍼즐로서 몇 개의 상을 수상했다.

해설

1974년에 발명되어 1980년에 출시되었으므로 정답은 (a)이다.

gizmo 기계 장치 | **ingenious** 독창적인 | **walk away with** ~을 수월하게 차지하다

25

Local actor Raphael Ramon is about to be swallowed up in this Friday's opening performance of *A Little Shop of Horrors* at Yu's Performing Arts Theater. Ramon, who depicted Laertes in *Hamlet* at the Barrymore Theater last year, plays geeky flower shop worker Seymour in an Asian take on this quirky cult musical by Howard Ashman and Alan Menken. The carnivorously-insatiable, man-eating plant Audrey is to be played by Cynthia Bechtold under the acclaimed director Marilyn Podawiltz. The show is the second this year for the theater with an ambitious schedule of eight productions in all. It also continues the theater's zany remaking of classic plays and musicals with an Asian spin.

Q: Which of the following is correct about *A Little Shop of Horrors*?
(a) Friday night is its encore performance.
(b) The leading man played Hamlet last year.
(c) The director is well respected nationwide.
(d) The plant is portrayed by Marilyn Podawiltz.

번역

지방 배우인 라파엘 라몬은 유스 공연 예술 극장에서 이번 주 금요일에 개막 공연하는 〈리틀 숍 오브 호러〉에서 자신이 가진 것을 모두 보여줄 예정입니다. 하워드 애쉬먼과 알란 멘켄이 만든 이 예측 불가능한 컬트 뮤지컬에서는 작년에 배리모어 극장에서 공연된 〈햄릿〉의 라에르테스를 연기한 라몬이 아시아 테이크 방식으로 엽기적인 행동을 하는 꽃가게 직원인 세이머 역을 연기합니다. 호평을 받고 있는 마릴린 포다윌츠의 감독 하에, 신시아 베치톨드가 육식 동물 같이 만족할 줄 모르는 식인 식물인 오드리 역을 연기합니다. 이 쇼는 모두 8개의 작품을 야심차게 계획하고 있는 이 극장에서 금년에 두 번째 작품입니다. 극장 측이 리메이크한 아시아 성향의 많은 고전 연극 및 뮤지컬이 계속 공연될 것 입니다.

Q: 〈리틀 숍 오브 호러〉에 대해 옳은 것은?
(a) 금요일 밤은 앙코르 공연이다.
(b) 주연 남자 배우가 작년에 햄릿 역을 맡았다.
(c) 감독은 전국적으로 높은 평가를 받고 있다.
(d) 마릴린 포다윌츠가 식물 연기를 한다.

해설

라몬을 소개하는 것으로 보아 금요일 밤에 개막 공연되는 〈리틀 숍 오브 호러〉에서 라몬은 주연 배우임을 짐작할 수 있다. 그는 작년에 〈햄릿〉에서 라에르테스를 연기했고, 마릴린 포다윌츠는 호평을 받고 있는 감독이다. 따라서 (c)가 정답이다.

swallow up 모든 것을 다 쓰다 | **geeky** 엽기적인 행동을 하는 | **take** 테이크 (영화에서 카메라를 중단시키지 않고 한번에 찍는 장면) | **quirky** 예측이 불가능한 | **carnivorously** 육식 동물 같이 | **insatiable** 만족할 줄 모르는 | **acclaimed** 호평을 받는 | **spin** 성향

26

Where else but in the frozen lands of Norway would you find the odd coupling of cross country skiing and rifle marksmanship? In 1861, the Trysil Rifle and Ski Club was formed to promote national defense even as the military had already been using skiing and marksmanship as regular exercise for its soldiers. Best known as the Winter Olympic Sport of biathlon, athletes test their endurance, stamina and shooting prowess on a 20 kilometer track. Competitors shoot four times at each shooting lane in the order of prone, standing, prone, and standing. Penalties of usually one minute are added to the biathletes final times for any missed target.

Q: What is true according to the passage?
(a) The Norwegian army utilizes skiing purely as sport.
(b) The biathlon started as a common military exercise.
(c) The modern Winter Olympics created the sport of biathlon.
(d) Biathletes must hone shooting accuracy more than skiing skills.

번역

노르웨이의 동토 말고 달리 어디에서 크로스컨트리 스키 타기와 소총 사격술의 기묘한 조합을 찾으시겠습니까? 군대에서는 이미 스키 타기와 소총 사격술을 군인들의 정규 훈련으로 이용하고 있었지만 국방을 장려하기 위해 1861년 트리실 라이플총과 스키 클럽이 결성되었습니다. 동계 올림픽 경기의 바이애슬론으로 가장 잘 알려졌으며, 선수들은 20km 트랙에서 자신들의 지구력, 체력, 사격 솜씨를 시험합니다. 선수들은 복사(엎드려 쏘기), 입사(서서 쏘기), 복사, 입사 순으로 각각의 사격 레인에서 4번 사격합니다. 맞추지 못한 표적에 대해서는 바이애슬론 선수의 전체 주행 시간에 보통 1분의 벌점이 추가됩니다.

Q: 지문과 일치하는 것은?
(a) 노르웨이 육군은 스키 타기를 순전히 스포츠로 이용했다.
(b) 바이애슬론은 일상적인 군대 훈련으로 시작되었다.
(c) 현대 동계 올림픽 경기로 바이애슬론이라는 스포츠가 생겼다.
(d) 바이애슬론 선수들은 반드시 스키타는 기술보다는 정확한 사격술을 연마해야 한다.

해설

노르웨이 군대에서는 스키 타기와 소총 사격술을 군인들의 정규 훈련 연습으로 이미 이용했고, 이것이 바이애슬론이라는 동계 올림픽 경기 종목이 되었으며, 시합에서는 스키타는 기술과 정확한 사격술 모두 중요하다. 따라서 정답은 (b)이다.

odd 기묘한 | **marksmanship** 사격술 | **endurance** 지구력 | **stamina** 체력 | **prowess** 솜씨 | **penalty** 벌점 | **hone** 연마하다

27

As the use of paper increased in the 19th century, so did the demand for a paper fastener. Interestingly enough, the first stapler was a hand-crafted tool made in France for King Louis XV. Unlike today's stapler, each of king's staplers was inscribed with the royal insignia. Like many inventions, there were many contributors to the invention of the stapler. Three patents were filed in the 1860's in America and Britain for contraptions that were the precursors to today's staplers. However, Henry R. Heyl in 1877 filed a patent for the first machine that both inserted and clinched staples in one step, and thus is recognized today as the inventor of the modern stapler.

Q: Which of the following is correct about the modern stapler?
(a) It owes its existence to three famous British inventors.
(b) It has historical roots in the medieval royal courts of Europe.
(c) It has an unclear lineage up to the modern inventors of the 1860's.
(d) It saw an increase in demand in conjunction with paper's usage.

번역

19세기에 종이의 사용이 증가하면서, 서류철 끼우개에 대한 수요도 증가했다. 흥미롭게도, 최초의 스테이플러는 프랑스에서 루이 15세를 위해 손으로 제작된 도구였다. 오늘날의 스테이플러와 달리, 왕의 각 스테이플러에는 왕실의 휘장이 새겨졌다. 많은 발명품과 마찬가지로 스테이플러의 발명에 많은 사람들이 기여했다. 1860년대 미국과 영국에서 오늘날 스테이플러의 선도자 격인 기계 장치에 대해 세 건의 특허가 신청되었다. 하지만 1877년 헨리 헤일은 최초로 한번에 스테이플을 꽂아 고정시킨 기계에 대해 특허를 신청했고, 이로써 오늘날 현대 스테이플러의 발명가로 인정 받고 있다.

Q: 현대 스테이플러에 대해 옳은 것은?
(a) 3명의 유명한 영국 발명가가 발명했다.
(b) 역사적인 뿌리를 중세 유럽 왕실에 두고 있다.
(c) 1860년대의 근대 발명가에 이르기까지 계통이 불분명하다.
(d) 종이의 사용과 함께 수요가 증가했다.

해설

첫 문장 '19세기에 종이 사용이 증가하면서 서류 죔쇠에 대한 수요도 증가했다'는 내용에 미루어 스테이플러에 대한 수요 역시 증가한 것을 알 수 있으므로 (d)가 정답이다.

paper fastener 서류철 끼우개 | **inscribe** 새기다 | **insignia** 휘장 **contributor** 기여자 | **patent** 특허 | **file** 신청하다 | **contraption** 기계 장치 | **precursor** 선도자 | **clinch** 고정시키다 | **lineage** 계통 **in conjunction with** ~와 함께

28

Parliament's investigation into the demise of a major London brokerage house has come up against some exceptional challenges that may result in few or no criminal charges being filed against the ex-CEO, chairman and members of the board. Investigators have found glaring errors in their accusation that the former executives of the firm hid billions of euros of liabilities in its balance sheets, which made the bank appear that much more solvent. People affected by the firm's collapse are still planning further civil and criminal suits to recuperate their losses which amount to billions of euros and, for many, their entire retirement pensions.

Q: Which of the following is correct about the brokerage firm?
(a) It is experiencing difficult hurdles in their investigation.
(b) It had recently undergone a change in management.
(c) It is currently under investigation for price manipulation.
(d) People are upset with its solvency and low pension plans.

번역

런던의 한 주요 중개 회사의 폐업에 대한 의회의 조사로 전직 최고 경영자, 회장 및 이사들을 상대로 제기된 형사 처벌이 거의 없거나 전혀 없을 수 있는 결과를 낳을지도 모르는 이례적인 문제에 부딪혔다. 수사관들은 고소장에서 회사의 전직 경영진이 대차 대조표에서 수십억 유로의 부채를 숨긴 명백한 오류를 발견했고, 이로 인해 은행의 지불 능력이 훨씬 큰 것으로 보였다. 회사의 붕괴로 수십억 유로에 달하는 피해를 본 사람들과 대부분의 경우 퇴직 연금 전액을 되찾기 위한 사람들이 추가 민사 및 형사 소송을 여전히 계획하고 있다.

Q: 중개 회사에 대해 옳은 것은?
(a) 조사 과정에서 어려운 장애를 경험하고 있다.
(b) 최근 경영진이 교체되었다.
(c) 현재 가격 조작에 대해서 조사를 받고 있다.
(d) 사람들은 중개 회사의 지불 능력과 낮은 연금 제도에 화가 났다.

해설

조사 자체가 어려움을 겪고 있다는 언급은 없으며, 대차 대조표를 허위로 작성한 경영진에 대해 의회의 조사가 이루어지고 있으므로 (a)와 (c)는 정답에서 제외된다. 연금을 받을 수 있을지 없을지에 대한 소송은 있지만 낮은 연금에 대한 언급은 없으므로 (d)도 정답에서 제외된다. 전직 최고 경영자, 회장, 이사들을 상대로 형사 처벌 혐의가 제기된 것으로 보아 회사의 경영진이 교체되었음을 알 수 있다. 따라서 정답은 (b)이다.

demise 종말 | **brokerage house** 중개 회사 | **criminal** 형사의 **glaring** 명백한 | **accusation** 고소장 | **executive** 경영진 | **liability**

29

There are some competing explanations behind the namesake "teddy bear." The true story by consensus is that it originates with President Theodore Roosevelt who was an avid outdoorsman and hunter. After three days on an unsuccessful bear hunting excursion, his aides tracked down an old bear and tied it to a tree for the president to shoot. Roosevelt refused to be so unsportsmanlike and a political cartoonist captured the story in a cartoon. Later, a novelty store owner put two stuffed bears on display and asked the president for permission to call them "Teddy's Bears". The touching story and catchy name stuck and a new category of children's toy was born.

Q: Which of the following is correct about the teddy bear?

(a) It is named after President Franklin Roosevelt.

(b) There are variations to the story of its origins.

(c) It was the original name of two stuffed toys.

(d) There are several derivations for the name.

번역

이름이 같은 '테디 베어' 뒤에는 대립되는 설명들이 있다. 많은 사람들이 동의하는 이야기는 이것이 야외 생활을 좋아하는 열렬한 사냥꾼인 시어도어 루스벨트 대통령과 함께 유래한다는 것이다. 곰 사냥 여행에서 실패한 후 삼 일 뒤 그의 보좌관들은 늙은 곰 한 마리를 찾아내어 대통령이 사격할 수 있도록 곰을 나무에 묶었다. 루스벨트는 그렇게 공정하지 않은 일은 거절했고, 정치 만화가가 그 이야기를 만화에 담아냈다. 후에, 한 장난감 상점 주인이 박제 곰 두 마리를 전시했고, 대통령에게 그것을 '테디의 곰'이라고 부르기를 허락해 달라고 요청했다. 이 감동적인 이야기와 기억하기 쉬운 이름이 사라지지 않고 있다가 새로운 어린이 장난감 종류가 생겼다.

Q: 곰 인형에 대해 옳은 것은?

(a) 프랭클린 루스벨트 대통령의 이름을 따서 명명되었다.

(b) 그 유래에 대해 다양한 이야기가 있다.

(c) 두 개의 봉제 완구의 원래 이름이었다.

(d) 이름에 대한 몇 개의 파생어가 있다.

해설

첫 문장에서 '테디의 곰'라는 이름의 배경에 대한 설명이 몇 개 있다고 하므로, 테디 베어의 근원에 대한 여러 변형된 이야기가 있음을 알 수 있다. 따라서 정답은 (b)이다.

competing 대립하는 | **namesake** 이름이 같은 사람[것] | **consensus** 합의 | **outdoorsman** 야외 생활을 좋아하는 사람 | **aide** 보좌관 | **track down** ~을 찾아내다 | **unsportsmanlike** 불공정한 | **capture** 담아내다 | **novelty** 자그마한 싸구려 장난감 | **derivation** 파생어

30

Many experts in the industry believe we are not too far from that moment when computers surpass humans in intelligence. Watson, the new IBM supercomputer, showed how a super computer can beat the world's best contestants on the hit show "Jeopardy." What is even more impressive is the fact that this proves how computers are now capable of learning "natural language," the process of disassembling and parsing an input of words and sentences. This is considerably more complicated than the opposite process of assembling output because input can often contain unexpected and unknown features. This is the cutting edge of artificial intelligence to date.

Q: Which of the following is correct about today's level of computer intelligence?

(a) It has attained its theoretical maximum potential.

(b) It has resulted in computers smarter than humans.

(c) It may exceed human intelligence in the near future.

(d) It can be useful for news gathering and reporting.

번역

산업계의 많은 전문가들은 컴퓨터가 인간의 지능을 능가하는 시기가 그리 멀지 않았다고 믿는다. 새로운 IBM 슈퍼 컴퓨터인 왓슨은 인기 쇼인 '제퍼디'에서 슈퍼 컴퓨터가 세계 최고의 경쟁 상대들을 어떻게 이길 수 있는지 보여 주었다. 더욱 인상적인 것은 이로써 오늘날 컴퓨터가 입력된 단어와 문장을 분해해서 분석하는 과정인 '자연 언어' 학습 능력이 있는가를 증명한다는 사실이다. 이 학습은 출력을 조합하는 그 반대 과정보다 상당히 복잡한데, 입력에는 흔히 예상치 않고 알려지지 않은 특징이 포함될 수 있기 때문이다. 이것이 현재까지의 최첨단 인공 지능이다.

Q: 오늘날 컴퓨터 인공 지능 수준에 대해 옳은 것은?

(a) 이론적으로 가능한 최고의 잠재 수준에 도달했다.

(b) 인간보다 더 영리한 컴퓨터가 나오게 했다.

(c) 가까운 미래에 인간 지능을 초월할 수도 있다.

(d) 기사 수집과 보도에 유용할 수 있다.

해설

오늘날 컴퓨터가 복잡한 자연 언어 학습 능력이 있음을 증명했다는 내용으로, 첫 문장에서 많은 전문가들이 컴퓨터가 인간의 지능을 능가하는 시기가 그리 멀지 않았다고 믿고 있는 것으로 보아 정답은 (c)이다. 슈퍼 컴퓨터가 세계 최고의 선수들을 이겼다고 해서 전반적인 분야에서 인간보다 더 영리하다고 할 수는 없으므로 (b)는 정답이 아니다.

surpass 능가하다 | **contestant** 경쟁 상대 | **disassemble** 분해하다 | **parse** 분석하다 | **cutting edge** 최첨단 | **artificial** 인공의

31

The lighter side of this dismal economy was

witnessed at today's speech given by former Chase Bank CEO and current Banking Minister Franklin Torres. Comedy relief was had when he tried to explain how the economy was getting better thanks to his department's bailout interventions and interest rate cuts. When reporters complained about increasing prices for staples such as food and gas, the minister responded by saying, "you can buy a smart phone with double the power for the same price today as two years ago. Let's keep everything in perspective." Loud outbreaks of laughter and murmuring resonated the auditorium and prompted one reporter to ask rhetorically, "you can't eat a smart phone, can you?"

Q: Which of the following is correct about the minister's speech?

(a) It was given at an economic forum by the Bank Minister.

(b) The speaker's comment resulted in unexpected anger and hostility.

(c) The speaker was convincing the crowd about economic changes.

(d) Its intent was to reassure the public about an ailing economy.

번역

전직 체이스 은행의 최고 경영자이자 현직 금융부 장관인 프랭클린 토레스가 오늘 한 연설에서 침울한 경제의 밝은 면이 보였습니다. 그가 금융부의 긴급 구제 개입과 금리 인하 덕에 경제가 어떻게 좋아지고 있었는가 설명할 때는 코미디 릴리프를 가질 수 있었습니다. 기자들이 식품과 가스와 같은 중요 상품의 가격 인상에 대해 불만을 제기했을 때, 장관은 '지금은 2년 전보다 성능이 두 배인 스마트폰을 같은 가격에 살 수 있습니다. 모든 것을 균형 있게 바라봅시다.' 라는 말로 응수했습니다. 폭소와 중얼거림이 강당에 퍼졌고, 어떤 기자는 수사적으로 묻지 않을 수 없었습니다. '스마트폰을 먹을 수는 없잖아요?'

Q: 장관의 연설에 대해 옳은 것은?

(a) 금융부 장관이 주최한 경제 토론회에서 연설했다.

(b) 연사의 논평이 예상치 못한 분노와 적개심을 초래했다.

(c) 연사는 경제 변화에 대해 군중을 납득시키고 있었다.

(d) 연설의 의도는 병든 경제에 대해 대중을 안심시키기 위한 것이었다.

해설

금융부 장관의 연설에 대한 보도 내용이다. 가격 인상에 대한 불만에 장관의 응수가 의도와 달리 사람들은 납득하기 어려운 코미디 처럼 들렸기 때문에 폭소와 중얼거림이 퍼졌고, 어떤 기자는 재치있게 응수했다는 내용이다. 따라서 정답은 (d)이다.

dismal 우울한 | comedy relief 코미디 릴리프 (코미디가 가져오는 긴장 완화 효과) | bailout 긴급 구제 | intervention 개입 | interest rate 금리 | staple 중요 상품 | perspective 균형감 | outbreak 발생 murmur 소곤거리다 | resonate 울려 퍼지다 | prompt 자극하다 rhetorically 수사적인

32

Animal behavior researcher Josh Klein has invented a way to make money with trained crows. Klein argues that crows are some of the smartest animals, even exceeding chimpanzees and dolphins. He points out that they often use ingenious methods for getting food. For instance, crows will wait for a traffic signal to change to drop acorns or other nuts onto the street. After the nuts are run over by vehicles, they will again wait for the lights to change to retrieve their reward. Klein has cleverly designed boxes that dispense peanuts when a crow drops a coin into a slot. He hopes to gather some of the estimated $250 million in loose change lying around New York City.

Q: Which of the following is correct according to the passage?

(a) Klein has made millions with his peanut dispenser.

(b) Crows are much easier to train than chimps or dolphins.

(c) Klein has his crows collecting coins to obtain peanuts.

(d) Crows prefer eating peanuts to acorns or other nuts.

번역

동물 행동 연구가 조쉬 클라인은 훈련 받은 까마귀로 돈을 버는 방법을 고안했다. 클라인은 까마귀는 가장 영리한 동물 중 하나로 침팬지나 돌고래도 능가한다고 주장한다. 그는 까마귀가 종종 먹이를 구하기 위해 영리한 방법을 사용한다는 점을 지적한다. 예를 들어, 까마귀는 도토리 또는 여타 견과류를 도로에 떨어뜨리려고 신호등이 바뀌기를 기다린다. 차가 도토리를 밟고 지나간 뒤 까마귀는 그 보상물을 다시 가져오기 위해 다시 신호등이 바뀌기를 기다린다. 클라인은 영리하게도 까마귀가 구멍 안으로 동전을 떨어뜨리면 땅콩을 내주는 상자를 설계했다. 그는 뉴욕 여기저기 땅에 떨어진 동전으로 약 2억 5천만 달러로 추산되는 금액을 모을 것으로 기대하고 있다.

Q: 지문과 일치하는 것은?

(a) 클라인은 땅콩 디스펜서로 수백만 달러를 벌었다.

(b) 까마귀는 침팬지나 돌고래보다 훈련시키기가 훨씬 쉽다.

(c) 클라인은 까마귀들이 땅콩을 얻기 위해 동전을 모으게 한다.

(d) 까마귀는 도토리 또는 여타 견과류보다 땅콩 먹기를 좋아한다.

해설

지문에 의하면 클라인은 훈련된 까마귀가 동전을 가져오면 땅콩을 내어주는 상자로 약 2억 5천만 달러를 벌 것을 기대하고 있으므로 (a)는 정답이 아니며, 까마귀는 침팬지나 돌고래보다 영리할 수 있지만 훈련시키기 훨씬 용이하다는 내용은 없으므로 (b)도 정답에서 제외된다. 따라서 정답은 (c)이다.

ingenious 기발한 | acorn 도토리 | retrieve 되찾다 | reward 보상 dispense 내주다 | loose change 동전

33

A longbow is ideally made from yew, although white woods such as elm, ash and hazel were often used because of their availability. It can be as tall as a man and be deadly at over 300 yards. A skilled archer could release twelve rounds in a minute whereas a crossbow can only shoot three. Many armies won battles due to their relentless showers of longbow arrows. Imagine incessant volleys of thousands of arrows descending upon your forces twelve times a minute. Today, archery survives as a sport, for hunting, and still in some cultures as a main weapon of defense.

Q: What can be inferred from the passage?
(a) Archers were not highly respected in the past.
(b) Bows has always been common as a sport.
(c) White woods have similar characteristics as yews.
(d) Militaries treated archers as only supplemental forces.

번역

큰 활은 그 유용함 때문에 보통 느릅나무, 서양물푸레나무, 개암나무와 같은 하얀 목재로 만들어졌지만 원칙적으로 주목으로 만든다. 큰 활은 성인 남성 키만할 수 있고, 300야드 이상 거리에서 생명을 빼앗을 수 있다. 숙련된 궁수는 1분에 12라운드를 쏠 수 있는 반면 석궁으로는 단지 3라운드를 쏠 수 있다. 많은 군대가 큰 활로 무자비하게 화살을 소나기처럼 퍼부어 전투에서 승리했다. 당신의 병력 위로 1분에 12번 수천 개의 화살이 쉴새 없이 일제히 날아 오는 사격을 상상해 보라. 오늘날 양궁은 스포츠로, 사냥으로, 아직도 몇몇 문화에서는 방어를 위한 주요 무기로 남아있다.

Q: 지문에서 유추할 수 있는 것은?
(a) 과거에 궁수들은 존경을 많이 받지 못했다.
(b) 활은 항상 스포츠로 일상적인 것이었다.
(c) 하얀 목재는 주목과 유사한 특징을 가지고 있다.
(d) 군대에서는 궁수들을 보충 병력으로만 취급했다.

해설

원칙적으로 주목을 사용하지만 흰색의 목재를 사용해서 큰 활을 만들었다는 내용으로 미루어 두 목재의 특성이 유사하다는 것을 알 수 있다. 따라서 정답은 (c)이다.

longbow 큰 활 | **yew** 주목 | **elm** 느릅나무 | **ash** 물푸레나무 | **hazel** 개암나무 | **availability** 유용성 | **crossbow** 석궁 | **incessant** 끊임없는 **volley** 일제 사격 | **force** 병력

34

It was my first ice fishing excursion on a lake in the bone-chilling cold of a Minnesota winter. Jake stopped his truck and walked up to my window to tell me to follow him on the lake at least thirty feet behind his vehicle to prevent cracks due to sonic alignment. And my fears were not quelled when he said I had to keep my windows open in case I broke through the ice. Nevertheless, when we got to the fishing shack, I was pleasantly surprised. There were two beds, chairs, a propane wall-mounted heater, diesel generator and even a satellite dish. It was certainly far from the preconceived "roughing it" experience I had imagined.

Q: What can be inferred from the passage?
(a) The writer's fears of hardship did not come true.
(b) Ice fishing can often be fatal for its participants.
(c) Ice fishing is a very popular activity in Minnesota.
(d) The writer and companion were new to ice fishing.

번역

그것은 뼛속까지 스며드는 미네소타의 겨울 추위에 호수 위에서 나의 첫 얼음 낚시 여행이었다. 제이크는 트럭을 세우고 나의 차창가로 걸어와 음의 정렬로 인해 균열이 생기는 것을 방지하기 위해 최소한 자기 차의 30피트 뒤에서 따라오라고 말했다. 내가 얼음이 깨져서 빠지는 경우에 대비해 차창을 계속 열어 두어야 한다고 했을 때 나의 두려움은 가라앉지 않았다. 그럼에도 불구하고 우리가 낚시꾼이 머무는 오두막집에 도착했을 때 나는 즐거운 놀람을 맛보았다. 그곳에는 침대 2개, 의자와 벽에 설치된 프로판 히터, 디젤 발전기에 위성 방송 수신 안테나까지 있었다. 그것은 확실히 내가 상상했던 미리 예상한 '잠깐 동안의 불편한 생활' 경험이 결코 아니었다.

Q: 지문에서 유추할 수 있는 것은?
(a) 고생에 대한 글쓴이의 두려움은 실현되지 않았다.
(b) 얼음 낚시는 종종 낚시꾼에게 치명적일 수 있다.
(c) 미네소타에서 얼음 낚시는 매우 인기 있는 활동이다.
(d) 글쓴이와 친구는 얼음 낚시를 처음 하러 갔다.

해설

글쓴이는 낚시를 하면서 불편한 생활에 대해 우려하고 걱정했지만 현실은 결코 그렇지 않았다는 내용이다. (b)와 (c)는 지문에 없는 내용이며 지문 내용으로 보아 글쓴이의 친구는 얼음 낚시 경험이 많은 사람이라는 것을 알 수 있으므로 정답은 (a)이다.

crack 금, 틈 | **alignment** 정렬 | **quell** 가라앉히다 | **shack** 오두막집 **generator** 발전기 | **satellite dish** 위성 방송 수신 안테나 **preconceive** 미리 생각하다 | **rough it** 잠깐 동안 불편한 생활을 하다

35

Despite Brazil's stellar involvement in the global economy, its labor laws are hampering it from reaching its full potential. Imagine the case of a businessman and his partners who purchased a chain of pharmacies. Upon possession of ownership, the employees sued the businessman for back wages amounting to about half a million dollars. Without proper records, the businessman lost the suit and subsequently his ownership. Brazil's archaic labor laws are set out in 900 articles and were derived from the corporatist labor code of Mussolini's Italian era. Even when owners and employees mutually agree on a change, it is virtually impossible to go through with it because of the rigidity of these cumbersome labor laws.

Q: What can be inferred from the passage?
(a) Brazil's labor laws are a model for emerging countries.
(b) Mussolini's Italy respected owner's rights over laborer's rights.
(c) Brazil's economy could do better with labor law reform.
(d) Owners in Brazil have strong rights thanks to Mussolini.

번역

세계 경제에 대한 브라질의 적극적인 관여에도 불구하고 브라질은 자국의 노동법 때문에 잠재력을 최대한 발휘하지 못하고 있습니다. 약국 체인점을 매수한 사업가와 그의 동업자를 생각해 봅시다. 그가 소유권을 보유한 후 종업원들은 약 50만 달러에 달하는 밀린 임금에 대해 사업가를 상대로 소송을 제기했습니다. 제대로 된 기록이 없었기 때문에 사업가는 패소했고 그 뒤에 소유권을 잃었습니다. 브라질의 고대 노동법은 900개의 조항으로 규정되어 있고 이태리 무솔리니 시대의 협동조합주의자 노동법에서 유래했습니다. 소유주와 종업원들이 법 수정에 상호 합의를 해도 다루기 힘든 노동법의 경직성 때문에 성사되기 실질적으로 불가능합니다.

Q: 지문에서 유추할 수 있는 것은?
(a) 브라질의 노동법은 신흥국을 위한 모델이다.
(b) 이태리의 무솔리니는 노동자의 권리보다 소유주의 권리를 존중했다.
(c) 노동법을 개정하면 브라질 경제는 더 좋아질 수 있다.
(d) 브라질에서 소유주는 무솔리니 덕분에 강력한 권리를 가지고 있다.

해설

약국 체인점을 매수한 사업가가 종업원들이 자신을 상대로 제기한 소송에서 패소해 소유권을 잃은 것을 예로 들면서 노동자에게 유리한 노동법 때문에 브라질이 잠재력을 충분히 발휘하지 못하고 있다는 내용이다. 따라서 정답은 (c)이다. (a), (b), (d)는 지문과 반대되는 내용이다.

stellar 뛰어난 | **involvement** 관여 | **hamper** 방해하다 | **back** 밀린 **sue** 소송을 제기하다 | **corporatist** 협동조합주의자 | **go through with** ~을 거치다 | **rigidity** 경직성 | **cumbersome** 다루기 힘든

36

It was all colorful balloons and fireworks at the groundbreaking ceremony of the new Caterpillar facility at Greenhill. Mayor Thomas Wadden dug the first hole with Jim Hanson, CEO of Northern Contractors. The new building will be a state-of-the-art green energy facility and the builders are vying for a LEED platinum certificate for green construction. Innovations such as wind mills, solar panels and rainwater-catching basins will guarantee that this building leaves a nominal carbon footprint. Locals are happy to see the return of the tractor giant after last year's F5 tornado demolished the old complex. Furthermore, the re-employment of over a hundred of the townspeople was the jolt this sleepy town's economy desperately needed.

Q: What can be inferred from the passage?
(a) Caterpillar is a major employer in the community.
(b) LEED is a consumer rights certification organization.
(c) The new facility will only consume green energy.
(d) Hundreds of townspeople will become unemployed.

번역

그린힐에서 있었던 캐터필러 사의 신축 기공식은 형형색색의 풍선과 불꽃놀이였다. 토마스 바덴 시장은 노던 컨트랙터스 사의 최고 경영자인 짐 핸슨과 함께 첫 번째 구멍을 굴착했다. 신축 건물은 최신의 친환경 에너지 시설이 될 것이고, 건축업자들은 친환경 건축에 대해 친환경 건물 인증을 받기 위해 경쟁하고 있다. 풍차, 태양 전지판, 빗물 집수조와 같은 혁신적인 시설들은 이 건물이 아주 적은 탄소배출량을 남기는 것을 보장할 것이다. 주민들은 작년에 5등급의 토네이도가 예전 단지를 무너뜨린 후, 트랙터 업계의 거인이 돌아온 것을 반가워한다. 더욱이 백 명이 넘는 도시인을 다시 고용한 것은 이 생기 없는 도시의 경제가 몹시 필요로 했던 충격이었다.

Q: 지문에서 유추할 수 있는 것은?
(a) 캐터필러 사는 지역 사회에서 중요한 고용주이다.
(b) LEED는 소비자 권리 인증기관이다.
(c) 신축 시설은 친환경 에너지만을 소비할 것이다.
(d) 수백 명의 도시인들이 해고될 것이다.

해설

그린힐에 있는 캐터필러 사의 신축 기공식을 보도하는 기사로, 도시가 토네이도의 피해를 입은 뒤 대형 트랙터 업체인 캐터필러 사가 다시 돌아와서 백 명이 넘는 도시인들을 고용할 것이라는 내용이다. 따라서 정답은 (a)이다.

groundbreaking ceremony 기공식 | **dig** 굴착하다 | **green energy** 친환경 에너지 | **LEED platinum certificate** 친환경 건물 인증 | **wind mill** 풍차 | **rainwater-catching basin** 빗물 집수조 **nominal** 아주 적은 | **carbon footprint** 탄소 배출량

37

Science fiction is becoming science fact as technology continues its exponential pace of growth. Humankind has been tinkering with machines and finding better ways to exploit them ever since the first caveman picked up a tool. However, revolutionary new work has opened the way for microchip implants in humans. Back in 1998, British scientist Kevin Warwick performed the first sub-dermal transponder implant by inserting a microchip in his hand. The microchip enabled him to open doors and turn on lights in his building. Other proposed uses for such implants are for verifying personal identification as well as providing medical information such as existing conditions, allergies, and medications being taken. This information would be useful to paramedics.

Q: What can be inferred from the passage?
(a) Microchip implants will save many lives in the future.
(b) Technology allows us to mimic science fiction movies.
(c) Kevin Warwick's test received tremendous praise.
(d) Human-machine interface has become a reality.

기술이 급속한 성장을 계속하면서 공상 과학 영화가 과학적 사실이 되고 있다. 최초의 원시인이 도구를 집어 든 이후 인류는 기계를 만지작거려서 더 나은 이용 방법을 찾아내고 있다. 하지만 혁신적인 새로운 작업을 통해 인체에 마이크로칩을 심을 수 있도록 길을 열어 주었다. 과거 1998년 영국의 과학자 케빈 워윅은 마이크로칩을 자신의 손에 삽입해 최초의 피하 무선응답기 이식을 시술했다. 그는 마이크로칩으로 자신의 건물 내에서 문을 열고 전등을 켤 수 있었다. 그러한 이식에 대해서 제안되고 있는 다른 용도로는 기존의 몸 상태, 알레르기 및 복용하는 약과 같은 의학 정보의 제공은 물론 개인의 신원 확인이 있다. 이 정보는 준의료 활동 종사자에게 유용할 것이다.

Q: 지문에서 유추할 수 있는 것은?
(a) 마이크로칩 이식으로 미래에 많은 생명을 구할 것이다.
(b) 기술을 이용해 공상 과학 영화를 흉내 낼 수 있게 되었다.
(c) 케빈 워윅의 실험은 엄청난 찬사를 받았다.
(d) 인간과 기계 간 인터페이스가 현실이 되었다.

기술 발전으로 마이크로칩을 이용한 인체 내의 무선응답기 이식으로 건물 시설의 편리한 조작이 가능해졌고, 인체에 이식된 마이크로칩을 의학 정보의 제공과 개인의 신원 확인에 이용하자는 제안이 있다. 이것은 인간과 기계 간의 상호 작용이 가능해진다는 것을 의미하므로 정답은 (d)이다.

exponential 급속한 | **tinker** 어설프게 만지작거리다 | **caveman** 원시인 | **open the way for** ～에게 길을 열어 주다 | **implant** 이식 | **subdermal** 피하의 | **transponder** 무선응답기 | **identification** 신원 확인 | **paramedic** 의료 보조자 | **tremendous** 엄청난

38

You want those fifteen minutes of fame to last a little longer? (a) Well, the first thing to do is get your foot in the door by taking a lot of risks on a reality show. (b) TV companies are always looking for people to do outlandish and wacky things on television. **(c) This type of entertainment has long been the bread and butter of the major networks.** (d) Once you're on a reality show, like the one where you have to live with a group of strangers, don't make friends but instead play the black sheep of the cast and you'll be guaranteed more interview talk time.

15분간의 명성이 좀 더 지속되길 바라십니까? (a) 그렇다면 먼저 상당한 위험을 무릅쓰고 리얼리티 쇼에 발을 들여 놓으십시오. (b) 방송사들은 TV에 나와 이상하고 엉뚱한 짓을 해줄 사람을 항상 찾고 있습니다. **(c) 이러한 종류의 오락은 오랫동안 주요 방송사의 재정 수단이 되고 있습니다.** (d) 일단 리얼리티 쇼에 나가면 여러 낯선 사람들과 함께 살아야 하는 장소에서처럼 친구를 만들지 말고, 그 대신 출연자들 중에서 말썽꾼 역할을 하십시오. 그러면 당신에게 더 많은 면담 대화 시간이 보장될 것입니다.

(a), (b), (d)는 TV 쇼 출연자가 좀 더 인기와 주목을 끌기 위해 해야 할 일에 대한 정보인 반면, (c)는 방송사가 선호하는 프로그램에 관한 내용이다. 따라서 정답은 (c)이다.

take a risk 위험을 무릅쓰다 | **outlandish** 이상한 | **wacky** 엉뚱한 **black sheep** 말썽꾼 | **cast** 출연자

39

Excalibur is the mythical sword of King Arthur Pendragon, son of Uther Pendragon. (a) King Arthur was recognized as the rightful heir to the throne when he pulled the magical sword from the stone. (b) He and his fearless and trustworthy Knights of the Round Table had many battles and quests, with the ultimate quest being the search for the Holy Grail. (c) Arthur and his knights ruled over all of Britain and resided within the golden walls of Camelot, their fortress city. **(d) In the end, King Arthur's heart was broken by Guinevere when she had a scandalous tryst with Sir Lancelot.**

엑스칼리버는 유더 펜드래곤의 아들인 아서 펜드래곤 왕의 상상의 검이다. (a) 아서 왕은 바위에서 마법의 검을 뽑았을 때 정당한 후계자로 인정되었다. (b) 그와 용감하고 신뢰할 수 있는 그의 원탁의 기사단은 많은 전투를 하고 원정을 갔었는데, 최후의 원정은 성배를 찾는 것이었다. (c) 아서와 그의 기사들은 영국 전체를 지배했고, 그들의 요새 도시이며, 황금의 벽으로 둘러싸인 카멜롯에 거주했다. **(d) 결국 기네비어가 랜슬롯 경과 수치스러운 밀회를 가졌을 때 마음의 상처를 입었다.**

(a), (b), (c)는 아서 왕의 공적인 행동인 반면, (d)는 아서 왕의 사적인 면에 관한 내용이므로 (d)가 정답이다.

mythical 상상의 | **heir** 후계자 | **throne** 왕위 | **quest** 탐색 | **Holy Grail** 성배 | **fortress** 요새 | **scandalous** 수치스러운 | **tryst** 밀회

40

Dumplings are commonly thought of as some meat or vegetable filling wrapped in a dough covering and then steamed, boiled, or fried. (a) There are hundreds of different types of dumplings in many different countries, varying in their ingredients and names. **(b) They are very versatile and can be enjoyed regardless of the season.** (c) From a Georgian lamb and beef filled Khinkali to a Chinese shrimp stuffed Har Gow, everybody has a dumpling to choose from. (d) Some believe that the modern dumpling was invented about 500 to 600 years ago in China and from there spread throughout the world.

번역

일반적으로 만두는 고기나 야채로 소를 싼 가루 반죽 외피를 찌거나 끓이거나 기름에 튀긴 것으로 여겨진다. (a) 여러 나라에 재료와 명칭이 다양한 수백 가지의 만두가 있다. **(b) 만두는 용도가 매우 다양하며 계절에 관계없이 즐길 수 있다.** (c) 조지아산 새끼 양고기와 소고기가 든 킨칼리에서부터 중국 새우를 넣은 새우 딤섬에 이르기까지 모든 사람이 선택하여 먹는 만두가 있다. (d) 어떤 사람들은 오늘날의 만두가 약 500~600년 전 중국에서 처음 만들어져 전 세계로 퍼졌다고 믿는다.

해설

만두를 소개하는 글로, (a)는 다양한 나라의 다양한 만두 재료와 이름이 있다고 하며 (c)에서 그 예를 들고, (d)에서는 만두의 기원인 나라가 중국이라는 내용이 이어지고 있다. (b)는 만두의 다양한 용도를 언급하므로 흐름에 맞지 않다.

dumpling 만두 | **filling** 소 | **dough** 가루 반죽 | **versatile** 용도가 다양한

Actual Test 05

⇒ 본책 P 162

Part I

1 (d)	2 (b)	3 (a)	4 (a)	5 (c)
6 (c)	7 (c)	8 (d)	9 (a)	10 (b)
11 (c)	12 (d)	13 (d)	14 (a)	15 (c)
16 (b)				

Part II

17 (b)	18 (d)	19 (b)	20 (d)	21 (c)
22 (b)	23 (a)	24 (b)	25 (d)	26 (c)
27 (b)	28 (a)	29 (c)	30 (d)	31 (b)
32 (c)	33 (a)	34 (d)	35 (d)	36 (c)
37 (d)				

Part III

38 (b)	39 (c)	40 (c)

1

In an article called "The Role of Higher Education in Social Mobility," the authors state that while most Americans believe the notion that anyone with strong motivation and sufficient ability should successfully gain entry into America's universities, this simply isn't what the research is conveying. Income related gaps in terms of access to and success in higher education are ballooning. The pool of qualified youth is far greater than the number admitted and enrolled, meaning that it would be possible for universities to increase enrollment without _____.

(a) blemishing their affirmative action records
(b) targeting protected groups
(c) creating a diluted brand
(d) reducing the quality of the student body

번역

'사회적 유동성에 있어 고등 교육의 역할'이라는 논문에는 대부분의 미국인은 강한 동기 부여와 충분한 능력을 가진 사람은 누구나 미국의 대학교에 들어가는 것이 가능하다고 믿는다고 명시되어 있지만, 이는 그 연구가 전하는 바와 전혀 다르다. 고등 교육에의 접근과 성공 측면에서 소득 관련 격차는 급증하고 있다. 실력 있는 젊은 인력 집단은 입학 허가를 받고 등록 가능한 정원을 훨씬 초과하는데, 이는 대학이 학생 집단의 질을 떨어뜨리지 않으면서 등록을 늘리는 것이 가능할 것이라는 것을 의미한다.

(a) 그들의 차별 철폐 조치 기록에 흠집내기
(b) 보호 집단을 목표로 하기
(c) 약화된 브랜드 만들기
(d) 학생 집단의 질 떨어뜨리기

마지막 문장에서 대입 합격 기준을 충족시키는 젊은이의 수가 대입 정원을 초과한다고 말하고 있으므로, 대학에 더 많은 학생을 입학시켜도 등록한 학생들의 질은 떨어지지 않을 것임을 유추할 수 있다. 따라서 가장 적절한 것은 (d)이다.

social mobility 사회적 유동성 | **notion** 생각 | **convey** 전달하다
balloon 급증하다 | **pool** 이용 가능한 인력 집단 | **enroll** 등록하다
blemish 흠집을 내다 | **affirmative action** 차별 철폐 조치 | **dilute**
약하게 하다

2

Quotes encapsulate famous and memorable words from important and remarkable persons. Sometimes they can serve to _____. "Give me liberty or give me death" as quoted from Patrick Henry symbolizes revolutionary America's move for political autonomy. Apart from their historical context, some quotes are timeless and forever give us something to ponder about. "The unexamined life is not worth living" is cited as a lasting word of advice by Socrates. Of course, one quote alone often does not do justice to the full scope of a great person's life. And we must also be careful that so-called famous quotes are not really misinterpretations when removed from their context.

(a) remind us of our place in history
(b) represent an important moment in time
(c) give a summary of a person's life
(d) illustrate the lives of great thinkers in history

번역

인용구는 중요하고 비범한 이들이 남긴 유명하고 기억할 만한 말들을 요약한 것이다. 때로 인용구는 시간상 중요한 순간을 나타내는 것이 될 수 있다. '나에게 자유가 아니면 죽음을 달라'는 패트릭 헨리의 말에서 인용한 것으로 정치적 자치를 위한 혁명적인 미국의 운동을 상징한다. 그 역사적 맥락은 차치하고서라도, 일부 인용구들은 세월이 흘러도 변치 않고, 끊임없이 우리에게 뭔가 곰곰이 생각할 거리를 준다. '반성하지 않는 삶은 살 가치가 없다'는 소크라테스의 영구 불변의 충고로 인용된다. 물론, 단 하나의 인용구가 한 위대한 인물의 생애 전체를 정당하게 드러내지는 못한다. 그리고 소위 유명한 인용구들이 그 맥락에서 삭제되어도 실제로 잘못된 해석은 아니라는 사실에도 주의해야 한다.

(a) 역사에서 우리의 위치를 상기시키는
(b) 시간상 중요한 순간을 나타내는
(c) 한 인물의 삶을 요약해 주는
(d) 역사상 위대한 사상가들의 삶을 보여주는

해설

인용구의 정의를 설명하고, 그 성격에 대해 예를 들며 서술하고 있다. 첫 예로, 패트릭 헨리가 어떤 특정 시기에 말한 인용구를 들고 있고 바로 뒷문장에서 '역사적 맥락은 차치하고서'라며 시간에 관계없이 영구 불

변한 영향을 끼치는 인용구에 대해 서술하고 있다. 따라서 빈칸에는 중요한 시간상의 순간을 나타낸다는 (b)가 알맞다.

quote 인용구 | **encapsulate** 요약하다 | **remarkable** 비범한
symbolize 상징하다 | **revolutionary** 혁명적인 | **autonomy** 자치권
context 맥락 | **ponder** 숙고하다 | **cite** 인용하다 | **do justice to**
~을 정당하게 대하다 | **scope** 범위 | **misinterpretation** 오해

3

Although Leonardo Da Vinci and Michelangelo are known for being masterful painters, both listed their painting talents as subordinate to their other capabilities. Leonardo, while offering his services to the duke of Milan, gave primacy to his qualifications as a military and hydraulic engineer, architect, and sculptor before painter. Michelangelo also conveyed to Pope Julius II that he was first a sculptor and then a painter. Both possessed mammoth egos and contributed to the notion of a "Renaissance Man"—

_____.

(a) a person of broad knowledge and skill
(b) a man of humble yet respected knowledge
(c) a slightly crazed yet brilliant mastermind
(d) a coward with issues of abandonment

번역

레오나르도 다빈치와 미켈란젤로는 위대한 화가로 알려져 있음에도 불구하고, 둘 다 자신의 그림 그리는 재능을 다른 능력에 부수적인 것으로 간주했다. 레오나르도는 밀라노의 공작을 위해 일하는 한편 화가보다는 군사 및 수력 공학자, 건축가, 조각가로서의 그의 능력에 중점을 뒀다. 미켈란젤로도 교황 율리우스 2세에게 자신이 조각가임을 먼저 알리고 나서 화가임을 밝혔다. 두 사람 모두 엄청 강한 자아를 지녔으며 폭넓은 지식과 기술을 가진 사람이라는 '르네상스적 인간'이라는 개념에 기여하였다.

(a) 폭넓은 지식과 기술을 가진 사람
(b) 겸손하나 존경받는 지식을 가진 사람
(c) 약간 정신이 나갔지만 뛰어난 지능의 소유자
(d) 포기라는 문제를 가진 겁쟁이

해설

회화, 건축, 과학 등 여러 분야에 다재 다능했던 레오나르도 다빈치와 미켈란젤로를 예로 들어 르네상스적 인간이라는 개념을 소개하고 있으므로 (a)가 가장 적절하다.

masterful 거장[대가]다운 | **list** 간주[생각]하다, 리스트에 포함하다
subordinate 부수적인 | **capability** 능력 | **primacy** 으뜸
qualification 능력 | **hydraulic engineer** 수력 공학자 | **convey**
알리다 | **mammoth** 거대한 | **possess** 소유하다 | **contribute to**
~에 기여하다 | **notion** 개념, 생각 | **Renaissance Man** 르네상스적
인간 (특히, 문학과 회화를 비롯한 여러 분야에 능하고 관심도 많은 사람)
mastermind 조종하는 사람 | **abandonment** 포기

4

_____ that occur every 90 to 120 minutes throughout the night. While a transitional stage exists as you fall asleep, potentially adding another stage, it doesn't repeat, therefore, excluding it from being part of the cycle. During the first three stages your body's metabolic rate and temperature decreases, endocrine glands secrete growth hormones and blood is sent to muscles to be reconditioned. However, during the fourth stage in which Rapid Eye Movement (REM) occurs, your blood pressure increases, respiration becomes erratic and your involuntary muscles become paralyzed. This is when the mind is revitalized and your emotions are being fine-tuned.

(a) Your sleep cycle consists of four repetitive stages
(b) It is often said that people have mini-dreams
(c) Many couples have snoring episodes
(d) Sleep researchers conclude people feel warm spots

[번역]

수면 주기는 밤사이 90~120분마다 반복적으로 일어나는 4단계로 구성된다. 잠이 들 무렵에만 또 다른 단계가 더해지는 변환 단계가 하나 존재하지만, 그것은 반복되지 않기 때문에 수면 주기에서 제외한다. 처음 3단계 동안 신체의 신진대사와 체온은 떨어지고 내분비선은 성장 호르몬을 분비하며 근육을 원상태로 되돌리기 위해 혈액이 근육으로 보내진다. 그러나 급속안구운동인 REM이 일어나는 4번째 단계에는 혈압이 상승하고 호흡이 불규칙적이 되며 불수의근은 마비된다. 이때 가 정신이 활기를 되찾고 감정이 미세하게 조정되는 때이다.

(a) 당신의 수면 주기는 반복적인 4단계로 구성된다
(b) 종종 사람들은 짧은 꿈을 꾼다고 한다
(c) 많은 부부에게 코골이 일화가 있다
(d) 수면 연구가들은 사람들이 온점을 느낀다고 결론짓는다

[해설]

전체적으로 특정 시간마다 일어나는 수면의 4단계에 대해서 설명하고 있으므로, 주제 문장인 첫 문장에 가장 적절한 것은 (a)이다.

transitional 과도기의 | **potentially** 잠재적으로 | **metabolic rate** 신진대사율 | **endocrine gland** 내분비선 | **secrete** 분비하다 **recondition** 원상태로 되돌아가게 하다 | **Rapid Eye Movement** 급속안구운동 | **respiration** 호흡 | **erratic** 불규칙한 | **involuntary muscle** 불수의근 (의지와 상관없이 움직이는 근육) | **paralyze** 마비시키다 | **revitalize** 새로이 활기를 불어넣다 | **fine-tune** 미세 조정하다 **consist of** ~로 구성되다 | **repetitive** 반복적인

5

With an ever-increasing world population, _____. In terms of decreasing losses, researchers have been engaged in bio-engineering which began with the tinkering of plant DNA, adapting them to resist pests and disease. It was first achieved by cross-pollinating plants showing the desired resistance with the target plant. Later more sophisticated techniques were developed with which researchers cut and spliced each plant's DNA. With these techniques came the extremely challenging prospect of isolating the specific genes in plants that offered the traits needed by researchers.

(a) decreasing the crops that are prone to infestation is important
(b) increasing the number crops planted has become paramount
(c) scientists have striven to increase yields and improve crop quality
(d) the use of technology has taken a back seat to crop management

[번역]

증가하는 세계 인구에 비례하여, 과학자들은 수확량과 작물의 질을 향상시키기 위해 노력해 왔다. 손실 감소의 측면에서 연구원들은 식물이 해충과 질병에 견디도록 하기 위해 식물 DNA를 서투르게 만지기 시작하여 생명 공학에 참여해 왔다. 이것은 목표 식물에 훌륭한 내성을 보이는 식물을 타화 수분을 함으로써 처음 이루어졌다. 후에 좀 더 정교한 기술이 개발되었고, 그 기술을 이용하여 연구자들은 각 식물의 DNA를 자르고 접합했다. 이러한 기술로 연구자들이 필요로 하는 형질을 제공하는 식물의 특정 유전자를 분리시키는 의욕을 북돋우는 가망이 보였다.

(a) 기생충의 침입에 약한 작물을 감소시키는 것이 중요하다
(b) 재배 작물의 수를 늘리는 것이 다른 무엇보다 가장 중요해졌다
(c) 과학자들은 수확량 증가와 작물의 질 향상을 위해 노력해왔다
(d) 기술 이용은 작물 관리에 자리를 내줬다

[해설]

과학자들이 질병과 해충에 대한 식물의 저항력을 향상시키고 수확량을 늘리기 위해 생명 공학을 이용하여 어떤 노력을 해왔는지에 대한 내용으로 (c)가 가장 자연스럽다.

bio-engineering 생명 공학 | **tinker** 서투르게 만지다 **cross-pollinate** 타화 수분시키다 | **resistance** 저항력 **sophisticated** 정교한 | **splice** 접합하다 | **isolate** 분리하다 | **trait** 유전 형질 | **infestation** 〈기생충 등의〉 침입 | **paramount** 다른 무엇보다 중요한 | **strive** 노력하다 | **yield** 수확량 | **take a back seat to** ~에게 자리를 내주다

6

We at Driving 101 are dedicated to _____. We provide constructive feedback after every lesson. Through many years of instruction, we have identified the best practices in training individuals who are anxious about driving. Our experienced instructors teach you the various skills needed to be a good defensive driver. We also teach parking skills. Many of our learners are very surprised at how quickly they learn to parallel-park through us. Before a road test, we give you a mock test so that you know exactly what to expect. We get you results and our success rate is very high. Read about our courses on our website www.Driving101.com.

(a) helping you to pass written examinations
(b) training you to be a competitive racer
(c) equipping you with great driving skills
(d) teaching you to drive defensively

번역

드라이빙 101은 여러분이 훌륭한 운전 실력을 갖출 수 있도록 최선을 다합니다. 저희는 매 레슨마다 건설적인 피드백을 줍니다. 저희는 여러 해 동안 가르쳐오면서 운전을 겁내는 사람들을 훈련시키는 데 가장 효과적인 실습 방법을 찾았습니다. 숙련된 강사들이 훌륭히 방어 운전을 하는데 필요한 다양한 기술을 가르쳐 드립니다. 주차하는 법도 가르쳐 드립니다. 저희를 통해 많은 학생들이 얼마나 빨리 평행 주차를 배우는지 아주 놀라실 겁니다. 도로 주행 시험 전에 모의시험을 봐서 여러분이 정확히 무엇을 예상해야 하는지를 알려드립니다. 저희는 여러분이 좋은 결과를 얻도록 준비해드리기에, 합격률이 매우 높습니다. 저희 사이트 www.Driving101.com에서 수업 과정에 대해 읽어 보시기를 바랍니다.

(a) 필기시험을 통과하도록 도와드립니다
(b) 경쟁력 있는 레이서가 되도록 훈련시켜 드립니다
(c) 훌륭한 운전 실력을 갖추게 해 줍니다
(d) 방어적으로 운전하는 법을 가르쳐 줍니다

해설

운전면허 학원을 광고하는 글로, 운전 학원은 면허가 없는 사람들에게 면허 시험을 볼 수 있도록 여러 가지 운전 방법을 가르치기 때문에 가장 적절한 것은 (c)이다. (a)는 필기시험에 대한 언급이 없기 때문에 틀리며, 레이서를 위한 광고가 아니므로 (b)도 틀리다. (d)의 방어 운전은 교육의 일부로만 언급되었다.

dedicate 전념하다. 개관하다 | **constructive** 건설적인 | **identify** 확인하다 | **anxious** 불안한 | **parallel** 평행의 | **mock** 모의의 **success rate** 성공률 | **equip** 갖추게 하다

7

Originally coached by his Canadian father Walter, Wayne Gretzky, _____, played with 20 year olds in Brantford, Ontario at the age of only 14. Upon joining the Edmonton Oilers in 1979, he rose to unprecedented fame, shattering records and winning 4 Stanley Cups in 7 years. In 1988, however, he made a drastic move, agreeing to be traded to Los Angeles. Canadians were outraged. His agent at the time, Peter Pocklington, was burned in effigy and Gretzky was considered a traitor by many Canadians. However, years later, at his last game in Canada, he was honored and cheered by all as he left the ice forever.

(a) prohibited from playing full time in the NHL
(b) a late bloomer on the professional circuit
(c) seen by many as a classic ice hockey prodigy
(d) talented businessman, but not a good player

번역

많은 이들이 최고의 아이스하키 천재로 보는 웨인 그레츠키는 처음에는 캐나다인 아버지 월터에게 코치를 받으며 겨우 14살의 나이에 온타리오 브랜트포드에서 20살짜리들과 함께 경기를 했다. 1979년에 에드먼턴 오일러스에 들어가서 신기록들을 세우고 7년 동안 4번의 스탠리 컵을 차지하며 전례 없는 명성을 날렸다. 그러나 1988년 그는 로스앤젤레스로의 트레이드에 동의하는 극단적인 행동을 감행했다. 캐나다인들은 격분했다. 당시 그의 에이전트였던 피터 포클링턴은 인형으로 불태워졌고 그레츠키는 많은 캐나다인들의 배신자로 여겨졌다. 그러나 몇 년 후, 캐나다에서의 그의 마지막 경기로 영원히 얼음판을 떠날 때 모든 이의 예우와 응원을 받았다.

(a) NHL에서 전임 선수로 경기하는 것이 금지된
(b) 프로 연맹에서 대기만성형인 사람
(c) 많은 이들이 최고의 아이스하키 천재로 보는
(d) 재능 있는 사업가이지만 좋은 선수는 아닌

해설

웨인 그레츠키가 14살에 20살 선수들과 경기를 하고 스탠리컵을 4번이나 수상하며 전례 없는 여러 기록을 세운 뛰어난 아이스하키 선수임을 알 수 있으므로 (c)가 적당하다.

rise to fame 명성을 날리다 | **unprecedented** 전례 없는 | **shatter** 산산조각 내다 | **drastic** 과감한, 극단적인 | **trade** 〈스포츠에서 선수를〉 트레이드하다 | **outraged** 격분한 | **effigy** 인형 | **traitor** 배반자, 반역자 **late bloomer** 대기만성형의 사람 | **circuit** 연맹 | **prodigy** 천재

8

In 490 B.C. the out-armed and out-numbered Athenian and Plataea armies defeated the Persians, claiming victory for the democratic way of life. King Darius of Persia had sent his army to conquer Athens as a result of Athens interceding in revolt with other Greek city-states against Persian domination. Ennobled by their participation in their democratic society, their willingness to sacrifice all was paramount to their victory. The Greek armies fought with fervor, _____ hand to hand combat, archery and in seizing their enemies' ships.

(a) back-dropped by more soldiers and weapons for
(b) their submission to their enemy coming in

(c) but the Persian army were experts in
(d) refusing to be defeated and being decisively triumphant in

기원전 490년. 무기도 부족하고 수적으로도 열세였던 아테네와 플라타이아이군은 페르시아를 무찌르고 민주적 삶을 향한 승리를 거두었다. 아테네가 페르시아의 지배에 맞선 다른 그리스 도시 국가와 함께 반란을 중재한 결과로 페르시아의 다리우스 왕은 아테네를 정복하기 위해 군대를 보냈다. 그들의 민주적인 사회 참여로 인해 모든 것을 희생하려는 그들의 의지는 승리에 있어 무엇보다 중요했다. 그리스 군대는 패배를 거부하고, 육탄전과 궁술, 적의 배를 점령하는데 있어서 결정적으로 성공하며 열렬히 싸웠다.

(a) 더 많은 병사와 무기로 인해 후퇴한
(b) 다가오는 적들에 대한 그들의 굴복
(c) 그러나 페르시아 군대는 전문가들이었다
(d) 패배를 거부하고 결정적으로 성공하며

민주주의를 위해 모든 것을 희생했던 그리스군의 의지에 대한 글로, 마지막 문장에서 그리스 군대가 열렬히 싸웠다고 하므로 문장을 이어주는 표현으로 (d)가 가장 적절하다.

out-armed 무기가 열세인 | **out-numbered** 수적으로 열세인 **conquer** 정복하다 | **intercede** 중재하다 | **revolt** 반란 | **domination** 지배 | **ennoble** 귀족에 봉하다 | **fervor** 열렬 | **hand to hand combat** 육탄전 | **seize** 점령하다 | **back-dropped** 후퇴한 | **submission** 항복 **decisively** 결정적으로

9

Harvard Business Review blogger Ron Ashkenas is telling managers to leverage their top performers or risk losing them. Inept managers often unintentionally dampen exceptional employees, telling them to "slow down" or "research more" because they feel threatened, fearing a subordinate will steal their thunder. In contrast, however, managers should embrace a top performer, stretch him or her to their limit and offer assignments that take their careers to the next level. By doing so, the manager will be recognized for _____, in addition to having the skills to develop people for the good of the company.

(a) having an eye for talent
(b) targeting non-performers
(c) profiteering on the backs of others
(d) building solid fundamentals

〈하버드 비즈니스 리뷰〉 블로거인 론 애시케나스는 관리자에게 최고 실적을 거둔 직원을 이용하든지 아니면 그들을 잃는 위험을 감수하라

고 이야기한다. 서투른 관리자는 부하 직원이 공을 가로챌 것을 두려워하며 위협을 느끼기 때문에 우수 직원에게 '천천히 하라,' '더 조사하라'고 말하며 의도하지 않게 그들의 기를 꺾는다. 그러나 관리자는 이와 반대여야 하며 최고 능력의 직원을 포용하고 그들이 능력을 최대한 발휘하며 경력을 다음 단계로 끌어 올릴 수 있는 업무를 주어야 한다. 그렇게 되면 관리자는 회사에 필요한 인력을 개발하는 기술뿐만 아니라 재능을 알아보는 눈도 가졌다는 인정을 받게 될 것이다.

(a) 재능을 알아보는 눈을 가짐
(b) 업무 미수행자를 대상으로 삼음
(c) 다른 이를 속여 부당 이득을 취함
(d) 견고한 기반을 세움

뛰어난 관리자란 우수 직원이 능력을 발휘할 수 있도록 도와주어야 한다는 내용으로, 뛰어난 관리자가 인정을 받는 것은 직원의 능력을 알아보는 것이라는 (a)가 가장 적절하다.

leverage 이용하다 | **inept** 서투른 | **unintentionally** 고의가 아닌 **dampen** (기세를) 꺾다 | **exceptional** 우수한 | **subordinate** 부하 **steal someone's thunder** ~몫의 성공을 가로채다 | **stretch** (능력 등을) 최대한 발휘하다 | **profiteer** 부당이득을 취하다 **fundamental** 기본

10

The Rocky Horror Picture Show began as a stage play in London around 1973. Capturing the attention of Lou Adler, an American producer, the show was brought to the big screen by him a year later. Critics and movie-goers alike ridiculed the movie at first; however, _____ grew over the years. Today, it is the longest running theatrical movie in history and watching it with the right audience can be one of the most rewarding experiences one could hope for. As it is often shown at midnight, fans dress up like their favorite characters and scream along with the actors on the screen.

(a) government censoring
(b) a small cult following
(c) funding for new movies
(d) touring theatrical performances

〈록키 호러 픽쳐 쇼〉는 1973년경 런던의 한 연극 무대에서 시작했다. 이 공연은 미국인 제작자인 루 애들러의 관심을 사로잡으면서 일년 후 루에 의해 대규모 영화로 만들어졌다. 처음에 비평가들과 영화 팬들은 하나같이 그 영화를 조롱했으나, 해가 거듭되며 소규모의 광신적인 추종자들이 늘어났다. 오늘날 역사상 가장 오랫동안 상영되는 극장 영화이며, 제대로 된 관객들과 그 영화를 보는 것은 누구나 바라는 가장 보람 있는 경험 중의 하나일 것이다. 영화가 종종 한밤중에 상영되기 때문에 팬들은 그들이 가장 좋아하는 등장인물처럼 차려 입고 화면의 배우들과 함께 소리를 지른다.

(a) 정부 검열

(b) 소규모의 맹렬한 추종자들

(c) 새로운 영화에 대한 자금

(d) 연극 공연의 순회

영화가 처음에는 인기가 없고 평이 좋지 않았다는 내용 이후 however 가 나왔으므로 뒷부분은 이와 대조적인 내용이 연결되어야 한다. 내용 상 대중적 인기에 관련된 것이 자연스러우므로 (b)가 가장 적절하다.

critic 비평가 | **ridicule** 비웃다 | **theatrical** 공연의, 연극의 **rewarding** 보람 있는 | **dress up** 옷을 갖춰 입다 | **censor** 검열하다 **cult** 숭배하는 | **following** 추종 세력

11

Shakespeare's *Hamlet* _____, focusing on the quagmires stemming from love, death and betrayal. Particularly frustrating is the fact that no clear positive resolutions present themselves due to the vagueness of Hamlet's world and his all-consuming insecurity. From scene to scene, he seems certain of one thing but later doubts what he has experienced. Others in the play seem to be able to act on their thoughts whereas he simply seems dumbfounded.

(a) was a distinguished gentlemen with a penchant for hunting

(b) was a landlord of sorts

(c) is a truly ambiguous and exasperating tragedy

(d) is an enthralling journey of self-discovery

셰익스피어의 〈햄릿〉은 사랑, 죽음, 배신에서 비롯된 끔찍할 수 없는 곤경에 초점을 둔 진실로 다의적이고 분통이 터지는 비극이다. 특히 좌절감이 드는 것은 햄릿의 모호한 세계와 그의 소모적인 불안감으로 인해 분명하고 긍정적인 결심이 없다는 사실이다. 장면마다 햄릿은 어느 한 가지에 대해 확신하는 듯 보이지만 나중에는 자신이 경험한 것을 의심한다. 극중 다른 인물들은 그들의 생각대로 행동할 수 있지만 햄릿은 말을 못 하는 듯하다.

(a) 사냥을 애호하는 뛰어난 신사였다

(b) 일종의 지주였다

(c) 진실로 다의적이고 분통이 터지는 비극이다

(d) 자신을 발견하는 마음을 사로잡는 여행이다

셰익스피어의 〈햄릿〉이 어떤 연극인지를 quagmire, vagueness, dumbfounded 등의 어휘를 사용해 설명하고 있는 것으로 보아 애매모호하고 답답한 비극이라는 내용의 (c)가 가장 적절하다.

quagmires 곤경 | **stem from** ~에서 기인하다 | **betrayal** 배신 **resolution** 결단 | **vagueness** 애매모호함 | **dumbfounded** 말문이 막힌 | **penchant** 애호 | **ambiguous** 애매모호한 | **exasperating** 분통이 터지는 | **enthralling** 마음을 사로잡는

12

_____ water intoxication. It occurs when water dilutes the body's sodium levels in the bloodstream, causing an imbalance of water in the brain. Symptoms can include a feeling of nausea, excessive fatigue, and in extreme cases, hallucinations or possibly even death. Water intoxication is most likely to occur during periods of intense athletic performance when athletes try to re-hydrate too quickly. The daily recommended amount of water is eight cups per day; however, not all of this water must be consumed in the liquid form as most foods also contribute to the body's water intake.

(a) The simple addition of rum leads to

(b) Recent dehydration problems refer to

(c) Oxygen–infused water can cause

(d) Drinking too much water can lead to

수분 과잉섭취는 물중독을 유발할 수 있다. 물중독은 물이 체내 혈액 순환의 나트륨 수치를 희석시키며 뇌에서 물 불균형을 일으킬 때 발생한다. 증상으로는 메스꺼운 느낌과 과도한 피로, 심한 경우 환각 증상이 나타나며 사망에 이를 수도 있다. 물중독은 격렬한 운동을 하는 동안 운동선수가 지나치게 빨리 수분을 재흡수하려 할 때 일어날 가능성이 가장 높다. 일일 수분 권장량은 하루에 8컵이지만, 대부분의 음식물이 체내 수분 섭취에 도움이 되기 때문에 하루 권장량이 모두 액체 형태로 소비되어야 하는 것은 아니다.

(a) 럼주를 약간 추가하면 ~을 초래한다

(b) 최근의 탈수 문제는 ~을 나타낸다

(c) 물에 녹아있는 산소는 ~을 초래할 수 있다

(d) 수분 과잉섭취는 ~을 유발할 수 있다

지문에서 물중독은 운동선수들이 너무 빨리 물을 재흡수하려고 할 때 일어날 가능성이 높다고 했으므로, 수분 과잉 섭취로 인해서라는 내용의 (d)가 가장 적당하다.

intoxication 중독 | **dilute** 묽게 하다 | **sodium** 나트륨 | **imbalance** 불균형 | **nausea** 메스꺼움 | **excessive** 과도한 | **fatigue** 피로 **hallucination** 환각, 환영 | **intense** 격렬한 | **re-hydrate** 물을 주어 원상으로 돌아가게 하다 | **intake** 섭취 | **dehydration** 탈수 | **infuse** 스미다

13

Aaliyah _____ Madonna, Mariah Carey, Beyonce, and others. An R&B singer, dancer, fashion model and actress, she was most known for her hit songs and collaborations with other musical giants, her modeling, and her acting in two motion pictures. Upon her success as an R&B singer, she was offered to further her career in motion pictures and was slated to appear in the two sequels to *The Matrix* as a supporting actress amongst other high-profile roles. However, the budding actress and accomplished singer's life was tragically cut short in 2001 when she died in a plane crash at the age of 22.

(a) was an investor in studios and real estate with mentors such as

(b) was a key player in the early success of women in show business, like

(c) struggled to find success in her early twenties, very similar to

(d) **was an aspiring professional on the cusp of joining the ranks of**

번역

알리야는 마돈나, 머라이어 캐리, 비욘세 등의 서열에 장차 합류하려는 출발점에 있는 포부가 큰 프로였다. R&B 가수이자 댄서, 패션 모델, 배우였던 그녀는 히트곡과 음악계 거장들과의 공동 작업, 모델 활동, 영화 두 편에서의 연기로 가장 잘 알려졌다. 그녀가 R&B 가수로 성공하자 영화계에서 경력을 발전시킬 기회가 주어졌고 이목을 끄는 역할들 중 조연으로 〈매트릭스〉 속편 두 편에 출연할 예정이었다. 그러나 갓 싹트기 시작하는 배우이자 뛰어난 가수는 2001년 22살의 나이에 비행기 추락에 의한 비극적 죽음으로 짧게 생을 마감하였다.

(a) 멘토들과 함께 스튜디오와 부동산에 투자한 투자가였다

(b) 연예 사업의 초기 여성의 성공에 중요 역할을 한 사람이었다

(c) 매우 유사하게 이십 대 초반에 성공하기 위해 몸부림쳤다

(d) 서열에 장차 합류하는 출발점에 있는 포부가 큰 프로였다

해설

지문은 22살에 생을 마감한 미국의 가수이자 배우였던 알리야에 관한 내용으로, 생전에 막 싹트기 시작한 배우이자 성공한 가수였다는 내용이 유명인들과 같은 서열에 올라가는 출발점에 있었다는 (d)와 연결된다.

collaboration 공동 작업 | **motion picture** 영화 | **further** 발전시키다 | **slate** 계획하다 | **sequel** 속편 | **amongst** ~중에 | **high-profile** 이목을 끄는 | **budding** 신예의 | **accomplished** 기량이 뛰어난 | **aspiring** 포부가 큰 | **cusp** 출발점

14

Czar Nicholas II, planning to revoke the onerous laws of his predecessors, was overthrown and killed by the Russian working class group called the Bolsheviks who desired more rapid reforms. Though his entire family was thought to be executed, rumors of a surviving daughter began to surface. One woman, Anne Anderson, steadfastly insisted that she was his daughter. She claimed that she was rescued by soldiers, but later left destitute in Germany. Scores of the Czar's relatives, ex-servants and acquaintances grilled her, with many saying she resembled the daughter. However, it was finally decided in court that _____ so her inheritance claim was denied.

(a) **there was a lack of conclusive evidence**

(b) she was the Czar's daughter

(c) the Czar had her out of wedlock

(d) there was nothing remaining in the Czar's estate

번역

전 황제들의 성가신 법률을 폐지하려고 계획하던 러시아 황제 니콜라스 2세는 좀더 신속한 개혁을 열망했던 볼셰비키라는 러시아의 노동 계층 집단에 의해 권좌에서 추방되고 죽임을 당했다. 황제의 모든 가족이 처형되었다고 생각되었지만 생존한 딸에 대한 소문이 떠돌기 시작했다. 앤 앤더슨이라는 여자는 자신이 황제의 딸이라고 계속 확고하게 주장했다. 그녀는 병사들에 의해 구조되었으나 후에 독일에서 궁핍하게 남겨졌다고 주장했다. 여러 황제 친척들과 전 하인들, 지인들이 그녀를 다그쳤고 그녀가 황제의 딸을 닮았다고 하는 사람들도 많이 있었다. 그러나 마침내 법정에서 결정적 증거가 부족하다는 결정이 나고 그녀의 유산 상속 청구는 기각되었다.

(a) **결정적 증거가 부족했다**

(b) 그녀는 황제의 딸이었다

(c) 황제는 결혼하지 않은 상태에서 그녀를 낳았다

(d) 황제의 재산이 아무것도 남아있지 않았다

해설

지문에서 앤 앤더슨이라는 여자는 자신이 황제 니콜라스 2세의 딸이라고 주장했으나 유산 상속에 대한 청구가 기각된 이유가 법정에서 그의 딸이라는 것을 증명할 수 없었기 때문이라는 것을 유추할 수 있다. 따라서 (a)가 가장 적절하다.

czar 황제 | **revoke** 폐지하다 | **onerous** 성가신 | **predecessor** 전임자 | **overthrow** 뒤엎다 | **reform** 개혁 | **execute** 처형하다 | **surface** 표면에 떠오르다 | **steadfastly** 변함없이 | **destitute** 궁핍한 | **grill** 다그치다 | **inheritance** 상속 | **conclusive** 결정적인 | **wedlock** 결혼 상태 | **estate** 자산

15

Dear Mr. Smith,

Thank you for the order that you have placed for the full team kit. We wish to confirm that the order will consist of 12 red and white striped jerseys (size large) and 12 white shorts (size large). We envisage that the delivery time on this order will be approximately 3 weeks from the date of this letter. _____, please be aware that we have experienced a slight delay on recent orders and there is a possibility that the order may take an additional 2 weeks beyond the expected date. Once again we thank you for your order and should there be any problems, please do not hesitate to contact me.

Kevin Song

(a) Fortunately
(b) Then
(c) However
(d) Of course

번역

스미스 씨께

팀 유니폼을 주문해 주셔서 감사합니다. 주문해 주신 내역이 적색과 흰색 줄무늬 셔츠 라지 사이즈 12벌과 흰색 반바지 라지 사이즈 12벌임을 확인해 드립니다. 이번 주문의 배송은 이 편지를 작성한 뒤 약 3주 후 일 것으로 예상합니다. 하지만 최근 주문에 대해 다소 지연이 있어서 예상 일자보다 2주 더 소요될 수 있음을 염두에 두십시오. 다시 한번 주문해 주신 것에 감사하고, 주문에 문제가 있다면 주저하지 말고 연락 주십시오.

케빈 송

(a) 다행히
(b) 그러면
(c) 하지만
(d) 물론

해설

스미스 씨가 주문한 내용을 확인하고 배달이 늦어질 수 있음을 알리는 편지이다. 빈칸 앞에서는 원래 예정된 도착 날짜를 알려주고 빈칸 뒤에서는 주문이 지연될 경우 배송에 2주가 더 걸릴 수 있다고 하였으므로, 역접의 접속사 (c) However가 알맞다.

place 〈주문 등을〉 하다 | **kit** 복장 | **envisage** 예상하다 | **hesitate** 주저하다

16

It is no secret to gardeners that cold and frost are the enemies of plants and vegetables. With the Age of Discovery and the industrial production of glass, greenhouses for housing tropical plants and growing fruits and vegetables have taken root especially in the colder climates of England and the Netherlands. _____ glass enclosures are rather expensive to construct and maintain, cheaper plastic coverings have made large-scale greenhouse gardening affordable. Improvements in durability have extended the life of the material to several years or even a decade, increasing the convenience and productivity of agriculture in parts of the world and extending the growing season year-round.

(a) In that
(b) Whereas
(c) As though
(d) Since

번역

추위와 서리가 식물과 채소의 적이라는 것은 정원사 모두가 알고 있는

공공연한 사실이다. 발견의 시대와 유리의 공업 생산으로, 영국과 네덜란드처럼 특히 더 추운 기후에서는 실내에서 열대 식물과 과일 및 채소를 키우는 온실이 뿌리를 내렸다. 유리 울타리 막은 건설과 유지에 비용이 다소 많이 드는 반면, 더 저렴한 비닐 덮개로는 적정한 가격으로 대규모의 온실 정원을 만들 수 있다. 내구성 향상으로 식물의 수명이 몇 년, 심지어 10년까지 연장되었으며, 세계 일부에서는 농업의 편리성과 생산성을 높이고 생장기가 연중 계속되도록 연장시켰다.

(a) ~라는 점에서
(b) ~인 반면
(c) 마치 ~인 듯
(d) ~때문에

해설

온실 재배에 대한 지문으로, 빈칸이 들어간 문장에서 유리를 이용한 울타리 막과 비닐 덮개를 이용한 온실의 특징에 관해 비교 설명하고 있다. 유리는 건설과 유지 비용이 많이 들고, 비닐은 더 저렴하다는 점에서 서로 대조해 말하고 있으므로 빈칸에 들어갈 접속사로 가장 적절한 것은 (b) Whereas이다.

frost 서리 | **greenhouse** 온실 | **take root** 뿌리를 내리다 | **enclosure** 울타리를 친 장소 | **affordable** (가격이) 적정한 | **durability** 내구성 | **growing season** 생장기 | **year-round** 연중 계속되는

17

The untrained eye may be forgiven for assuming that a piece of sheet music constitutes the final form of a musical work. What with all the clefs and key signatures, not to mention the articulation marks for pizzicatos and crescendos, the work of the performer would seem to be indubitably laid out in a clear-cut notation. And yet such is not to be the case when the original inspiration of the composer's muse precipitates onto the written medium to be read by another soul, another spirit driven by its own irrepressible sensibilities and tendencies. Then what may be recast or left unheard through the prism of accent marks and dotted notes is what is ineffable and evanescent in the music.

Q: What is the main topic of the passage?
(a) the difficulties of performing a musical work well
(b) why any musical notation can be reinterpreted
(c) how to listen for the original intent in any music
(d) a call to reinvent today's system of scoring music

번역

훈련 받지 않은 시각으로 한 장의 악보를 음악 작업의 최종 산물로 추측하는 것은 무리가 아닐 수도 있다. 피치카토와 크레센도를 위한 조음표는 물론 모든 음자리표와 조표가 표시된 것은 그 연주가의 작품이 의심할 여지 없이 명백한 표기로 배치된 것처럼 보일 수 있다. 그럼에도 그렇게 기록된 것은 작곡가의 최초 영감이 종이 위의 매개체로 갑자기 떨어져서, 고유의 억누를 수 없는 감수성과 성향에 의해 돌출된

또 다른 정신, 또 다른 영혼에 의해 읽혀지는 것은 아니다. 그리고 음악에서 강세 부호와 점음표의 프리즘을 통해 개작되거나 듣지 않고 남겨진 것은 말로 표현할 수 없고 순간적인 것이다.

Q: 지문의 주제는?
(a) 음악 작품을 잘 연주하는 데 있어서의 어려움
(b) 어떤 기보법이든 재해석될 수 있는 이유
(c) 어떤 음악이든 본래의 의도를 듣는 방법
(d) 오늘날 작곡 시스템의 재창조에 대한 요구

[해설]
악보 한 장이 작곡가의 최종 산물이라고 생각할 수 있지만, 작곡가가 가진 본래의 영감이 제대로 읽히는 것도 아니며, 순간적이고 형언할 수 없는 영감이 제대로 종이 위에 구성될 수 없다는 내용이다. 따라서 지문의 주된 논제로 가장 적절한 것은 (b)이다. 본래의 의도를 듣는 방법에 대한 내용은 나오지 않았으므로 (c)는 틀리다.

clef 음자리표 | key signature 조표 | articulation 조음 | indubitably 의심할 여지없이 | clear-cut 명백한 | notation 표기 | inspiration 영감 precipitate 〈갑자기 어떤 상태에〉 떨어지다 | irrepressible 억누를 수 없는 tendency 성향, 기질 | recast 개작(改作)하다 | dotted note 점음표 ineffable 형언할 수 없는 | evanescent 순간의 | musical notation 기보법(손으로 직접 쓰거나 인쇄 또는 다른 수단을 동원해서 음악을 시각화시키는 방법) | score 악보에 기입하다

18

Dear Ms. Dornier,

Reflecting upon my tour of your facility in Thailand last week with your delightful staff, I would like to convey my admiration for such a well-run factory. I was especially impressed with your floor arrangement and personnel. I don't believe I have ever viewed such a cost efficient and smoothly run manufacturing process. Additionally, all of your employees were extremely courteous and made a fantastic effort to explain various functions and answer my inquiries. Finally, I would be most appreciative if you would extend a special thank you to Mr. Borat from me. He was most hospitable during my visit and I really enjoyed our discussions over dinner the night before my departure.

Yours faithfully,
George Eliot
General Manager

Q: What is the main purpose of the letter?
(a) To report on an overseas factory and its current status
(b) To thank Mr. Borat for his hospitality and helpfulness
(c) To critique the facility and staff in the Thailand location

(d) To express gratitude for hosting a visit by the author

[번역]
도르니에 씨께

지난주 귀사의 유쾌한 직원들과 함께한 태국 시설 시찰에 대해 돌아보며, 훌륭히 운영되는 공장에 대한 존경심을 전하고 싶습니다. 특히 귀사의 층 배치와 직원들이 인상적이었습니다. 그렇게 비용 절감이 되고 매끄럽게 진행되는 제조 과정은 본 적이 없습니다. 또한 귀사의 모든 직원은 매우 정중했으며, 굉장히 열심히 여러 기능에 관한 설명을 해주었고 제 질문에 답변해 주었습니다. 마지막으로, 보랏 씨에게 제 감사를 전해주시면 정말 감사하겠습니다. 저의 방문 기간 동안 보랏 씨가 가장 친절했고 출발 전날 밤 저녁식사 중에 한 토론은 정말 즐거웠습니다.

총지배인, 조지 엘리엇

Q: 편지의 주된 목적은?
(a) 해외 공장과 현황에 대해 보고하기 위해
(b) 보랏 씨의 환대와 도움에 감사하기 위해
(c) 태국 지사의 설비와 직원을 비평하기 위해
(d) 글쓴이의 방문을 맞이해준 것에 고마움을 표하기 위해

[해설]
편지를 보낸 사람은 태국의 어떤 회사를 방문한 후 시설을 둘러보도록 도움을 준 회사 직원들에게 감사 인사를 전하고 있다. 따라서 정답은 (d)이다.

arrangement 배치 | personnel 직원 | inquiry 문의 | appreciative 고마워하는 | hospitable 친절한 | critique 비평하다

19

Heading up the Northern Renaissance in art, the Flemish artists of the 15th century such as Jan van Eyck were masters of oil painting in the tradition of northern Gothic art. A detailed naturalism and richness of color characterize their art. Their religious altarpieces as well as more secular works have remained admired for their virtuosity and realism. The style is in the tradition of verisimilitude to nature without a preoccupation with linear perspective as in some of the Italian landscape paintings of that era. It can be said that these paintings with their shallow or even ambiguous perspective are most at home in the context of the sculptural and architectural elements of a gothic cathedral setting.

Q: What is the main topic of the passage?
(a) Comparing northern and southern styles of renaissance art
(b) Characterizing the artistry of the Flemish masters
(c) Appreciating the techniques of medieval Flemish art

(d) Placing Gothic art and architecture in its historical context

미술에 있어 북부 르네상스로 가보면, 얀 반 에이크 같은 15세기의 플랑드르 화가들은 북부 고딕 미술의 전통에 있어서 유화의 대가들이었다. 상세한 자연주의와 풍부한 색감 표현이 그들 그림의 특징이다. 보다 세속적인 작품들은 물론 제단 뒤의 종교적인 작품들은 그들의 기교와 사실주의로 인해 찬사를 받는다. 그 시대에 몇몇 이탈리아 풍경화처럼 직선 원근법에 집착하지 않고 자연의 모습에 가깝게 표현하는 전통에 그 스타일이 있다. 피상적이고 심지어 애매모호한 원근법을 가진 이런 그림들은 고딕 양식으로 된 대성당의 조각적이고 건축적 요소라는 맥락에서 가장 그 본거지에 있다고 할 수 있다.

Q: 지문의 주제는?
(a) 르네상스 미술의 북부와 남부 스타일 비교
(b) 플랑드르 미술 대가들의 예술적 기교의 특징
(c) 중세 플랑드르 미술의 기법 감상
(d) 역사적 맥락에서의 고딕 미술과 고딕 건축

북부 르네상스의 플랑드르 미술에 관한 내용으로, 그들의 그림에 나타난 특징과 그들 작품이 찬사를 받고 있는 이유 및 작품 속 스타일을 순서대로 설명하고 있다. 따라서 지문의 주제로 가장 적절한 것은 (b)이다.

head up ~로 향하다 | **altarpiece** 제단 뒤의 그림 | **secular** 세속적인 **virtuosity** 기교 | **verisimilitude** 그럴듯함 | **preoccupation** 심취 **linear perspective** 직선 원근법 | **shallow** 피상적인 | **artistry** 예술적 기교 | **medieval** 중세의 | **context** 맥락

20

Teaching autistic children in school requires a little extra skill and effort. Here are a few ideas to help teachers handle autistic children in their classroom. For one thing, students with autism like to have a fixed time table for the day as it helps them feel comfortable. Teachers also need to be flexible to the different learning styles of autistic students. Students with autism may also need some extra time to do their assignments. Some students with autism who struggle with group activities can be given an option of working independently for group projects. A lot of children with autism may need some additional care from teachers to be able to keep up with regular students.

Q: What is the passage mainly about?
(a) Helping autistic students get along with peers
(b) Supporting students suffering from autism with assignments
(c) Punishing autistic students that misbehave
(d) Helping teachers teach children with autism

학교에서 자폐아를 가르치는 데는 별도의 기술과 노력이 약간 필요하다. 교사가 반에서 자폐아를 다루는 데 도움이 되는 아이디어가 몇 가지 있다. 우선, 자폐증이 있는 학생들은 온종일 정해진 시간표를 좋아한다. 그것이 이들을 편하게 해주기 때문이다. 교사도 그들의 다양한 학습 유형에 맞추는 유연성을 가져야 한다. 자폐 학생들은 과제 수행에 보다 많은 시간이 필요할 수도 있다. 그룹 활동을 어려워하는 자폐 학생에게는 그룹 프로젝트 시간에 혼자 할 수 있도록 선택권이 주어져야 한다. 많은 자폐아들은 일반 학생들에게 뒤떨어지지 않도록 교사로부터 보다 많은 보살핌이 필요하다.

Q: 지문에서 주로 언급하고 있는 것은?
(a) 자폐 학생들이 또래와 잘 지낼 수 있도록 돕기
(b) 자폐 학생들이 과제하는 것을 돕기
(c) 말썽 피우는 자폐 학생들 벌주기
(d) 교사가 자폐아를 가르치도록 돕기

지문은 자폐아들을 가르치고 과제를 수행하도록 돕는 데 교사가 알아야 할 점을 소개하고 있으므로 답은 (d)이다.

autistic 자폐증의 | **for one thing** 우선 첫째로 | **flexible** 융통 있는, 유연한 | **assignment** 과제 | **peer** 또래 | **misbehave** 못된 짓을 하다

21

The public face of the UN may be the high-profile functions of urgent international matters such as peacekeeping and international law. But the more run-of-the-mill administrative operations of the multi-national organization have been questioned as another example of runaway overhead. Given that the number of annual meetings can run in the tens of thousands and the number of reports published in the hundreds of thousands, some see redundancy and inefficiency as a concern. The yearly budget of $5 billion excludes the money spent on military operations worldwide, which, if accounted for, is estimated at closer to $20 billion.

Q: What is the best title for the passage?
(a) How to Streamline UN Operational Costs
(b) The Causes of Inefficiency in Running the UN
(c) Estimates on the Organizational Cost of the UN
(d) Concerns about the Public Image of the UN

UN의 대중적으로 알려진 일면은 평화 유지와 국제 법률 같은 시급한 국제적 문제에 대한 세간의 주목을 끄는 기능일 것이다. 하지만 다국적 기관으로서 지극히 평범한 행정 운영은 급격히 오르는 간접비의 또 다른 예로 문제시되어왔다. 연례 총회 횟수는 수만 차례에 이르고 발간되는 보고서는 수십 만 건에 달한다는 점에서 불필요한 중복과 비효율성에 대한 우려의 시선이 있다. 전 세계 군사 운영 비용을 제외하고 연간 50억 달러의 예산은 소요 경비를 말하자면 200억 달러에 가까울 것으로 추산된다.

Q: 지문에 가장 잘 어울리는 제목은?
(a) UN 운영 비용을 능률화할 방안
(b) UN 운영 비효율화의 원인
(c) UN 조직 운영 비용 추산
(d) UN의 대중적 이미지에 대한 우려

해설

UN의 예산 사용에 있어서의 불필요한 중복과 비효율성에 관한 우려가 있다는 내용으로, 마지막 문장에 UN의 연간 예산과 추정 비용을 제시하고 있는 것으로 볼 때, 지문의 제목으로 가장 적절한 것은 (c)이다.

high-profile 세간의 이목을 끄는 | run-of-the-mill 지극히 평범한 | administrative 행정상의 | operation 작전, 활동 | runaway 고삐 풀린 | redundancy 불필요한 중복 | inefficiency 비효율 | account for ~의 지출 내역을 말하다 | estimate 추산하다 | streamline 능률화하다 | operational cost 운영 비용 | organizational 조직적인

22

The fact is your personal information is vulnerable to falling into the wrong hands. If you shop online, your personal information such as your credit card account, a bank account, a job is out there. If your information is used fraudulently, you may not find out about it for months or even longer, depending on how closely you monitor your credit report. At Identity Ensure, we help guard you against more than just credit fraud. We alert you whenever we detect your personal information being used to apply for wireless services, retail credit, utilities, check orders & reorders, and mortgage loans within our extensive network.

Q: What is the main purpose of the passage?
(a) To warn about the dangers of identity theft online
(b) To advertise a credit protection agency
(c) To inform how people have their identity stolen
(d) To criticize the system of a credit card company

번역

여러분의 개인 정보가 나쁜 사람의 손에 들어가기 쉽다는 것은 사실입니다. 온라인 쇼핑을 하면 신용 카드 계정, 은행 구좌, 직업 등과 같은 신상 정보가 노출됩니다. 만약 개인 정보가 사기에 이용되더라도 꼼꼼히 신용카드 내역을 살펴보지 않으면 몇 달 혹은 심지어 더 오랫동안 알아내지 못할 수도 있습니다. 아이덴티티 인슈어는 단순한 신용 사기 그 이상으로부터 여러분을 보호합니다. 저희의 광범위한 네트워크를 통해 여러분의 개인 정보가 무선 서비스, 소매 신용 구입/ 판매, 공공 서비스, 수표 신청[재신청], 담보 대출 등을 위해 사용되는 것이 감지될 때마다 알려드릴 것입니다.

Q: 지문의 주된 목적은?
(a) 온라인상의 개인 정보 도용의 위험을 경고하기 위해
(b) 신용 보호 대행사를 광고하기 위해
(c) 사람들이 어떻게 개인 정보를 도용 당하는지 알리기 위해
(d) 신용카드 회사의 시스템을 비판하기 위해

해설

사기에 이용되기 쉬운 개인 정보에 대해 아이덴티티 인슈어라는 회사가 온라인상에서 보호 서비스를 제공한다는 내용으로 정답은 (b)이다.

vulnerable 취약한 | fraudulently 사기용으로 | monitor 감시하다 | ensure 보장하다 | mortgage 담보 대출 (융자) | extensive 광범위한

23

Malcolm Gladwell in his book *Blink: The Power of Thinking Without Thinking* would put forth the case that quick judgments made based on a slice of information available can be just as good or even better than slow judgments based on extensive deliberation. The argument goes that information overload hinders and not helps the cause of reaching a decision. Compounding the problem would be subconscious biases skewing the process, or conflicting forces causing paralysis by analysis. A caveat to all this is that this near-instant analysis would have to be built on the foundation of extensive prior knowledge. Detractors may even accuse this approach of glorifying intuition.

Q: Which of the following is correct according to the passage?
(a) Prejudices can slowly worsen decision making over time.
(b) Intuition is the way to reach a carefully considered decision.
(c) Critics of the book claim that the author is inconsistent.
(d) This theory argues against too much education is useless.

번역

말콤 그래드웰은 그의 저서 〈블링크: 첫 2초의 힘〉에서 이용할 수 있는 하나의 정보를 토대로 한 빠른 결정이 폭넓은 숙고를 바탕으로 한 느린 결정만큼이나 훌륭하거나 심지어 더 나을 수도 있는 경우를 제시하고 있다. 정보의 과부하는 결정에 도달하지 못하게 하고 도움을 주지 못한다고 주장한다. 문제를 악화시키는 것은 사고의 과정을 왜곡시키는 무의식적인 편견이나 분석으로 인한 무기력을 야기하는 상충하는 힘이다. 이런 모든 것에 대해 주의할 것은 폭넓은 경험 지식을 바탕으로 거의 즉각적인 분석이 이루어져야 한다는 것이다. 이를 비방하는 사람들은 이런 접근법이 직관을 미화하는 것이라고 비난할지도 모른다.

Q: 지문에 따르면 다음 중 옳은 것은?
(a) 편견은 시간을 두고 내리는 결정을 천천히 악화시킬 수 있다.
(b) 직관은 신중하게 고려된 결정을 내리는 방법이다.
(c) 책의 비평가들은 저자가 일관성이 없다고 주장한다.
(d) 이론은 너무 많은 교육이 쓸모없다는 것에 반대한다.

해설

말콤 그래드웰은 심사숙고 끝에 내린 결정보다 순간적인 직관에 따른

결정이 더 나을 수 있으며, 지나치게 많은 정보와 분석이 의사 결정을 방해하거나 도움이 되지 않을 수 있으므로, 갖고 있던 지식을 토대로 즉각적인 결정을 내려야 한다고 말하고 있다. 지문의 중반부에 무의식적인 편견이 문제를 악화시킨다고 하므로 옳은 것은 (a)이다.

put forth 제시하다 | **extensive** 폭넓은 | **deliberation** 숙고 | **overload** 과부하 | **hinder** 방해하다 | **compound** 악화시키다 | **subconscious** 무의식적인 | **bias** 편견 | **skew** 왜곡하다 | **conflicting** 상충하는 | **paralysis** 무기력 | **caveat** 주의할 점 | **detractor** 비방하는 사람 | **glorify** 미화하다 | **intuition** 직관력 | **prejudice** 편견 | **inconsistent** 모순되는, 일관성 없는

24

If it is to be taken as valid that people form deep emotional bonds with their pets, then the old cliché that a pet is a part of the family could also be accepted. From a sociological point of view, a pet really does alter family dynamics in that different family members would have different relationships with the pet. People can be classified according to whether they treat a pet as merely an animal or as a family member. To put it simply, pets could become a point of contention in the family. On the other hand, pets could act as intermediaries in the way, for example, children might in keeping families together.

Q: Which of the following is correct according to the passage?
(a) Adults accept pets as part of the family more than children do.
(b) Families can possibly grow apart from owning a pet.
(c) Pets almost always lead people to form deep emotional bonds.
(d) Children and pets may fight for affection within a family.

사람들이 애완동물과 깊은 정서적 유대를 형성한다는 것이 타당한 것으로 여겨진다면, 애완동물은 가족의 일원이라는 오래된 진부한 표현도 인정할 수 있다. 사회학적 관점에서 볼 때, 식구들마다 애완동물과 각기 다른 관계를 맺는다는 점에서 애완동물은 실제로 가족 관계의 역학을 변화시킨다. 애완동물을 그저 동물로 대하는지, 식구로 대하는지에 따라 사람을 분류할 수 있다. 간단히 말해서, 애완동물들은 가족 내에서 논쟁의 쟁점이 될 수 있다. 다른 한편으로는 아이들이 가족을 단합시키듯 애완동물이 중재자 역할을 할 수도 있다.

Q: 지문에 따르면 다음 중 옳은 것은?
(a) 어른들은 아이들보다 더 애완동물을 가족의 일원으로 받아들인다.
(b) 애완동물 소유를 두고 가족들이 분열될 가능성도 있다.
(c) 애완동물들은 거의 항상 사람들이 깊은 정서적 유대감을 형성하도록 이끈다.
(d) 가족 안에서 아이들과 애완동물이 애정을 두고 싸울 수 있다.

가정 내에서 애완동물이 가지는 특징과 역할에 관한 글로, 애완동물을 가족의 일원으로 생각하는지 여부에 따라 가족 관계의 역학이 달라질 수 있으며 가족 내에서 논쟁의 쟁점이 될 수 있다고 하므로, 지문에 따른 내용으로 옳은 것은 (b)이다.

valid 유효한, 정당한 | **bond** 유대감 | **cliché** 진부한 표현 | **sociological** 사회학적인 | **alter** 바꾸다 | **dynamics** 역학 | **contention** 논쟁 | **intermediary** 중재자 | **keep together** 단합하다 | **affection** 애정

25

Dear Mr. Brown,

This is with reference to your letter for my conditional hire within your organization as a copy writer. I am very much delighted to get this good news from your side and I would like to thank you for providing me the chance to prove my capabilities by serving in your organization. Though I would like to join you as soon as possible, I need to clarify that, as per our discussion, I am already working in an organization and require a little time to resign from my current employment. Barring any issues, I should be available to start on Tuesday, October 8th. Thank you most sincerely for your time and consideration.

Sincerely,
James Conn

Q: Which is correct about the person receiving this letter?
(a) Since he already gets another job, he is rejecting the offer.
(b) His company wants to purchase the sender's company.
(c) The sender is supposed to send him a letter of resignation.
(d) He has hired the sender to work at his company.

브라운 씨께

귀사에 제가 카피라이터로 조건부 채용되었다는 편지와 관련하여 답장을 보냅니다. 이런 좋은 소식을 듣게 되어 매우 기쁘고 귀사에 근무함으로써 제 능력을 증명할 기회를 주심에 감사 드립니다. 되도록 빨리 근무하고 싶지만, 의논한 바와 같이 제가 이미 다른 곳에서 일을 하고 있고 현 직장에서 사직하려면 시간이 좀 필요하다는 것을 분명히 하고 싶습니다. 다른 문제가 없다면, 10월 8일 화요일에 일을 시작할 수 있을 것입니다. 시간 내어 배려해 주셔서 진심으로 감사 드립니다.

제임스 콘

Q: 편지의 수신자에 대해 옳은 것은?
(a) 이미 다른 직장을 구했기 때문에 제안을 거절하고 있다.
(b) 그의 회사는 발신자의 회사를 사기를 원한다.

(c) 발신자는 수신자에게 사직서를 보내야 한다.
(d) 발신자를 회사에 고용했다.

해설

편지를 보내는 사람은 채용되어 브라운 씨의 회사에서 일할 기회를 얻게 되어 감사하고 기뻐하고 있으므로 (d)가 정답이다.

with reference to ~와 관련하여 | **conditional** 조건부의 | **as per** ~에 따라서 | **resign** 사임하다 | **barring** ~이 없다면

26

The boll weevil is an insect that destroys cotton plants, and has been a menace to every American state in which cotton is grown. Boll weevils eat the silky fibers in the seedpods of cotton plants and the buds of cotton flowers. Four or five times during a single season, female weevils lay their eggs inside the cotton buds, proliferating their population exponentially. The government would like to get rid of the boll weevil by spraying a powerful poison over the cotton fields, but this spraying is believed to also kill spiders and other useful insects. The one positive effect that has come from the boll weevil is that it has forced many farmers to raise alternative crops from which they have thrived.

Q: Which of the following is correct about boll weevil according to the passage?
(a) They are impervious to any chemical spray.
(b) Only the seeds of the cotton plant are eaten.
(c) They can reproduce several times a year.
(d) Spiders are their main natural enemy.

번역

목화 바구미는 목화를 망치는 곤충이며, 목화를 재배하는 미국의 모든 주에 위협적 존재가 되어왔다. 목화 바구미는 목화 꼬투리의 부드러운 섬유질과 목화 꽃봉오리를 먹는다. 암컷 바구미는 한 계절에 4 또는 5회 목화 꽃봉오리 안에 알을 나아서, 그 수를 기하급수적으로 증가시킨다. 정부는 목화밭에 강력한 독을 살포해서 목화 바구미를 제거하려 하지만, 이런 살포로 거미와 다른 유용한 곤충들도 죽는다고 한다. 목화 바구미로 인한 긍정적인 효과 하나는 이 바구미 때문에 많은 농부들이 대체 작물을 재배하지 않을 수 없었으며, 이로 인해서 농부들은 성공했다.

Q: 지문에 따르면 목화 바구미에 대해 옳은 것은?
(a) 어떤 살충제에도 영향을 받지 않는다.
(b) 목화씨만 먹는다.
(c) 일 년에 수 차례 번식할 수 있다.
(d) 거미가 주요 천적이다.

해설

Four or five times during a single season 이하를 통해 정답이 (c)임을 알 수 있다. powerful poison으로 박멸할 수 있고 목화씨가 아닌 꼬투리의 섬유질과 꽃봉오리를 먹으므로 (a)와 (b)는 옳지 않으며 (d)에 대한 언급은 없다.

boll weevil 목화 바구미 | **menace** 위협적인 존재 | **seedpod** 꼬투리 | **proliferate** 증식하다 | **exponentially** 기하급수적으로 | **alternative crop** 대체 작물 | **imperious** ~에 영향받지 않는 | **reproduce** 번식하다

27

The old adage that truth can be stranger than fiction still often succeeds in winning acceptance. When looking around for extrasolar planets, or exoplanets, analogous to the ones we know, the physics often turn out to baffle us once again. The Kepler "Planet Hunter" space telescope set out in 2009 to orbit the sun and look at star systems in the Northern Cross. Since then, it's been transmitting back data that has scientists going back to the drawing board. Whole collections of planets closer to their star than thought possible have heads being scratched. And with the number of possible planets detected at over 1,200, estimates say that nearly one-fifth of all stars in the universe have planets orbiting them.

Q: Which of the following is correct about extrasolar planets according to the passage?
(a) Scientists think one-fifth of them have planets in orbit.
(b) Some are detected unexpectedly close to their stars.
(c) The Northern Cross has approximately 1,200 of them.
(d) Physicists find them analogous to ones already known.

번역

사실이 허구보다 더 이상할 수 있다는 오랜 속담은 아직도 종종 받아들여지고 있다. 태양계 밖의 행성들 즉, 우리가 아는 것과 유사한 태양계 외행성을 찾기 위해 여러 곳을 둘러볼 때, 물리학은 또 다시 우리를 어리둥절하게 만든다. 2009년 태양 궤도를 돌며 북십자성의 행성계를 관찰할 케플러의 '플래닛 헌터' 우주 망원경을 설치했다. 그 이후로, 과학자들을 다시 연구의 처음으로 되돌아가게끔 하는 자료가 전송되고 있다. 가능하다고 생각했던 것보다 항성에 더 가까운 행성들의 집합체가 곤혹스럽게 한다. 그리고 가능한 행성의 수가 1,200회 넘게 발견되어, 추정치를 통해 우주의 모든 항성 중 거의 1/5이 그 주위를 도는 행성을 갖고 있다는 사실을 말해준다.

Q: 지문에 따르면 다음 중 외행성들에 대해 옳은 것은?
(a) 과학자들은 외행성의 1/5이 그 궤도 안에 행성을 갖고 있다고 본다.
(b) 뜻밖에 항성 가까이에 있는 행성 몇 개가 발견되었다.
(c) 북십자성은 약 1,200개의 행성을 가지고 있다.
(d) 물리학자들은 그것들이 이미 알려진 것과 유사하다는 사실을 발견한다.

해설

태양계 외행성에 관한 연구에서 우주 망원경이 전송하는 자료로 인해

과학자들이 다시 연구하고, 생각보다 항성에 더 가까이 붙어 도는 행성들이 발견되면서 머리를 긁적이게 되었다는 내용으로, 사실이 허구보다 더 이상할 수 있음을 이야기하고 있다. 지문의 후반부에 생각했던 것 보다 항성 가까이에서 도는 행성들이 발견되었다고 했으므로 옳은 것은 (b)이다.

adage 속담 | exoplanet 태양계 외행성 | analogous 유사한 | baffle 어리둥절하게 만들다 | Northern Cross 북십자성 | transmit 전송하다 go back to the drawing board 처음부터 다시 시작하다 | scratch one's head 곤혹스러워하다 estimate 추정치 | unexpectedly 뜻밖에 | approximately 대략

28

Today, January 1st, I'm announcing my candidacy for mayor. Over the past five years, we have seen the deterioration of our community as the incumbent mayor has allowed our infrastructure to reach a state of disrepair with pot-holed roads, underfunded transit lines and inadequate power supply. Well, I would like to change all of that! By voting for me, you are voting for a positive change in our community. My first priority as Mayor will be to revitalize our community through a partnership with the private sector to pave new roads, improve upon transit and most importantly, increase power generation through the use of wind turbines in the Windy Hill region of our town. So, please vote for me in September and we will again build a community we can be proud of.

Kevin Jenkins
Mayoral Candidate for Smallsville

Q: Which of the following is correct according to the passage?

(a) Wind power is promised to supplement the town's energy supply.
(b) Jenkins will begin his campaign for mayor in September.
(c) The town of Smallsville is located on Windy Hill.
(d) Upkeep of the town's infrastructure is not an election issue.

번역

1월 1일 오늘 저는 시장 출마를 선언합니다. 우리는 지난 5년간 현재 시장이 움푹 파인 도로와 자금 부족을 겪는 운송 노선, 부족한 전기 공급으로 사회 기반 시설이 황폐해짐에 따라 지역 사회의 악화를 지켜봐 왔습니다. 저는 이 모든 것을 바꾸고 싶습니다! 저에게 투표 하신다면, 우리 지역 사회의 긍정적인 변화를 위해 투표를 하는 것입니다. 시장으로서 저의 최우선 순위는 우리 지역 사회를 다시 활성화시키는 것이며, 이를 위해 사기업과 협력하여, 새 도로를 포장하고, 운송을 향상시키고, 그리고 가장 중요한 윈디 힐 지역의 풍력 발전용 터빈을 이용하여 전력 생산을 높일 것입니다. 9월 선거에서 저에게 투표하십시오. 그러면 자랑스러워 할 수 있는 지역 사회를 우리가 다시 세울 것입니다.

스몰스빌 시장 후보 케빈 젠킨스

Q: 지문에 따르면 다음 중 옳은 것은?
(a) 풍력 발전은 시의 에너지 공급을 보충할 가망이 있다.
(b) 젠킨스는 9월에 시장 선거 운동을 시작할 것이다.
(c) 스몰스빌 시는 윈디 힐에 위치한다.
(d) 시의 기반을 유지하는 것은 선거의 논점이 아니다.

해설

케빈 젠킨스가 스몰스빌의 시장 선거에 출마를 선언하는 글이다. 시의 현 문제점을 지적하며 공약 중 하나로 풍력 발전용 터빈을 이용해 전력 생산을 높여 지역 사회를 다시 활성화시킨다고 말하고 있다. 따라서 풍력 발전으로 인해 시에 에너지를 공급할 수 있다는 (a)가 정답이다.

deterioration 퇴보 | incumbent 재임 중인 | infrastructure 사회 기반 시설 | disrepair 황폐 | pot-holed 도로가 움푹 파인 underfunded 자금 부족을 겪는 | transit 운송 | inadequate 부족한 revitalize 재활성화 시키다 | pave 포장하다 | candidacy 입후보

29

From the lens of two millenniums gone past, it may not be readily noticeable just how inventive an ancient and venerated work of literature is. *The Records of the Grand Historian* by the historiographer Sima Qian is at once a classic book on history as well as an innovative document. Even as the *Shiji* has been a template for many future works ever since the Han Dynasty when it was written, it departed from its precedents which mainly served to glorify their dynastic reigns. It is a monumental book which encompasses not only the standard chronicle of significant events but also has a section that portrays in vivid human detail the important personages who comprised these events.

Q: Which of the following is correct according to the passage?
(a) The history respected the point of view of rival dynasties.
(b) Every single history book since the Shiji has copied its style.
(c) Important historical figures are described in a separate section.
(d) The author Sima Qian does not glorify the dynasty he chronicles.

번역

지나간 2천년 역사의 렌즈를 통해 볼 때, 고대의 존경 받는 문학 작품이 얼마나 독창적인지는 선뜻 눈에 띄지 않을 수 있다. 역사가 사마천이 쓴 〈사기열전〉은 역사에 관한 고전서인 동시에 혁신적인 기록이기도 하다. 〈사기〉는 그것이 집필되었던 한(漢)왕조 이후 많은 작품들의 본보기가 되기는 했지만, 주로 그 왕조의 치세를 찬양하는데 주력했던 기존의 책에서 벗어난 책이다. 이 책은 중요한 사건의 표준 연대기를 아

우를 뿐 아니라 이런 사건들에 나타난 중요 인물들을 생생하고 상세히 묘사하는 부분도 있다는 점에서 기념비적인 책이다.

Q: 지문에 따르면 다음 중 옳은 것은?
(a) 역사는 경쟁 왕조들의 관점을 중히 여겼다.
(b) 사기 이후에 모든 역사서는 그 방식을 모방했다.
(c) 역사적으로 중요한 인물들이 별도로 기술되었다.
(d) 저자 사마천은 그가 기록한 왕조를 찬미하지 않는다.

해설

역사 고전인 동시에 획기적인 기록이기도 했던 사마천의 〈사기〉에 대한 지문으로, 그 왕조의 치세를 찬양하는 데 주력했던 전례에서 벗어나 연대기적인 사건 기록뿐 아니라 그 사건 속의 인물들까지 생생히 묘사했다는 점에서 기념비적인 책이라고 했으므로, 별도로 역사상 중요한 인물이 설명되어 있다는 (c)이다.

venerated 존경 받는 | historiographer 역사가 | template 본보기 | depart from ~에서 벗어나다 | precedent 선례 | glorify 찬미하다 | reign 치세 | monumental 기념비적인 | encompass 아우르다 | chronicle 연대기 | personage 인물 | comprise 구성하다

30

Commuter highway routes display a curious impediment to their traffic flow that doesn't have to do with highway design. In the event of a visually outstanding scene of an accident, and even if the vehicles in questions are off to the side of the road, newscasters almost obligatorily mention the gaper's delay which at times increase commute times by not a negligible amount of minutes. The sight of a spectacular crash or the flashing lights of police cruisers attract the gaping of on-lookers and their concomitant slowing down their own speeds even without any obstacle on the road. This curiosity about a car crash is perhaps inevitable. With this almost invariable delay, the best choice is often to use an alternate course.

Q: Which of the following is true according to the passage, ?
(a) A gaper's delay actually increases the danger of driving.
(b) More lanes on a highway can help remedy gaper's delay.
(c) Flashing police lights do not contribute to gaper's delay.
(d) Human nature is to the ultimate cause of gaper's delay.

번역

통근용 고속도로에서 그것의 속성에 부합하지 않게 교통 흐름을 방해하는 기이한 일이 있다. 외관상 도드라져 보이는 사고 현장의 경우, 문제 차량들이 길 옆으로 빠져있음에도 무시할 수 없는 몇 분이나 통근

시간을 늘리는 구경 정체에 관해 뉴스 진행자들은 줄곧 빠짐없이 언급하고 있다. 대단한 충돌 사고나 경찰 순찰차의 반짝이는 불빛을 입 벌리고 바라보는 구경꾼들로 인해 도로에 별다른 장애가 없지만 속도가 늦어진다. 교통사고에 대한 이런 호기심은 아마도 피할 수 없는 것이리라. 지체가 불가피할 경우 종종 다른 길을 이용하는 것이 최선책이다.

Q: 지문에 따르면 다음 중 옳은 것은?
(a) 구경 정체는 실제로 운전의 위험성을 증가시킨다.
(b) 고속도로의 더 많은 차선이 구경 정체 현상 해결에 도움이 될 수 있다.
(c) 경찰차의 반짝이는 불빛은 구경 정체 현상의 원인은 아니다.
(d) 인간 본성이 구경 정체 현상의 궁극적인 원인이다.

해설

통근 도로에 교통사고가 발생할 경우, 많은 이들이 넋을 놓고 구경하기 때문에 발생하는 구경 지체 현상으로 차량의 속도가 줄면서 정체가 되고 결국 통근 시간에 늦게 되는 상황에 관해 이야기하고 있다. This curiosity about 이하를 통해 구경 자체를 inevitable이라고 표현한 것으로 보아 (d)가 적당하다. 운전의 위험성이나 차선에 대한 언급은 없으므로 (a)와 (b)는 오답이다.

commuter 통근자 | impediment 장애물 | obligatorily 의무적으로 | gaper's delay 구경 정체 (넋 놓고 바라보는 구경꾼들로 인한 정체) | negligible 무시해도 될 정도의 | cruiser 순찰차 | gape 입을 딱 벌리고 보다 | concomitant 수반하는 | inevitable 불가피한 | invariable 불변의 | remedy 개선하다

31

Our philosophy here at Olsen Trading is to follow the exemplar tactics of the best traders. The key to their success is rather simple. Instead of believing in using complex formulas for supposedly beating the system, wise traders adhere to the firm principle of looking long-term. This is because the markets are not predictable in the short-term. When markets are erratic, an even keel can weather the storm. In fact, successful traders don't do many trades. They also make trades that may run counter to the trend. Naturally, they are humble since they know they don't beat the markets all the time. Keeping this attitude in mind, we trust that your working with us at Olsen can be mutually beneficial for all.

Q: Which of the following is recommended for making profitable trades?
(a) Look at the trends and go in the opposite direction.
(b) Resist the urge to react to sudden market fluctuations.
(c) Use simple formulas only for making many humble trades.
(d) Look to the long-term but act on the short-term.

(c) Its products can help distinguish a company from the rest.

(d) It sells corporate gifts which are certified by the Green trend.

녹색 흐름을 반영하는 회사 증정품을 제공함으로써 귀사에 매력을 부여하고 강한 환경 의식을 보여주세요. 환경친화적인 회사 증정품은 귀하가 더 큰 대의를 믿는다는 것을 보여주기에 귀사를 차별화시켜줍니다. 귀하의 사업에 단순한 도덕적인 면을 더하는 것 이상으로 의미 있게 만들 것입니다. 많은 공급자들이 한정된 환경친화적인 제품을 보유하는 데 반해, Branding-it-right.com은 대규모 선택의 여지가 있습니다. 특별 선택품목으로 곡물 플라스틱으로 만든 자연 분해성 제품과 재활용품으로 만들어진 물건이 있습니다. 뿐만 아니라 유기농 마케팅 제품들과 에너지 절약 증정품도 있습니다.

Q: 광고에 따르면 다음 중 Branding-it-right.com에 대해 옳은 것은?
(a) 사무실에서 자연 분해성 재활용 제품을 쓴다.
(b) 온라인 재고품 목록이 타 경쟁사보다 많다.
(c) 회사를 타사와 차별화시키도록 해주는 제품이 있다.
(d) 녹색 흐름에 보증된 회사 증정품을 판다.

해설

Branding-it-right.com은 친환경 제품으로 구성된 회사 증정품을 판매하는 회사로, 고객 회사가 환경친화적인 증정품을 통해 타사와 차별화될 수 있다는 내용의 광고이다. 따라서 Branding-it-right.com에 대해 옳은 것은 (c)이다.

allure 매력 | **differentiate** 차별하다 | **cause** 대의명분 | **relevant** 실제적으로 중요한[가치 있는] | **array** 집합체, 모음 | **featured** 특색으로 한 | **biodegradable** 자연분해성의 | **organic** 유기농의, 유기적인 | **inventory** 재고(목록) | **certified** 보증된

번역

저희 올슨 트레이딩의 철학은 최고 트레이더들의 모범 전략을 따르는 것입니다. 그들의 성공 비결은 꽤 간단합니다. 현명한 트레이더는 체계를 무너뜨릴 만한 복잡한 공식 적용을 믿는 대신, 장기적 관점에 입각한 확고한 원칙을 고수합니다. 이는 시장을 단기 예측할 수 없기 때문입니다. 시장 변동이 심할 때는 용골도 폭풍우를 견뎌낼 수 있습니다. 실제로, 성공한 트레이더는 거래를 많이 하지 않습니다. 추세를 따라가지 않는 거래를 하기도 합니다. 물론 그들은 항상 시장을 이기지 못한다는 것을 알기 때문에 겸손합니다. 이런 자세를 마음에 새기며, 올슨에서 저희와 함께 일한다면 모든 면에서 상호 이득이 되리라 믿습니다.

Q: 다음 중 수익성 있는 거래를 위해 추천되는 것은?
(a) 동향을 파악한 후 그 반대로 가라.
(b) 급작스러운 시장 변동에 대해 급히 반응하지 않도록 하라.
(c) 단순한 공식을 이용해서 보잘것없는 거래를 많이 하라.
(d) 장기적으로 전망하고 단기적으로 행동하라.

해설

올슨 트레이딩 회사의 거래 철학에 관한 글로, 예측할 수 없기 때문에 단기보다는 장기를 관망하는 확고한 원칙을 고수하며 추세를 따라가지도 않고, 시장을 이길 수 없다는 겸손한 자세로 임하기 때문에 함께 일하면 상호 이득을 얻을 수 있을 것이라고 말하고 있다. 따라서 추천할 만한 내용으로 적절한 것은 (b)이다.

exemplar 모범 | **tactic** 전략 | **trader** 입각한 | **formula** 공식 | **adhere to** ~을 고수하다 | **erratic** 불규칙한 | **keel** 용골(선박 바닥의 중앙을 받치는 길고 큰 재목) | **weather the storm** 폭풍우를 견뎌내다 | **counter to** ~에 어긋나는 | **mutually** 상호간에 | **beneficial** 이로운 | **fluctuation** 변동

32

Lend your company allure and show eco-consciousness by providing corporate gifts that reflect the Green trend. Environmentally-friendly corporate gifts differentiate your company, as they show you believe in a greater cause. More than adding a simple moral aspect to your business, these also make your enterprise relevant. While many suppliers have a limited selection of environment-friendly products, Branding-it-right.com has a massive array to choose from. Featured options include biodegradable items made of corn plastic and others made from recycled materials. There are organic marketing products and energy-saving corporate gifts as well.

Q: Which of the following is correct about Branding-it-right.com according to the advertisement?

(a) It uses biodegradable and recycled products in its offices.

(b) Its online inventory of items is larger than any of its competitors.

33

The Paleozoic era of geologic history begins with the Cambrian period with its seeming profusion in the diversity of life forms on Earth. This system of chronology is not accidental as the very term "Paleozoic" derives from Greek roots for "ancient" and "life." The Paleozoic saw the evolution of all the major phylum of multi-cellular organisms as we know them today, the appearance of the first fishes, insects, and reptiles dating back to around 500 million years ago. This is to say that the initial migration of life onto land happened in this era as far as the ancient and incomplete fossil records can tell us. Subsequent eras include the Mesozoic with its dinosaurs and the Cenozoic with its rise of mammals.

Q: What can be inferred about the Paleozoic era from the passage?

(a) It was so designated for its diversification of life forms.

(b) Most of the species from this era have largely died out by now.

(c) It is preceded by both the Mesozoic and Cenozoic eras.

(d) The ancient Greeks first came up with this categorization.

번역
지질학 역사상 고생대는 지구에 생물 형태의 다양성이 외견상 풍성해진 캄브리아기로부터 시작된다. '고생대'라는 용어 자체가 그리스어 어원인 '고대'와 '생물'에서 유래한다는 것으로 보아 이러한 연대기 체계가 갑자기 만들어진 것은 아니다. 5억 년쯤 전으로 거슬러 올라가면 고생대에는 초기 어류, 곤충, 파충류 같은 오늘날 우리가 알고 있는 문(門)에 속하는 모든 주요 다세포 생물들의 진화를 볼 수 있다. 이것은 이 시대 생물들이 처음 육지로 이주했음에 대해 고대의 불완전한 화석 기록이 우리에게 알려줄 수 있는 것보다 많은 것을 알려준다. 뒤이어 공룡이 살았던 중생대와 포유류가 번성한 신생대가 나타난다.

Q: 지문을 통해 고생대에 대해 유추할 수 있는 것은?

(a) 생명 형태의 다양화로 확실히 지정되었다.

(b) 이 시대의 종 대부분은 지금까지 대개 멸종되었다.

(c) 중생대와 신생대 모두에 뒤이은 시대이다.

(d) 고대 그리스에서 최초로 이 분류를 제시했다.

해설

고생대의 어원 및 그 시기의 특징을 설명하는 글로, 고생대는 생물의 다양성이 풍부해진 캄브리아기와 함께 시작된다고 했으므로, 생명의 다양화로 지정된 것으로 볼 수 있으므로 유추할 수 있는 내용으로 옳은 것은 (a)이다.

Paleozoic era 고생대 | **geologic** 지질학의 | **seeming** 외견상의 **profusion** 풍성함 | **chronology** 연대기 | **derive from** ~에서 파생되다 | **phylum** 문(門: 강의 위이고 계의 아래인 생물 분류 단위) **multi-cellular** 다세포의 | **organism** 생물 | **migration** 이주 **subsequent** 이후의 | **Mesozoic** 중생대 | **Cenozoic** 신생대 **designate** 지정하다 | **diversification** 다양성 | **die out** 멸종되다 **precede** ~에 선행하다 | **come up with** 제시하다 | **categorization** 분류

theoretically available, adequate distribution remains only theoretical.

Q: What can be inferred from the passage?

(a) Shortages in food, water, and energy are only theoretical.

(b) The world's population explosion runs its course for now.

(c) It is difficult and pointless to predict future trends.

(d) **The world will be severely overcrowded around 2050.**

번역

인구 증가와 관련하여 끊임없이 지구 최후의 날을 예측하고 있음에도 불구하고, 2011년 언젠가 70억 번 째 사람이 태어나는 것을 세계는 지켜보게 될 것이다. 60억 인구 도달이라는 획기적 사건은 불과 새천년 전환기에 발생했다. 1960년에 인구는 고작 30억이었다. 현재 추정되는 인구는 이번 세기 중반까지 80~90억 명이다. 세계 인구의 약 75%는 도시 구역으로 계속 확대되고 있는 몇몇 지역과 도시에 살게 될 것이다. 미래 예측은 늘 위험한 일이지만, 이 문제에 있어 식량, 물, 에너지 부족에 대한 매우 심각한 예측은 지속되고 있다. 이론적으로 자원을 충분히 구할 수는 있지만, 적절한 분배는 이론상으로만 가능한 일로 남아있다.

Q: 지문을 통해 유추할 수 있는 것은?

(a) 식량, 물, 에너지 부족은 이론일 뿐이다.

(b) 세계의 인구 폭발은 우선 진행 중이다.

(c) 미래 추세 예측은 어렵고 무의미한 일이다.

(d) **2050년경에 세계는 심각한 인구 과밀이 될 것이다.**

해설

인구는 끊임없이 증가하고 있으며 이번 세기 중반인 2050년까지 세계 인구가 80~90억 명으로 증가할 것이라고 예측하는 것으로 보아 지문을 통해 유추할 수 있는 내용으로 가장 적절한 것은 (d)이다.

perennial 지속되는 | **doomsday** 지구 최후의 날 | **milestone** 획기적인 사건 | **prophesy** 예언하다 | **dire** 매우 심각한 | **prognosis** 예측 | **persist** 지속되다 | **distribution** 분배 | **run its course** 자연스럽게 전개되다

34

Despite the perennial doomsday predictions about population growth, the world will have seen its 7 billionth person being born sometime in 2011. The previous milestone of 6 billion was only reached at the turn of the millennium. The number in 1960 was a mere 3 billion. Current estimates foresee 8-9 billion by mid-century. Approximately 75% of the world will be living in cities with some regions becoming huge continuous urban zones. Prophesying the future has always been a risky business, but the dire prognosis of food, water, and energy shortage forever persist in relation to the issue. Although enough resources are

35

The so-called Big Three Bailout, the federally-assisted bankruptcy and restructuring of the top three US automakers in the wake of the 2008 Credit Crisis, provided ample opportunity for finger pointing. If it wasn't for the executives with their private jets and hefty bonuses, it was the labor unions with their plush benefits and job security. Lest it be about the old head-butting between labor and management, it was reiterated time and again that the terms and conditions for the automotive unions then-existing were negotiated and agreed upon decades back by all parties involved.

Q: What opinion would the writer most likely agree with?
(a) The bailout was necessary to keep the economy stable.
(b) All sides only used the opportunity to play the blame game.
(c) Labor and management never get along and never will.
(d) People would do well to maintain historical perspective.

2008년 금융 공황의 결과 미국 상위 세 개 자동차 회사에 대해 연방 정부가 원조한 파산과 구조 조정, 소위 빅 쓰리 긴급 구제가 지탄을 받을 만한 충분한 빌미를 내주었다. 전용 비행기와 두둑한 보너스를 챙긴 경영진이 아닌, 아주 안락한 혜택과 고용 보장을 받는 노동 조합이 그 지탄의 대상이었다. 노사간의 케케묵은 대립이 될까 봐, 당시 있던 자동차 노조를 위한 계약 조건이 모든 관련 당사자들에 의해 수십 년 동안 협상 및 합의되었다는 것을 몇 번이고 되풀이하였다.

Q: 글쓴이가 가장 동의할 만한 주장은?
(a) 긴급 구제는 경제 안정을 유지하기 위해 필요한 것이었다.
(b) 모든 편이 남 탓을 하기 위해 기회를 이용할 뿐이다.
(c) 노사는 결코 서로 잘 지내지 못하고, 앞으로도 그럴 것이다.
(d) 사람들은 역사적 관점을 유지하는 것이 좋을 것이다.

미국 내에서 상위를 차지하고 있는 자동차 회사에 대한 연방 정부의 긴급 구제로 나타난 현상에 관한 내용으로, 조합을 위한 측면에서 계약 조건에 수십 년 동안 협상과 합의가 되었다는 비판으로 볼 때, 글쓴이가 동의할 만한 내용으로 가장 적절한 것은 (d)이다.

bailout 긴급 구제 | **restructuring** 구조 조정 | **in the wake of** ~의 결과로서 | **Credit Crisis** 금융 공황 | **finger pointing** 비난 | **hefty** 많은 | **plush** 안락한 | **job security** 고용 보장 | **lest** ~하지 않도록 | **head-butting** 박치기 | **reiterate** 되풀이하다 | **stable** 안정된

36

Some might believe that winning at a game such as chess is simply a matter of using perfect logic to make the correct moves and avoid mistakes. Others might counter that beating another human player takes as much humanity as possible, cunning and illogic included. This would-be philosophical debate was put to the test when IBM's Big Blue supercomputer was pitted against the reigning world champion Garry Kasparov in a series of matches in 1996-1997. Estimated to be able to look a dozen or two moves ahead, the machine nonetheless only barely edged out its flesh-and-blood opponent.

Q: What can be inferred about the Big Blue supercomputer from the passage?

(a) It can calculate how any one move will eventually end the game.
(b) The contest with Kasparov proved that logic is all-important in chess.
(c) It won a few matches but also lost a few to its opponent.
(d) Non-logical or deceptive moves are also within its capability.

어떤 사람들은 체스 같은 게임에서의 승리란 완벽한 논리를 이용해 정확하게 움직이고 실수를 피하는 단순한 문제라고 생각할지도 모른다. 다른 이들은 인간인 상대 선수를 이기려면 교활함과 비논리를 포함해 인간적 면모를 가능한 많이 가져야 한다고 반박할 수도 있다. 이런 철학적일 수도 있는 논쟁은 IBM의 블루 슈퍼 컴퓨터가 1996-1997 세계 챔피언 게리 카스파로프와 일련의 경기를 펼치면서 시험대에 오르게 되었다. 기계가 여러 움직임을 예측할 수 있을 것으로 보이지만, 그럼에도 불구하고 살아 있는 인간인 상대 선수를 몰아내지는 못할 것이다.

Q: 지문을 통해 빅 블루 슈퍼 컴퓨터에 대해 유추할 수 있는 것은?
(a) 어떻게 하나의 움직임이 결국 게임을 끝낼지 계산할 수 있다.
(b) 카스파로프와의 대결은 체스에서 논리가 가장 중요함을 입증했다.
(c) 상대에게 몇 번 이기기도 몇 번 지기도 했다.
(d) 비논리적이거나 속이는 움직임 또한 컴퓨터의 능력이다.

체스 같은 게임에서 인간과 기계의 대결에 관한 논쟁이 체스 세계 챔피언 게리 카스파로프와 슈퍼 컴퓨터의 경기로 시험대에 오르게 되었지만, 기계가 몇 수를 앞서 내다볼 수 있다 해도 인간인 상대를 몰아내기는 쉽지 않을 것이라고 한다. 따라서 슈퍼 컴퓨터가 계속 이긴 것은 아님을 유추할 수 있으므로 (c)가 가장 적절하다.

counter 대응하다 | **put to the test** ~을 시험대에 올리다 | **pit** 겨루게 하다 | **reigning** 군림하는 | **edge out** 몰아내다 | **flesh-and-blood** 살아있는 인간 | **all-important** 가장 중요한 | **deceptive** 속이는

37

As vast and empty as all of outer space may be, the zone of orbital space in which satellites and space stations can operate is predetermined by the physics of the planet we inhabit. Within this useful range of low Earth orbits there lurk not only micro-meteorites but also an increasing amount of man-made space debris. The smallest of these estimated 600,000 orbiting space particles are one reason for the metal foil coverings and other protective armor on space vehicles. The larger of a centimeter or more, though tracked to the best of our ability, today represent the greatest risk to any space mission. The International Space Station, the MIR Station, and the Space Shuttles all show the markings of collisions on panels, windows, and solar cells.

Q: What can be inferred about orbital space particles from the passage?
(a) Satellites can maneuver around them most of the time.
(b) Metal foil and armor on spacecraft protect them adequately.
(c) They are meteorites found throughout our solar system.
(d) Even small ones are a significant threat to astronauts.

번역
전 우주 공간이 거대하고 텅 비어있다 해도, 위성들과 우주 정거장들이 작동될 수 있는 우주 궤도 구역은 우리가 살고 있는 지구의 물리에 따라 정해진다. 낮은 지구 선회 코스로 유용한 영역 내에는 우주진뿐만 아니라 증가하고 있는 인공 우주 파편들도 도사리고 있다. 600,000개로 추산되는 궤도를 선회하는 가장 미세한 우주 입자들로 인해 우주선에 금속박 덮개와 기타 보호 외장 처리를 한다. 보다 큰 1센티미터 이상의 것들은 인간의 능력으로 완벽히 추적한다고 해도 오늘날 우주 임무 수행에 최대 위협이 된다. 국제 우주 정거장과 MRI 스테이션, 우주 왕복선 모두 그 패널, 창문, 태양 전지에 충돌의 흔적을 갖고 있다.

Q: 지문을 통해 우주 궤도 입자에 대해 유추할 수 있는 것은?
(a) 위성들은 대부분 입자들을 처리할 수 있다.
(b) 우주선에 금속박과 외장이 우주선을 적절히 보호한다.
(c) 우리 태양계를 통틀어 발견된 운석이다.
(d) 작은 것조차도 우주 비행사들에게 큰 위협이 된다.

해설
우주 공간에 우주진뿐만 아니라 인간이 만든 우주 파편들로 인해, 우주 정거장과 MRI 스테이션, 우주 왕복선의 패널과 창문, 태양 전지에 충돌의 흔적이 남아 있다고 한다. 이를 통해 볼 때, 우주 궤도에 있는 입자들에 관해 유추할 수 있는 내용이므로 가장 적절한 것은 작은 파편들도 우주 비행사들에게 큰 위협이 될 수 있다고 하는 (d)이다.

orbital space 우주 궤도 | predetermined 미리 결정된 | lurk 도사리다 | micro-meteorite 우주진 | debris 잔해, 쓰레기 | collision 충돌 | solar cell 태양 전지 | maneuver (교묘하게) 처리하다 | meteorite 운석

38

Even the Caesars of ancient Rome were famously occupied with managing the already teeming capital of their far-flung empire. (a) The Eternal City over the years has done nothing if not proven that urban upkeep itself is an eternal work. **(b) The ancient city center has perhaps never seen better days after the barbarians took over than today.** (c) Today's millions of inhabitants are but too numerous to all find accommodations in the ruins of the original site as the medieval population had done. (d) Contemporary urban sprawl surrounds the ancient municipality and puts pressures on it.

번역
고대 로마의 황제들조차 멀리 떨어진 제국의 인구 밀도가 이미 높은 수도를 관리하는 일에 여념이 없었다는 사실은 유명하다. (a) 영원의 도시 로마는 도시 유지 자체가 끝없는 일이라는 것이 입증되지 않았다면 수년간 아무 일도 되지 않았을 것이다. **(b) 고대 도시의 중심부는 야만인이 점령한 이후 오늘날보다 더 좋은 날이 없었을 것이다.** (c) 중세 사람들처럼 오늘날의 수백만 주민 모두가 본래 유적지에서 살 곳을 찾기에는 그 수가 너무 많다. (d) 오늘날의 도시 확산 현상은 고대 지방 자치 구역을 에워싸며 압력을 가하고 있다.

해설
고대 로마 시대에도 황제들은 과밀화된 도시 관리로 바빴고, 오늘날 유적지에는 주민의 수가 너무 많아 거주민 모두가 살 곳을 찾기 힘들며, 무분별한 도시 확장이 고대 도시 구역에 압박을 준다는 내용으로 이어진다. 도시 인구 과밀에 대한 전체 맥락에 어울리지 않은 문장은 (b)이다.

be occupied with ~에 여념이 없다 | teeming 바글거리는 far-flung 멀리 떨어진 | Eternal City 영원의 도시 (로마의 별칭) barbarian 야만인 | inhabitant 주민 | accommodation 거처 ruin 유적지 | contemporary 현대의 | urban sprawl 도시 확산 현상 (무분별하고 불규칙한 도시의 교외 개발) | municipality 지방 자치 구역

39

Skiing is not only one of the most popular sports in the world but is also one of the oldest modes of transportation. (a) Remains of skis that date back to 4000 B.C. have been found in Altai and Scandinavia, while ancient cave drawings in the Norwegian area depict the story of an ancient tribe if skiers from the north attacking a village over 8,000 years ago. (b) These days, skiing is a big industry that is the main source of revenue for many mountain regions. **(c) Some mountain areas are remote and only accessible by skies.** (d) While in the past, skiing was once an elitist sport of the rich, now it is enjoyed by a broad spectrum of society.

번역
스키는 세상에서 가장 인기 있는 스포츠 중 하나일 뿐만 아니라 가장 오래된 운송 방식 중 하나이기도 하다. (a) 기원전 4000년으로 거슬러 올라가 알타이와 스칸디나비아에서 스키 유물이 발견된 한편 노르웨이 지역의 고대 동굴 그림은 8000년 전 북쪽의 고대 스키 부족이 한 마을을 공격하는 이야기를 묘사하고 있다. (b) 오늘날 스키는 여러 산악 지역의 주수입원이 되는 큰 사업이다. **(c) 어떤 산악 지역은 외져서 스키로만 접근이 가능하다.** (d) 과거의 스키는 한때 부자들의 엘리트 스포츠였지만 지금은 폭넓은 사회에서 사람들이 즐긴다.

해설
가장 오래된 운송 수단 중의 하나이자 가장 인기 있는 스포츠 중 하나인 스키에 대한 내용으로, 외진 산악 지역의 접근성에 대한 (c)는 전체 흐름에 맞지 않는다.

mode 방식 | transportation 운송, 수송 | remains 유적 | depict 묘사하다 | revenue 수입 | remote 외진 | elitist 엘리트주의의 spectrum 영역

40

The suburbs developed in response to several social forces. (a) The multi-lane freeways that go around the perimeter of the city spurred the development of suburban places along the city's rim. (b) Now rather than going from the suburb to the central city to work, shop, see a doctor, or enjoy a movie, suburbanites can obtain the same services by driving along the outer belt from one suburban community to another. **(c) Suburban shopping malls and industrial centers have bright new facilities and ample parking.** (d) Another factor has been the decentralization of jobs with manufacturing plants and distribution centers relocating to the outer rings of the city.

번역

교외 지역은 몇 가지 사회적 영향력에 대응하여 발전되었다. (a) 도시를 돌아가는 다차선 고속 도로는 도시의 가장자리를 따라 교외 지역의 개발을 활성화했다. (b) 이제 교외 거주자들은 일하러 가거나 쇼핑하러 갈 때, 병원에 가거나 영화를 즐길 때 중심 도시로 가기보다는 한 교외 지역 사회에서 다른 지역 사회로 외곽 지대를 따라 운전해 가서 동일한 서비스를 받을 수 있다. **(c) 교외의 쇼핑몰과 산업 센터에는 깔끔한 새로운 시설과 충분한 주차 공간이 있다.** (d) 또 다른 요인은 제조 공장과 유통 센터가 도시의 외환부로 이전함에 따른 일자리 분산이다.

해설

도시 주변의 고속 도로, 일거리의 분산화 등 교외 지역에 영향을 미친 요인에 대한 내용으로, 교외 지역의 쇼핑몰과 산업 센터의 특징에 대한 (c)는 문맥에 어울리지 않는다.

force 영향력 | **perimeter** 주변 | **spur** 활성화하다 | **rim** 가장자리 **suburbanite** 교외 거주자 | **decentralization** 분산 | **distribution** 분산 | **outer ring** 외환부

텝스 1+
정상을 향한 필독서

How to
TEPs
실전
900 독해편

텝스 정상을 향한 독해 고득점 비법 특강
최신 기출문제를 재구성한 Actual Test 5회분
수준 높은 주제와 어휘의 고난도 독해

서울대 텝스 관리위원회 최신기출 Listening | 서울대학교 TEPS관리위원회 문제 제공 ·
넥서스 TEPS연구소 해설 | 320쪽 | 19,800원
서울대 텝스 관리위원회 최신기출 Reading | 서울대학교 TEPS관리위원회 문제 제공 ·
넥서스 TEPS연구소 해설 | 568쪽 | 24,800원
서울대 텝스 관리위원회 최신기출 스피킹 · 라이팅 | 서울대학교 TEPS관리위원회 문제 제공 ·
유경하 해설 | 340쪽 | 28,000원
서울대 텝스 관리위원회 최신기출 i-TEPS | 서울대학교 TEPS관리위원회 문제 제공 ·
넥서스 TEPS연구소 해설 | 296쪽 | 19,800원

독해 · 청해 · 문법

How to 텝스 독해 기본편 | 양준희 · 넥서스 TEPS연구소 지음 | 312쪽 | 17,500원
How to 텝스 독해 중급편 | 장우리 지음 | 360쪽 | 17,500원
How to 텝스 독해 고난도편 | 넥서스 TEPS연구소 지음 | 324쪽 | 17,500원
How to 텝스 청해 중급편 | 양준희 지음 | 276쪽 | 18,500원
How to 텝스 문법 고난도편 | 테스 김 · 넥서스 TEPS연구소 지음 | 160쪽 | 12,500원

텝스 기출모의 1200 | 넥서스 TEPS연구소 지음 | 456쪽 | 18,500원
How to TEPS 실전력 500 · 600 · 700 · 800 · 900 | 넥서스 TEPS연구소 지음 |
308쪽 | 실전력 500~800: 16,500원, 실전력 900: 18,000원
서울대 텝스 관리위원회 텝스 실전 연습 5회+1회 | 서울대학교 TEPS관리위원회 문제 제공 |
200쪽 | 9,800원
텝스 기출모의 5회분 | 넥서스 TEPS연구소 지음 | 364쪽 | 14,500원

어휘

서울대 최신기출 TEPS VOCA | 넥서스 TEPS연구소 · 문덕 지음 | 544쪽 | 15,000원
How to TEPS VOCA | 김무룡 · 넥서스 TEPS연구소 지음 | 320쪽 | 12,800원
How to TEPS 넥서스 텝스 보카 | 이기헌 지음 | 536쪽 | 15,000원
How to 텝스 어휘 기본편 | 고명희 · 넥서스 TEPS연구소 지음 | 304쪽 | 15,500원
How to 텝스 어휘 고난도편 | 김무룡 · 넥서스 TEPS연구소 지음 | 296쪽 | 17,000원

How to TEPS 시크릿 청해편 · 독해편 | 유니스 정(청해), 정성수(독해) 지음 |
청해: 22,500원, 독해: 14,500원
텝스, 어려운 파트만 콕콕 찍어 점수 따기(청해 PART 4 · 문법 PART 3,4) | 이성희 ·
전종삼 지음 | 176쪽 | 13,000원

고급 (800점 이상)

How to TEPS 실전 800 어휘편 · 청해편 · 문법편 · 독해편 | 넥서스 TEPS연구소
(어휘, 청해, 독해), 테스 김(문법) 지음 | 어휘: 12,800원, 청해: 19,000원, 문법:
16,000원, 독해: 19,000원
How to TEPS 실전 900 청해편 · 문법편 · 독해편 | 김철용(청해), 이용재(문법),
김철용(독해) 지음 | 청해: 17,000원, 문법: 16,500원, 독해: 17,500원

How to TEPS L/C | 이성희 지음 | 400쪽 | 19,800원
How to TEPS R/C | 이정은 · 넥서스 TEPS연구소 지음 | 396쪽 | 19,800원

How to TEPS Expert L | 박영주 지음 | 340쪽 | 21,000원
How to TEPS Expert GVR | 박영주 지음 | 520쪽 | 28,000원
How to TEPS Expert 고난도 실전 모의고사 | 넥서스 TEPS연구소 지음 | 388쪽 |
21,500원